Life After Life

Life After Life

'I'd been 20 years in the nick.
I never dreamed the sheer, mad joy of
freedom was going to be
even crazier than life inside...'

Norman Parker

JOHN BLAKE

Published by John Blake Publishing Ltd,
3, Bramber Court, 2 Bramber Road,
London W14 9PB, England

www.blake.co.uk

First published in paperback in 2006

ISBN 1 84454 221 1

British Library Cataloguing-in-Publication Data:

A catalogue record for this book is available from the British Library.

Design by www.envydesign.co.uk

Printed in Great Britain by Bookmarque Ltd

3 5 7 9 10 8 6 4 2

Papers used by John Blake Publishing are natural, recyclable
products made from wood grown in sustainable forests.
The manufacturing processes conform to the environmental
regulations of the country of origin.

contents

'If only it were all so simple. If only there were evil people somewhere insidiously committing evil deeds, and it were necessary only to separate them from the rest of us and destroy them. But the line dividing good and evil cuts through the heart of every human being. And who is willing to destroy a piece of his own heart?

During the life of any heart this line keeps changing place; sometimes it is squeezed one way by exuberant evil and sometimes it shifts to allow enough space for good to flourish. One and the same human being is, at various ages, under various circumstances, a totally different human being. At times he is close to being a devil, at times to sainthood. But his name doesn't change, and to that name we ascribe the whole lot, good or evil.'

Alexander Solzhenitsyn

For Samantha

LIFE AFTER LIFE

I'm not like you, straight fucking people!

And it isn't merely a matter of criminality; more a peculiar aspect of the soul.

You see, 'the Beast' is strong in me. Has been since as long as I can remember, although I didn't recognise it as such then. Youthful innocence euphemistically labelled it 'rage' or 'hatred' or 'self-destructiveness'. I indulged it and used it in alliance with 'courage' to carry me through dangerous and threatening situations. In truth, it was so strong I could hardly resist it.

With hindsight, I now clearly see that it used me. That evil side of my nature caused me to commit two killings, although I take full responsibility for my crimes. I could no more distance myself from them than one part of my heart could distance itself from another. Nor would I seek to.

In my defence (and what you are about to read is undoubtedly a defence), I have achieved great things. For a man to turn around his heart, to imprison 'the Beast', must surely be the greatest of achievements.

Thus far though, it has all been largely academic. In prison, the scope for evil is inhibited. In such a closed community, dark deeds are recognised as such and retribution is immediate. Evil flourishes best in conditions of total freedom. And soon I am to be free again. Then we will see to what extent I have truly imprisoned 'the Beast'.

LIFE
AFTER LIFE

the spirit is willing

After 20 years and a couple of months, the Home Office finally sent me to open prison. My relief was tinged with trepidation. Two decades of identical days kaleidoscoped together in a dull blur of pain and frustration. A protective reflex of memory prevented individual incidents from tormenting me but, at an almost subliminal level, I ached unceasingly. Long years spent with no pleasure whatsoever had stripped me down to a basic bedrock of merely surviving. And I had truly become a survivor.

If that which does not kill you makes you stronger, then I had become immensely strong. Not living in any meaningful way, just functioning from day to day. I had switched off all emotion and denied fond feeling. Just as a sophisticated computer might switch off unneeded functions when taken from a highly complex task to a simple one, I had switched off many human levels of experience.

There was no loving or touching or caressing or belonging in my world. The awful loneliness brought about by 20 years of solitude had permeated my very soul.

In order to protect my besieged sanity I had retreated into the castle, pulled up the drawbridge and stood on the battlements, surveying that great body of the human race that I was no longer a part of. In some ways it made me feel safe, and oh so strong. Nothing could touch me now, nothing could hurt me.

Physical pain had long since become merely a transient sensation, leaving no lasting image. Twenty thousand hours spent punishing my body in gruelling workouts had fired a will that the Jesuit, Saint Ignatius Loyola, would have been proud of. Regular periods of meditation had given me a mental strength and detachment that few but the most dedicated monks could hope to achieve. I lived much in my thoughts now.

However, I remained aware that mine was an unnatural state. To embrace loneliness like a creed was to deny the warmth and the healing power of love. But love had no place in my world. If I had become cold and detached and something less than human, then it had been forced on me. If I now had an arrogance based on fanatical self-belief, then that was precisely what was needed to survive where so many other strong men had gone under. I would make no apologies for what I had become; the triumph was that I was still there at all. For, whatever my crimes, to keep a man in solitude for 20 years is exceedingly cruel.

This gave me further strength and a feeling of superiority in that I felt the moral high ground now belonged to me. Especially when taken in conjunction with the knowledge that I had turned my heart around. Only those who have been a part of evil can appreciate its true nature. And only then if they have progressed to a comparative state of grace.

* * *

The change had started barely five years into my sentence. Parkhurst Prison in 1975 had seemed like one of the levels of the descent into hell. In penal terms it was the end of the line, filled with men whom the system had given up on. Strength and violence was everything, loss of face the ultimate nightmare. I saw strong men, damaged men, men fired with a spirit so fierce and so troubled that it caused them to ricochet around colliding with other men. But, far worse, I saw myself.

Fortunately, I was able to observe my surroundings objectively, dispassionately. I had often pondered on the true nature of evil. What I had once thought to be merely an adjunct to my personality, something I could call upon at will whilst maintaining a strict control over, I now began to recognise to be a powerful and uncontrollable force. Something that existed outside of me as a cosmic force in its own right, yet something that undeniably had a strong foothold in me.

I observed its effect on other older, more mature men. Without exception, it had corroded them like some powerful vitriol and often shaped them in its own image. I had been forced to conclude that evil was antipathetic to life, that its aim was always the destruction of all living things. Rationality alone dictated that I must resist it.

Parkhurst particularly, and prison in general, wasn't the best of places to achieve this. It was akin to trying to attain a non-violent, peace-loving state in a war zone. I resolved to maintain the outward form of the warrior, but underneath I would battle for my soul.

My strategy would depend on what I determined the true nature of evil to be. Was evil purely an external force that could invade the host like an evil spirit? Or was it rather a negativity of the soul, a succession of small, evil acts that cumulated in the negative charging of the spirit? Perhaps it was even a combination of the two.

If it were the former, I immediately had a profound philosophical problem. To acknowledge the existence of a force for evil I must also acknowledge a force for good. The existence of the Devil also meant the existence of God. Yet in my pursuit of an all-powerful will, one that would safely carry me through the interminable years, I had denied the existence of any superior force. In my breathtaking arrogance, my monumental self-belief, I could acknowledge no God and most certainly bend no knee to him in an act of worship. That would be akin to weakness and the start of the long, slippery slope towards oblivion.

So, there would be no prayers from me. I resolved to commit no evil acts just for the sake of it and would take no pleasure from cruelty, but that would be situation normal anyway. My violence was never gratuitous, always in reaction to some attack or injury.

Further, when I could, I would do good and kindly deeds. I could hardly walk about Parkhurst like some latterday St Francis though. That would be taken as a sign of weakness by others and invite trouble. But when there was an opportunity to help discreetly some deserving soul, I would take it. Perhaps, in time, that would positively charge my soul and reverse the process of negativity.

However, the state of my soul notwithstanding, I still had to survive physically living in prison. In long-term jails, trouble is never far away, the pressure incessant. It took all my concentration just to survive. Not only was I a committed rebel, I was also a determined escaper. I was constantly being moved from jail to jail. Very slowly, the years passed — but they did pass.

* * *

Fifteen years on and nearing the gates of Ford Open Prison my philosophy had matured somewhat. This came about not through any blinding revelation. More from confronting new, unique life-situations that caused me to modify my outlook.

It was 1990, a serious, life-threatening illness three years earlier had weakened me in ways other than the physical. That I, Norman Parker, could fall ill had undermined my fanatical self-belief. Illness was for weaker, lesser spirits. The reality was that for the first time in my life I knew humility and came face to face with my own mortality.

It had literally come right out of the blue. I was at The Verne, a bleak, windswept Category C prison on the isthmus of Portland in Dorset. I had been there for over seven years, something of a record for a lifer in a semi-open prison. Yet I had been a victim of the Thatcher years, of the increasingly punitive penal policies. Political expediency had become all whilst pragmatism and rationality had withered away. I feared I would never be released.

I had been waiting just over a year for my parole answer when it finally arrived. Perhaps I could expect something now. I had served just over 18 years, the last seven of them in semi-open conditions. I had been in no trouble for several years. I kept myself to myself to such an extent that I could certainly be considered a loner, without being thought of as withdrawn or eccentric.

However, it had obviously all meant nothing. I was refused parole, to be reviewed again in two years' time. In the meantime, I was to be moved 'sideways' to another Category C prison.

Within a week, a senior Home Office official came on his rounds. Mr Brown had dealt with my case for several years and was one of those decent, career civil servants to whom the political machinations of Thatcher were anathema. He sympathised, but could offer no solutions.

The knock-back had hit me hard, though I did my best not to show it. In my frustration, I rounded on him and said angrily, 'Is there no optimum time for my release, Mr Brown? At least I've got a home to go to at the moment. Do you want to wait until my family all die so there's nowhere for me to go?'

Brown paused, a hurt look on his face. 'Parker, I only sit on the Parole Board as an observer. I can only recommend. What you must realise is that there are those on the Board who believe that it is a question of "if" rather than "when" you should ever be released.'

That served to focus my mind wonderfully. If after 18 years in prison it was a question of 'if' rather than 'when' I would ever be released, then the future was bleak indeed. That thought tormented me all my waking hours. I could see myself dying in prison, an old and broken man. They would have beaten me, I would be a failure, and that was what I couldn't live with.

I had always been incredibly fit and healthy. For the past five years, seven days a week, I had worked as a gym orderly. For a fitness fanatic like me, it really was a case of letting the alcoholic into the brewery. Hard days were those with three, hour-long workouts; easy days were those with just two. I was fitter than an Olympic athlete, because the latter rest and take days off. I had hardly missed a day's training for the past 18 years.

I had always considered myself quite knowledgeable about diet and nutrition. I had been a vegetarian for many years and bought vitamin pills and health supplements from the canteen. My one dietary weakness was sugar. I knew its harmful effects, but still I put lots in everything. I rationalised that, living healthily in every other way, I could survive it. There was also a degree of arrogance that I had made myself so strong, it wouldn't harm me.

The weekend had been the same as hundreds of others I had spent at The Verne. On Friday and Saturday evening I had puffed with a couple of pals, the only times I ever took any drugs. I found the cannabis relaxed me, but, more importantly, gave me a different mental perspective. The pressure and madness of the week temporarily receded, allowing me a more balanced look on what was, by any standards, a bizarre existence. There had been the usual score of hostile confrontations, brought about by too many frustrated and angry men confined in unsuitable conditions. But I had handled them. It was brinkmanship. I would have followed through if I had had to. But another conviction for serious violence would have kept me in jail for the rest of my days. Therefore, it was incredible pressure. For me, every dangerous situation could turn into a life or death scenario.

Yet I couldn't back down. Because of my record, both in prison and outside, everyone knew who I was. Many potential tough guys, screw or con, would consider me a challenge. I kept a low profile, holding my head up, without swaggering about. Yet if some mug could confront me over something and get me to back down, that would make him look the more tough and so increase his standing with his mates.

Bullshit, total macho bullshit, but unfortunately it was the predominant philosophy in the world in which I lived. If I did back down, then there would be a queue of lesser mugs lining up to have a go at me to improve their reputations. In short, my life would become a bigger misery than it already was, an intolerable misery. A misery that would affect my spirit, my will-power, my self-belief and my pride. Ultimately, it would undermine my strength to survive and I would go under. So it was a threat to my very existence.

The mere physical side of any challenge didn't particularly bother me. The Verne wasn't like many of the long-term jails where there were many tough and dangerous inmates. By the time that men reached semi-open prison, they had settled down somewhat. They had come to terms with their sentence and tended to avoid unnecessary trouble. And trouble at The Verne would mean being sent back to much worse conditions in a higher-security jail.

The occasional yobbo still got through, though. Usually doing a comparatively short sentence and already on his way out, he was still looking for something to prove. In physical terms, they were often far from being mugs, either. Guys in their early twenties, football hooligans or local hard men that regularly fought for a reputation, they were a force to be reckoned with in their locality.

They weren't demented killers though. My basic stance was that I didn't fuck with anyone unnecessarily and no one was going to fuck with me. The world I lived in was so cold, so inhospitable, so filled with pain, that I could barely tolerate it. It would be a very foolish man indeed who would stand in my face and become the focus of all my hatred.

Then I would stand back just for a micro-second and examine this spirit before me. The conflict would become timeless and move to an almost mystical level. Men facing each other in a life or death situation as they have down the ages. No bluster, no posing or concession to style, even speaking would become superfluous. I would go and get my blade and he would get his. We would meet where we wouldn't be disturbed, in the recess or some small room, and conflict would begin.

For my part, I would attack and self-destruct all in the same action. After years of holding it back, I would release 'the Beast'. Like some primal force, it would take me over and carry me into battle.

Through fear, through self-preservation, past horror and even over pain itself, it would propel me. For the moment I would go unquestioningly, for the prime objective was the combat, the intent to kill and the personal survival.

But a small part of me would cry, because I would know that I had lost everything. I now had knowledge. I now had understanding. I had come, through many years of self-examination and discipline, to know the number of 'the Beast'. And in so doing, I had become a better, more complete, happier person.

Facing me would be another spirit posessed of 'the Beast' and we would destroy each other for its greater glory. For me, there would be no winning or losing, for I had already lost. I had let 'the Beast' back into my soul!

Mercifully, the vast majority of men could perceive Armageddon in my eyes and gave me space. Nevertheless, it was still pressure. The weekend was some small respite. Apart from being out of it on puff, I would carbo-load with peanut butter or banana sandwiches. The 'munchies' would add impetus to an already voracious appetite trying to keep up with a phenomenal work-out programme.

That Sunday evening I ate a not unusual eight sandwiches, sixteen thick slices of home-made prison bread, which had been freshly made that morning and was always quite yeasty. It was washed down with several cups of honey-sweetened coffee.

As I swam up to consciousness early Monday morning, the usual wave of depression and despair washed over me like an acid tide. The parole knock-back of a month earlier coloured all my waking moments now. Whereas before there had been some hope of better things to come, now all was darkness. How could I motivate myself to drag myself through another day of mindless boredom yielding so little return? Shortly, I would be moving to another Category C jail, but one where the conditions would be worse than at 'The Verne'.

The terrifying thing was that I was in the grip of a system that cared so little for me that it would drive me to my death. So many others had run out of strength in the face of such an awful existence, that they had done away with themselves. I had always managed to resist feelings of self-destruction, but I wasn't so arrogant as to assume that my strength was infinite. The possibility existed that they would open my cell one day to find me hanging lifeless behind my door. But for the moment, my spirit was still strong.

Beyond the tart taste of the early morning despair, there was another sensation that troubled me this Monday. I searched around in my semi-conscious world of pain for its origins.

My hands felt strange. Perhaps I had lain on them as I slept or they had grown cold outside the covers, but the sensations my brain was receiving definitely informed me that something was wrong. I rolled over and examined them.

I often said that I was beyond surprises now. So much grave misfortune had befallen me that such a statement wasn't based on self-pity. Yet as I stared at my hands, I certainly felt surprised. Overnight, my fingers had swollen to twice their normal size and were very red and sore. Moreover, my hands were half-clenched, claw-like, and I could neither fully extend my fingers out straight nor close them into a fist. I examined them more closely.

With the swollen fingers of my right hand I tried to force back the fingers of my left, but it was too painful. There was also evidence of some powerful metabolic movement during the night. Whereas my other fingers were swollen but still relatively straight, both of my thumbs and forefingers had been permanently twisted out of shape. There were bony, gnarled protruberances around the joints of my thumbs.

What could have happened? Had I had some kind of a stroke in the night? All the rest of me seemed fine, apart from the usual early morning aches and pains. Could one have a stroke that was confined only to the hands?

Lying there that Monday morning, my feelings weren't that this was some new and interesting situation that had just arisen. Among all the other nightmares of my existence, it seemed that I now had some serious illness. On those rare occasions I thought of God, I thought of Him with rage and hatred. I reviled Him for being a vengeful, punitive deity. Undoubtedly, my crimes had invited punishment, but if His was the overall plan, why had He cast me as the key player in this tragedy?

Moreover, I knew there were far worse than me. Neither of my victims were innocent or unprovoking. In jail, I had never gone out of my way to make others' lives a misery. On the contrary, my friends all regarded me as a decent, loyal and honourable man, who would never betray them. Admittedly, I wasn't over-friendly to strangers, but I often went out of my way to help weaker, deserving spirits and was generous. It was all part of my grand plan to positively charge my soul.

I looked up in the general direction of where this awesome deity might reside. 'What next?' I demanded cynically. 'In addition to all the pain and misfortune, you have decided to cripple me as well, you bastard.' There was no reply and I hadn't expected any. I climbed out of bed to confront the day.

Shaving and showering was difficult. With fingers like sausages, delicate movements were impossible. Serving breakfast on the hot-plate raised other problems. My hands provoked sympathetic comment from both con and screw alike, but I was in no mood for commiseration. No one referred to them again, making me even more aware of my perceived rabid state. Everyone knew of my knock-back. I was like a condemned man. My presence was a confirmation of their own mortality and there was silence until I had passed.

I went into the gym as usual, to begin my work as an orderly. The gym screws briefly remarked on the state of my hands, then let it rest. I reflected that a couple who resented my independence might have been secretly pleased. Sweeping and mopping was no problem, but when I came to do my weights workout I found it was impossible to grip the bar. I compromised by doing a circuit and running.

Obviously I would have to report sick, but the only decent, committed GP held his surgery on a Thursday. For the rest, it was the crisis school of medicine. They would wait until the problem was acute, then rush you to an outside hospital. In the meantime, you would have to do with Aspirin water.

Thursday seemed to take an age to come around. In the meantime, the problem had spread. The talus bone in my right foot had become very sore, preventing me from running. My right knee was also stiff and swollen; there would be no circuits or even step-ups.

This was a completely unique situation for me. All my life I had dissipated my excess energy, my frustrations, through fitness. It was the basic axiom of the man I was, a personal statement of faith. Life immobile, confined to a wheelchair perhaps, was the cruellest fate imaginable for someone like me. I directed a blast of sheer malice at that baleful deity who had brought me to this.

There was a further consideration. In the jungle I now inhabited, the strong preyed on the weak. In my weakened, semi-crippled state, men who had resented me but feared me might feel emboldened to attack. I couldn't make a fist to punch with; I couldn't grip a knife to stab with; how was I supposed to defend myself?

The Thursday morning doctor was his usual sympathetic,

professional self. He examined my hands, questioned me, then took a blood sample. He expressed the hope that I didn't have rheumatoid arthritis, which would see me permanently in a wheelchair. I awaited the test results almost as I had awaited my parole result.

The test came back negative. In the cold light of day, this turned out to be little consolation. For, call it what you will, I was already partially crippled and growing less mobile by the day.

My friends, mostly other lifers, were all supportive, but amongst even these I detected a kind of embarrassment. It was as if they realised I was doomed and could do nothing. I could imagine a time when they would speak of me in the past tense. 'Poor old Norm. What a way for him to go, dying in a wheelchair like that and in prison, too.' For all of us lifers, our greatest secret fear was to die in prison.

Just over the horizon loomed another awesome threat. I would soon have to move to my new jail, Littlehey. There, I wouldn't even have the comfort of my friends and familiar screws. Further, I had heard that the régime was strict and unsympathetic. But at least I would be away from The Verne where I had assumed the status of some moveable tragedy. It wasn't that I was ungrateful, it's just that it's much more difficult to fire up your spirit when everyone's being so damn sympathetic.

By now, my mother was becoming quite frantic. These past eighteen years, whatever the season and in whichever part of the country, she had visited me every month. Now she hadn't seen me for six weeks and I was continuing to put the visit off. In my phone calls and letters to her, I explained that I wanted to get the knock-back out of my system. I mentioned the arthritis in passing, but didn't say that it had nearly crippled me.

She was over 80 now, any more stress might finish her. I ended by saying that the trip to The Verne was long and arduous. She might as well wait the few weeks until I was in my new prison, where the journey would be easier.

My transfer day duly arrived and I said my farewells. I found I had mixed feelings at leaving. You can't spend seven-and-a-half years of your life in one place without leaving a small piece of yourself behind when you leave. Especially if the place was as wild, as beautiful and deeply spiritual as Portland. Six hundred feet above sea level, at the end of a narrow isthmus of land and scoured by some of the wildest winds in the world, I had developed an affinity with the island, if not the prison. Now, I hobbled around the course I used to run most mornings. As I left in the transfer coach, I tried not to look back.

There was a night in Winchester, a chaotic local jail. Half-crippled, I had difficulty climbing the stairs to the fours with all my kit. The following day saw the onward coach journey to Littlehey, near Huntingdon.

It was a brand-new jail, open barely two years. Although it had a Category C security classification, its security was more like a tight Cat B. You were banged up for all meals and the young, newly trained screws even put the bolt across, something that was only done at night in the top-security jails. There was also a large population of nonces, making up about half of the inmates, and we were warned that, if we harmed them in any way, we would be moved out to a worse jail.

The conditions and the prison politics hardly concerned me at the moment. My utmost priority was to address the problem of my health. In due course, like all 'receptions', I was called up to see the Principal Medical Officer, the most senior health official in the jail. He had a reputation among the cons as being a cold, uncaring individual who was only concerned with the detail of management.

I hobbled into his presence and he absentmindedly waved me to a chair. He continued to write in a large ledger for several seconds, allowing me to observe him covertly. For the first time in my life, I would desperately need something from a prison official, so I would need to weigh him up as best I could.

He was in his late fifties and of medium build. A full head of short, dark hair was peppered at the sides with grey. Tinted, gold-rimmed glasses concealed his eyes. So far, I had learned nothing.

Finishing with the ledger, he looked up. 'Right,' he said, reaching for a bulky record folder at the edge of his desk. Briefly, he scanned the name, frowning momentarily at the thickness of the folder. 'Been about, have we, Parker?'

The tone was enquiring rather than sarcastic. In earlier days, I would have erred on the side of prejudice and insulted him, but he virtually had the power of life and death over me.

'Not so much in the last ten years, Doctor,' I replied evenly.

'Just give me a minute, will you?' He began to skim through my file. Several minutes later, he looked up again. His expression said many things, and nothing, but whatever it was, it was beyond the remit of the present situation. He cleared his throat, at the same time as clearing his face, and no doubt his mind.

'Any immediate health problems, Parker?' He was firmly in medical mode again.

I explained about the arthritis. He gave me a full examination, tested my grip and read through the medical reports from The Verne.

'Had any other illnesses?'

'Before this I was disgustingly healthy, Doctor, never been ill in my life.' I paused. I would only get one chance, so I had better mention everything even if it was only a rash that mostly affected my legs. 'I have suffered from psoriasis since I was a teenager, though.'

'Oh,' said the doctor sitting back with a thoughtful look in his eye. He leaned forward again, so quickly it caused me to jump. 'You've got psoriatic arthritis,' he informed me quite undramatically. 'Twenty per cent of people who suffer from psoriasis go on to develop the arthritis as well.' He stated it like some interesting fact.

Figuratively, I raised my eyes to that malignantly mischievous deity who plagued my very existence. 'Gee God, thanks, a five to one shot and my horse ran in first.' The doctor was still looking at me. Quickly, I put that last thought out of my head. There was a far more important question to ask.

'Will my condition get worse, Doctor?' Only I was aware of the slight quaver in my voice.

The doctor looked at me carefully, examining me. His expression said, 'Is he man enough to take the truth?' He didn't want a situation in which I ran screaming from the room or later topped myself.

Coming to a decision, he spoke. 'Yes it will. In all cases, the condition deteriorates. I can give you some tablets that will take away some of the pain and stiffness. There will be some side-effects, though, and they will only delay the inevitable.' And he was finished.

Taking a deep breath, I got up. 'Thank you, Doctor,' I muttered, my mind on his last remarks. As I hobbled to the door I couldn't help but think that, bearing in mind how crippled I already was, to 'get worse' would be virtual paralysis.

I returned to my cell and lay on my bed. Never in all my life to date had I felt so low and defeated. If I was the hero of a book or a film, I would have felt reassured. We all know that the hero always comes through. But I was only the hero in my own life, and my life might be a tragedy. There was no guarantee whatsoever that I would pull through.

But although God had cursed me through the sheer awfulness of my experience, He had also blessed me with great strength and determination, not to mention intelligence. Knowledge was power. I had studied to gain my degree, so I knew how to research data. Our prison library was linked to all of Cambridgeshire's libraries. I would research this arthritic condition of mine in the knowledge that my very life depended on it.

First, I read all the books on arthritis. Mainstream medicine seemed unanimous that it was incurable. The only hope was to delay its advance through patent medicines and surgery. Both were quite costly.

The more I read, though, the more I came across dissenting voices. Some eminent men and women suggested that there was a strong link with diet, that certain foods broke down in one's system to form uric acid. This acid then found its way into joints and damaged tissue to cause swelling and pain, *ergo* arthritis.

I read scores of books on diet. It seemed that the problematic foods were those high in yeasts and sugars, causing a yeast overgrowth in the gut. These were the conditions that favoured the production of uric acid. Confident that I had identified the enemy, I declared total and unconditional war on him. I would put no food in my gut that would encourage the growth of yeast.

The immediate problem was that I didn't have much choice over what I ate. There were only so many variations of official prison diet and a 'no sugars, no yeasts' wasn't among them. I would have to get a job in the prison kitchen. There, I could eat what I wanted.

There was some surprise on the labour board when I asked to go into the kitchen. I was officially Grade 2 labour and could have lain in my cell all day. However, it was approved. I was put to work in the icy-cold veg room. Prepping the vegetables in tanks of freezing water did wonders for my arthritis. Tears of pain ran down my face as I hand-peeled the eyes from the spuds.

Most prison kitchens are tightly run and the cons are only allowed certain extras. But I wasn't too worried about this, because all I wanted was plenty of raw veg, salad and soya bean, stuff most cons would refuse. By an amazing irony, Littlehey's was the most lax kitchen I had ever seen. The inmate kitchen staff could help themselves to whatever they fancied. I often saw a single con cook a whole chicken just for himself.

If anything, this served to fire my will even more. For every breakfast, dinner, tea and supper, solidly for eight consecutive months, I ate a meal of either raw vegetables mixed with non-citrus fruits or soya bean stew.

Mindful of the damage that uric acid does to joints, I realised that I would somehow have to find a way to keep fresh, cleansing blood flowing. Yet I was unable to do exercise. However, as part of my fitness programme, I had always done stretching workouts. This opened joints up to their maximum extent, allowing fresh, oxygenated blood to wash away inflammation and small particles of bone, so regenerating growth. I rationalised that this would help dislodge the uric acid from my joints.

So, for 70 consecutive nights after bang-up, I would get down on a mat on my cold, concrete cell floor and stretch. Stretching and extending the joints was always painful even when I was an athlete; now, as an arthritic, it was excruciating. Again, tears of pain ran down my face. I focused my mind until I could call up the cognitive map of the particular stretch like a plan on a video screen. I focused out the pain. I developed a fanatical determination born of the will to survive.

It did not kill me. I was already a strong and determined man. It made me stronger, almost frighteningly strong. I knew that, if I so desired, I could make myself do anything.

I had never been particularly religious in the accepted sense. I was far too arrogant for that. I had been born a Jew, but had never practised outside jail. I went to *schul* (synagogue), if one was held in whichever prison I was in, but I despised Zionism in general and Israel's foreign policy in particular. I often said that I had more in common with a good muslim than I did with a bad Jew.

At about the same time I renewed my stretching routine, someone gave me a Jewish Prayer Book. A cynic would say that, with my back against the wall, I was trying anything. It was more fundamental than that. I, who had never pleaded for anything in my life, who had never bent a knee to any superior power whatsoever, at last knew some humility.

It was a tacit admission that perhaps my arrogance was part of the problem. I moved from the doctrine that 'man is God' to an acknowledgement of a superior being. I wasn't about to go out and evangelicise the world, preach to the faithful, declare myself a born-again anything or walk about clutching a Torah. But every night, before I climbed into bed, I would kneel down and recite two Psalms of David, Psalm XXIII and Psalm CIII. With a *kapel* on my head and a shawl round my neck, I would ask God to protect my mother and restore me to good health. I felt strangely embarrassed when I did this, to the extent that I would cover the spyhole up lest anyone should see me.

A couple of months of this new dietary, spiritual and stretching routine passed. There was a dramatic improvement. The swelling in my hands had gone down and the stiffness in other parts of my body had decreased. My eyesight had improved to the extent that I no longer needed glasses to read with and a slight fuzz of hair had grown back on my usually bald head. More importantly, I took great satisfaction in the knowledge that I could now control this illness.

Several more months saw me back in the gym doing weights workouts. Running was still too much for me, but I could play the occasional game of badminton. Although I had lost some weight, I was looking quite healthy.

After a year, I felt well enough to leave the kitchen. I had been able to broaden my diet enough to get by on a special medical diet. I involved myself in the general life of the prison again. I finished my degree and was allowed out with an escort to attend the degree ceremony at Ely Cathedral. I helped with community work.

My parole review came around again and I was duly assessed. I waited 12 months for an answer and was delighted to hear that I would go to open prison in six months' time. This was a definite commitment to release me. In any event, if things didn't go right there, I could release myself. There were friends abroad who would help me.

The six months passed surprisingly quickly. As I left for Ford Open Prison, I mused on the events of the three-and-a-half years at Littlehey. I had learned a lot about myself. I had arrived merely a physical man, albeit a damaged one. Now I was almost whole again through diet and stretching, but there was an entirely new dimension to me. I still continued to get down on my knees and pray every night. I was now a spiritual man.

LIFE
AFTER LIFE

It was late afternoon as the transfer coach from the Scrubs finally neared Ford. There were 25 potential 'receptions' on board and no doubt the move meant different things to each of us. I was sure that I had been away from conditions of freedom the longest. There were no lifers on the escort and, even if there had been it would have been unlikely that any of them would have had to serve 20 years before getting to open prison.

There was no feeling of triumph. It had been so long in coming that it was almost a Pyrrhic victory. But like some wise and wily old lion, I did savour the moment.

Other than a disaster, I was now going to be free. It was two years before my next review and I would wait at least a year for an answer but, all other things being equal, the parole board and the Home Secretary would have to find a very good reason to keep me in jail any longer.

There had been instances when lifers got a knock-back in open prison and did another period in a different open prison, but these were extremely rare. I knew that I was a special case *par excellence*, but by the time I finally received my answer, I would have served 23 years. Add on 12 months on the hostel and that would bring it up to 24. Surely that would be enough. I had to assume that it would be.

I assessed my strategy. Many cons looked on open jail as a time for self-indulgence. There would be illicit booze, drugs, clandestine trips to the local village, midnight parties, all the stuff of open prison legend. But not for me. For any lifer, the open prison period was the one most fraught with danger. For if he was caught out doing anything, he would be sent back to a closed prison and have to await another parole review before being sent back to open prison again. This could take anything from three to five years. I just didn't think that an illicit drink or a shag was worth that price. Especially when, if I just waited, I could have it all with no risk.

No, I wasn't looking forward to my time at Ford from a social point of view. If anything, it would be more lonely than my time in closed jails. I would have to be careful who I mixed with. A clown could self-destruct and take me with him. I would walk my usual lonely path and keep myself to myself.

On the plus side, though, I could secretly scheme about my release plans. Outside, the free world was the big picture. Who cared who was cock of the walk in the village pond that was Ford?

I took stock of my situation. I was 46 years of age, with a muscularity and athleticism that had me looking ten years younger. I certainly didn't feel 46. In the gym, I could outperform men half my age. I wasn't a contender, but I could handle myself in a row. My spirit was still young and fierce and although a tear-up with a blade was the last thing I wanted, I was sure I could crank up the necessary bottle if push came to shove. More importantly, my mind was still clear and sharp. Studying for the degree had kept me on my toes mentally.

But I was aware that there had been a significant change in me. It wasn't that I was tired, or broken or weaker in spirit, but I really didn't want to hurt anyone any more. Perhaps it was the regular prayers or even a natural process of maturation, but the rage, the hatred — 'the Beast' — just didn't seem to be as fierce. So perhaps I should be thankful for that.

As I faced reintegration into straight society, I began to appreciate just how much of an outsider I really was. If, in a community of criminals like Ford, my two killings put me very much beyond the pale, how much further out would it place me among ordinary men and women?

Would ordinary people shun me, fear me, point me out to each other? Never in my life had I felt ashamed or embarrassed by my crimes, but then I had spent all my life among criminals. By the inverted logic of the underworld, my crimes were almost like badges of merit. But I had come to reject the flawed standards of the underworld, too.

I would have to be very careful, otherwise my whole value system would fall apart. My very self-belief rested on a certain bedrock of core values. However, I would stick by those tried and tested tenets that had sustained me over the years. OK, so I really didn't want to hurt or kill anyone ever again, but that didn't mean I had to change my whole philosophy. As I moved into a less violent society, I would myself become less violent. But the self-belief, the arrogance that had sustained me over the years, I would retain a large measure of that. Even if it wasn't so obvious.

One thing I was determined about, there would be no sackcloth and ashes. Remorse is an intensely personal thing and happens internally. Whatever my crimes, I had done my time. I wouldn't return to society with a swagger, but I wouldn't hang my head in shame either.

I was well aware that the society to which I was returning wasn't exactly Plato's republic. Greed, aggressive self-interest and indifference to others all seemed to play a part in modern business. I was under no illusions. I would have to scramble and fight like the rest. But what exactly would I do?

I would be 50 by the time I got out. I had no actual work experience of anything. Even with a good honours degree, what company would take me on at my age and with my background? I could put as optimistic a slant on it as I liked, but it was unlikely that I would make it in straight business now.

I did have a network of pals who had grown very rich through the drugs trade and ran straight businesses. Maybe one of them would put me in, but there was hardly much of a career in it.

Over the years, from as long back as the horrors of Parkhurst in 1975, it had been my secret wish to write. Not the usual, semi-literate, self-glorifying rubbish that blighted the genre of ex-con authors, but something meaningful. Was it just my arrogance again, my self-belief, or could I really become a good writer? I certainly had a tale to tell.

Studying for my degree had brought me into contact with the great writers — Balzac, Turgenev, Lawrence, Zola — they all had their great strengths, and some weaknesses. By reading them, I learned the 'nuts and bolts' of writing. No, I didn't want to write like any one of them. I was too arrogant for that. I wanted to write like myself, in my own unique style.

I would be eclectic. I would take some of the physical description of Balzac without overwhelming the reader with a mass of data. Similarly, I would inject the unspoken, psychological undercurrents of Lawrence, but avoid the emotional whirlpool he so often created. It would be a synthesis of styles rather than a plagiarisation. I was quietly confident that it would be great, but what if it wasn't. Moreover, what if it was great, but didn't get recognition or reward? I wouldn't be the first writer to starve in a garret.

So if I really was going to take stock of my situation, all I could count on was what I actually had. My mother would have me come and live with her. In fact, it was part of my official release plan. However, she lived in a one-bedroom flat in Wimbledon. She had saved some money for me, bless her, but a couple of thousand pounds wasn't going to set me up for good. Clearly, I would have to have a second strategy.

I didn't come to this conclusion by means of abstract thought, but rather by sound pragmatic observation. Shortly before I had left Littlehey, the Governor had taken me out on a walk around the nearest town. St Neots in Cambridgeshire wasn't exactly home to the fleshpots of Babylon, but the distinction between rich and poor was clear to see.

I was aware that I had exactly nothing in my pocket. Should that still be the situation on the day of my release, I would enter society again right at the bottom rung. From a prisoner's point of view, freedom was always a great and valued thing. But not freedom to be poor or hungry. Fuck that. I hadn't survived 20 excrutiating years just to come out and live in some hovel on the dole.

Which brought me right back full circle. At heart, I was really a thief. Not some petty, jealous no-talent who coveted my neighbour's ass. Rather, a full-blown, ideological rebel against an unfair, post-capitalist society.

The robber barons had carved the spoils up hundreds of years before I was born. Now their ancestors reaped the benefits. It was nothing personal against them but, like Marx, I wanted to redistribute some wealth. Same general idea, but different ideology. Instead of taking from the privileged few to give to the masses, the masses would have to fend for themselves, as they had done all through history. I would steal from the rich in order to join them.

* * *

Now, with regard to crime, I was quite a rich and talented man. I knew hundreds of wealthy, clever and influential criminals. More to the point, they also knew me. And that was the important factor. Other than surviving in quite good shape, I didn't have much to show for 20 years in jail, but I did have a very good name. In criminal terms this meant that I was known to be honourable, trustworthy, courageous, intelligent and loyal. You can't ask much more of a prospective crime partner. I was sure I would be of some value to someone. Over the years, I had kept in touch with several key players. Now would be the time to renew the acquaintance. But first I would settle into Ford.

As I expected, there were quite a few people there I already knew. Several lifers had preceded me from Littlehey. As luck would have it, I found myself on the same landing as Fred, a lifer who had been on the same landing as me at Littlehey. We weren't bosom pals, but we had more things in common than many prison pals. He would do as a companion at Ford.

Fred was a well-built man who was nearing 60. He had been a successful road-haulier who merely dabbled in crime, before getting involved with a major drug smuggling gang. The leader was a megalomaniac who had started killing couriers. Fred was only on the fringes, but when the whole mess collapsed it took him down with it. He hadn't actually killed anyone himself, just passed on a gun. A less naïve man would have kept his mouth shut. As it was, his admissions got him a life sentence. Received wisdom was that he had got it for next to nothing.

Not really being the business, his chosen persona in prison was to act the business. Not that he was violent and disruptive, he was too intent on being a model prisoner for that. Instead, he was all-knowing in an Arthur Daley way, complete with the exaggerated cockney accent spoken from the corner of his mouth.

But he was all right. There was no harm in him. He was friendly and generous, with no vindictive side to his nature at all. Most importantly, Fred would never grass you. I didn't plan to continue the friendship outside, but for Ford, it would do.

The first three months in my new jail were largely an anti-climax. Low fences notwithstanding, if you were not allowed outside the perimeter and didn't escape, Ford was much the same as many semi-open jails.

There was a structured plan for lifers and I realised that I would have to go through it like anyone else. At the three-month mark I would be taken on a town walk by my case officer; a month later I could take a town walk on my own; and after six months, I would be allowed to work outside three days a week on community work.

They had recently instituted a privilege called a 'town visit' for all inmates of open prisons. After a suitable period of time in the jail, a visitor could come up once a month and take you out for up to six hours, staying within a 25-mile radius of the prison. Lifers had to be in the prison for six months before they could have a town visit.

After nine months, if everything had gone smoothly, the lifer would be allowed out for a weekend's 'home leave'. This was a major element in the 'lifer release plan'. The man would leave the jail early Friday morning, spend the weekend at home with his family, then return Monday evening. Needless to say, all lifers looked forward to this privilege the most.

While I waited for these various landmark events to come round, I got a job in the kitchen. Cooking the special diets was clean and interesting enough work. It also allowed me access to my own special diet and extra periods in the gym.

Time passed, I made a couple of close friends but, by and large, kept myself to myself, and I was civil to those few staff I came in contact with. Secretly, I contacted a couple of 'the chaps', successful criminal pals, to let them know that I would be out on the street again soon. All was going smoothly enough.

My 'town walk' came and went and it was every bit the massive anti-climax I expected it to be. My 'case officer' was a pleasant-enough, middle-aged screw, who had been hand-picked for me by Ford pals who ought to know. At the end of the day, we were just two middle-aged men in civvies, walking along the wet and windy sea-front at Littlehampton.

We went into a café and had egg and chips among other working-class men who were massively indifferent to us. If they had known the real situation, that this was officially my first day of freedom for over 20 years, perhaps they would have reacted differently. But they didn't. It all brought home to me that reality was very much in the eye of the beholder.

Lest my cynicism suggests that I, too, was massively indifferent, I should point out that I was carefully observing everything. Without passion, without excitement, without any sense of special occasion, I was observing the minutiae of people's everyday lives.

I was acutely aware that I had hardly lived in society at all. Incarcerated at 18, home by 23, away again at 26 and not home yet at 50, clearly I had had little adult life-experience. I had no history of living in a flat with wife and kids and holding down a job. I had never visited in-laws at weekends, picked the kids up from school, gone on family holidays. I didn't really know what a 'life' was, yet I would have to put one together soon. It was interesting to see how other people were doing it.

At first sight, it was all a great disappointment. There were people I saw who I could have tolerated pieces of their lives. But when I worked out the implications of the rest, the 24-hours-a-day, seven-days-a-week bit, I was sure it wasn't for me. I had mountains to climb, kingdoms to conquer, secrets to discover. The mundane would be my deadly enemy. If growing up meant growing boring, then I would forever remain a juvenile. But whatever life I decided to lead, I would need money to make it work.

The 'town walk' on my own was little different to the one with my case officer, other than I went entirely where I wanted. Littlehampton didn't offer too many options; you can only eat a finite amount of egg and chips (my special diet precluded more esoteric fare). Soon I was bored and returned to the prison early.

The approaching 'community work' did excite my interest though. Men from Ford would be loaned to local charitable and quasi-charitable organisations to work for free, three days a week. You were taken to the job by car and introduced to the civilians you would be working for. Thereafter, you would be issued with a bicycle by the prison, and cycle there and back. You were cautioned on the dangers of drinking, becoming romantically involved with civilian females and smuggling contraband back into the jail. My diet and my self-discipline ensured that I was tempted by none of the three.

I was given the job as handyman to Littlehampton Scout Hut. An immediate problem was that, when it came to building repairs, or any other kind for that matter, I was anything but handy. My mother laughed when I told her over the phone.

'You never so much as knocked a nail in for me,' she chortled.

Clearly, I would have to bluff and make it up as I went along.

In the event, I was agreeably surprised. The Scout Hut was a one-storey, pre-fabricated building that stood on its own grounds in a residential Littlehampton street. It was in a reasonable state of repair. The other bit of good news was that there were no scouts. Or rather, I never saw them. They only used the place in the evenings, when I was safely back in Ford.

However, the Scout Hut was used during the day as a nursery and crêche. There were several nursery assistants, local women with a child-care qualification. The children were all local, pre-school kids who were dropped off by their mothers before they went to work.

For a large part of my adult life, I hadn't been around women at all. For the past 20 years I had rarely talked to one. This would be good experience for me. I was far too proud and well-mannered to be pushy, but if and when they talked to me, I would take great pleasure in responding.

In truth, it was much more fundamental than that. The more I saw of free-world society, the more I realised just how much prison had damaged me. Yes, I was the strongest, most disciplined con who had ever walked a prison landing. I was the world champion control freak who was totally in command of every facet of my life. I had no weaknesses at all, or none that I allowed to hinder me. Except one — my very strength was a weakness. I was an absolute and complete island. No one in the whole wide world, except perhaps my mother, was close to me. I embraced loneliness like a creed and was too proud to admit that it bothered me. But I was so lonely, I often felt as though I was the only man on the planet.

In jail there was no other option. It was not in my nature to have emotional relationships with men. I knew that the only way for me to drive this coldness from my soul was to love a woman in the free world. Perhaps she could heal me and take away the pain.

But it wouldn't be a Littlehampton mum. Not that I was being élitist. From early on, I could see that some of them were very sweet and attractive. I had bigger fish to fry. I wasn't ready to settle into a Littlehampton life just yet, and to drag a mum and a couple of kids with me wherever I wanted to go would be a distinct disadvantage for all concerned.

At first, I tried to keep out of the way as much as possible. I was uncomfortably aware that all the adults must know that I was a convicted murderer. OK, it was another gangster I had killed and if anyone came near the kids and tried to harm them I would literally have died in their defence. But they didn't know this. As far as they were concerned, the genus 'murderer' might be a threat to everyone, including children. If one of the mums or dads had confronted me and told me to stay away from their kid, I would have died of shame. For the first time in my life, I almost felt like a nonce.

But the nursery assistants well knew that my offences weren't against women or kids, otherwise I wouldn't have got the job. To my surprise, not only were they very open and friendly with me, they actively encouraged me to play with the kids.

I had been away from children for so long, I had forgotten what an utter delight they can be. With adults in jail I had to be forever on my guard. But these child-spirits were naïve and unsophisticated and friendly without reservation and trusting and not at all evil. I could totally and utterly relax with them. But there was danger. Not for them, but for me. I, who on a daily basis, through aggression and hard stares, managed to create a distance between myself and other prison inmates, was suddenly overwhelmed by small people who thrust themselves into my world.

Then there was the touching. No one touched me. Perhaps my mother, once a month on a visit, might briefly hug me, but no other human made physical contact with me. Suddenly, these warm bodies would grab my hand and pull me, or grab my leg and demand my attention and it was all very confusing for me. I always conducted interaction in isolation, with no tactile element whatsoever. How could I concentrate on the conversation, when there was this strange feeling of human contact on my leg?

Within a very short space of time, the kids all loved me. Admittedly, many were from one-parent families or had dads who were too busy to play with them, but it was something more. I was good with kids. The women all agreed. Time after time they remarked on how their daughter would never approach other men, even sometimes their own fathers, but they would come to me. They couldn't figure it out.

I knew the answer immediately. I had a clear heart. I had 'the Beast' totally under control and there was no evil in me. In their childish innocence, the kids could feel that. They had no fear of me.

It was all so good for me, so healing. I felt myself becoming whole again. I still had a very long way to go, but my time at the Scout Hut was the happiest, most positive period in recent memory. On the three days a week I attended, life at Ford was but a distant memory.

As the six-month period arrived, I also became eligible for town visits. I reserved the first one for an influential, old criminal pal. I had met Gary in the early days of my sentence. Then, I was the senior 'chap', and he'd been a little in awe of me. I had helped him in a dire situation, lending him a blade and standing close to deter a dangerous enemy. He had never forgotten it. Now he was a leading member of the second most powerful drugs gang in London. He was certainly in a position to help me when I got out.

On the day of the visit, I was called to the gate-lodge, then crossed the road to search for my visitor in the car park. A face wreathed in shadow called to me from the window of a dark family saloon. The years had been as kind to Gary as they had to me. He was fatter around the face than I remembered him, but he still had the dark, Irish good looks and a mischievous smile around the corners of his mouth.

It had been 16 years since we'd last seen each other at the Scrubs. He slipped from behind the driver's seat and hugged me. I smiled as I saw the increased girth. 'Yeah, I know, Norm, fat cunt, ain't I?'

'Have to get you into some of the old fitness routines when I get out, mate,' I laughed in reply.

'Too fucking old, Norm. Too fucking old, mate. Jump in.'

We drove out of the car park and headed towards Littlehampton.

'Where do you want to go?' he asked.

'How the fuck do I know? I've only been out twice in the last 20 stretch.'

Gary laughed. 'OK, I'll take you to Brighton.'

'It's outside the 25-mile radius, we could both get nicked.'

'With all the other things I'm involved in, that's one nicking I could stand.'

As we drove, we talked. Gary brought me up to date with all the gossip on the street. I had already heard much of it in the nick. If you were staunch, staunch people tended to confide in you. It seemed that he was doing very well, but he didn't go into detail. He cautioned me on letting people know my business. He admitted that he was on a strong firm and sang the praises of his business partners. I added that I had heard nothing but good about them myself.

'What you gonna do when you get out, Norm?'

'The same as you, with a bit of luck, mate. I don't intend to be skint.'

'Just take your time,' he warned. 'You don't want to go straight back in.'

'Well, perhaps you can point me in the right direction. I ain't a ponce. I don't want any free handouts. Maybe you can suggest something.'

Gary paused, a thoughtful look on his face. 'You know, I'm gonna help ya, but maybe you can help yourself. You're an intelligent guy. You know lots of people. If you can find a way to get puff from a source country to anywhere on mainland Europe, I guarantee I can get transport there and pay you £600 a key.'

'I've got a pal of mine in Thailand ...'

'Don't say any more, see what you can put together. It's a while before you get out anyway.'

With my mind now at rest, I set about enjoying the visit. With Gary, money wasn't a problem. We went into some of the best places in Brighton. As he dropped me off at the jail several hours later, I was far more confident about the future.

LIFE
AFTER LIFE

E very jail has a kind of rhythm, a beat, a centre of power around
which the population resonates. Usually, this is a particularly
officious group of screws or a dominant and influential set of cons.
The rest of the inmates dance to their tune.

Ford wasn't at all like this. For a start, the screws were almost
invisible. Because it was an open prison, staffing levels were at an
absolute minimum. The only times you ever saw them on the
landings was when they did a roll check.

In normal circumstances, in any closed prison, this would have led
to a growth of prisoner power. But in the conditions of freedom that
existed at Ford, prisoners could find hardly any common ground
between them. The only thing they had in common was that they had
all been convicted of some crime. If this led to any feelings of
solidarity, then it wasn't immediately apparent.

A very large percentage of the cons were 'white collar' criminals,
professional men who had never been in trouble before in their lives.
Many were quite élitist about their offences and didn't consider
themselves to be 'real' criminals. Moreover, because famous and
wealthy businessmen came to Ford virtually direct from the court,
there was a buzz about the place, almost as if Ford was some bizarre
extension of the City.

It was all largely academic as far as I was concerned. I was sure
that I wouldn't have to rely on anyone at Ford to sort out a living for
me when I got out. But many of the cons acted as if they would,

hanging around some of the more successful businessmen in the hope of a favour.

My natural arrogance and aggressiveness still served me well even at Ford. I didn't have to bash anyone, but soon everyone treated me with the basic degree of respect and caution that I had grown accustomed to. It certainly made living in jail easier.

Three days a week I cycled to my job at the Scout Hut, and the rest of the time I worked in the kitchen. Recreation was divided between gym workouts, long walks around the extensive grounds and sitting talking to selected pals.

There was also a well-attended *schul* at Ford. Although very much a spiritual man now, insofar as I believed that one's spiritual development was paramount, I wasn't much into outward shows of faith. However, I did attend services a couple of times a week.

Relations with the Rabbi were always difficult. From his manner it was clear that he found it very hard to accept that a Jewish boy had committed murder. Fortunately, I wasn't seeking his acceptance. Further problems would have arisen had he questioned me about my faith. Although I described myself as a Jew, because I had been born one, that really didn't tell you anything about my belief system. It certainly wasn't Judaism, more an eclectic mix of New Age-style spiritualism centred on myself.

Not that I was messianic, I didn't want to lead anyone anywhere. I was just convinced that I had a strong and powerful spirit, one that had a definite destiny mapped out for it. My goal was to follow that spirit wherever it led me.

Whatever Fred was, he wasn't in the least spiritual. Had I discussed such things with him, his reaction would have been very predictable. On occasions when I had touched on matters that were even borderline abstruse, he would sit back, stare at me for several seconds, then say, Daley-style, 'Are you fucking sure? 'Ere, you're cracking up mate,' and all out of the corner of his mouth. Needless to say, I didn't discuss the origins of the universe with Fred.

He was very clever with his hands, though. He was forever making useful contraptions out of wood. One day he suggested to me that he could make a roller-coaster, a childrens' ride, if he could get the wood. Ford was very strong on community work. Every day, men went out to help local communities in their fêtes and fund-raising activities. Fred said that once the roller-coaster was made, we could take it out around the villages and use it at their fêtes to raise money.

It was an interesting proposition.

In *schul*, I approached a wealthy businesman and he donated £2,000 worth of wood. Fred went to work in a spare shed he was given for the purpose and set about making the roller-coaster. Initially, I tried to help him, but he could be a grumpy fucker at times and I didn't like being told what to do. In the end, he largely made it himself.

The finished article was a revelation. There was a 4ft square heavy stand with rails around the sides. A set of steps led up to a platform that was 4ft from the ground. From the edge of the platform a railed track dipped sharply towards the ground, then ran a further 80ft over carefully constructed humps and dips, culminating in a buffer contraption at the end. Small carts, 4ft long and 2ft wide, ran on small wheels along the track. The whole apparatus was brightly painted in fairground colours.

Although it was for small children, an adult could just squeeze into one of the carts. I tried the ride myself and found it stimulating. The initial steep descent was quite scary and the subsequent bumps caused you to grip the sides of the cart tightly. For a child, it would be an exciting ride.

The Governor was well pleased with it. He could see it earning him some headlines in the local press. Local fêtes, shows and rallies were advised of the roller-coaster's existence and bookings poured in. Every weekend during the summer months, a group of seven of us would be picked up at the gate and taken to some small village to take part in their fête.

Apart from the fact that it was very enjoyable to see kids have a good time, it was also educational for me. Working at the fêtes was exposing me to village life that had hardly changed over decades. It was breaking me in easily for the culture shock that living in a big city would present.

* * *

Irresistably, inexorably, my first home leave drew close. It was to be much more than just a quick trip home for the weekend. What with my case officer and Ford's probation department involved at one end, and my civilian probation officer at the other, there was an element of ritual about the whole process. From their point of view, this would be a big test for me.

I didn't see it like that at all. I knew I would be able to handle it, easily. I wasn't going to get roaring drunk (my anti-yeast diet prevented me from drinking), neither was I going to run amok at the first perceived insult. I was just going to pay a visit to the real world to see how and where I fitted in.

On one level, it had already brought me right down to earth. Whereas I was quite a celebrity in the nick, on first-name terms with all the notorious villains, out on the street it was all about money. It was quite embarrassing not to have any. Not that I was completely skint. My mother had two grand for me and my pals who had visited had contributed another couple of grand.

Being in jail for the last 21 years, I had no street clothes. I had bought bits and pieces over the previous few months, but my wardrobe was far from complete. It was beginning to dawn on me just how much I had lost by being in prison for so long, how far behind I was and what I would have to do to catch up. It was a daunting task.

Early Friday morning I dressed in reception, then shared a cab with a couple of others to the station. In civilian clothes I was indistinguishable from other early-morning commuters on the platform, but I still felt that I stood out. Perhaps it was the sense of occasion. After all, it was my first trip home in 21 years.

The train pulled into Victoria and I took the Tube to Wandsworth. London hadn't really changed much. The crowds and the traffic were more dense, and here and there new buildings thrust themselves through the old backdrop, but it was still the old anonymous, unfriendly big city that I had left two decades before.

I found the probation office and was soon in the presence of my probation officer. Alan was a slim, balding man in his late thirties, partially crippled by a childhood bout of polio. He carried one hand bent up in front of him, praying mantis-style. But he was quite pleasant. He made it clear he wasn't going to give me a hard time. I guessed that he must have been every bit as intimidated by me as most other straight-goers I'd met.

He had been down to visit me a couple of times at Ford and I liked his attitude. He actually felt that he had a duty to help me as much as he could. Some probation officers merely see their role as a regulating one and put the parolee back inside at the first sign of trouble.

One fact about Alan that I wasn't too pleased with was that he lived in the same block of flats as my mother, only two floors above her. Just my form, eh? I wouldn't get too much privacy in my comings and goings.

Just outside the probation office, I caught the bus that would take me to Wimbledon. I had never seen my mother's flat. She moved there after I went into prison, but I had seen photographs. Now I was standing on the lawn, staring up at the tall, white tower block. A multitude of emotions washed over me. I never thought I would see the day when I would be standing here, waiting to meet her again. I loved my mother dearly, she was the only thing that had kept me going through the long years. Through the solitude, the numbing loneliness, hers was the love that had sustained me. My constant dread was that she would die while I was still in jail.

Like a scene from a film, I was in the lift, then I stood before the flat door. As it opened, my mother reached for me, crumpled and cried. I walked her inside and was immediately struck by how small and dingy it was. I suppose I should have realised that, at her age and on a pension, it wouldn't be a palace. But it was still a shock. It didn't quite fit in with my over-romanticised view of myself as some heroic figure returning after a long absence. If there was some special destiny reserved for me, could it really be launched from such uninspiring surroundings? I consoled myself that it would only be temporary and further fired my resolve to make a success of myself very quickly.

By now it was early afternoon and my mother bustled about preparing a meal for me. I realised it was an important ritual for her, gave some meaning to her life, so I sat back in an armchair and phoned a few friends. I was due to go out that evening with two old friends; in the meantime, I had a couple of hours to kill.

Immediately, I encountered my first significant problem. For 20 years I had been sitting about trying to pass away time. But that was in jail. Now I was free, however temporarily. It seemed sacrilege just to pass time, waste time or whatever else you called it. I wanted to be doing meaningful things, important things, exciting things. Things that free people do. But it began to dawn on me that there would be times when I could do things like that, but for the most part I would be just like everyone else and spend long periods just sitting about.

Perhaps the tension showed, maybe I was fidgeting, but Mum kept popping back into the room to ask if I was OK. I assured her that I was and made a conscious effort to try to relax. I didn't succeed, but at least I stopped fidgeting.

I ate the meal with Mum and it was all very pleasant, but the taste of anti-climax was like a sour taste in my mouth. I caught myself thinking that, thankfully, I would only have a weekend of this, and immediately felt guilty.

I owed much to my mother and didn't want to seem ungrateful, but prison had made me into a driven man. Whatever she wanted for me, there were things I just had to do. I would take care of her now, as I had promised myself I would, but the pressure to fulfill whatever destiny awaited me was irresistable.

She had been fussing around me like the proverbial mother hen, something I wasn't at all used to and found intensely annoying. However, there were things I would have to put up with. Gently, I tried to tell her that for years I had been doing everything for myself. She nodded as if she understood, but I could tell she felt that now she could do it for me. It was another thing that dawned on me. I would have to get to know this strong-minded, grey-haired old lady all over again.

We talked a long while and, suddenly, it was early evening. I found myself dressing for the night out. My suit, shirt and shoes were all well made and expensive, so that made me feel better.

The downstairs buzzer went and Mum let someone in. The doorbell announced that they were outside. I heard the footsteps in the hall and then a great bulk filled the doorway. I rose to my feet and hugged my old pal.

Other than for one town visit, I hadn't seen Johnny Morris for 20 years. He was a legend around Notting Hill as a hard-drinking, hard-fighting thief who had never done a day's work in his life. He had always been massively built, but with the extra stones of flab that the years had added, he looked enormous.

Time hadn't been too kind with his face either. His corpulent features were red and deeply lined. But he had a rough and ready air, a devil-may-care attitude and laughed constantly. Central casting would have engaged him as a pirate.

''Allo, mate. Been behaving himself, has he, Mrs Parker?' He turned to embrace my mum.

Pleasantries were exchanged, but I wanted to get away as quickly as possible now. I had investigated the limits of the 'home' scenario, and now I was eager to examine the Friday night out with the 'chaps' one.

'Everything OK?' he asked as we drove away in his car.

'Yeah, just a bit bored, mate, really.'

'Must give yourself time, Norm. We're all like that straight out of the nick. Anyway, there's a nice night ahead. I thought we'd start out at the "Vol".'

With that he slipped me two £50 notes. The 'Vol' I knew to be his local pub, so no doubt it was to be an evening drinking.

I hadn't told him of my no booze diet yet.

As we drove, he told me of all the local scandal. I found I wasn't interested and hoped the day would never come when the details of other people's lives would become important to me. John went on to complain about how hard it was to earn a few quid now. All the old games were finished, it was exclusively about drugs. I guessed from this that he had no good drugs contacts himself.

We pulled up in a dingy back street. The British Volunteer was a small, grimy pub that looked like it hadn't been painted since before I had gone away. There were 10,000 just like it up and down the country. Inside, it hadn't changed much either. Dark-stained tables, chairs and bars all added to the general impression of gloom.

There was music playing, but absolutely no movement to go with it. Half-a-dozen untidily dressed men sat at tables, another half-a-dozen sat at the bar. Most were middle-aged or older. I didn't recognise anyone, but then I had never been a drinker, even in the old days.

Each man had a drink in front of him. Several sat silently, staring into it, as if fascinated by what they saw there. There was mimimal interaction. A couple of those at the bar chatted listlessly, but that was it. Over in the far corner, a group of teenage girls put records on a sound system. That looked marginally more interesting, but when I looked closer I saw that they were hardly more than children.

Our entrance had hardly caused a stir. I felt it would have needed something much more than that. In some ways, the setting seemed almost timeless, as if the same scenario had been played out countless times over a long period. Several men turned to nod at John, a few mumbled greetings. There was nothing hearty about it, though. I discerned that a couple looked wary at his arrival.

If he had noticed any of this undercurrent, John didn't show it. He grunted a couple of greetings and ambled over to the bar. I followed close behind. He ordered a pint and was surprised by my mineral water. We went to sit at one of the brown-stained tables.

John introduced me to two drinkers sitting nearby. They looked slightly more interested when he said that it was my first night out in

20 years, but I wished he hadn't mentioned it. I wasn't going to hide my past, but I didn't want to become a freak-show either.

And that was it, really. We sat there, occasionally sipping our drinks, making desultory conversation. From time to time, someone else came in, or someone left. The music played, no one danced, there were no high points, or even low points for that matter. I suppose you could have called it a social setting, but there was very little socialising. I guessed that those present felt it preferable to sitting at home on their own. It was quite a revelation when I realised that, up and down the country, there must be millions more sitting just like this.

Not me, I vowed. Not fucking me. This was another part of 'life' that I didn't want. If this was your local pub, you could keep it.

Perhaps John could see that I was restless, perhaps he finally realised that not an awful lot was going on at the 'Vol'.

'Fancy a move to somewhere else, Norm?'

'Yeah, that'll do,' I replied, trying not to sound too keen. We had ben at the pub for an hour, and it had seemed like a week.

The Tavern, half-a-mile away, was an entirely more lively place. It was well-lit, noisy and quite crowded. We were due to meet Ernie here. He was supposed to be an old pal, but in truth I couldn't remember him. I remembered several brothers with the same surname, but I couldn't put a face to Ernie.

John and I pushed through the crowd and suddenly there were cries in front of us. A group of six, three men, three women, all middle-aged, were warmly welcoming John. He waved me into the group and introduced me. Thankfully, this time he didn't mention the 20 years.

A tall, florid-faced man who introduced himself as Ernie made a fuss of me, but I didn't recognise him. I had been told many times that I hadn't changed much over the years, but then I wasn't carrying stones of extra weight. I tried to picture Ernie as a youth, but still couldn't put a face to the name.

A round of drinks were bought and I now stood in a group of eight. Conversation was still awkward, but it was an improvement on the 'Vol'. I mused that there must be an art to pub conversations. How do you stand about for hours, talking to people who are almost strangers, without it becoming boring? The answer, of course, was to drink heavily while you are doing it. I noticed that a couple of the group were so inebriated they laughed at anything. In fact, they often laughed in the wrong places, but no one seemed to care.

I forget what I talked about. Afterwards I couldn't remember one conversation, yet I was stone-cold sober. All around me, the general noise level rose steadily as drunken people chatted noisily.

I felt very awkward, not a part of it at all. Strangely, I didn't want to be a part of it. It seemed a particularly unproductive way to spend one's evening.

By now, John was very drunk, but he seemed to be enjoying himself. He stared blearily at his watch. 'Half-past ten,' he announced to no one in particular. 'If we hurry, we can get afters in the "Vol".'

I wasn't at all sure what this meant. The others in the group obviously did. Ernie nodded enthusiastically as a fierce argument broke out between two of the couples. John staggered out into the night, followed by Ernie and myself.

Back at the 'Vol', the music was louder and some of the conversations seemed marginally more animated. But people still sat about staring into their pints. John and Ernie rushed to claim a place at the bar. Almost in desperation now, I decided to drink vodka. Perhaps I was missing something, or rather needed to blot something out.

An hour later, my sense of urgency seemed to have gone. It no longer seemed to be such a waste of time just hanging around the 'Vol'. I found that I could now listen to conversations without absorbing any of their content. Last and by no means least, some kind of drunken cameraderie had grown around John, Ernie and myself. It was almost as if we had been old drinking partners for years. At closing time, the three of us staggered outside.

'We know a couple of birds round the corner who are up for a fuck if you give 'em a couple of quid,' slurred John.

It had been a long time, but what of all my resolutions? It wasn't sex I had missed, I soon learned to handle that appetite. It was love. I had thought long and hard about my future partner and was sure we would share something beautiful. It was an ideal, every bit as pure and romantic as the destiny I searched for. Was I really going to start out on the quest with some sordid, drunken, fumbling grope with an anonymous whore? Where would that leave all my discipline?

'Not tonight, John, I'm too pissed.'

'OK, boy, let's get you home.'

As we pulled away, we nearly collided with a passing car. John and Ernie shouted abuse, but the driver shouted back. As he drove off, I noticed that he was black.

'Oi, Ern, don't stand for that. Get after the black cunt,' growled John. Ernie raced away in pursuit.

Suddenly, even through the alcoholic haze, I experienced an incredible sense of déjà vu. We were all 18 again and racing through the streets of Notting Hill in the drunken pursuit of a black man.

We rounded a corner, nearly colliding with another car and the adrenalin rush brought me to my senses. What the hell was I doing here? My first night out on parole and already I was in a dangerous situation. Moreover, I had long ago grown out of the racism thing. Why were we pursuing this innocent fella?

John must have seen the concern on my face.

''Ere, hold up, Ern. Hold up, mate. I forgot about Norman. He can't get involved in this sort of thing. Let's drop you home, mate,' he said, looking at me.

In the event, I got a cab. On the journey home, I mused on the events of the evening. Had I enjoyed myself? Not really. Would I do it again? Definitely not. And had John and Ernie been doing the same thing these past 20 years? I was sure they had. How boring. How fucking boring. Whatever I wanted for my new life, it certainly wasn't that. So far I hadn't seen too much that I liked. Perhaps life at 50 was all like this. But it was only Friday. I still had the rest of the weekend to go.

* * *

I awoke the following morning and immediately wondered where I was. From the amount of light flowing into the room, I knew I wasn't in a cell. I arose, put away the sofa bed, washed, shaved and dressed, all before my mother awoke. I felt quite embarrassed that I should be sharing a flat with my mother at my age.

My mother got up and promptly set about making me breakfast. I reasoned that this was the role she had set her heart on, so I wasn't going to argue. It would have been ungenerous to point out that I had been fending for myself the past 20 years.

She asked how my night out had been and I said that I had enjoyed myself. That gave me the opportunity to tell her that I had arranged to see John again that morning. He was going out with me to get some clothes. She seemed genuinely pleased that I had a friend to go out with. No doubt she realised that I didn't want to sit indoors on my first weekend out.

I met John in Notting Hill just after noon. He took me to a tailor all the 'chaps' used and paid for a suit for me. Then we drifted about, looking at some of the old places where we used to hang out. It was all quite sad really. They were times gone with nothing to show for them. Those few people I saw who I remembered from old were much changed, and not only physically. Before, we were young people in pursuit of fun, of a good time; now you could see that they spent all their energies just trying to survive life. If anything, John and I reminded them of the carefree youths they had been and in the remembering came the realisation that they had settled for so much less than their original aspirations. Not that John and I were doing much better than they, but at least we still had the free, challenging, searching spirit.

It was all useful stuff for me. You can theorise all you like in jail, but there is nothing like real life to test out your plans. The more I saw, the more I realised I would have to get some money quickly. It was reassuring that that evening I was meeting Gary and his wife for a meal.

While the previous evening with John had been merely a diversion, I viewed the impending evening with Gary as a definite career opportunity. He was an old friend, clearly in a position to help me out of a dire situation. A word from him in the right quarter could set me up.

We met in a restaurant in the Fulham Road. It was expensive without being pretentious. I had never met Gary's wife before, but I knew he had been with her for many years. It soon became apparent that Gary never discussed business in front of his wife. So I settled down to a relaxed evening in pleasant company.

We worked our way through several courses, talking all the while. Surreptitiously, I examined the other diners. All were well dressed and looked successful. It seemed that a meal in good company was quite an acceptable way to spend a Saturday evening.

As if he had just read my thoughts, Gary said, 'I often spend an evening in a good restaurant. Sometimes we go to a show, but I didn't know what you'd fancy, so I left it.'

'This is OK, Gary,' I replied, 'it's just good to be out.'

'The novelty will wear off, Norm. Things have changed an awful lot. Also, you're a different age now. Us old folks don't go tearing around like we did when we were young.' Gary laughed and turned to his wife, who was also laughing. I laughed along with them, but more out of politeness than agreement. Back in the nick there had been little difference between me and the younger men. We worked out side by side in the gym, we ran, did circuits, gambled. If we argued, my age was never a factor and should a punch-up have ensued, then I didn't doubt that I would have been able to hold my own or, at least, give a good account of myself.

It occurred to me that here was another way in which I was very different. Not only did I have a very young outlook, fortunately I had the constitution to go with it. No doubt I had a lot of growing up to do, but to be a boy in a man's body wasn't necessarily such a bad thing. In some ways, it was like being born again at 50. My spirit was still strong. I would explore this new world and see where my spirit led me.

* * *

As much as I was driven by the desire to use my home-leave as constructively as possible to further my career on release, there were other priorities. My mother had also been serving a sentence. Her whole life for the last 20 years had been geared to supporting me wherever I was in the penal system. Whether it was writing, visiting, sending stuff in, petitioning the Home Office on my behalf or just being there for me, she had shared my pain.

In my darkest hours, often as I lay in solitary in some ill-lit dungeon in the bowels of some decrepit Victorian jail, the thought that sustained me was that somewhere out there was one person who truly cared for me. It was, quite literally, a lifeline for me. I lived in constant dread of her not being there.

Often in my daydreams — you daydream a lot in conditions of deprivation — I saw myself walking with her across Wimbledon Common. Such a simple thing for a man to take his mother for a country walk, yet so singularly unattainable for me in my position. But not now.

There was a brief protest. She argued that women didn't go much on the common now because there had been several attacks. I smiled indulgently. I pointed out that I had walked the landings with some of the worst beasts in the system, yet they had cowered from me. Was I really going to let some nonce prevent me from taking my mother for a walk on the common? I didn't think so.

She huffed and puffed, then quickly prepared the ingredients for lunch. Secretly, though, I could see she was pleased. For many years, her friends had enjoyed their children around them, while she had been alone. Now, ironically, her friends' children had grown up, married and moved away, leaving them on their own, while she had her son back.

Even though I had been in the countryside this past year, the common was very beautiful. Leafy pathways criss-crossed each other and we hardly saw another soul. I mused that this common hadn't changed for centuries. I could almost see the spirits of ancient travellers passing beneath the trees.

Now and again I stole a secret glance at my mother. She was picking her way through the paths, placing her feet carefully, but she seemed to be content. I enclosed her spirit in mine and felt a great surge of warmth. I owed this woman so much, I loved her so much. I hoped I could make her proud of me.

There was a sudden flutter of fear in my stomach. I knew I had to do what I had to do, it was my destiny. We are all prisoners of our own particular personality and mine was a harsh master who drove me unmercifully. I could no more resist it than I could stop drawing breath. I hoped I wouldn't hurt her again. But for the moment, all was idyllic. I had realised my most precious dream. I was together with my mother again.

I suffered the ritual of Sunday lunch, sitting in the crowded lounge of my mum's council flat. The phrase 'humble beginnings' played over and over in my mind, but I reflected that I was nearly 50 now and should have been further along the road. Most men are thinking of retirement at 50 and here was I starting out in life again.

After lunch, a neighbour of Mum's came in. I was introduced and was as polite as I possibly could be, but suddenly I felt stifled. I just had to get away. I still had two other priorities to accomplish and, with luck, I could get them both in before I had to return to Ford in the morning.

I called a mini-cab, saying I wanted to go to Shepherd's Bush. My mother didn't ask who I was going to see, so I didn't have to lie. The truth, at the very least, would have disturbed her.

Once in the cab, I changed the destination to Mortlake Cemetery. The driver didn't suspect any subterfuge. No doubt, fares often changed their minds and it wasn't uncommon for people to go to cemeteries on a Sunday to pay their respects. However, as with most things in my life, for me it just wasn't that simple.

Mortlake was where Susan was — Susan whom I had shot to death back in 1963 when we were both 18. The passing of almost three decades had done little to dull the memory of the trauma and paralysing grief. I carried it with me and it still coloured everything I did. Often I felt so guilty that I should have a life when all Susan had was the grave. It was of little consolation that my life had been so dire since. More than once I had felt that, when misfortune had come my way, it was my penance and no more than I deserved.

The cab dropped me at the gates of the cemetery. As I walked past other mourners I averted my eyes lest they should see my guilt. The killer had returned to visit his victim. If they had known the truth, would they all turn on me and denounce me? Moreover, while they might be welcomed by the spirit of the deceased they visited, what welcome could I expect?

One day, I knew I would have to face the spirit of Susan again, and that prospect filled me with mortal dread. I was safe in my miserable life in the land of the living, but once I entered the realm of darkness, who knew what terrors awaited my soul?

I walked through the cemetery in the general direction of where I thought the grave to be. I had visited it once when I had come home from my first sentence, but that was over 20 years ago. There was a strong possibility that I wouldn't be able to find it. But I had to. There was a synchronicity about what I was doing. On the spiritual path that I was treading, I knew that this was an important step.

At the far end of the cemetery, three massive fields of graves spread over an area the size of many football pitches. Serried ranks of gravestones marched to the middle-distance, the legends of the deceased partially obscured on their time-worn façades. Where would I begin? If I went from stone to stone it would take several hours and then there was a possibility I might miss it.

Wide tarmac pathways separated the fields of graves. Fortunately for me, this part of the cemetery was deserted, save for one elderly man wearing a cloth cap. He stood at the corner of one of the paths, a clipboard in his hands, surveying the ranks of stones.

Secretly, I cursed; I wanted to be on my own for the coming search. In my paranoia, I feared that every onlooker could discern my intent. Perhaps he was some kind of cemetery inspector. Maybe he would ask me what I was doing here. I turned my back on him and started along the first rank of stones.

Within seconds, I had lost myself in my task. Anonymous names leapt at me from weather-beaten stones only to be analysed and discarded. 'No, I'm sorry, spirit, it isn't you I have come to see. Go back to your long sleep, perhaps someone will come in a while.'

I walked and turned and walked again. Countless stones I passed, but I didn't see Susan's. Suddenly, the futility of it hit me. I stopped and looked around. I was halfway through the central field of graves, the stones surrounding me like corn in a field. I would need assistance to find Susan.

The old man in the cloth cap still stood at the junction of the tarmac paths. Only, to my surprise, he wasn't an old man at all. As I looked closely now I could clearly see that it was a portly, middle-aged woman wearing a head-scarf, but still carrying a clip-board.

How could I have made such a mistake? There was nothing wrong with my eyesight. I had clearly seen an old man. Spiritual I might be, but I wasn't in the least superstitious. Never, in my whole life, had I seen anything even slightly supernatural.

It did shake me and I realised that perhaps this was to be an unusual day. A disturbing *frisson* of fear played around the base of my spine.

Although 50 yards away, the woman looked up and her gaze met and held mine, enquiringly.

'Er ... is there an office around here? Somewhere I can check a name against a grave?' I was embarrassed now.

'Who are you looking for?' she called back.

The question shocked me; it was precisely the one I would have avoided. What if she knew that the particular grave I was searching for belonged to someone who had been murdered?

I turned away, ignoring the question, looking beyond the fields of graves to a collection of small buildings. Perhaps these would have some information, if they were open on a Sunday.

I paused momentarily. Just before I was to set off in their direction, something caused me to look down. My mouth fell open as I involuntarily drew a long, deep breath. I felt an icy chill all down my back and a minor tremor shook me. I was standing on Susan's grave.

I was a rational man, a true child of the scientific age. If I couldn't see it, touch it or measure it, it didn't exist for me. But what I had just experienced was beyond explanation. There were literally thousands of graves all around me. What were the odds of my stopping by chance on precisely the grave I was seeking?

My thoughts returned to the old man who had turned into a

woman. It certainly was becoming an unusual day. More importantly, perhaps this was to be the day I realised that there was another world apart from the corporeal.

Still in mild shock, I turned back towards the woman in the headscarf. She was still looking at me enquiringly.

'It's OK. I've found it,' I shouted across at her.

Now it was her turn to look surprised, even uncomfortable. She stared and said nothing.

Slowly, my surprise turned to gratitude. I had found my Susan again. All the old emotions stirred and I realised I still loved her and missed her as much as I had the day she died. I had lived with so much pain, I had become an expert at pushing it away.

I knelt on the grave and felt warm tears come to my eyes. But in this intensely personal moment, something was intruding. I didn't turn to look, but I was sure that the lady with the scarf was still staring over at me. I busied myself with another task.

I had bought a bunch of flowers by the cemetery gate. There was a small flower vase built into Susan's stone. It was both empty and dry. I looked across the fields of graves and saw a stand-pipe at the intersection of several paths. I picked up the metal flower holder and set off for the stand-pipe.

As I neared it, I saw that the woman was heading to meet me.

'Who was it you were looking for then?' she asked.

I bent my head as I filled the vase and ignored the question. It was as if contending mystical forces held the field and to prevaricate would be a sacrilege.

The woman carried on seamlessly. 'There are a lot of interesting names in this cemetery, you know. Two separate clans of Callaghans, and several Brownlows. I'm over from Canada to search for the grave of my father. I haven't been here for 20 years.'

Almost as if a bell had chimed, there was a resonance to the 'twenty years'. Of all the other amazing coincidences, how strange that two people who hadn't been to that cemetery for 20 years should both visit on the same day.

The vase now full, I smiled at the woman and backed away. In truth, I was now totally unnerved by the whole situation. It was as if I had somehow stepped into a medieval morality play. Various characters were elemental forces personified. I wondered who the woman with the scarf might represent.

I hurried back to Susan's grave and put the red roses in the vase. I sat in a moment's reverie and focused on the message on the stone: 'One by one we meet again, as God will link the broken chain.' To others that might sound like a promise, but in my state it had all the echoes of a threat. I had to be gone.

'I'm sorry, Susan. I'm really sorry.' I placed one hand on the stone and kissed the head of the angel carved into its side. Then I strode off between the graves without looking back.

There were dozens of squirrels scampering about the graveyard in the bright autumn sunlight. Perhaps this was the nearest thing to countryside they could find in the big city. I smiled a cheerless smile at the thought that something living could find a home here.

Several yards in front of me, a large grey squirrel stood in the grass at the side of the path. For some reason I looked at it and saw that it was looking at me. As I got closer, it started to move towards me, never once taking its eyes off me.

As a confirmed townie, I had always thought that squirrels were timid creatures in the presence of humans. On any other day I would have ignored it. However, in my heightened state everything now seemed to assume some mystical significance. I found myself wondering what spirit could be embodied in the squirrel and whether it meant me any harm.

I crossed to the other side of the path and hurried by. The squirrel sat, just looking at me. Had it scampered after me I would undoubtedly have run. On any other day, I would have smiled at the thought of tough Norman, the scourge of Parkhurst, fleeing from a squirrel. But today it all made sense. As I passed through the gates of the cemetery, I felt a profound sense of relief.

✳   ✳   ✳

That left just one more mission to accomplish on this home leave. Ian had been one of my closest friends in jail. There had been three of us. We were inseparable. Through the direst of situations we stuck together. Our loyalty was our strength.

Davy and Ian had both been released from jail years before me. Davy visited me once before losing contact. Through the grapevine, I heard that he had had drug problems; he'd beaten up his long-suffering wife and pulled several shabby tricks on friends. I would search him out in time, but it wasn't a priority.

Ian, a couple of years younger than me, had been doing 25 years.

Of small, wiry build, his courage was legendary. A confirmed rebel against the screws, he regularly went out of his way to help less fortunate cons. It often got him into trouble.

After one prolonged spell in solitary, his mind had cracked. He would take to staring at the ground for long periods and became quite unpredictable. Prison is the most unforgiving of places. Weakness becomes a fatal flaw, something to be exploited by all save the closest friends. Everyone turned against him. He became reclusive.

At the time, there was nothing I could do. I roasted on the spit of my own agony. It was as much as I could do to survive myself. I swore I would search Ian out when, or rather if, I was released.

Now I had the opportunity. The last I had heard was that he was living in his mother's flat over by the Caledonian Road. His crazy, drug-raddled behaviour had driven his mother from the flat. Not long afterwards, she had died. No doubt, Ian lived in his own private purgatory.

That I should search him out spoke volumes about my place in the world. Unlike free men, I had no extended family, no network of friendships built up over the years. Other than my mother, and my father who was in a home, all my relatives had disowned me, including my sister. What could I say? I could hardly condemn them. It couldn't have been easy having a double killer in the family.

Thus, my network of prison friends had become my family. No researcher could have discerned even the remotest of blood lines, but my friends liked me and I liked them. We enjoyed each other's company and would help each other out in times of trouble. And perhaps that's more than could be said for most families. I believed that you didn't have to be related to have kin.

The Tube took me to the top of Caledonian Road. I knew the name of the tower block and that it was white. I scoured each side of the road, occasionally asking directions of passers-by. I was surprised that so many of them were of various ethnic origins. However, they spoke English as well as me and certainly knew the area better.

After nearly an hour, just as I was considering failure, I found it. The white façade belied the untidy interior. The stairwells and landings were strewn with rubbish.

At the end of a long, wide corridor, I saw the number I was looking for. I pressed the bell, then stood back. I waited for several minutes. Finally, the door opened.

A slim, elderly-looking man with pure white hair stepped out. I was about to ask for Ian.

'Norman, Norman, it's you!' The white-haired man was smiling, a look of utter surprise on his face.

I peered more closely at him. As if from under some stage make-up, I made out the features of the Ian I used to know. I reflected on what a cruel caricaturist time can be. We threw our arms around each other and hugged tightly.

'When did you get out?' Ian demanded excitedly.

'I'm only on my first home leave, I've got to go back tomorrow.'

Ian's face dropped with disappointment. Gathering himself, it was as if he reminded himself that, at least, he had me for now. He beamed again. 'Come in, Norm.'

Even in the semi-darkness, I could see the flat was a mess.

'No electric, mate.' Ian scrunched up his face by way of apology.

'Don't worry about it, Ian. It's fine,' I reassured him.

He led me into a dingy kitchen, with dirty crockery piled high by the sink. We sat either side of a formica-topped table. There was a moment's silence.

'Want a cup of tea, Norm? We've got gas.'

I ran my eyes over the grimy cup by the sink. 'No thanks, Ian. What you been up to then?'

Ian's shoulders slumped and he lowered his head to his chest. 'Not too good really, Norm, not too good at all. But I'm getting better. I've got all my paintings in the other room. I'll show ya.'

The change of subject was welcome. I followed him into the adjoining room. In the gloom, I could discern a large, unmade bed. Propped all around the room were unframed and often unfinished oil paintings. They stood on chairs, cupboards, small tables and the floor. The lighting was hardly ideal, but from the limited amount of detail I could see, they didn't look very good.

Suddenly, something moved in the gloom by the bed. At first, it was a darker black than the surroundings, like some enormous furry cat. Then, looming beneath it like some pale moon, a face.

I looked at Ian, embarrassed.

'That's Lana, my girlfriend,' said Ian, grinning uncomfortably.

As I turned back to say 'hello', I saw that Lana had lifted herself up on one elbow. A pretty, child's face smiled weakly at me from beneath a tangled Afro. The hairdo was the only concession to her mixed-race origins; her features and skin tone were decidedly European. Her eyes were bloodshot and unfocused. Her mouth hung partly open and around its sides I could discern several angry-looking spots. She was obviously a junkie and she didn't look a day over 16.

We retreated from the room to sit either side of the kitchen table again. Ian started to explain, but I held up a hand to silence him. I hadn't come to sit in judgement. I was a mate, come to help.

Suddenly, a teenage girl flounced into the kitchen. Her mixed-race origins were more readily apparent in her darker skin, and she was stunningly beautiful. An almond-shaped face was framed by a tight Afro. Her tall, slim figure was tightly encased in a short, sheath dress. Her face was pretty, intelligent and cheeky. She looked at me enquiringly, as if to ask what I was doing here.

'This is Abigail,' said Ian, by way of an introduction.

With studied arrogance, Abigail ignored him. She looked me up and down, noting my smart clothes and confident manner. 'Who are you?'

I had heard that Ian had taken to frequenting the bars around King's Cross when he'd got out and that he had taken some of the street girls back to his mother's flat. No doubt, this Abigail was one of the King's Cross Posse. I guessed she would be like all the rest — streetwise, mercenary and ruthless.

You could see that Abigail was used to getting her way with men. I opened my mouth to reply, when another girl ran in. This one was of a similar age, but decidedly plumper. 'Oh,' was all she managed to get out.

'Girls, this is Norman. He's just done 20 years in jail,' Ian blurted out.

Given the circumstances, I wasn't too put out. Among these girls it could only enhance my reputation. And, in the short time I would have with Ian, I wanted to shore up his position as best I could.

I stood up and shook hands with Abigail and then with the tubby girl who introduced herself as Jemma. Both smiled, embarrassed by the formal handshake. Regaining their composure, they looked me up and down again, assessing me. But they had nothing for me. They were obviously both street and drug girls. Not only did I have an inordinate fear of AIDS, I still had this romanticised concept of my future love partner. I had no intention of tarnishing it with either Abigail or Jemma. I sat down again.

'Look, girls. This man here is a good friend of mine. He was a force to be reckoned with in the nick. Now I want you to look after him.' Both girls were nodding in agreement now. 'I'll be back in a couple of month's time and I don't want to hear that any liberties have been taken. OK?' Both girls nodded in agreement again.

Suddenly, there was a ring at the door and the spell was broken. An extravagantly dressed young black guy swaggered in. He didn't have to carry a sign saying he was a drug dealer. The two girls immediately lost interest in everything else. They entwined themselves around the newcomer. Ian was also on his feet, slapping the guy on the back. The guy ignored him, taking quite a liberty seeing as it was Ian's flat, then led the two girls upstairs. Ian sat, deflated, back in the chair. There was silence. We sat quietly for quite a while.

'I was very lonely when I got out, Norm. Too much chokey, I suppose, too much solitary living. I just had to have someone around me. I brought a lot of these girls in here, but they just take the piss. They've stolen all my clothes, sold everything worth selling. A couple of the "chaps" gave me some money when I got out, but I gave it all away. My brother comes round from time to time, but as soon as he turns his back they steal everything. Little Lana in there is the only one who is any good.'

As hard as I had made my heart in the jail, a wave of emotion still swept over me. I could identify precisely with what Ian had said, because I felt exactly that way myself. The only difference was that I was too proud and too strong to admit it. Yeah, what did they think would happen to a man when they put him in a dungeon for 20 years. Didn't Erich Fromm argue that, just as a man had a basic need for food, drink, warmth and light, so he had a basic need for love? Ian and I were two men starving to death from lack of love.

I reached across the table and grasped Ian's hand. 'Ian, I've got to go. I'm back to Ford in the morning, but you can write to me. I'm out again in a couple of months' time and I'll come to see you again. In the meantime, for fuck's sake be strong. Try to get back into some training again. When I get out I'll help you. Don't forget, I'll always be your pal.'

We stood and hugged each other. I reasoned that Ian was as close to family as I had, although I didn't know what my mother would make of that. As Ian opened the door, I heard the girls and the dude laughing upstairs. With a parting wave, I walked away along the corridor.

✳ ✳ ✳

One of the first people to seek me out on my return to Ford was my case officer. Many lifers came back from their home-leaves quite shell-shocked by the awful realisation that, having survived the traumatic experience of many years in jail, they were now confronted by the even more traumatic prospect of having to put their lives back together again in the outside world. Only now they were older, more tired, out of touch and quite damaged by the years inside.

With me, however, it was very much the contrary. I was pleased just to have the opportunity. I was hungry to try out my new personality on the world. Then there was this sense of destiny I felt. I didn't communicate these things to my case officer, though. I just told him how nice it was to see my mother again, of Sunday lunch at home and a walk on Wimbledon Common. He could see that I wasn't hung-over on drink or drugs and this account seemed to satisfy him.

Over the following weeks, I carefully analysed every detail of the weekend. What had happened, how I felt about it, how other people had felt about it and did I want that type of thing as part of my life?

The one factor that rose clearly above all others was that you could only make choices about the kind of lifestyle you wanted if you had money. Otherwise, you did what the poor people did — spend lots of time sitting in your flat watching TV or occasionally having a drink.

The other fact that was quite clear was that the whole crime scene had massively changed. Prior to my arrest, armed robbers ruled the first division of crime. All you needed were a couple of fellas with bottle, some guns and a 'bit of work'. The latter could range from a security van, to a bank or even a good jewellers.

My pals on the outside all assured me that that was all finished. The rise in technology meant that large cash transfers took place inside armoured vans that were almost impregnable. The IRA bombing campaign meant that many city streets were scanned by closed-circuit TV systems and an armed rapid response police unit could be lurking around every corner.

Then there was the money. It would take a team of around four or six to pull down a half-a-million-pound score. You'd get a hundred grand for your whack, but a 20 stretch if you got caught. And on a major bit of work like that, you could bet your life the police wouldn't stop looking.

In the drugs game, if you had the right connections, you could make literally hundreds of grands, comparatively easily, without stirring up too much heat. But the emphasis was on 'the right connections'.

The best move would be one from a source country where the drug was very cheap, all the way home to a first-world country. If it was that simple, however, everybody would be doing it. Obviously, an original move and a high degree of planning was called for.

In the criminal world, I was a past master at 'networking', building up connections between capable criminals who could contribute each part of the puzzle. Over the years, I had selected certain people whom I had kept in contact with. Now would be the time to re-establish contact.

Ivor was a tall, dapper, intelligent guy, who, like myself, was now the wrong side of 40. He was a Midlander who, through his motor racing connections, had travelled extensively around the world. He had come to drug smuggling quite late in life, but had had a good run before getting 12 years for hashish smuggling. We had been pals at Littlehey.

I got him up on a town visit and he came with his new girlfriend, a pleasant Birmingham woman with two chidren. When I managed to get him on his own, we compared notes. Only recently out himself, he was still struggling. However, it was interesting for me to compare Midland's prices with those of London and the south. Certain drugs were more or less available, at cheaper or dearer prices. I could see there was some scope for business. I put him in touch with a couple of pals of mine who were quite small players, but at least Ivor started to earn a couple of quid.

I explained that I had a pal in Thailand who could load and send a container of Thai grass for about £120 a key [kilo]. There was a minimum order of a ton, but the Thais would include an extra ton on credit, provided we would sell it for them at something less than the European market price. Bearing in mind that a key of decent Thai grass was fetching upwards of £2,200 per key in England at the time, the profit margin was very attractive. We would, of course, have to find someone to put up the initial £120,000 for the first ton.

In passing, I also explained that I had a pal who would send transport to any part of mainland Europe and buy off me at up to £600 per key. Ivor looked thoughtful.

'It's great if you can get one all the way home, Norm, but it's very difficult. You never really appreciate that England is an island until you try to smuggle something in. But mainland Europe's a big place. Some countries are very poor and backward. Some have just had revolutions and are in chaos. That would be the move. To get it into one of the former communist Eastern European countries.'

'Yeah, nice one, Ivor. What do we do? Go to the trade section of their embassy and say that we've got a new product for them?'

Ivor ignored the sarcasm. 'Like yourself, Norman, I know lots of people and they trust me. Not so long ago I did an Albanian guy a favour. I knew him from the nick and he was desperate to get a phoney passport to get back into his country. I got him one for nothing. He told me that I had virtually saved his life.'

'You're all heart, Ivor,' I said, playfully punching him in the ribs. 'That's why I like you.'

Ivor laughed and pushed me away. We had fallen into the easy-going relationship we had shared in the nick.

'Will you let me finish?' he said, serious now. 'Well, as luck would have it, he was on the other side in the revolution and his side won. Now he sits on the Revolutionary Council. The only problem is, now that he's in charge, he finds he's in charge of fuck all. The country's absolutely skint. People are literally starving in the streets. He's up for anything that would earn him a few quid.'

Ivor paused for breath and to sip his drink, but I wasn't going to interrupt him now. 'I've already spoken to him about what he can do. He's told me that he can do absolutely anything inside Albania. He said that for thirty grand we can have the docks in the capital. We can bring anything we like through, no questions asked.'

My mind was working very quickly now, weighing up the pros and cons. I knew where Albania was on the map; Greece, Bulgaria and Yugoslavia were all near neighbours. Then, further up, there was Germany. There were distinct possibilities.

Ivor interrupted my train of thought. 'The best part is that we couldn't be nicked. Provided that the Thai people send it OK, my man will escort it through the docks. He'll mind us all the time we're in Albania. If your mate can send lorries to pick it up, we will never need to step outside the country.'

I was listening, but I was also doing some mental arithmetic. If the grass was costing us £120 per key at source, allowing some costs for transport we could have it in Albania for about £150 per key. If I could than sell it on to Gary's people for £500 to £600 per key, that would represent a profit of around £400,000 grand per ton. Once we got a couple under our belt, we could sling it in ten ton at a time. Why send a part-empty container when you can send a full one? It looked like we had found a very useful project.

The next move would be to talk to Aran. Fortunately, he was coming home from Thailand for Christmas. I would have to get him up on a town visit.

With a promising project now in place, I felt slightly less worried about the prospects of release. However, in some ways I was pleased that freedom was still 18 months away. It would give me time to get everything properly in place.

*   *   *

Never one to put all my eggs in one basket, I now decided to concentrate on an alternative project. Criminal projects were all very well; I had the contacts and the reputation to pull them off, but there was always the possibility of getting nicked. I realised that, with my track record, the police would watch me very carefully on release. I wasn't too arrogant to think that I couldn't be nicked. And then where would I be? By the time I got out again, I really would be an old man.

That was why I had devised what I called my 'two-track' approach to freedom. There would be the criminal ventures, but there would also be straight ones. I was now ready to write.

The subject would have to be prison, of course. That was where I had spent most of my adult life. But what a fascinating subject. It was all about the human spirit in adversity. Troubled souls writhing in torment and a system that tried to keep them in check.

I was well aware of the sociological/criminological side to it. I had even written a few articles myself for appropriate journals. There would be a background of that to my work, but the main thrust, the hook that would grab the reader, was the amazing stories. I wouldn't have to invent anything. In jail, truth really was stranger than fiction. My dramas would be populated by fabulous characters who, if they didn't already exist, you would never dare to invent them. And these were all people I had known personally.

I chose a day to begin, gathered a collection of biros and a large foolscap pad, and then sat down to write. I was going to write about the Albany riot 16 years earlier. It was a great story, all about irresistible forces and immovable objects.

I found I had excellent recall; details came flooding back to me and, once again, I lay in solitary in Albany chokey. It brought home to me just how far I had come and how much my prospects had improved. I found that, through the writing, I could still taste the despair of my Albany days. Whenever it became too much, I would put down my pen and take a long walk around Ford's playing fields.

But it was hard work. The line of the story stretched out in front of me like the Great Wall of China. I could imagine a bricklayer with the first brick in his hand, looking into the distance to where he would eventually finish. It was a daunting task that curbed my enthusiasm for the project. Periods spent writing was like time in harness. If I had had any doubts about it before, I now realised that writing was hard work.

That Christmas, unusually for me, I was ill. One of the frequent bouts of 'flu had swept Ford and this time had claimed me amongst its victims. I lay in bed in my room, feeling quite sorry for myself. Friends occasionally dropped in, but I really wasn't in the mood for either festivities or company. I read, but was soon bored. I contemplated writing, but couldn't face it. I lay there, thinking.

Suddenly, I was back at Parkhurst. Part top-security jail, part mental hospital, it had been a bizarre and brutal experience. I thought of a particular episode, one that I had occasionally related as a story sitting in a cell somewhere, talking to pals. Maybe I should write it. I reached for my pen and pad.

Several hours later, I had a dozen or more foolscap sides of writing. The story hung together well. Writing was so much easier when taken in bite-sized chunks. Perhaps I should focus on short stories.

The following day, I thought of another Parkhurst episode and wrote it down. The third day saw me commit another Parkhurst tale to paper. At that point, an idea began to dawn. I wondered how many stories I could remember from my Parkhurst days.

Several hours later and I was looking at a list of 23 headings representing incidents that had happened at Parkhurst. Clearly, I should write a book of short stories, just linking each with some narrative. And the title? It came to me just as clearly: *Parkhurst Tales*.

Now I had the outline of my project firmly in my sights, I got down to some serious work. My self-discipline stood me in good stead now. I made sure I wrote for at least a couple of hours each day. Within a few months, I had a 280-page manuscript. I began to feel like a writer.

At least, I did in private. I didn't intend to let the prison authorities know what I was doing. They had a peculiar attitude towards ex-cons writing. They tried to claim that everything was protected by the Official Secrets Act and couldn't be divulged. My argument was that I hadn't signed it.

Secretly, I showed my writing to some of my pals and they loved it. Not only were the stories enjoyable, they were pleased that, at long last, someone was telling it as it was and giving our side of the story.

One thing led to another; someone knew a writer and a TV producer outside. I sent them some of my stuff. It met with an enthusiastic response. They wanted to see me.

Jess was a likeable Scots guy who had been a successful photographer before becoming a scriptwriter. He had lost his house, his business and all his money on a failed film project. Now he served up grams of coke to his former business associates around clubland, while still trying to write.

I met him one weekend when I was out with the roller-coaster. I immediately liked him and we got on well. He warned me about the million slags and wankers in media-land, and that mostly they would waste my time or try to steal my ideas. He said that he could help me, steer me through. He didn't want anything for it, just the satisfaction of seeing a decent guy make it.

By now I had managed to get a complete manuscript of *Parkhurst Tales* out, so the authorities were presented with something of a *fait accompli*. I now 'went public' to my case officer and the lifer Governor. I pitched it as a solid career opportunity. I showed them a letter from a top TV producer who Jess had managed to interest in my writing. Trix, the producer, was asking to meet me in London to discuss the project.

The lifer Governor was in a quandary. If his role was truly to encourage lifers to make a success of themselves, he could hardly stifle my fledgling writing career. He approved the meeting.

I found it hard to restrain my natural pessimism as I took the train to London, *Parkhurst Tales* clutched firmly under my arm. It really looked like things were beginning to happen for me, although I was sure that, at some point, they would go wrong. They always had before.

The meeting itself, at The Groucho Club, was almost a cliché in literary terms. Everybody who was anybody in the media world met there. I was confident I could handle it, but was sure I was unique in that there wouldn't be any other murderers out on parole there.

Piccadilly was bustling; and Soho was quite confusing, but I managed to find my way to Groucho's and waited in reception for Trix to arrive. He was ten minutes late when he hurried in.

He was all apologies as he ushered me into the bar. As Trix ordered drinks, I weighed him up. He was clearly of West Indian extraction, quite portly and very short. He had a pleasant, open face and a cultured intelligent voice that had echoes of the street. He was dressed smartly but casually and had a small, leather hat perched on his head. On many people it would have looked ridiculous, but on Trix it looked cool. I guessed he was about ten years younger that me.

Very soon we were quite relaxed around each other. He intimated that he still had brothers over in South London who ducked and dived. I guessed that this was where the street echoes in his diction came from. He enthused about my work; he was a successful writer himself and admired my style. He was sure it had potential for film or TV.

We dined, discussed the world in general and crime trends in particular, and agreed that he would investigate possible media opportunities for my writing. On the train back to Ford that evening, I felt that I had achieved something.

I didn't let it completely go to my head though, as I was still intent on my 'two-track' policy until the writing really came to something. Over the following months I continued to have the chaps up on town visits. I saw Aran and confirmed the Thai connection. Ivor spoke to his Albanian pal. When I saw Gary, he seemed pleased with the way it was all going.

* * *

Back in the spiritual world, though, all was far from settled. I had read somewhere that once a man has been awakened to the spiritual, everything else became irrelevant. Undoubtedly, I was now on a mission of self-discovery. I realised I would always live in the shadow of my past — if nothing else, the writing would ensure that. Even my readership would be aware of the existence of 'the Beast'. In many ways, I had become an observer of my own life.

Set reading for my degree course and the arrogance that came with being a writer myself served to put me off reading. I read absolutely no novels. Somehow I came into possession of *The Occult* by Colin Wilson and found myself lost in a world of mysteries and alternate religions. It would all serve to enlighten me and aid me in my quest to further understand the cult of Norman.

For that was how I had come to view myself. As some flawed but powerful spirit, driven towards a destiny that I couldn't comprehend. If I were to ever drown out the cries of my victims, to rescue myself from abject failure with only destruction as my epitaph, I would have to achieve greatness. I was a late starter, with a considerable handicap, but I would achieve something or die in the attempt.

I came across the work of Israel Regardie, sometime associate of Crowley, though I didn't hold that against him. He had broken away early. I wouldn't have tolerated anything negative. I had found darkness myself and was now on a journey to the light.

I ordered two of his books through the library. Neither were available, and I was very disappointed with the title they did send. *The Art of Making Talismans* promised little I would be interested in. In retrospect, it was fate that it should come to me.

As I read, I learned that this was far more than some New Age guide to making some lucky trinket. There was a whole philosophy behind the ancient art of talismans. Or perhaps I should refer to it as a theosophy, for much was based on ancient religion.

There were charts, much like astrological charts. The time and date of one's birth were paramount. The finished article could protect, but when constructed towards some purpose, it could empower one towards that goal. The mystical writer in me felt compelled to seek its assistance. I had never been one for lucky charms, rabbits' feet, medallions, whatever, but this did strike some chord in me. I set about making my talisman.

From the charts, I found that my shape was a triangle and my colour was red. I cut a small, equilateral triangle from a red plastic tray.

My *kamea* was the 'Kamea of the Sun'. The numbers were disturbing. Ironically, my lucky number was 6, although on many of the times it had featured in my life it had been anything but lucky, but that wasn't what caused me concern. On the back of the talisman I had to inscribe four numbers. One in each of the three corners of the triangle and the last in the centre. According to the 'Kamea of the Sun', my four numbers were 6, 36, 111 and 666.

Now, I was well aware of the number of 'the Beast' and it came as a considerable shock to find it in my chart. But several years previously, I had had an expert in numerology in the next cell to mine. He had said that 444 was a worse number and 666 could be extremely bad, but sometimes it could be extremely good too. I was reassured by Regardie's reputation as a 'white magician', but it was with some trepidation that I inscribed the numbers on the back of the triangle.

The front was less problematic. Three numbers — 1, 5 and 9 — were to go in each corner and my name, written in Hebrew, was to be inscribed with the letters in a circle.

As a Jew, I reflected on the use of Hebrew as quite apposite for me. However, I was aware that Hebrew was the ancient language of mysticism. In *schul* I approached a Hebrew scholar. I didn't explain my full intent, but I got him to write out a close approximation of my name in Hebrew. I inscribed it on the front of the triangle.

All I needed now was a silver chain to hang it from. My mother gave me one she used to wear, remarking that she didn't much like the use to which it was being put. I drilled a small hole in the top corner of the triangle, threaded the chain through and I had my talisman.

According to Regardie, the wearing of the talisman gave it power towards the required goal. The more it was worn, the more powerful it would get. Ideally, the wearer should never take it off. I didn't much fancy running about the gym with it swinging in full view. There would be some ribbing and sensible people would think that I was cracking up. But I was intent on my mystical path and determined to wear it as often as I could.

* * *

Several months passed and I hadn't made as much progress through Trix as I would have liked. In fact, at times it was difficult even to communicate with him. Resident experts at Ford, and there were several for every profession, advised that I should get an agent.

But how? How many agents would be willing to represent someone with my background. With the *schul* being my fall-back position whenever I encountered a problem, I asked the businessman who had donated the wood for the roller-coaster.

Solly was held in awe by the other Jews at Ford, and by many of the other cons as well. He was a very wealthy and powerful businessman. His case having held the headlines for several months. This all meant nothing to me. I had long ago ceased to judge a man on his possessions.

Even in prison grey, without a coin, Solly was a man of stature. He conducted himself with dignity and didn't seek those favours from the authorities that others in his position could have garnered. His father had originally come from the East End and there was still something of the East End boy about Solly. He was unpretentious and completely down to earth.

All the other Jews fawned on him. At first, I ignored him, then just treated him civilly. Perhaps he was impressed by my straightforwardness. We grew to like each other and he admitted that he was impressed by my strength and the determination which had sustained me through my sentence.

He read some of my writing and liked it. He recommended a friend of his who was a top agent and sent her copies. She wrote to me, asking to see me.

Once again, I travelled to London clutching *Parkhurst Tales*. Anita's office was in Shaftesbury Avenue and, as I waited in the anteroom to her office, I realised how privileged I was to have some of her time.

I was ushered into the presence of a dark, slim, well-dressed woman with a disarmingly friendly smile. Immediately, she did her best to put me at my ease. She emphasised how highly she thought of Solly, her manner suggesting that we all shared a Jewish background.

Within minutes, we were joined by a portly, florid-faced man in his fifties. Long years of living in England couldn't disguise the Celtish whisper in his voice. He introduced himself as Frank Delaney, writer, broadcaster and then consultant editor at Random Century. He enthused about my writing.

'Norman, your work is great. You write at two levels, you analyse and you observe. You've got enough work here for several years. I'm going to recommend to Random Century that they make you a star author and give you a two-book contract. I'm so pleased I've come across your stuff.'

The confirmed pessimist in me stifled any exhilaration. I was immediately suspicious of this man's credentials. Yet Anita was a top agent and would only have dealt with people at the pinnacle of their profession. Anyway, I had heard of Frank Delaney and he had a considerable reputation. I had experienced so many let-downs in the past, I feared a cup of nectar turning into a poisoned chalice. I wouldn't get too excited, just in case.

However, I did feel excited on the train back. Whatever the outcome career-wise of the meeting in Anita's office, there was one thing that couldn't be denied; Frank Delaney thought that I was a great writer. He had positively enthused over my work and it hadn't been an act. In his exalted position, perhaps he knew what he was talking about. For a fledgling writer, all natural arrogance apart, who was still unsure of the quality of his work, it was very reassuring. A cocksure ex-killer had travelled up to London that morning; it was a quietly confident writer who had returned.

LIFE
AFTER LIFE

By now, the life I had settled into at Ford was just about as easy as could be found in prison. What with my work at the Scout Hut, trips out with the roller-coaster, town visits and occasional home-leaves, it wasn't exactly a stimulating existence but, in the circumstances, could be tolerated until full freedom arrived.

There was quite a high turnover of cons; each week there could be as many as 20 receptions. By and large, I took little notice. I had my own small circle of friends and I wasn't especially looking to expand it.

Just before Boy-Boy arrived, I received a message from Gary. He asked me to look out for a friend of his and see that he settled in OK. I was wary of getting involved with people I didn't know personally; an irresponsible fool could get himself and any associates thrown out of Ford. Gary assured me that Boy-Boy was a game, staunch fella, even if he could be a bit scatty at times. However, to help friends of friends in the nick was a duty, not a choice, I was committed to helping Boy-Boy, whatever he was like.

In the event, I was pleasantly surprised. The man who sought me out was a tall, slim, reserved guy in his middle twenties. He had a serious air about him and wasn't much given to fooling about. He made it clear he wasn't going to impose himself on me, realising that I had to steer a safe path in Ford.

Within a couple of weeks, I grew to quite like him. Everything was very much understated about Boy-Boy. Although very capable, he wasn't at all boastful. You literally had to drag the detail out of him.

It transpired that his family had lived in Notting Hill for decades. His father was a wealthy and successful drugs importer who had been in the game for 20 years. Boy-Boy, though, wanted to make his own way and was reluctant to accept help from him. It also transpired that he had been a champion boxer. Further, he was very capable and dangerous in a tear-up and was feared and respected all across West London. You would never have thought so to look at him and I found this out from others, which made me respect him the more. We didn't hang around together all the time, but I got him on the roller-coaster party and we became friends.

As part of my 'two-track' release plan, I had long thought that, should all else fail, I could always get a job in a gym. Not only was I very knowledgeable about all aspects of gym work, I also had a well-developed physique. However, I was aware that, to work in most gyms, you needed a professional qualification. I found out that they did an appropriate course called 'Recreation and Leisure Management' at a college in nearby Worthing. I would have to attend one day a week, on a Monday. The education department approved my application. If nothing else, it would get me out of the prison for one more day a week.

On the first Monday of term, I travelled to Worthing with another potential gym instructor. Barry was a young ex-squaddie who was trying to come to terms with the fact that the Army had been the one chance he had had to get away from the northern squalor he had grown up in, but he had blown it. He was full of crazy ideas and ill-thought out plans. Within the first ten minutes, I realised that he wasn't to be taken seriously.

We sat in class, him revelling in the fact that he was from the nick, me, slightly embarassed by it. I cautioned him about telling the others I was a lifer. I wasn't there to create an impression, socialise or have a good time, I just wanted the qualification with a minimun amount of fuss.

The first shock was that the rest of the dozen or so students were little more than teenagers. The oldest fella was 23, then there was an eight-year gap to the second-oldest student beside me — Jackie.

Jackie was interesting and very attractive. I really wasn't looking for courtship. There would be little opportunity and any prospective catch could well be intimidated by my background. That didn't mean that I wouldn't enjoy chatting and socialising with women, though. If nothing else, it would be good practice for me.

It turned out that Jackie was more embarrassed by the age difference between herself and the rest of the students than I was. Quite pretty and delightfully shy, after first keeping her distance she found she had more in common with me than the others. Slowly, we became friends.

She explained that she was married, with three boisterous boys. Her husband, whom she had been with since teenage years, was a bricklayer in Littlehampton. She worked part-time in the local leisure centre.

I didn't actually drag this informtion out of her; everything was extremely low-key between us, but slowly, over the passage of several months, we began to share details of our lives.

Jackie was highly intelligent and something of a dreamer. She realised that her life was just slipping past and wanted more. But she was trapped. Littlehampton, a husband and three children all stood in the way of an exciting career.

She found my history fascinating, if somewhat horrifying. She had never met anyone who had ever been to prison before, let alone a criminal of my ilk. She was never judgemental and always careful not to hurt my feelings. However, she thought the prospects of my coming release very exciting.

Relations were all decidedly proper between us. Not only was I shy and awkward with women, I had fallen into 'perfect gentleman' mode with her. She never encouraged me and I would never push myself on her uninvited. We sat together in class and stayed together on field trips, but neither of us considered it a romance.

That isn't to say that I wouldn't have liked it to be so. Of the women I had seen so far, Jackie certainly seemed very suitable. She was pretty, had a good figure from working out in the gym, was intelligent and shared many of my interests. She also seemed shy and unworldly. A more sophisticated and precocious woman would have intimidated me. The only problem was that she was married and didn't seem interested in me romantically.

However, it wasn't a problem. Mondays out at college were only a sideshow to the grand scheme of things. When I left Ford on my writer/outlaw's mission into the great wide world, no doubt Littlehampton Jackie would be a forgotten irrelevance.

* * *

It had taken time, but my liaison with my new agent was at last beginning to bear fruit. She had brought Trix into line and had interested a major player. She wanted to bring him down to see me.

Received wisdom from the professionals at Ford was that this was a significant coup. Mike Mansfield was a wealthy and famous record and video producer. For him to come all the way to Sussex to see me could only mean that he was seriously interested in the project.

Mike Mansfield and his assistant duly arrived with Anita. As we sat around a table in the visiting room, I hoped the novelty of the situation wouldn't detract from the seriousness of the negotiations. I realised that this was a major opportunity. However, I was still a prisoner of my natural arrogance and self-belief. I was confident in the quality of my work, as evidenced by the comparatively quick show of interest. I was sure I was going to make it one way or another.

Anita did the introductions, then Mike launched into an enthusiastic explanation of why he thought there were good prospects for a TV series based on *Parkhurst Tales*. I listened attentively. All self-confidence notwithstanding, I realised that, as a unknown writer, my position wasn't a strong one. I would need the help of powerful and established allies to get my first piece of work off the ground.

They weren't going to get 'writer-as-artist' from me. I wouldn't fight for total editorial control over my work. I rationalised that I wasn't a one-trick pony, I would write other things. If necessary, I would sacrifice some artistic integrity over *Parkhurst Tales*. My only question would be, 'How rich and famous are you going to make me, so that on my next project I will have editorial control?'

I sat there quietly proud of my pragmatism. Mike burbled away about amalgamating certain characters to make them more recognisable for the viewers. An image sprang to mind of those silent ranks of morons who populated prison TV rooms, gazing vacantly at the screen. A major reason I had retained my sanity was that I had never become a TV buff in jail.

Suddenly, I focused on what Mike was saying. 'I see *Parkhurst Tales* as something like ...' he paused, searching for words, it couldn't have been effect '... er, *Coronation Street* set in prison.'

If he had leaned across the table and punched me in the face, I couldn't have been more insulted. Writer/outlaw I might be, but I believed passionately in my work. That was the whole essence of it. It was true, real, factual, the way it had actually happened. There was no ideology involved, this wasn't a partial convict's version of what went on in prison.

Parkhurst Tales was a cautionary tale. Nothing was glorified: I didn't want any young man to come away feeling that there was something glamorous or exciting about spending one's life in jail. And yes, it was a savage indictment of the system. I was writing in that greatest of traditions, the writer informing society of a rottenness at its core. That was my main motivation, the basis of my spirituality, not some quick way to make a few quid through some trashy TV series. If it had been, I would have written it completely differently, complete with easily recognisable heroes and villains.

There was a brief surge of anger, prison mode asserted itself in my mind as I contemplated launching myself across the table at this outsider who would make a mockery of my work. But I had great self-control now. It all registered as merely a flicker in my eye.

'You know the medium, Mike,' I heard myself say, 'I'll leave that up to you.' I smiled at Anita, who smiled back approvingly.

Later, I cursed myself. I wasn't even out of prison, yet I was already compromising my values. I had needed a strong value-system to get myself through. You had to become a philosopher in prison if you were to make any sense of things and retain your sanity. Living in an emotional and social vacuum, surrounded by so much negativity, you could only believe in absolutes: honesty to one's beliefs, loyalty to one's friends and a determination to do good rather than evil acts.

'But what of your continuing criminality?' I hear you say. 'Define your terms,' I reply.

The directors and shareholders of the drink and tobacco conglomerates lose little sleep over the death and disease their products cause. The manufacturers of Prozac and other psychotropic drugs never agonise over the moral implications of their products. Why should I baulk at breaching a culturally based embargo on cannabis, a comparatively harmless drug?

* *. *

My parole review came around again and all the usual reports were made. Everyone said that I should get my release date this time. However, there was some reservation. The then Tory government was firmly in a law and order mind-set. It was purely political expediency rather than penal pragmatism. I could just turn out to be one of those 'special cases' they drew the line at. I was concerned, but not overly so. I had talked to my pals about it. If I got another knock-back they would help me to settle abroad. I faced the future with an air of inevitability.

Several weeks had passed since my meeting with Anita and Mike Mansfield, when a letter arrived. Anita was suggesting the setting up of a company called Parkhurst Tales Ltd. The shares would be divided four ways, with Trix, Mike, Anita and myself having 25 per cent each.

I consulted the Ford professionals. I thought that, seeing as how *Parkhurst Tales* was 100 per cent created by myself, one quarter share didn't represent a fair share. They agreed. Perhaps I should have accepted part of a sure 'something'.

The project still continued; it was taken to the networks, but three of them rejected it. The 'professionals' remarked that, with Mike's background in music video and Trix's in comedy, perhaps the networks didn't think they were up to heavy drama. Anyway, Trix and Anita expressed their continuing interest. It was something outside my control, so I concentrated more intensely on criminal projects.

The months rolled by, town visits and home-leaves came and went. I was gradually re-establishing contact with all my old friends. Steve had served 16 years of a life sentence; we had been comrades through many hard times. Now he had returned to Worthing, where he lived with his childhood sweetheart who had waited patiently for him. They ran an old folks home between them and seemed content.

Many a Monday, out at college, I met him at lunchtime. We had puffed together in the nick, and it was quite a novelty to slip away to his flat now and have a couple of pipes. If the outside world was surreal enough to me under normal conditions, it became absolutely fantastic when off my face. Travelling about became like some magical mystery tour through a fantasy land. I was sure it was all very mundane to the rest of Worthing's inhabitants, but when I returned to the jail it was as if from an amazing adventure. I was still just visiting the world, digesting it in easy, bite-sized chunks, then returning to the safe haven of Ford, to assess my experiences.

Jim was another lifer pal. He had been just 17 and a game young East End kid when he had got his sentence. In jail, we had much in common, sharing many of the same values and hopes on release.

One home-leave, I took the Tube to Plaistow. We met at his run-down council flat. I had heard that he'd had a hard time. Early financial success had come complete with a heavy coke habit. Soon he had done his money, his friends and his reputation. Skint and out of favour, he was struggling at the moment.

He had always been a bit of a ladies' man and Julie was no disappointment. Stunningly beautiful, her immaculate clothes and grooming seemed quite out of place in the surroundings. I was faultlessly polite, but she seemed reserved and sullen. I guessed there might be problems between them.

Jim was pleased to see me, but was quick to stress that these were hard times.

'You'll see, Norm. No one gives you a chance. It's not like the old days,' he cautioned.

As far as I was concerned, nothing had changed between us. I realised we couldn't be 'all boys together' out here, the presence of wives and girlfriends prevented that. But surely we were still mates who would see each other regularly and look out for each other.

But this was a different world. I had only ever been used to the all-male prison society. Men moved in groups there. The basic unit was your closest pals, everything revolved around that. Out here, the basic unit was the man and his woman, almost to the exclusion of all else. I realised that this was something that I would have to come to terms with. Perhaps things would be different when I had a regular girlfriend myself.

In many ways, he was still the same old Jim, lively, irreverent and restlessly energetic. But underneath, something was missing. There was little of the old warmth, the genuineness. There was something superficial, even seedy about him. This was soon confirmed.

'What size shoes you take, Norm?'

'Seven I suppose, Jim,' I said slightly embarrassed. Buying clothes was still quite personal to me.

'I've got something for you,' he said, disappearing out of the room. I heard him speak to Julie next door. He returned with a pair of black leather shoes in his hand.

'I've only worn them a couple of times, paid sixty quid for them. Try them on.'

They looked OK, plain, quite reserved. But I didn't wear second-hand shoes, not even in the nick. More embarrassed now, I put them on. They fitted well enough.

'OK?' Jim asked.

I nodded in reply. 'Normally, Norm, I'd give 'em to ya, but we're skint and Julie says I've got to ask you for something. I'll take thirty quid for them.'

I was deeply embarrassed and angry both at the same time. What could I say? This was a man who had been a close friend in the nick. We had stood by each other in times of great danger; our friendship had sustained us against a soulless existence where every man's hand seemed to be against you. Now he had tricked me into buying a pair of poxy second-hand shoes at a price you could have bought new ones in a sale.

Inwardly, I flinched. Jim's friendship was very important to me. I didn't want to start off out here by falling out with people. I saw my future as one where I was surrounded by a network of supportive friends. The alternative would be the loneliness of the jail.

With as good grace as I could manage, I handed over £30. Jim muttered a subdued 'Thanks'. It was unspoken, but he knew that he had taken a liberty. It would pass for now. Perhaps he really was on hard times and would change as his situation improved. For now, though, I had to get away. I said my goodbyes and left.

Within months, he and Julie had moved to Brighton. Perhaps the change of environment agreed with him. I often visited him on town visits. He seemed calmer, but it was still obvious he had a coke problem. It was my first real experience of the phenomenon. It seemed that coke could change your personality and make you selfish. I swore that it would never have me.

* * *

Things were going really well with Gary now. With my parole answer imminent and all the elements of the Albanian move in place, he was a regular visitor. On home-leaves I had begun to meet with him and the rest of the firm he was with.

It was generally recognised that the Joneses were the second-most powerful firm in London. South London-based, they were prolific importers of drugs. They were extremely wealthy and well organised, with several ex-army minders on the firm. They were a force to be reckoned with.

Billy and Barry Jones hadn't got carried away by their success. People said they were still the unassuming, good-natured fellas they had always been. I certainly got on well enough with them. We never spoke about the Albanian coup, but I knew that Gary had mentioned it to them. Whenever we met, they always forced wads of money into my pockets. On one occasion I came away with four grand. I didn't know it for a fact, but it certainly looked like they were grooming me for a place on the firm. In straight-world terms, I suppose that was a bit like Merryl Lynch head-hunting you for a top position. With just a minimum of effort, the calibre of the company would almost guarantee your future success.

By now, Boy-Boy had been released and I also saw him on home-leaves. His father was still doing well and had given him a chunk of money, but, by coincidence, he had joined up with the other most powerful firm in London. The Taylors were even more successful and well organised than the Joneses. They were also more dangerous.

It was a strange liaison really. Boy-Boy had been close to Gary and was friendly with the Joneses. Yet the Taylors were the Joneses' sworn enemies. There had been several confrontations, with the Taylors taking the leading role. I vowed not to get involved. Both the Taylors and the Joneses had a reputation for being honourable. I saw no problem in my being friends with both of them.

In fact, it considerably improved my criminal standing. I was already well in with the Joneses, and I now had a close pal who was right on the firm with the Taylors. Home-leaves were heady times. One day I would be standing with Billy and Barry Jones in South London. The next I would be with Boy-Boy and Perry and David Taylor in their City bar.

Back at Ford, I was growing increasingly frustrated. I really wanted to be out on the street now. I cringed at every gangland swoop that might threaten my 'help'. But I was still months away from receiving a parole answer.

As if to signal that it might be an end to an era, the second year of my college course drew to a close. I would miss the Mondays in Worthing. Surprisingly, I found that I would also miss Jackie. Still without the slightest hint of romance between us, we had come to share each other's hopes and fears. When we met, we would relate the details of the previous week. We laughed together and found that we both valued each other's opinions.

On the penultimate week, I summoned up my courage and asked her to have lunch with me the coming Monday. Shyly, she agreed. The King's Hotel in Bognor had seen better days, but it was still the most prestigious hotel in the town. Out of season now, the lunchtime dining room was almost deserted. Jackie confessed that the only time she had ever been in a big hotel was when she was abroad on holiday.

That was little consolation to me — I hadn't been in one for over 20 years. The formalities and etiquette of ordering a meal and making polite conversation loomed like a nightmare. I was anything but relaxed.

Somehow, we stumbled through our meal. Like two teenagers who had just met, every subject seemed embarrassing. She admitted that she didn't love her husband any more and wanted a divorce. He was the only man she had ever known since she was 17. In some ways she was starting out all over again, just like me.

For my part, I said that I didn't know what to expect if and when I got out, but that I had enjoyed her company and would like to stay in touch. She looked at me with tears in her eyes and I took her hand. I reflected that neither of us would have been out of place in a Jane Austen novel.

It was a timeless moment, one I didn't want to end. But she had to go and pick the kids up and I had to get back to jail. We said a sad 'goodbye'. Awkwardly, I kissed her on the cheek.

I felt exhilarated on the way back to the prison. Nothing much had happened, certainly not by some of today's standards. However, merely through a form of words, I now felt more complete, more happy. There was no deep commitment, but we obviously felt something for each other. I suppose I could now say that I had a woman in my life. It did something to assuage the aching loneliness.

I had often wondered about the moment of hearing about my release. What would be the circumstances? How would I feel? But not obsessively. That way lay madness. Merely, would it be an auspicious day, magically marked in some way? Would I wake on the morning feeling different and know that this was the day? As with most things in prison, having been awaited so long, when it did arrive it was something of an anti-climax.

I had gone to the dining hall at lunchtime as usual and seen my name on the the call-ups board, which signified that the lifer Governor wanted to see me. It could have been anything. Something to do with my work, my writing, an unusual letter. However, bearing in mind that I had been waiting 11 months and 18 days for my parole answer — you could start expecting to hear something after about six months — I did get a nervous feeling in my stomach.

If it was my answer, so much would depend on it. Either it would be pressure off and the delightful prospect of putting my life back together again, or the nightmare of absconding at 50 and living on the run on the continent. Fifteen years earlier I would have welcomed the challenge and excitement of the latter. But now I couldn't help but feel that it was too late for all that.

The lifer Governor was a tall, reserved, polite man, a career civil servant who was often mystified by the vagaries of the system. Knowing I would be nervous, he dispensed with any preliminaries.

'You've got your release date, Norman. You go to the Scrubs hostel in two weeks' time for nine months' hostel, then you will be released.'

There was no explosion of emotion in me. I didn't feel like jumping up for joy, but I did feel very relieved. I immediately thought how pleased my mother would be. I was aware the Governor would be watching my reaction. There were so many apocryphal tales of men breaking down in tears. There would be none of that from me. Strength in all things had become an obsession with me. I had resolved that, whatever the news, I would handle it with dignity.

I shook the Governor's hand and took the piece of paper which was the official notification of my parole result. It was barely four lines.

I didn't rush around telling my pals. Fred and Boy-Boy had both been recently released and I hadn't bothered to make new friends. As I lay on my bed, I couldn't help but reflect on a system that had held me for 23 years, then gave me only two weeks' notice that I would be free.

Now that I was leaving, I began to look at Ford with different eyes. It had been good for me, had given me some respite and allowed me to gather my strength against the challenge of freedom. Physically, I was much better. Other than a stiffness about the knees, I was nearly back to full health. However, I still had to stick rigidly to a special diet.

From a mental point of view, I was still phenomenally strong, disciplined and focused. No doubt that would serve me well in the outside world. However, I was well aware that there were massive gaps in my experience of life. In some ways it was like being born again at fifty.

I would miss the Scout Hut and the kids. The goodbyes were sad, especially when the children presented me with gifts from their parents. I promised I would come back and see them from time to time.

There were only a couple of farewells to be said at Ford. I packed up what was left of my kit. I had taken most of it with me when I went on my last home-leave. Then I just waited.

After 23 years of waiting, the two weeks passed quite quickly. I took the train to London and made my way to the hostel.

Wormwood Scrubs Hostel was situated outside the prison, but right next to the main gate. As I turned left into the hostel building, sundry screws, visitors and deliverymen carried straight on to the prison proper. I didn't exactly experience a sense of *déjà vu*, just a cold feeling down my spine at the thought of starting my time all over again.

The hostel warden was an old Senior Officer. He was assisted by two other former screws, all of them in civilian clothes. He explained the rules, quite an extensive list. There was a tiredness about his eyes and his manner. I guessed that he had played out this exact scenario with so many others, who had then gone on to mess it up and be put back inside.

He took me upstairs and put me in a large room containing three beds. I would be sharing with two others. I put down my kit, then he showed me around the hostel.

Apart from several rooms identical to my own, there was a TV room, a dining room and a small kitchen. I reflected that I wouldn't be seeing too much of them. I would leave as soon as I could in the morning and return as late as I could at night. I intended to use the hostel just to sleep.

Hostel residents had to work at least five days a week. A percentage of their wages was paid to the hostel. They could leave at 6.00am and had to be back in the hostel by 10.45pm. Those who had somewhere to go could leave the hostel every Friday morning and be back by 10.45pm on Sunday evening. For those who had done a long time inside, it was intended to be the last step before the responsibility of full freedom.

I had already arranged my job. I would be working for a property management company owned by Gary. In truth, I would only go there each Friday to pick up my £150 wage packet. That would leave me plenty of time to work on my other plans.

By now it was Friday afternoon and the warden had completed all his paperwork for me. He told me to go home and be back by Sunday evening. Three buses later, I was at my mum's flat.

A dozen or more home-leaves had blunted the excitement of home-coming somewhat, but my mother still cried and hugged me at this new stage in my journey to freedom. I put my stuff away and sat down in the lounge. Almost immediately there was a problem.

I should have been able to relax, take a deep breath and sit back, thanking all the gods of fortune for delivering me from a hellish existence. I should have been able to exult in my freedom, in the fact that, should I so wish, I could walk out of the flat and go for a stroll across the common.

Instead, my mind was in a turmoil. I didn't actually fidget, but mentally I couldn't stay in one place. I was a driven man. Why, I demanded of myself, after spending so many years just sitting about, was I now sitting about in my mum's flat? And that was a further source of discomfort. I was embarrassed to be fifty years of age and living in my mother's one-bedroomed flat.

My friends had all told me to take my time. But I was Tough Norman, Tearaway Norman, the Peter Pan of the prison system. I hadn't sat about all those years merely to exist at a basic level. That might be OK for some lifers, those who had been burned out by the endless years. Perhaps all they were fit for now was to idle away their declining years in poverty.

Not for me, though. That was why I had fought the system so fiercely. I had come out to achieve something, make something of myself. Only that would detract from the sense of failure at having wasted so much of my life.

I quickly phoned around and made appointments to see several of my friends. They were excited that I was home, albeit on the hostel, and promised some eventful nights out. I spoke to Gary and he sounded strangely reticent. He pleaded pressure of work and said that he wouldn't be able to see me for a while. I dismissed my suspicions as prison paranoia.

By most people's standards it was an eventful weekend. Friday evening saw me in several pubs in the East End. Old friends and new hugged me and rushed to buy drinks. A significant problem was that, because of the arthritis, I didn't drink. Therefore, not only did I feel strange and out of place in, what was for me, unusual surroundings, I had to suffer it stone cold sober whilst others got drunk. After a while, it got quite boring.

The women, however, did fascinate me. Not only was there the strong sexual attraction, there was also the possibility of getting close to another spirit after so many years of solitude. In truth, I would have passed on the pubs, the parties and the clubs, just to sit in a small room with a woman and warm myself at the altar of her spirituality. The sex would have been important, but not as important as exploring each other's minds, sharing the immediate experience, giving and receiving pleasure and reassuring the other spirit that she could relax safe in the knowledge that she was loved and cared for and would have someone to look out for her in the coming years.

But that didn't happen all in a second, and certainly not across a noisy East End pub. I didn't make it easy for myself either. Where my pals were all at least 20 years younger than I, so were the company we were in. I found I wasn't in the least attracted to women of my own age. Their sophistication and experience seemed to intimidate me and remind me of my own inexperience. In some ways, it would have been like going out with my mother.

Further, I could see through their eyes that they had suffered the death of too many dreams. Each new affair had become a cold exchange, an almost inevitable expectation that it would all go wrong too soon, leaving one or the other feeling used. I was still young at heart and romantic. No doubt they, in their world-worn pragmatism, their down-to-earth common sense, would find it all a bit silly. But I wasn't ready to give up my dream of destiny yet.

Young, attractive women, however, seemed to know their worth in the modern market place. They demanded young, attractive fellas and a good time. Older men needed a successful background to be taken seriously. Not only was I nearly skint, I didn't even have my own flat. Short of buying loads of drinks and handing out lines of coke, I wasn't going to have much early success with these type of women. And even if I had, in those circumstances, would I meet the woman I was looking for? Clearly, it was going to take some time.

Saturday morning saw me out with big John, buying a car from a friend's showroom. For £2,000 I got a little red Vauxall Nova that was guaranteed to last. I knew that I would need to be able to get about and public transport was too inconvenient and expensive. I had recently passed my driving test while still at Ford. It didn't prepare me for the London traffic, though.

That afternoon, I joined a local gym. What had worked for me in prison would work outside. I was quite proud of my physique and fitness, and I didn't intend to let it go. Furthermore, it was the basis of my self-discipline. The local YMCA had a well-resourced gym. The women were a novelty for me; I had never worked out alongside women before, and I was sure I would get used to it. Anyway, I would be focusing on the workout. I hadn't joined a gym to socialise.

Saturday evening saw me out with Nick. He was the epitome of what all the young fellas thought they should be. He must have been the original 'tall, dark and handsome' of many women's dreams. He was smart, confident, articulate, funny and something of a successful criminal. He charmed most women without even trying. It would be interesting watching his moves.

We went to several pubs and clubs, then headed for Browns, supposedly the best club in London. Nick, of course, was close friends with Jake, the owner. Not only did we walk straight past the waiting queue, soon we were sitting in the exclusive VIP suite.

I examined some of the people around me. There were a couple of well-known pop stars and one film star I recognised. Nick let slip that I was fresh out of jail after 20 years and that served to excite their interest. Conversation was animated and intense.

During lulls, I looked at some of the women. All were stunningly beautiful and exquisitely groomed. Whenever I went to the bar to buy drinks, several looked at me with interest. I caught a couple looking intently at my watch. It was an expensive one and had come from a batch that had been stolen. It had been a gift from a friend. I was immediately paranoid. On returning to the group, I asked Nick about it.

He threw back his head and laughed.

'Norman, there's some right shrewd little cows up here. They're out for anything they can get. Before they go out with you, they want to make sure you've got some money. That's why they look at your watch. If it's an expensive one, they're interested. If not, not.'

I was beginning to discover just how naïve I was. After so many years in the poisoned society that was prison, I just didn't want to believe that the straight world was similarly flawed. Surely, that was what criminality was all about? Criminals were mostly bad people with bad ways; conversely, honest people should all be good people, with nice ways.

Of course, I didn't really believe that. But, on a spiritual level, I wasn't ready to accept the alternative. If I had to buy these girls in Browns, then I wasn't interested. What I could buy, so could anyone else. And when the money ran out, well then so would they. Discouraged but not disheartened, I came home from Browns alone.

I had a Sunday drink with Boy-Boy, but he seemed much changed. Gone was the reserved, laid-back manner, and in its place was an aggressive, thrusting, in-your-face attitude. He seemed under pressure and extremely paranoid. An old and mutual friend offered an explanation.

'He ain't been the same since he's been on the firm with the Taylors,' he confided. 'Don't say that I said so, but he's bang on the coke, too.'

I spent a frenetic couple of hours around him. He seemed to be the centre of attention, with dozens of people coming and going. He did talk to me occasionally, but for long periods of time he seemed indifferent to my presence. He told me to come round to his house the following morning at 10.00am, then I left.

On Sunday evening, lying in my bed in the hostel, I had a lot to think about. This new world was very confusing. My main concern was how I was going to make a living. The job with Gary was only for the period of the hostel and I wouldn't get far on £150 a week anyway. Through Jake, a couple of people were interested in seeing my writing, but film or publishing deals were a long way off.

It was worrying that I hadn't touched base with Gary yet. One would have thought that he would have been one of the first to see me, even apart from the Albanian coup. Boy-Boy was supposed to be my pal and had promised to help me, yet he had been almost dismissive when I had seen him that afternoon. I would have to see what he said when I saw him the next morning. With that thought, I fell into a troubled sleep.

Monday set a pattern. I was up at 5.30am, shaved, showered, dressed and was out of the hostel by 6.00am. With my car parked just around the corner, I was home in Wimbledon eating my breakfast by just after 7.00am.

I left at 8.30am for my rendezvous with Boy-Boy. Arriving at his house early, I sat outside reading a paper until just before 10.00am.

His wife answered the door. She explained that he had gone out just after 9.00am and didn't say where he was going. He hadn't left a message for me either. She didn't know what to suggest, but her manner indicated that this wasn't the first time it had happened.

Instantly, I felt deflated. The 'chaps' didn't make meetings with each other and not show up. It was the gravest discourtesy, especially as he hadn't even left a message. I tried to convince myself that there must have been some kind of emergency, that he had had to leave in a hurry.

He had told me that I could always find him in the afternoons in the Taylors' City wine bar. It was too early yet, so I went to a local café for a late breakfast.

Cottons was close to Ludgate Circus. It was something between a wine bar and a restaurant. The décor was decidedly American, all shiny brasswork and polished wood. Around the walls were a selection of Americana, legends of Harley Davidsons and Thunderbirds.

The clientele were mostly city types, smart, soberly dressed young men and women, out from their offices for a quick lunch. I wondered if they knew who the proprietors of the establishment were.

The fare seemed to be mostly fast food, with various burgers and fries prominent on the menu. There was a central bar area manned by a brace of barmaids whose brittle beauty and hard eyes spoke of an East End upbringing. The manager had an aura of toughness unusual for the catering trade. I guessed he had other functions other than the culinary.

I asked after Boy-Boy and there was wariness in his eyes as he appraised me. Perhaps something in my manner reassured him, somewhat. Almost grudgingly he conceded that he hadn't been in yet, but was expected later. I sat at the bar, waiting.

City-type customers came and went, their gaze fluttering around the bar, pausing momentarily when their eyes met mine only to quickly break away again. Occasionally, some hard-faced type would settle at the bar. Their gaze was more challenging, surreptitiously lancing about until our eyes met, then communicating a thinly veiled aggression and paranoia.

After about an hour, Boy-Boy came in together with an athletically built blonde man in his mid-thirties. I guessed this to be Perry Taylor and that was how Boy-Boy introduced him to me. There was an aura of power, of confidence about him, but he was friendly enough. He indicated that he had heard of me and bought me a drink.

Boy-Boy dealt with the abortive early-morning meeting almost dismissively, explaining that he had to go out in a hurry. I felt it uncharitable to suggest that he might have left me a message, but let it pass. We sat, talking about the ways of the modern criminal world.

'I've got a grand for you here, Norm,' he said, passing me a wad of money. Almost embarrassed, I took it. I wasn't a ponce, I didn't want to live off hand-outs from my pals, but there was a tradition that, fresh out of prison, your pals would give you money. It wasn't something that would last much longer. I looked forward to the opportunity to earn my own money.

As if he had read my mind, Boy-Boy launched into an unsolicited explanation. With a quick look at Perry he said, 'There's not a lot we can do for you, Norm. If we gave you 200 key of puff, you wouldn't know what to do with it. You could easily give it to the wrong people who'd go through the slips. Then we'd have to look for them and get it back. We're looking for someone to mind a warehouse for a few days. There's a ton of puff there and we need someone to give it out, a couple of hundred key a time. But if you got nicked there, everyone would blame us for putting you in the frame. It's a job for half a mug really. We have talked about it but, at the moment, we can't do anything for you.' He looked at Perry and Perry nodded in agreement.

I felt bitter disappointment, but what could I say? They had made their decision and I wasn't going to beg for help. Perhaps the situation would change. Boy-Boy had just given me a grand, so it would have seemed ungrateful to complain. In the meantime, I would just have to make the most of the connection and hope I could come up with something that would let me in.

Suddenly, a tall, slim, dark-haired man was standing by the table. 'Norman, this is my brother David,' said Perry.

I stood to shake his hand and was immediately impressed by his open, friendly manner. He had a softness around the eyes which smacked of compassion rather than weakness. He seemed to be genuinely pleased to meet me. There was no reserve, no feeling each other out.

Perry stood and led David away. Moments later, he returned and passed me a wad of money. I demurred, I didn't know them and had never met them before. But as a friend of a friend, custom demanded that they should give something to a man just out of jail.

We talked about recent events in the criminal fraternity. It was clear that they trusted me; they spoke quite openly. I felt quite privileged to be party to the inside story. Soon, however, they pleaded pressure of business. They slipped away and I left soon afterwards, £1,500 the richer, but no nearer to knowing how I was to earn a living.

What was I going to do now? It was still only early afternoon and I had empty hours to fill. I reflected that, for most of my adult life, my existence had been structured by the prison. Every hour of every day had been planned out for me. I had deadlines of set meal times, roll checks and recreation periods to meet. Now I was in a totally unstructured world where I could do what I pleased and go where I wanted. But all to no set purpose. It was very confusing.

✳   ✳   ✳

I knew that, at some stage, I would need a mobile phone. If you wanted to be in the game you had to be contactable. The technology was unfamiliar to me, but I left the phone shop half-an-hour later with the latest model. I made a point of phoning around all my friends to give them the number. Suddenly, I felt slightly less isolated, less cut off from the rest of the world. I was only a phone call away from my friends.

There was one moment of numerologically induced paranoia. I totted up my ten-digit phone number and it came to 51. 51, of course, adds up to 6, the number I called my lucky number and which had figured so prominently in my life and in my kamea of the talisman.

All in the greater cause of networking, I now decided to go and see Fred. He was living at his mother's flat in Camden Town. I phoned and then drove over.

It was an untidy set of mansions and I reflected that Fred could be hardly more content with his present situation than I was. Especially as he was now fully out, whereas, at least, I was still on the hostel.

The flat was clean but cluttered. A kindly looking, grey-haired old lady was ensconced in a chair in a corner. She rose to her feet to shake my hand as Fred introduced us, then sat to continue watching the TV.

In domestic mode, Fred was entirely less gruff and Arthur Daleyesque. I guessed it was a persona unknown to and unfamiliar to his mother. I could imagine her asking him why he was talking like that and smiled at the thought. In private, though, he still talked out of the corner of his mouth, however there was less confidence about him, he seemed slightly deflated. No doubt he had already come up against some of the disappointments that I was encountering.

We compared notes. Back at Ford we had briefly discussed the possibility of our becoming business partners, of co-operating in various criminal ventures, but we both thought that, with our considerable network of friends and acquaintances, we could make it on our own. Now, I realised that I quite liked Fred. He was a decent, honourable man who had many strengths. He hadn't been a tearaway in prison. Far from it, in fact, his pursuit of model prisoner status had become something of a joke. But there was nothing 'wrong' about him and he knew more than I did about the drugs game. Between us, we just might come up with something. We didn't exchange contracts or anything, but we did decide to work together for a while.

The problem was that there wasn't much to work with. By the very nature of the business, there were no hard and fast delivery systems or distribution networks. In the constant game of cat and mouse with the police, old operations were 'busted' and new ones sprang up. That meant there were always opportunities for new ideas. We were both intelligent and well trusted, supremely important attributes, and had a wide network of influential friends. On the downside, we were new to the street and had no money to invest in projects.

I told Fred an outline of the Albanian move, without going into either personalities or too much detail. Fred told me tales of potential transport. There was always talk of lorry drivers who would carry stuff, airport workers who could bypass security and docks personnel who, for a consideration, could guide a container through unhindered. It was like having one part of a jigsaw puzzle. The other part would be someone who could supply the contraband at the other end. But as the stuff would be coming to us, the hard part would be not only to convince them that the scam would work, but also that we could be trusted to hand over their share. Luckily, we both had good reputations in that regard.

From what had been an inauspicious start, I had managed to turn the day around into a constructive and positive experience. I left Fred's confident that I now had someone to share the worry of making a way in this new and confusing world with. That thought in mind, I drove home.

On one level, I found it reassuring to have somewhere to return to that was home. The prison had been my home for so long that to set me free in the world was tantamount to letting a caged bird free from its cage. On another level though, I realised that it was unnatural for a man of nearly 50 to live with his mother. Not that I didn't enjoy her company or was uneasy around her. I quickly adapted to her fussing around me, no inconsiderable feat when you consider that for years I had lived alone. My whole philosophy had centred around being hostile and pushing people away. In prison, familiarity really did breed contempt. To make close friends inevitably ended in sadness as they went out and you were left to do your time in greater isolation. I realised that it would be a long time before I was comfortable with letting someone get close.

And then there was this general pessimism about the way I handled relationships. I always loved too deeply, needed the other too much and lived in terror of losing them. Now I was so strong, though.

I had survived for over 20 years in total isolation. I wasn't an island, but only a narrow isthmus connected me to the rest of mankind. As much as I yearned for the closeness of a relationship, the warming, healing power of love, I also feared it. How strange, that a man, fired in the icy loneliness of the institution, one who feared nothing, not even death, could be terrified of love. Violence and extreme pain couldn't touch me. Only love could kill me.

I had observed others in the street, young men and women, insular in their togetherness. Cocooned in love you could shut the world out, but only when you were young. Older couples seemed more distant, as if they were more aware of just how hard life could be and what a struggle it was.

I saw older men with their families. The wife, her figure often ravaged by child-bearing, shepherding the kids along like some mother duck. The man inevitably looked trapped, tethered to this place in life by the demands of his family. I knew I couldn't tolerate such restrictions. I would have to have some financial success first before I attempted to build a family. In the meantime, life with my mother was the only option.

Meetings with my probation officer soon revealed that the local council had a policy of refusing accommodation to single males. There would be no council flat for me when I finished my hostel period. I could always get one privately, then get the social to pay for it. But I had never rented a flat in my life and didn't know how to go about it. Also, the intricacies of the social security system were a mystery to me. I was glad the problem was still several months away.

Considering the problem, however, revealed to me a shortcoming I had previously been unaware of. For a man who valued strength above all other virtues, it came as quite a shock. I found that I actually feared the prospect of living in a flat alone. Not so much just being alone there, more the returning to an empty flat. I rationalised that living alone in a cell for 20 years was the cause. If that was the only detrimental effect, perhaps I was lucky. I hoped I would grow out of it in time.

* * *

Now that Fred was my business partner, at least it gave some structure to my day. At least once a day, I would drive over and discuss any developments. At other times, I did the rounds of my pals. There were literally dozens of these, men who had good reputations in the jail.

Most of these were almost in the same position as I was, planning major moves while in the meantime trying to earn a living by selling various drugs on at a profit. I thought of the parallel with the City — we also were commodity brokers, except for the fact that we dealt in illegal drugs.

Considering the risks and the responsibility, profit margins were remarkably small. Puff was making about £2,250 per key wholesale at the time. You would be fortunate to get it for £100 to £150 less than that and have to take 50 to 100 key. You would be responsible for over £200,000 worth of gear, all to earn £10,000–£15,000 grand. But if all went smoothly, you could do that in a week, but there were always problems with quality and losses.

There was some hypocrisy over dealing in certain types of drugs. Some made a big thing about only dealing in puff, others admitted to trading in coke and ecstasy. Virtually everyone was agreed that heroin was beyond the pale. Certainly, few of the 'chaps' knew anyone who took heroin.

A normal hostel day for me would be to leave the hostel early and drive straight to my gym. After a vigorous workout, a sauna and a shower I would go home for breakfast. I could sit still long enough to read the paper, then I would be off, ricocheting around London, from one 'chap' to the next. Often, I would get home in the evening and wonder what I had achieved. However, as long as I was in perpetual motion it didn't seem to matter.

One advantage I had was that my pals weren't just confined to London. I knew someone in virtually all the major cities. So if London was flooded with a particular drug and the price went down, then there might be a market for it elsewhere.

Occasionally, I would drive up to Birmingham at weekends and stay with Ivor. His girlfriend and her two children offered me typical Midlands hospitality, and made me feel part of the family. Ivor was well-known in the area. He had been a smuggler for many years. His speciality was knowing what types of car, in which year, had a place where puff could be hidden. He would buy the car and convert it, then find an unlikely-looking couple to drive it to Spain. He would pay for the holiday and give them a couple of grand on top. They would part with the car for a day for it to be loaded up. Then they would come back with 40 or 50 key well-hidden in the bodywork. The secret to his succes wasn't so much the choice of hiding place, but the people. He had one couple who were at least 60, the woman with her neck in a brace. They had never been stopped.

Ivor's problem was that he had difficulty raising all the money to finance each trip and he rarely had a good source to buy from. I set about looking for a Spanish supplier for him.

He was also friendly with a Midlands-based biker gang. Through these he had a good market for speed. These were all good 'clues' for me.

Finally, after two weeks, I managed to arrange a meet with Gary. We met in the car park of his property management company. He explained that he had been very busy, but the old intimacy was missing. When I asked about the Albanian coup he dismissed it saying that his firm had recently bought 40 tons in Holland. It wasn't a good enough explanation in the circumstances really. I had spent almost a year planning the move. I couldn't figure out what had changed. He had been my main hope.

I asked if there was something else I could do with him and his group and he said there wasn't anything at the moment. His manner throughout had remained distant, bordering on the unfriendly. Almost as an afterthought, he passed me a bundled-up plastic bag he was carrying.

'There's five grand there, Norm. It should keep you going for a while.'

I tried to figure out what was going on, something wasn't quite right. Gary had been one of the most honourable, loyal men I had ever met. His voice was saying one thing and his eyes were saying another. It seemed like the £5,000 was a personal apology for letting me down. But he wasn't going to explain. I shook his hand and he walked away.

I still saw Boy-Boy, when I could catch up with him. Life with the hottest firm in town was frantic and he was permanently stuck in gangster mode. At times, though, it was as if he had lucid moments and was his old self for a while. He wondered aloud if he was doing the right thing and feared impending disaster. It was reassuring that he still confided in me. We had been close pals at Ford.

In turn, I told him about the meeting with Gary. He smiled knowingly and shook his head. 'He's probably heard that you've been seen at Cottons with me and Perry. Perry hates the Joneses and slags off any of their firm he meets. That's probably why you're out of favour with them.'

Mentally, I kicked myself. I was aware of the importance of 'politics' in prison, every jail was riven with it. I hadn't realised it extended outside. Still, it was too late to do anything about it and, fuck it, I would speak to whoever I wanted. My aim was to be as eclectic as I possibly could be in pursuit of a 'clue'. In this instance, it had worked against me, but, in the long run, it was a sound policy. Because of the huge number of people I knew, I was sure it would be possible to bridge between people or groups who might not normally do business with each other.

Tom was a classic example of someone the 'chaps' would not normally touch with a barge pole. I had originally met him through a prison training partner of mine called Alf. Alf was a local boxing champion from Luton. What he lacked in brains, he more than compensated for in loyalty and courage. To describe him as 'simple' was merely a comment on his unsophistication. He was one of the most genuine men I had ever met and we had become firm friends.

Tom was also from Luton, but was as different from Alf as it was possible to be. His adopted persona was that of the town-bred 'Hooray'. He had a fearsome reputation for drinking, drugs and women, all carried out to excess in pursuit of his own particular version of *A Rake's Progress*.

Physically, he was quite unimpressive. Although still in his twenties, years of dissolute living had left him with a slim build, bordering on the skinny. The visage was pure Mr Bean, yet he was certainly a ladies' man. He was always to be found in the company of at least one, and often two, beautiful and very sexy young women. He was certainly obsessed with sex, the pursuit of which was undoubtedly his prime motivation.

The amazing thing was that he was extremely intelligent, yet sought to dissipate his talents with drug and alcohol abuse. He was also breathtakingly arrogant, which, when coupled with an innate selfishness, made him very difficult to deal with. However, he was something of a physical coward, so often held back from major put-downs lest someone bash him.

At first sight, the casual observer wouldn't be aware of any these qualities. He was a consummate amateur psychologist who had the knack of making everyone seem special to him. He would carry this to such lengths that he generally managed to convince everybody. However, his selfishness and drug-induced ineptitude often led him to take liberties with his friends. Then there could be a serious falling out.

My interest in him was purely criminal; ineptitude, drug-induced or otherwise, was anathema to me. Crime was a very serious business and Tom just didn't focus enough. He had never been in prison though. I reflected that a spell inside would have focused his mind wonderfully.

I knew he had made a lot of money in the past as a young music entrepreneur, even if he had blown it all in riotous living. Perhaps because of this he had some amazing contacts. These led to him becoming involved in some clever scams involving major contacts in drugs and banking. I was sure that, if I could get him sober long enough, I could provide the other part of the puzzle that would get us a fortune.

On the literary front, I was still trying to promote *Parkhurst Tales*. Never a week went by without having a meeting with a publisher or TV producer. From a social point of view, it was all interesting stuff, but nothing concrete came of it. Until, that is, Nick introduced me to a newspaper reporter who specialised in crime. He passed me on to a small publisher in King's Cross. Suddenly, a publishing deal was in the offing.

The publisher was very interested when I told him what Frank Delaney had said about my writing. He asked me if Delaney would be willing to write a Foreword. I phoned him and he agreed to do it. He also confirmed this to Anita, who was still acting for me, and the publisher. So, with that as a condition, I was given a £3,000 advance and a publishing deal.

It was very satisfying, at long last, to be able to think of myself as a proper writer. I had always believed in my work, but getting a deal seemed to be more about who you were rather than the quality of your writing. It was quite undignified traipsing around from publisher to publisher trying to sell your work like some travelling salesman. It was partly in reaction to that that I had returned to criminal mode. I valued my independence and, if it was to be the independence of the outlaw, then so be it.

LIFE AFTER LIFE

If I found it a problem to find enough to do on weekdays, then weekends were a nightmare. At least people were about during the week. At weekends they went into family mode. Everyone seemed either to have a permanent girlfriend or a wife and kids. It's not that I wasn't welcome, it's just that I felt out of place. In prison, my mates were always available to hang out with.

By now I was seriously worried by the direction my life was taking. This wasn't at all the world I had expected to come out to. I had expected problems fitting in but, in the world I had found, I didn't want to fit in. Moreover, running around trying to eke out a living in the drugs game was pressure. I was well aware that many of the people I was seeing would be known to the police and possibly under observation. In short, I could get nicked at any time. I had no alternative, because a life on the breadline was intolerable for me. It was with something of a death wish that I went on my rounds each day.

But I always had the talisman to protect me. I still wore it towards the greater goal of getting my book published, but it had also assumed the role of good luck charm, too.

I continued to read in pursuit of spiritual knowledge and development, and among the things that particularly interested me were ley lines and sources of natural energy. My arthritis was still doggedly inflaming my joints. Progress was sure but slow.

I rationalised that if I could boost my own natural vitality by standing at a source of natural energy, it would improve my condition. After all, many churches and temples had been built on ley lines and there were ancient tales of the sick going there to be healed.

One Sunday I drove down to Stonehenge. I was herded along with crowds of tourists and never got closer to the stones than about 50 yards. I reasoned that that wouldn't do me much good. I scoured the books for less well-known sites.

Wandlebury was the hilltop site of an ancient Roman encampment. A local archaeologist called Lethbridge had found remains of an even earlier temple and excavated large figures carved in the chalk. There was a triumvirate of Gog, Magog and a demonic figure. It was rumoured that sacrifices had taken place there at various festivals.

Early one Sunday I set out on my mission, for that was how I had come to see it. If life was about spiritual development, then that would be my priority. In truth, I could make little sense of a life spent watching TV, drinking in pubs, going to football matches and many other trivial pastimes that seemed so important to so many people. There had to be more to it than that. Otherwise, you were wasting time just as surely as if you were sitting in a prison cell.

Was it only I who could see this, or was it the curse of the muse? My writing talent had to have come from somewhere. Did artistic people look deeper for meaning than normal folk? Was this why so many writers, poets, painters and sculptors had killed themselves? Did they tire of the mundane, trivial existence that sufficed to divert their less discerning brethren?

The book had spoken of Wandlebury only in general terms, that the exposed figures could be seen from a certain village. I found the village a few miles to the south of Cambridge, at the end on the M11. There was no sign of the figures.

I drove around the village streets to no avail. I couldn't contemplate failure. I must find the place, I was sure it was all part of the plan. Finally, I stopped a lone pedestrian, the village seemed strangely deserted. By coincidence, he was a local school teacher and knew of Wandlebury. He gave me directions.

Within ten minutes I was at the gates of Wandlebury. A large sign announced it to be a site of considerable archaeological significance. I parked alongside scores of other cars in a large car park and joined throngs of earnest parents and their children as they hurried along country paths. A combination of upper-class accents and green

Wellington boots served to alert me that this was a favourite haunt of the well-heeled at play. I was on more serious business, though.

I examined a schematic drawing in a glass case. It detailed the Roman encampment, the walls, the buildings and the fortifications. In a large open space to the south of the encampment was a reference to the figures. I headed in their general direction.

The book had said that the figures had been allowed to grow over, that they were now covered by grass again and could only be seen as shallow depressions. I scoured an uneven hillside and couldn't discern anything that looked remotely artificial.

I went so far as to enter the encampment, thinking the scale of the drawing had been wrong, and joined the crowds thronging the paths between the Roman ruins.

After about an hour, I returned to the uneven hillside almost in despair. I must find the figures, but except for a few girls in a souvenir shop, there seemed to be no one who I could ask.

I loitered on a path as streams of visitors swept past me. Suddenly, I saw a strange figure coming towards me. He was a tall, slim, elderly chap with a cadaverous face, dressed from head to foot in country tweeds that were tailored much like a uniform. He wore a deer-stalker hat of the same material. I reflected that, other than for the missing pipe, he could have been Sherlock Holmes. Perhaps by way of compensation, he was pushing an ancient, black bicycle.

It was an incongruous figure by any standards. Certainly, no one else was dressed remotely like him. Even a townie like myself could recognise him as a countryman.

'Excuse me,' I said in as cultured a voice as I could muster, 'do you know where Lethbridge's figures are to be found, the ones carved in the chalk?'

The voice was so thick with country brogue as to be almost a caricature. 'Aye, they be over there, just beyond the brow of that hill.'

I wasn't having that at all. It was OK for these country folk to discern differences in terrain, but to me it was all fields.

'Where exactly, please?' I was more insistent now.

He pointed more directly, using particular bushes as locations and giving the approximate distance in yards. I thanked him and studiously followed his directions.

I found myself standing on the same uneven hillside, the encampment above and a line of fir trees below. There was an area of undulations, shallow depressions centred around the spot that old

Sherlock had directed me to. This had to be it, but there was little to be seen really. I tried to imagine the outline of the figures, but thick grass obscured all detail. If I looked carefully, I could just make out three large depressions. I sat down on the edge of the largest depression.

It was a bright, dry, sunny day, the light bringing everything into sharp contrast. I tried to imagine ancient ceremonies on this very spot. In olden times it must have been charged with the prayers and spirits of many believers. I willed that ancient power into my body, closing my eyes and opening myself to facilitate the flow.

I can't say that I felt anything, except for a sense of achievement in that I had accomplished that which I had set out to do. Strangely elated, I drove back to London.

✳ ✳ ✳

Spiritual missions weren't the only ones that occupied me at this time. I was still looking for Ian. I still hadn't located him after he moved from his mother's flat. However, I tracked down his estranged brother who gave me an address in Hackney.

It took me to a basement flat in a street lined with dilapidated houses. The rubbish-strewn steps led down past a neglected and filthy front garden. A barred gate stood in front of a wooden door that hadn't seen a coat of paint for many a year. An adjacent window was similarly heavily barred, a grimy sheet hanging as a curtain behind its cracked and dirty panes.

I rapped sharply on the wooden door with my knuckles, hearing the sound echo in the passage beyond. There was silence. I rapped again. Suddenly, the grimy curtain moved and an elderly, time-ravaged black face peered at me. It immediately disappeared and I heard a voice shout, 'Ian ... Ian,' in a throaty rasp.

I heard approaching footsteps and the inner door opened. Dressed only in grimy white underpants which stood out against his pale, unnaturally white and emaciated body, with an untidy grey beard that ran into his long white hair, it could have been Ben Gunn — except for the fact that he would have had to have spent the last year in a dungeon, for little sun had touched this body.

'Ian?' I asked tentatively.

Recognition dawned. Whichever drugs had befogged his brain gave him temporary respite and he smiled broadly.

'Norman? Norman?'

'Open the gate, Ian, before you catch your death of cold.'

Fumbling on the floor for a key, he unlocked the gate. I followed him along a short passageway, past piles of rubbish and strips of wallpaper hanging like vines. We entered a room that was in total darkness.

'Hang on, I'll turn the light on.' Ian disappeared into the Stygian blackness.

'Why the fuck didn't you write to me to let me know where you were, Ian?'

The mumbled reply was indecipherable.

Suddenly, the light came on. To my surprise, incongruous lumps stirred under blankets and coats strewn across sofas and chairs. Sleep-wrinkled faces blinked and stared at me. There was a rough bed made up over in one corner. Ian climbed into it and propped himself up on one elbow, looking at me.

'Well, you know how it is, Norm. I had it hard for a while.'

I refrained from remarking about the present conditions, because things didn't look too good right now. Especially as all four of the others were now sitting up looking at me.

'This is Judy,' said Ian by way of an introduction, indicating a strikingly pretty young black woman.

'Hi, Norman, Ian's told me all about you.' Her perfect teeth formed the bright centre to a warm smile.

It was infectious and I smiled in return.

'You've already met Abigail.'

Ian waved to the slim, mixed-race girl I had seen at his mother's flat. The passage of more than a year had seen her pass from slim to skinny, her deep-set eyes bordered by dark shadows. Quite indifferent, she stared at me and through me.

'This is Georgie.'

A well-built, young black woman hoisted herself from an armchair and moved past me.

'Hello, Norman,' she waved at me and smiled mischievously. 'Must have a piss.' She disappeared from the room.

'I'm Charlie,' said a stocky black guy. He stood and made a small ritual out of shaking my hand.

'You've got quite a family, mate.' The remark was humorous rather than sarcastic.

'Well, you know how it is, Norm. You must try to help people out.'

I reflected that I didn't know how it was but it was a sorry state of affairs that this was the only place that such young people could find to live. It reconfirmed my determination to make something of myself.

Ian explained that, after being thrown out of his mother's flat, he had lived rough for a while, and had then been given a place in a hostel. This present place was a council flat he had recently been allocated. The histories of Judy, Abigail, Georgie and Charlie were an unmitigated catalogue of disasters. That so much grief, so much ill-fortune, had befallen ones so young almost beggared belief. There were deaths, rapes, illnesses and periods of imprisonment, all compounded by drug addiction. I reflected that, had such misfortune befallen me, I could well have turned to drugs. Then I instantly rejected it. I had been through far worse than all of them, yet I had survived. It was purely a question of how you dealt with it.

Ian made a pot of tea, making sure I saw him clean a cup specially for me. We sat around drinking it. Judy and Georgie were good company. There was nothing wrong with their intellects and living on the street had made them articulate and sharp. They were funny too. Very soon, they were making fun of themselves, Ian, Charlie and me. Abigail remained sullenly aloof and went back to sleep. I found myself laughing and relaxing.

Suddenly, I realised that I was at ease with these people. Of all the social situations I had been in since I had been out, this was the most natural and informal. No one was trying to create an impression or score points. I felt I had nothing to hide or explain away. My time in prison didn't hang in the air like a guilty secret.

Perhaps it was their irresponsibility I liked, however short-sighted and juvenile it was. I had no intention of sharing either their lifestyle or lack of ambition, but for a period of light relief, they were good company. I now had a place I could drop into whenever I was bored or had nowhere else to go.

Also, all insanity apart, I still felt close to Ian. The mind might twist, but the outward form remained the same. I remembered the strength I had drawn from our friendship in prison. He used to be good company and, with him at my side, I had had nothing to fear. Perhaps we could renew our comradeship. Maybe I could help heal his mind. At the very least, it was my duty to try. I knew that, in similar circumstances, he would have done the same for me.

Good company they may have been, but I didn't look at the girls at

Ian's as potential partners. I clung determinedly to my vision of my ideal mate. Not only wasn't I ready, but the girl of my dreams wasn't going to be a junkie. There was always the possibility of sex and I did consider it, but it would have besmirched my romantic ideal and I was totally paranoid about AIDS. Just my luck to survive a 24-stretch and contract AIDS in my first six months out. I would wait.

Perhaps the experience at Ian's struck a chord. That evening I phoned Jackie. I felt a distinct thrill of pleasure as her cheery, little-girl voice answered. She sounded pleased to hear from me, questioning me excitedly about events since I had been home. I filled her in on the general details and she opined that I was leading such an exciting life.

Just for a moment I did pause and thought of all the places I had been and all the people I had met, of the book deal and prospects in general. For a normal man, I suppose it would have been quite exciting. But I was far from normal. I was at a loss to explain to her the almost insane ambition that fired me.

She asked me if I had met anyone. I said I hadn't, and that I had been concentrating on my career. She told me that she had got her husband to leave and she was now living on her own with the boys. It had been a trying time, but it was something she had had to do. Now she was single again, a couple of local men had shown an interest. But it had only extended to having a good time and they had baulked at taking on another man's three kids. So, at present, she was just biding her time and looking around.

There was an implied invitation there and I said I would like to come down and see her. She replied that she would like that, too. Evenings were a problem, because of the kids. We arranged to meet during the day, the following week.

It lifted my spirits and improved my general mood. The world didn't seem quite so dark and I didn't feel nearly so driven. I wondered if my condition was exacerbated by extreme loneliness. Perhaps it was a form of post-traumatic stress disorder. I recalled that soldiers in Vietnam had suffered it after only comparatively short periods of extreme stress. Well, 24 years in jail had certainly been extremely stressful, I could attest to that. Maybe the symptoms were a need for constant excitement and stimulation.

By the following day, the moment was past and the black mood was back upon me again. It lifted slightly when Fred phoned and said that something was happening and he wanted to see me.

We met at his flat, but he insisted on leaving before he would talk. We circled the block, Fred filling me in on the details through the corner of his mouth.

It transpired that he had just made contact with an old pal he had known in the nick. He referred to him only as 'Fatty', a less than respectful nickname and I guessed that, by prison standards, Fred had out-ranked him in status. Out here, though, the notoriety of your last conviction meant nothing at all. It was all about how much money you had. And 'Fatty' had a big garage and car showrooms over at Sunbury, with a large house and grounds in the nearby countryside.

He was also bringing in large quantities of drugs from Holland. Fred said we could have coke, speed or puff. The important thing was that we could have it on credit. With coke at around £30,000 a key and speed at £3,000–£4,000, this was a considerable concession.

We drove over to the East End and arranged to have the use of an empty council flat belonging to a pal of Fred's. It was in a tower block just off the Mile End Road. With a hat pulled down around my ears, I took the lift to the twelfth floor to check it out.

It had obviously been a family flat. Children's wallpaper in a small bedroom and a box of toys confirmed that. I knew that Fred's mate was separated from his wife. I guessed that a lot of dreams had died there.

I searched around for a good hiding place. I didn't want some casual visitor stumbling across the stash. Although the flat wasn't being used, it was best to be safe.

In a larger bedroom, I found a heating vent. Gloved hands removed retaining screws to reveal a heating duct that disappeared inside the wall. There was space to conceal several keys. I replaced the vent and left the flat.

That evening, as I lay in my hostel bed, I thought about the challenge that tomorrow would bring. This wasn't just planning to do something: I would be driving about with a large consignment of drugs with me. Should I be caught, the resultant punishment would be tantamount to a death sentence. I would get ten to twelve years and my licence would be revoked. I really would be an old man if I got out again. Death would be preferable.

The following morning I was on edge as I ate breakfast at my mother's. I snapped replies to her questions, thinking how she would take it if I were nicked later that day. All her hopes and dreams would go up in smoke, too. My bad temper was almost an attempt to drive her away, somehow to lessen the blow should she lose me again.

I had phoned Gary the previous evening, saying I needed to see him urgently. We met near where he lived at Hendon. I explained that I had to pick something up that morning and I needed some insurance. I begged the loan of a gun; at least it would give me the chance to get away.

He could see the desperation in my manner. He had been a true and trusted friend in the past. He couldn't say no to a mate in trouble.

He told me to wait for a while and drove off. Twenty minutes later he returned, and handed me a small, cloth-wrapped bundle.

'There's a .38 there with six shots, Norm. Keep it. Just don't tell anyone I gave it to you.'

I thanked him and drove away. With the gun on board I seemed to have a heightened sense of awareness. Strangely, I wasn't nervous any more. There was a sense of resignation, of what would be would be. If this was my day to go down, then so be it. At least it would be the end of all the pain and turmoil. It wasn't that I was overtly suicidal, just terribly self-destructive. I reflected that I probably felt like this because I had made such a fuck-up of my life.

As I drove over to Sunbury, I ran through in my mind what I would do if I were to be stopped. I sincerely didn't want to hurt anybody. It was just that I wouldn't be taken. As a last resort, I would shoot a copper in the leg, but the .38 was really for myself. Faced with impending death in prison, I would shoot myself.

It brought home to me just how driven I was to be going on what was, in truth, a suicide mission. On one level it was reassuring that my bottle hadn't gone after all those years in jail. I still had the courage to go on a heavy bit of work. On another level, it just showed how desperate I had become.

I found the garage on the outskirts of Sunbury and drove round the back. Fred was waiting by an open car bay. I drove in and Fred pulled a door shut behind me. As I got out, a burly man hurried up and handed me a large sports bag.

'There's four key of coke and four of speed there, Norm,' said Fred over his shoulder.

I quickly slung the bag in front of the passenger seat, got back in and drove out again. The whole operation had taken only a couple of minutes.

I focused on trying to relax as much as possible. Impatience could cause an accident, with dire consequences for me. Irrationally, I felt like I was the centre of the universe, as if everything else was revolving around me. The bag lay on the floor beside me. It might as well contain a powerful bomb; its contents could certainly destroy me.

As I neared central London, the traffic grew thicker and the pressure increased. Police cars passed me by and occasionally I heard sirens. What if it was for me? My heart quickened at the thought of a chance encounter. What a strange thing fate could be. In a couple of hours' time, would I be sitting safe indoors drinking a cup of tea, or lying dead in the street?

With some relief, I pulled up near the Mile End tower block. I was nearly safe now. I went up to the flat, stashed the drugs and the gun in the ducting, wiped down anything I might have touched, then left.

I felt so alive and exhilarated as I drove over to Fred's. The adrenalin rush still coursed through my system. But I was safe now. Even if the stash was found it couldn't be connected to me — until I went back to collect something the next time, that is.

Over the next week or so, Fred and I sold all the coke and speed between us. I ferried it about, a key at a time, every trip another suicide mission. It played havoc with my nerves, pushing me ever closer to the edge. Self-destructiveness had become a way of life for me.

We made £1,000 each on every key of coke and £700 each on the speed. For just over a week's work, I had earned myself £5,400. But to do so I had risked my life a dozen times. I reflected that I must have been mad to do so, but, when you are at the bottom of the ladder, these are the risks you have to take. At least I now had a regular source of income. We paid the money we had collected to 'Fatty' and picked up another consignment. My chosen profession now was to run suicide missions on a daily basis. I consoled myself with the thought that things could only get better.

* * *

By comparison, days when I wasn't ferrying consignments of drugs around seemed quite relaxed now. Often, I would drop into Ian's and see how he and the 'street people' were doing. None of them worked, so, other than for some money from the social, each had some game or scam whereby they got a few quid. Mostly, the girls were 'hoisters', although that term implies a degree of professionalism at shoplifting that they didn't have. Forays out were all too desperate, fuelled by the need for drugs.

Abigail made no bones about the fact that she was a 'brass'. A few hours down King's Cross would bring her the couple of hundred quid she needed to get through the day. Georgie admitted to 'clipping' punters from time to time, taking their money, then running off.

Charlie fancied himself as something of a credit card fraudsman. Yet he wasn't nearly as clever as he thought he was and often had to run out of shops. He would return to the flat all breathless, to blurt out how he had just avoided arrest. Then he would try to borrow money off the others to buy the drugs he needed.

An entirely smoother operator was Juby, the elderly black guy who had seen me through the front window on my first visit. His forte was credit cards, too. Although raddled by a 20-year heroin habit, he would dress up quite smartly for his forays.

He lived in the front room with a young mixed-race girl called Joanna. There was no furniture, just a mattress they shared on the floor. It was a strange relationship, even by the standards of the street. Joanna lay on the mattress all day, while Juby went out grafting.

Even in the gloom of the half-light of the basement room, you could see that she was quite beautiful. Yet her speech was slurred by years of heroin abuse and she was always sleepy. Like an orchid in a dungeon, it all seemed such a terrible waste.

Charlotte was unusual in that she was both white and worked at a regular job. A slim, sharp-faced woman in her mid-twenties, she often visited Ian's flat with her two children. There was a girl of about eight and a boy of around four. Both were clean and tidy and seemed unfazed by their squalid surroundings. They treated Ian like a surrogate father and chased him around the back yard in endless games of 'tag'.

Janice was like some marauding, dark spirit. A short, mixed-race girl with bushy black hair and a child's face, the baggy coats and jeans she mostly wore served to disguise an attractive figure. She too was a 'hoister' and often ventured into dark and dangerous buildings to buy her drugs. She had been raped when she was barely 15. The baggy clothes were an attempt to 'dress down' and disguise her figure.

Her expression too was far from friendly. She would sweep into the flat and sit herself down, dispensing with greetings and ignoring any offered. She was in her early twenties, yet was wise beyond her years. But it was a wisdom born of the streets and really, if you talked to her at any length, it soon became apparent that she was forever fixed in a juvenile mind-set.

Her life was an endless circle of stealing, selling the goods at knock-down prices, then buying drugs. There was no plan or discernible pattern to it. It was all done purely on the basis of immediate need. She never comtemplated saving to buy a larger quantity of drugs more cheaply. She just lived from hand to mouth.

Needless to say, like the rest of the girls, she regularly disappeared into prison for months at a time. She took it all in her stride, as part of the risks of her chosen profession. From time to time, I could sense a vulnerability, a softness under the hard exterior, as if she had also tired of this horrible world she lived in. But in a flash it would be gone and the flinty exterior would be back in place again.

All the 'street people', including Ian, needed a daily fix of heroin. It was only Abigail who injected though; all the rest 'chased' on pieces of tin foil. They didn't seem to enjoy their addiction, just sitting about, semi-comatose after the latest hit.

Their passion was for crack cocaine. Whereas heroin was a physical addiction, the crack was more psychological. The pursuit of it was almost like a mission. Once the idea was in their heads they would gather together to raise the necessary money. Then they would go to the nearest crack-dealer to make the purchase. Often they would get stung, always they would be given short measure, for these weren't criminals in charge of their lives, rather junkies who were the victims of their addiction.

I often watched in amazement. Perhaps, as a doomed spirit myself, I felt comfortable in the presence of more obviously doomed spirits. Perhaps it was a power thing. I regularly helped them out with lifts and money for food.

Wednesday promised to be a special day away from the madness. As I drove down to Sussex and my impending meeting with Jackie, I vowed to put all thoughts of the pressures of my city life out of my mind. It was a beautiful drive, through beautiful countryside. I reflected that Sussex was the first part of England that I had experienced through the eyes of freedom.

As I neared Ford, I dwelt on the time I had spent there and was surprised to remember it fondly. Almost as a gentler kinder time, free from the incredible pressure of the present. Arundel resembled some fairytale town, complete with turreted castle.

The Black Rabbit was a picturesque pub by the river, its stained timbers standing out starkly from the white plaster in the bright sunlight. It was almost surreal, as if dwarves and talking animals might appear any second from behind hedgerows.

I was early and parked at the far end of the car park. Suddenly, I was nervous. What would I say to her? I so wanted this to go well, yet I was still awkward around women. I wanted to impress her with my city sophistication, however, even with her limited experience she was far more sophisticated than I.

I still puffed, and not only at weekends as in prison, but occasionally during the week, too. Compared to the drink and drugs binges that virtually everyone of my acquaintance indulged in, it was a minor vice. I found that I had to have something in social situations, although the puff often made me more awkward, not less.

I had a quick puff as I waited. Immediately, the surreal quality of the day seemed to intensify. I was on the brink of a great adventure. Compared to the dull and empty days of prison, the imminent meeting promised pleasure beyond measure.

I recognised Jackie's car as it pulled into the car park and my heart quickened. I got out and strolled to meet her. As she came towards me, her eyes shyly downcast, I reflected on how pretty she was.

She said, 'Hello,' in her little girl's voice and I kissed her lightly on the cheek. It occurred to me that she might have been as nervous as me.

'Do you want a puff before we go anywhere?' I heard myself say. I was sure her life was a model of restraint, yet I remembered that she said she puffed very occasionally.

She giggled and looked around her. 'Where?' she asked.

I led her to my car. Like two schoolkids, we sat back in the seats and puffed at the little pipe. Suddenly, she coughed and her eyes filled with tears. We both laughed at her plight and it served to break the ice. We were strangers no more, just fellow conspirators.

We decided to eat first, then take her dog for a walk along the river. She had left it in her car. Ordering at The Black Rabbit was even more difficult off my face than it would have been straight. The consolation was that Jackie was quite out of it, too.

We giggled conspiratorially. We were both enjoying ourselves.

The food was good, the setting idyllic. I caught myself thinking that if life was all like this, there would be no pain. But that reminded me that the day would have to end. I pushed the thought from me.

We finished eating and talked for a while over coffee. She told me of the various liaisons she had had since being single. None had been what she was looking for. Most ended in awkward scenes. She said she was resigned to waiting until her children had grown up. Neither of us mentioned any possible future for ourselves together.

We collected the dog from her car, a delightfully soppy golden retriever with a pleasing personality that seemed to mirror her own. Then we walked by the river. But it was more than that. The very trees and bushes seemed to sing with joy under the warming sun. The river trickled and gurgled like some jolly infant. Birds swooped and called, as if exulting in the sheer pleasure of being alive. With a marked cadence, insects hummed and buzzed as a backdrop to our conversation.

Undoubtedly, some of it was the effects of the puff, but, for my part, it was more than that. It was all so beautiful. After the horrors of the past 20 years, it was as if my senses had been brought to the brink of overload. If I had died that moment, I would have died blissfully happy. I felt a great, warm bubble of caring envelop the woman who walked beside me.

We talked of love and loneliness and of the worries of mundane existence. Suddenly, I was holding her hand. It was as if we had both melded into one. I could feel her breathing, her heartbeat, her pulse, all through the tips of my fingers.

Talking became superfluous, we seemed to be able to experience each other's feelings. We walked in silence in slow pursuit of the shiny, golden creature that was her dog.

But time pressed on and soon she looked at her watch. She remarked that she had to pick her boys up shortly. Like coming out of a dream, the awful reality that it would end confronted me. But we had shared something today. I was sure it had been a memorable experience for both of us. As we walked back to our cars, I felt we now shared a bond.

We agreed to meet again soon. Demurely, she offered her cheek. I kissed her lightly and she was gone. It was with a considerable feeling of deflation that I drove back to London and my horrible life. I tried to picture what life would be like living with Jackie. At that point, I realised I was hopelessly in love with her.

While it filled a void in my life, it was a situation I wasn't at all pleased with. For someone who took great pride in his strength, it came as quite a shock to realise that here was something that controlled me. Fight it as I would, I couldn't get Jackie out of my mind. I threw myself into my city life with an even greater degree of self-destructiveness.

✳ ✳ ✳

Jess had become both a kindred spirit and a good friend. We shared both the profession of writer and that of the city drug dealer. He operated on a smaller, more personal scale than me. His life was less fraught in that he dealt in grams and the occasional ounce of coke. However, a complicating factor was that he was probably his own best customer.

He had a delightful wife, solidly in the 'earth mother' mould and twin boys who were quite a handful. I reflected that Jess must be under considerable pressure with the responsibility of such a family.

Often, I would meet him at his flat in South London, then we would go to Soho. He knew scores of young people in the music and media professions. Many of them were his customers.

Soho during the day was entirely less seedy and dangerous than Soho by night. Professional people thronged the bars and restaurants mostly at lunchtime.

On closer examination, their lives weren't as smoothly successful as they first seemed. Nearly all of them worried about their job, their relationship and their coke habit. While I had first thought that I had everything to learn from them, when they learned that I was totally in control of my vices, it seemed that it was they who could learn from me. It was some small consolation that they weren't happy with their lives either.

The call from the publisher shocked me out of my literary complacency. Frank Delaney was dragging his heels over the Foreword. He had been asked several times for his copy, but it hadn't been forthcoming. He was strangely elusive with me on the phone. Anita put it into perspective when she told me that he had just been offered *The Book Show* on Sky TV. Perhaps it would now be an embarrassment for him to link his name with mine.

The upshot was that the whole book deal was now in jeopardy. A condition had been Delaney's Foreword. As luck would have it, I had been close friends with Tom Mangold, the writer and TV presenter since he interviewed me for a piece on prisons many years previously.

He agreed to do the Foreword himself. The publisher seemed mollified. The deal was back on track.

With my feelings for Jackie rapidly turning into an obsession, I tried to get down to see her each week and phoned her regularly. If relationships are about power, Jackie soon realised that she was well in control. It soon became apparent that she wasn't nearly as naïve and unsophisticated as I had first thought.

One weekend, I drove down to Bognor to take her out. She admitted that she was seeing someone from a local nightclub, but said it wasn't serious. We drove along the coast to Brighton, to spend the evening with Jim and Julie. You could see that Jackie was quite fascinated by them, making for a stylish, interesting couple.

I had brought a few Es. We went out for a meal, then the three of us took them, but Jackie refused. She was strangely silent for the rest of the evening. As I took her home, she suddenly raged at me. She accused me of exploiting both Julie and Jim, as if they were junkies, dependent on Es. It ruined the night for us both and it took several phone calls before I managed to placate her.

On another weekend, I brought her up to London. Knowing how much it meant to me, Jess really put himself out. He booked a private room at Grouchos for her.

On the Friday, we dined, puffed then saw *Swan Lake* at Sadlers Wells. Saturday saw us shopping in Oxford Street and going to Browns with Nick in the evening. She did some coke with Nick, drunk more than she was used to and was thrilled to stand barely yards from George Michael at the bar. As I dropped her back at Grouchos, she made it clear that I wouldn't be spending the night with her.

The following day we lunched in Soho with friends of Jess. You could see that she was mightily impressed by such colourful and sophisticated people. That evening, I drove her down to her cottage near Arundel.

It was charmingly rustic, down a narrow country lane. She showed me round the simple but clean rooms. The boys' bedrooms were particularly poignant for me. It all smacked of a delightful domesticity. As I drove back to London I was sure that I would have given anything to live there with Jackie and the kids.

But she had made it quite clear there was no future for us. Apart from any other consideration, all her friends knew of me and my prison background, and she couldn't live with that. I cursed the weakness in me that didn't allow me to blot her out of my mind. If I had been in hell in jail, I was now in a worse hell of mental torment. I was sure it was just an over-reaction to being on my own for so long. But rationalise it as I may, the situation still tortured me.

I hadn't been around to Ian's for over three months. It was partly the obsession with Jackie and partly a reaction against a lifestyle that was so obviously doomed. I had tried to encourage Ian to pull himself together, but he was content to sink further in the mire. It was as if he was hiding from the world and wallowing in failure. He had been a first division armed robber, now his chosen companions were from the dregs of the underworld.

The front door was open as I descended the steps. I called out as I walked along the passage and heard Ian's answering shout. He was sitting in an armchair. Opposite him sat Janice. She still had a dour, sullen expression on her face. She nodded to me briefly as I sat down.

Ian explained that she had been in Holloway these past three months, by coincidence, virtually from the day I had last been there. They had let her out for the day to attend a drug rehab centre. She had absconded and come straight round to Ian's. He marvelled that we should both reappear on the same day.

She looked quite sad, slouched there in the armchair. Behind the hard exterior, she was still only a young girl. I new of the rigours of prison she had just experienced, the loneliness of being locked alone in a cell. Now she was on the run, with just the clothes she stood up in.

Suddenly, I looked at her more closely. When she relaxed, and didn't clench her jaw so tightly, she was quite pretty. Her bushy black hair formed a dark halo around her face. The clothes she was wearing were more feminine than usual. They revealed a petite figure that was perfectly in proportion.

An idea formed in my head. I realised I quite fancied this wild young girl. I had been out all of six months now and still I hadn't had sex. It was all very well saving myself in pursuit of my ideal partner, but would it be such a weakness to indulge my passion? If nothing else, it might take my mind off Jackie. Merely the thought of her caused me to flinch mentally.

I waited until Ian went into the kitchen, then followed him.

'Ian, I've got some Es on me. Do you think Janice would consider having a trade with me if I gave her some?' I screwed up my face in embarrassment.

Ian looked quite surprised, as if he hadn't remotely considered the possibility. He cocked his head to one side, obviously thinking.

'Janice doesn't bother with fellas much,' he confided, 'she's had a bad time with men and her boyfriend's in prison. But I think she likes you and she's right down at the moment.'

Instantly I felt guilty. Ian had hinted previously that sometimes she went down the Cross in an emergency to get money for drugs.

'I won't take a liberty with her, Ian.'

'I know you won't,' he smiled, 'I'll ask her.'

Really embarrassed now, I stayed in the kitchen while Ian went back in to ask Janice. Almost immediately he was back.

'That's OK,' he said, 'as I thought, she likes you.'

The front bedroom was empty. Juby and Joanna had recently moved on. And Ian had recently acquired a new double bed. I got some sheets from the wardrobe and remade it. Janice stood in the corner, watching me. We still hadn't spoken.

I wondered if she realised what was going through my head. She probably thought that I was just another randy geezer who wanted to fuck her. It was far more profound than that. I hadn't had communion with another spirit for over 23 years. A lesser man would have given in to the impulse and gone with a brass the first day he was free. But I was the mystic warrior, master of all my desires. I firmly believed that when you made love to someone you cared for, you touched their soul. That was what I desired, the ultimate sexual thrill. Anything else was merely a mutual using, hardly better than masturbation.

'I've got some Es for you here, Janice,' I said to break the ice.

She looked at me suspiciously. 'How many?'

'Will six do?' She put her hand out and I gave her the tablets.

'Here's another one to take now.' I put one in my mouth and handed another to her. I watched her swallow it. 'I've changed the sheets.' It was a superfluous remark, she had watched me do it.

It was rapidly becoming a bizarre situation. I was uneasy enough without a taciturn partner. 'Are you going to talk to me or what?' I suddenly asked, smiling.

She smiled in return. 'I just wanted to make sure you weren't a nutter. Ian told me you were in prison for a long time.'

I laughed openly now. 'Well, I suppose I am a nutter, but not that way, Janice. You've got nothing to fear from me.'

We both undressed and climbed between the sheets. I saw her glance at my body, carefully appraising it. 'Work out on the weights?'

she asked.

'All the time,' I replied, looking at her.

She had the most perfect, petite body. Her legs were slim and feminine and completely unmarked. Her waist was narrow and her stomach taut. Her breasts were in proportion to the rest of her and were high and firm. I now realised why she covered herself up with baggy, shapeless clothes.

I reached for her and she came easily into my arms. I was content just to talk to her for a while. As I nestled my face in her hair, we talked of our recent past. I could identify with her precisely. I, too, had experienced the trauma of arrest and the loneliness of the prison cell. I shared the delight of being free for the first day with her. I understood the fear of being caught and returned to prison. That night I would return to the Scrubs hostel.

Suddenly, I began to feel the E come on me. There was a heightening of the senses. I breathed in deeply and smelled her shampoo, her perfume and the musk of her body. They were delightful, stimulating smells and I felt myself become aroused all over. Not only in my dick, which was now fully erect, but right down to the tips of my fingers.

I felt a surge of pure power course through my body that set me tingling all over. I was strangely calm and perfectly in control. I would pleasure this woman quite unselfishly. And in the giving would be my greater pleasure. For a time, we would be two souls lost in the throes of our passion. As primal as any beastly copulation, yet as caring as the most spiritual union.

I kissed her breasts and licked them and felt her arch her back in passion. Suddenly, my lips found hers and we both gasped at the intensity of the emotion. We drank deeply of each other as a delicious shiver shook us to the core. And then I was on her.

Almost bemusedly, I felt her fight me off.

'Condom, Norman. Condom,' I heard her say. I had temporarily forgotten this essential part of twentieth-century loving. I reached for one I had placed by the bed and Janice helped me put it on. As she touched me, I thought I would burst.

Gently, she guided me into her. Twenty years spent wanking had made me large and she was only a small girl. Slowly I slid it home and heard her utter a little cry of pain. Then nature itself took over.

We were like two animals, totally unrestrained as we thrust and licked and kissed and bit at each other. With eyes closed, we writhed on the bed, completely oblivious to our surroundings. A cacophony of small, pleasurable sounds accompanied our every movement.

Like some carefully choreographed dance, I quickly changed position and took her from behind. As I gently bit into her neck, I thrust into her pussy at this different angle and felt her whole body convulse as she came. But I was far from done.

As we changed positions once more, her face was momentarily above me. Framed by her damp hair it was a picture of ecstasy. She looked so beautiful.

'You're beautiful, so fucking beautiful,' I gasped.

She stared into my eyes. 'So are you,' she replied, 'so are you.'

It was a magic and memorable moment and enough to give us both pause. The hard man of the prison examined the experience and found it utterly genuine. With all her experience of the streets, it had touched a nerve in Janice, too. Something had irrevocably changed between us. But for the moment, we were still caught up in our passion. I turned her on her back and entered her again. I thrust deeply and pulled her close to me. I felt her shudder again and then it was as if some higher force drove me. I spiralled ever upwards until at last an incredible brightness burst in my consciousness. Far below, I felt myself come.

We lay for a long time without speaking. Occasionally, Janice would nuzzle her face against my chest and I would kiss her neck gently. But it was all beyond words.

We made love again, then lay and talked. We must have snoozed for a while, then made love once more. When Ian finally disturbed us we had been in the room for seven hours. It hadn't seemed anything like that long.

As we dressed, Janice kept sneaking sly looks at me. I guessed what she was thinking. I took her in my arms.

'Janice, I'm going to look after you now,' I said.

* * *

We joined Ian in the other room and chatted for a while. I felt slightly guilty as far as he was concerned. All the girls came and went, just making a convenience of him really, and he never got to sleep with any of them. He had confided in me that Janice was a special favourite of his, that they were good friends. He would have liked there to have been more to the relationship, but the great advantage for all the girls of staying at Ian's was that they never got harassed sexually, as they did in so many other places.

But he seemed genuinely pleased for both Janice and me that we had found each other. I guessed that he was so lonely he just wanted to feel that he belonged. I suppose he envisaged that the three of us would now hang around together.

As the E wore off, so did some of the 'loved up' feeling. I could suffer the lows that followed the highs, but then I wasn't a confirmed junkie. The latter inevitably went in search of the next high.

I had noticed different moods in Janice before. Sometimes it was as if she had two different personae. However, as we rarely saw each other, I took little notice.

I now became aware of a change that had come over her. Her teeth were clamped together, altering the shape of her jawline. Gone was the mischievous light that had danced in her eyes. And the smile that had made her look so beautiful was as distant a memory as yesterday's sunshine.

'I need you to get me some gear,' she virtually growled at me.

'What?' I replied, as mystified by the request as the change in mood.

'I'm starting to cluck. I'm going to need some gear shortly otherwise I'm going to be ill.'

From sitting around Ian's, I knew that 'clucking' was heroin withdrawal. For someone like myself who was so fanatically strong around my needs and desires, I couldn't really identify with a need that could rule someone so utterly. However, I knew that even strong men had been cowed by heroin.

I wanted to help her, but my values were still very much of the 'old school'. Heroin was completely beyond the pale and anyone who gave it to his girlfriend was beneath contempt. But if I was going to look after her, I could hardly just sit there and watch her suffer.

Another consideration, though, was just how genuine our feelings were for each other. I was undoubtedly on the rebound from Jackie. Janice, like most girls from the street, was notoriously hard and mercenary around men. I had often listened to the girls laugh about how they had suckered some gullible 'punter', before disappearing with his money.

I was from the street, too, though, an active player in the game and at a far higher level than any of Ian's 'street people' ever would be. I had enough money to be able to be generous and believed it to be 'good karma' to help those less fortunate than myself. I was aware that I still suffered from 'prison paranoia', however I wasn't going to be taken for a mug by anyone. I would have to watch the situation closely.

Ian wanted to come with us, but it was suspicious enough for a couple to be in the areas we were going. I drove Janice to a dilapidated council estate in Stoke Newington and parked up.

'You can't come with me. They'll think you're Old Bill.'

I shrugged off what, in other circumstances, would have been a grievous insult. 'How much do you want?'

'A score will do.'

I handed her the money and with a grudging 'Thanks' she was gone. I watched her disappear up a darkened alleyway that I would have thought twice about entering, but in these, as in so many other things, she was utterly fearless.

This was the bit I hated, just sitting about waiting in such a run-down, depressing area. From time to time, various members of the dispossessed flitted from shadow to shadow. Sometimes they would steal a suspicious, wary glance at me. I would ignore them and continue staring into the middle distance. I felt no fear of them. They might have the desperation of the ghetto, but I was fit and healthy and fired with a courage they couldn't compete with. I was confident that, should it come to a tear-up, I would give a good account of myself.

After about 20 minutes, Janice returned and we drove back to Ian's. I watched as they chased the spluttering crumbs across the tin foil, sitting well back to avoid the noxious fumes. Calmer now, Janice lay back in an armchair. Ian dozed in the corner.

Like some impartial observer of the human condition, I reflected on the various life-worlds that people seemed to create for themselves out here. Was this one any more or less stimulating than some of the loveless, middle-class scenarios I had seen? I was still exploring this strange world and had yet to find anything remotely resembling Nirvana. Perhaps man's lot really was one of quiet desperation.

But I had to get back to the hostel and I stood to leave. Janice walked to the door with me. We kissed and, briefly, she clung to me. Then I was gone, into the night.

I had much to think about as I drove back to the Scrubs. Perhaps the most important thing was that I hadn't thought about Jackie all day. And when I did think about her, there was nothing there. I realised that I didn't particularly like her and didn't care if I never saw her again. Quite literally, it was as if a spell had been broken.

It was all very unnerving. I was a rational man, my philosophy firmly grounded in reality. What was happening to me? Why was I in such an emotional turmoil? It was obvious that, as much as I had thought that I had come through the long years unscathed, something very fundamental had happened to me. Yet there was no one I could talk to about it and probably no cure. I would just have to work it out for myself.

Suddenly my phone rang. The breathy, almost childish voice identified itself as Janice.

'Norman, I miss you already. Thanks for today, I really enjoyed myself. You will come round tomorrow, won't you?'

It felt so good to have someone want me, need me and care for me, even if it was just some junkie, street girl. But who was I, a jailbird killer, to look down on anyone? If it kept the loneliness at bay, if it banished the memory of Jackie, if it made me whole and healed me, why should I question it?

I examined my feelings for Janice and was sure that I didn't love her. It wasn't just that she wasn't 'suitable', didn't fit in with my romantic ideal. It was that there wasn't that deep longing to be with her; the thinking about her all the time and the wanting her to love me in return.

I resolved not to hurt this girl, not to use her and to look after her as best as I could. In return, I would enjoy her love. It all made me feel unusually mature. That the 'little boy' of the institution could be handling this situation in such an objective, 'adult' way quite surprised me. Perhaps I was starting to grow up.

'I miss you too, Jan,' (and, in truth, I did), 'I'll see you in the morning.'

'Please don't hurt me, Norman. I've been hurt lots before and I won't hurt you.'

If this girl was grafting me, she really was quite an actress and was playing the role to the full. But I had the feeling that she did care. And why shouldn't she? My confidence with women was low at the moment, but I was sure I had attractive qualities. I had more than held my own in the realm of men. I had lots of friends, was articulate and intelligent, was quite a successful criminal and was soon to be a published author. Janice would have reason to be proud of me.

'I won't hurt you, Jan. You just try to be strong now and get on top of those drugs, yeah?'

'I'll try, Norman. I'll try.'

'Bye now.'

'Bye. I love you.'

As I switched my phone off, I resolved to get Janice off drugs. Not only would I take nothing from her, when I eventually left, she would be stronger than before. That served to dispel further any thoughts that I might be using her.

* * *

The following day was Friday and I was due to spend the weekend with Ivor in Birmingham. I also had to deliver two keys of speed to him for the local bikers. Perhaps I could kill several birds with minimal stones. I phoned him and he agreed that I could bring Jan with me. Not only could we spend a weekend together in a village on the outskirts of Birmingham, it would also look less suspicious driving with Jan than if I was on my own.

Janice was asleep on the sofa when I arrived at Ian's. I shook her gently, but she started quite violently and fixed me with a baleful grimace. For a second I had to remind myself of the time we had spent together the previous day.

She wasn't going to be hurried and I realised that she probably wasn't feeling too well. I knew that mornings were bad times for junkies.

In her own sweet time, she got up, washed in the bathroom and changed into clean clothes. She was quite the little gypsy, carrying everything she needed with her. It was certainly a performance, intending to convey to me that she wasn't at my beck and call. When finally she sat down ready, I couldn't help but smile.

'What you fuckin' smiling at?' she demanded, her face a dark scowl.

I realised she was probably every bit as paranoid as I was, always expecting the worst. That had certainly been her experience. I further realised that I wasn't going to have it all my own way with her. She was very spirited and fiery. By the same token, I was a strong and fiery spirit myself, so it was a quality I wasn't going to hold against her. I reasoned that, when she got to know me and trust me, she would relax a bit. In the meantime, mutual friends could expect to witness pyrotechnics between us at times.

I chose not to answer, saying instead, 'I'm going to take you up to Birmingham to spend the weekend with me, Jan, if that's all right with you?'

She made a small play of considering the offer, as if her social diary was already quite full. I reminded myself not to smile again; I didn't want another outburst. Suddenly, it was all very funny. Here was I, Crazy Norman, the terror of the long-term jails, being intimidated by a mere slip of a girl.

'When we coming back?' she demanded.

'Sunday afternoon,' I replied.

'I'll need some toiletries and stuff if we're going to go out.'

'Don't worry,' I cut her off quickly, 'I'll get everything you need on the way.'

Somewhat mollified, she collected her things together.

Ian, who was fully awake himself now, looked thoroughly downcast. I was taking his little companion away, leaving him alone for the weekend. But I knew the 'street people' would be round. At weekends, Ian's was the centre of activity. Somewhere people could drop in to take whatever drugs they had with them.

He came out to the car with us and I hugged him goodbye. I walked around the car and got in. As I closed the door I heard him say quietly to Janice, 'Don't forget who put you on to it.'

Immediately, my paranoia flared. In jail, Ian had been the most loyal and honourable friend a man could wish for. Now, his chosen companions were the dregs of the underworld. I believed, nay hoped, that he still had his former principles, although much of his behaviour didn't support that contention.

So what was going on? Was there some kind of conspiracy between him and Janice? I suppose I was about £12,000 strong at the moment, with prospects of getting more. No great fortune in 'chaps' terms, but a considerable fortune by 'street people's' standards.

I cursed myself for being so trusting. Yet to receive anything worthwhile you first had to give. At least, that was the way I looked at it. Janice's love for me would all turn to ashes in my mouth if it were merely a ploy to graft me.

I said nothing as we drove off, deciding just to watch the situation carefully. I stopped at a local supermarket and got all the bits and pieces that Janice would need for the weekend. There was one nasty moment in the perfume section. I watched Janice hovering and suddenly realised who I was with.

'Oi, Janice,' I cautioned, 'don't you fucking dare. I've got the money to pay for everything. I don't need to be nicked for shoplifting, if you don't mind.' She glared at me and walked on.

Back in the car, I explained that even a minor offence could cause my life licence to be revoked and send me back inside for several years. It wasn't that my bottle had gone; I was quite active in my own right. But she would have to be careful when she was around me. Some of the irresponsible things she normally did could destroy me.

She looked at me dubiously as I explained all this, as if I was exaggerating.

'I wouldn't get you nicked,' she said stubbornly. 'It's just that I'm not used to having to look out for my partner.'

I accepted this explanation, realising that most of her boyfriends and partners must have been junkie petty thieves. It was quite amusing to think that, by the standards of the street, I was a considerable move upmarket for her.

But now I had to go into 'work' mode. I would be picking up the keys of speed shortly and, once again, I would be on a suicide mission. I resolved to leave the gun behind this time. I couldn't really take it up to Ivor's place with me. However, that hardly lessened the pressure on me. If I got stopped, it would be all over for me.

Janice was far too street-wise not to notice my change of mood long before we got to Mile End. I had decided not to tell her anything. What she didn't know about couldn't get her into trouble. If we were stopped, I would take full responsibility anyway.

I parked several streets away from the tower block. Even so, I was back within 15 minutes. I put the small, plastic-wrapped parcel in the boot and got in the car. Janice had turned the radio on and it was playing loudly. Turning it down, I drove away. Neither of us spoke.

I knew her well enough now to know she had the hump. In the circumstances, I just didn't care. I was focusing all my attention on driving and watching out for police cars. Girlfriends of the 'chaps' were often on offer, it went with the territory. If you enjoyed the money and the good times, you had to risk the bad.

Suddenly, Janice turned the radio up and loud music filled the car. We weren't a normal-looking couple by any means. She was a young, sexy-looking, mixed-race girl; I was white and obviously twice her age. We didn't need loud music to attract any more attention. Then there was the state of my, already overstretched, nerves. I turned it down again.

As she reached to turn it up again, I swatted her hand away.

'For fuck's sake, Janice. Leave the fucking music down, will ya?'

She recoiled from the mild slap as if she had been scalded.

'Oh fucking hit me, would ya? Is that the sort of geezer you are, you hit birds?'

I was trying to drive and look at her all at the same time. Nothing could have been further from the truth, though, and I couldn't let it go.

'I've never hit a woman in my life, Jan.'

'No, but you shot one though.'

Inwardly I cringed. I wasn't going to hide anything from her, but I hadn't realised that Ian had already told her. A brief suspicion of Ian's motives registered in my brain.

'Nice one, Janice. Thanks for throwing that in my face.' Now it was my turn to feel hurt.

As if realising that she had hurt me, she fell silent for several minutes. But it was plain that she was still seething.

'And another thing, if you're going to use me as smother, you should be paying me.' This was an obvious reference to the parcel.

She did have a point. If this was just a one-off trip, she ought to be paid.

'Janice, you're my bird. I'll buy everything for you, I'll take care of you, we're together. Do I have to pay you to be with me?' In truth, I was still over-paranoid about her trying to graft me.

'Well, I am working. And I should be paid,' she insisted stubbornly.

The exchange didn't exactly clear the air, I was far too tense to relax, but it did serve to broker an uneasy truce. Sullenly, we both sat there as the miles slipped past, the radio playing quietly in the background.

Once we were on the M1 and picked up speed, I did feel a lessening of the pressure. I wasn't home and dry by any means, but the chances of being randomly stopped had decreased considerably.

The village where Ivor lived was a typical Midlands conurbation, rows of identical houses lining the sides of very similar streets. I pulled up outside his girlfriend's house. As Janice and I approached the front door, Ivor opened it.

He was always relaxed and easy-going, with a charming manner. Knowing how paranoid Janice could be around men, I'd had reservations about their meeting. But he hugged her gently, kissed her lightly on the cheek and led her inside.

Bessie was a big-built woman in her early thirties, who had only been with Ivor for six months. Her previous boyfriend had knocked her about and she had developed a serious speed habit. She was naturally friendly and caring and seemed happy with Ivor. She was strong, both physically and mentally, but she doted on her two children.

Anna, the eldest, was an intelligent girl of about 13 who, although not particularly attractive, was big for her age. John was a year younger and lived in the shadow of his precocious sister.

Ivor did the introductions and Bessie and Janice immediately seemed to get along. In truth, I had explained the situation to him on the phone and no doubt he had briefed Bessie. Anna was absolutely fascinated by Janice. They weren't too different in size, but with her fuzzy Afro-style hair, pretty face and petite figure, she was all that Anna would wish to be.

It gave me the opportunity to leave Janice for a few minutes. I drove Ivor round to his own house, which was nearby, handed over the speed and carried Janice's and my stuff inside. Now I could relax.

After tea, we all went to the local bowling alley. I had never been in one before and didn't particularly take to it, but everybody else seemed to be enjoying themselves. Janice was like a different person. She laughed and scampered about and was totally at her ease. With Anna constantly at her side, she was like Bessie's third child. I reflected that years spent in prison and in servitude to heroin had stolen much of her childhood from her. Although so hard on the outside, she carried so much pain within. I suddenly felt very protective towards her.

She didn't neglect me, often breaking off from the game to run across and kiss me or cuddle. We were quite natural and relaxed with each other, and were obviously happy. I saw other couples look over at us, but didn't feel at all self-conscious. Whatever the age difference, it didn't bother us. I felt quite proud that such an attractive, vivacious girl as Janice should be with me. But suddenly I was afraid.

Everything I had ever loved I had lost. Every good time had turned into a nightmare. Pain and loneliness had become my constant companions. I feared that this relationship with Janice would turn into something I would cherish. The greater fear was that I would then lose it. But for now I would try to live for the moment, enfold myself in the unfamiliar happiness and damn what tomorrow might bring.

I awoke early next morning (prison habits die hard) and was immediately aware of Janice lying beside me. There was the warmth of her body and the pressure of her thigh against mine, but it was more than that. I, who was so attuned to loneliness, of waking up alone in a cold bed, could actually feel a spirit next to mine. I focused on the feeling and, although my eyes were tightly closed, could see a brightness where Janice's spirit was. But as I focused, the brightness faded and I was just aware of the physical warmth.

We had made love for a long time the previous night. Whatever else, we were certainly sexually compatible. She had confessed that she enjoyed sex, but bad experiences with men had turned her towards women. She assured me that I satisfied her, which was something of a relief. After so many years celibate, I had feared that I might not be able to keep up with her. But in my heart, I was confident I would. Long years focusing on health and fitness had finally paid off.

I was aware that I wanted her right now, but I knew how she hated being awoken early. I would wait until later. In the meantime I would exult in the thought of what a prize awaited me.

That afternoon we went shopping together in town. In the evening, we went to a local pub with Ivor and Bessie. Later, we danced in Bessie's front room. Not earth-shattering stuff, but we enjoyed ourselves.

We lay in quite late on Sunday morning. Janice was up before me and was suddenly missing. I wandered from room to room, but couldn't find her. As I stood before the kitchen window, a slight movement in the yard outside attracted my attention.

She was still wearing just knickers and a shirt that served as a nightdress, but was squatting down in the corner of the yard where the wall met the wooden fence. As I looked more closely I noticed her body shaking as she cried bitterly.

I ran into the yard and across to her. I squatted down next to her and hugged her to me. 'What's the matter, Jan? What the fuck's the matter?' My voice was thick with emotion.

Deep sobbing wracked her body and she was unable to answer.

'OK, OK. You're all right, nothing's going to hurt you while I'm around. Now, what's the matter? Please tell me.'

Long minutes passed and slowly she regained control. 'Your friends, they're so nice to me.' Her voice broke as she forced the words out.

I looked at this little girl next to me, her face all wet with tears, and wondered what sort of nightmare life she had had that simple hospitality could have such an effect on her. It occurred to me just how much we had in common and I felt my heart go out to her. But not too much. I had just been through the agony of Jackie. I was well aware that only love could kill me. To place my heart in the hands of this irresponsible girl would be an act of utter folly. In the greater plan, I was still the mystical warrior on a mission. Duty demanded that I save myself for greater things.

Late Sunday afternoon, we drove back to London and Ian's flat. If I had been in any doubt about the good time we'd had or its positive effect on me, Ian immediately dispelled it.

'Look at the two of you,' he enthused as we walked in the door. 'You're shining, the pair of you, positively shining.'

There was undoubtedly a degree of relief that we were back in his responsibility, but it did cause Janice and I to turn and look at each other. He was right. I wouldn't have described it as 'shining', but there was a brightness about our faces, a happiness that hadn't been there when we left.

Shortly afterwards, Janice led me into the other room. There was an unusual earnestness in her manner, emphasised by the fact that she gripped my arm tightly.

'Norman, Ian's right, you know. We are so strong together. If we stay together, nothing can hurt us.' Her brow furrowed with the intensity of her emotion. 'A lot of people will feel threatened by that though,' she continued. 'People will try to break us apart. So don't let them do it, eh?'

For once, Janice seemed very wise. I, who had so little experience of relationships, couldn't be expected to know. However, I couldn't deny that I was feeling something. We would just have to see how things turned out.

LIFE
AFTER LIFE

love on and off the rocks

Janice had now become a part of my daily life. I still had to do my bit of running around with Fred and occasionally go on other meets and, obviously, Janice couldn't be with me for this. I say 'obviously', but it was never obvious to her.

'I'm a thief, too, you know,' she'd say to me quite petulantly whenever I had something criminal to do.

I was sure the 'chaps' wouldn't have appreciated it at all, had I shown up with this wild-looking girl. To be frank, it would have instantly destroyed my credibility and their faith in my judgement. I would have been out of business.

I felt guilty about leaving her at Ian's, but I had few other options. Weeknights I had to return to the hostel to sleep myself and I could hardly take her with me, even if she hadn't have been on the run. There was one solution though.

I had taken her over to meet my mother on a couple of occasions and they had got on quite well. To be honest, my long-suffering mum would have welcomed the Whore of Babylon had I brought her home, she was that devoted to me. Further, she knew I needed someone and hoped that Janice would be good for me.

Whether she realised how off-the-wall Janice was was a moot point. She led quite a sheltered existence, only popping round to the local shops occasionally. She was hardly wise in the ways of the street. However, I did catch her taking sly looks at Janice when she thought she wasn't looking, weighing her up.

For Janice's part, she seemed so starved of affection that she positively glowed under my mum's fussing about her. Snacks, cups of tea and small presents that my mum had had for years all brought smiles of sheer delight to her face.

'She's nice, your mum,' she'd say as if daring me to deny it, and once, 'Your mum treats me better than my own mum.'

What could I say to that? I was just pleased that the three of us seemed happy together. I'd leave Jan with my mum when I went off to meet Fred. In the evenings when I returned to the hostel, she would sleep in my bed in Mum's lounge. It was quite an imposition on my mum, but nothing was too much trouble for me.

There were a couple of worrying moments. Mum pulled me aside one evening and told me how Jan had acted suspiciously in the local chemists, as if she was going to steal something. Further, that she had searched the flat and that some of Mum's things had been disturbed. But nothing was missing and there were so many other major worries in my life that I let it go.

The more time I spent with her, the more I became aware of how dependent on drugs Janice really was. There was the heroin dependency of course, but that wasn't too much of a problem as she could go for days without it as long as she had some Valium. In fact, at times she seemed more addicted to the Valium.

There was something called Rohipnal that she regularly craved, and various other tablets to bring her up if she was coming down, or to bring her down when she was too high. She needed a whole range of patent medicines just to stabilise her between the illegal drugs she took. I reflected that a chemist would have had a full-time job just managing her moods.

Obviously, these patent drugs couldn't be bought over the counter, so much of our day was taken up going from one run-down flat to another, either buying what she needed or swapping some other drug for it.

The most serious problem was the crack cocaine. She could go for days and days without even thinking about it, but once it was in her head it was like an obsession. I refused to buy it for her, saying it was killing her. She would go into her other persona when on it and become morose and paranoid. It was also phenomenally expensive. There just wasn't enough money in the world to maintain a crack habit.

So she would just disappear. Sometimes she would storm off, and at other times just slip away. She would shoplift until she had enough to buy what she wanted, then go in search of the 'rocks' or 'stones'. She would return several hours later, sullen but apologetic. I grew to accept it as a weakness she had no control over. However, it was a constant source of friction between us.

The North London drugs scene was a whole new world to me. That such an extensive drug-dependent underclass existed seemed amazing. There had been nothing remotely resembling it when I was last out. The mystical warrior in me couldn't help but reflect that it was a harbinger of the apocalypse. By comparison, at least I had a mission. As writer–outlaw I would avoid the ranks of the doomed.

I was still very suspicious of Janice's motives. She seemed to have an easy familiarity with many of the young, and not so young, male druggies whose flats she frequented. I agonised over imaginary scenarios where she traded sex for drugs when I wasn't there.

I was nothing if not inordinately proud. It was a fault with me, but had sustained me through the years in jail. The thought that my girlfriend was being unfaithful behind my back was my worst nightmare. It fed my paranoia and I regularly took it out on Janice.

Janice was extremely touchy about anything to do with sex. The merest suggestion that I might suspect her of being unfaithful was enough to provoke a towering rage.

'I'm with you, ain't I?' was her answer, as if it was all self-evident.

Well, it wasn't self-evident to me. I was already quite conscious of our age difference. As far as I was concerned, I was flying about just like any other young 'chap' on the street. I was as brave and proud as anyone. My girl should bring respect for me, too.

Janice had been quiet for several hours. I thought it was either a mood or that she wasn't feeling well. In the event, it turned out that she had been thinking.

'I've been thinking, Norman,' she said suddenly in a manner that dared me to suggest that she hadn't. 'This isn't any good. I really love you and I want to give our relationship a chance. I want to give myself up, so that when I come out we can settle down properly.'

On a purely selfish level, I would miss her. I had got used to having this little spirit, albeit a troubled spirit, around me. Despite all the frustrations and jealousies, she had been keeping the loneliness at bay. Further, with all the phenomenal pressure I was under, the suicide missions and all, time spent alone with Janice was often pure bliss.

On a more pragmatic level, however, it wasn't a bad idea. She had ten weeks left to serve, I only had four more weeks on the hostel. So at least I would be fully free when she came out. Further, it was difficult to divide my attention between working with Fred and looking after Janice. One slip and it would all be over for me. With Janice safely back in prison, I could focus on 'work' and, hopefully, be on my feet when she got out.

But it had to be her decision. I hated prison and all it stood for. I could hardly encourage this girl I cared for voluntarily to enter a world I was just escaping. I would stand in the meal queues with her, share the loneliness of her cell at night and bridle under the unkindness of the screws. She had been through it all before admittedly, although that wouldn't necessarily make it any easier. However, at least she would have me to visit her this time and to be waiting for her when she got out.

As if she had read my mind, she suddenly clutched at my arm. 'You will wait for me, won't you?' All the tough exterior was gone now. There was fear bordering on despair in her eyes.

I pulled her to me and hugged her tightly. 'Of course I will. I promise.'

'And visit me regularly? I'll get through easy if I have visits.'

She had often bemoaned the fact that her mother had refused to visit her in prison. I always had regular visits, but had observed the effect on others who hadn't.

'I'll visit you every week, I swear to God, Janice. You don't really know me very well yet. But anyone who knows me will tell you that I'm an honourable man, a man of my word. Loyalty is the finest quality. I'll be there for you. You just try to sort your drugs problem out.'

'It would really help if you could bring me up some Valium from time to time. Ian will bring it in for me.'

'You know I won't let you suffer, Jan. I've got to be a bit careful, what with my life licence and all. But I'll find a way to get you what you need.'

This seemed to reassure her somewhat, but she continued to cling to me. She said that she would need to pick up some things from her mother's, then it would just be a matter of phoning the jail to let them know she was coming.

For our last evening together, we wanted to be on our own. She picked the clothes up from her mother's while I waited downstairs in the car. She said 'Goodbye' to Ian and told him how to wrap the Valium she would need. Then we went for a meal.

The candlelight and soft music smacked of cliché, but we were oblivious to it all. We held hands across the table and stared into each other's eyes, Janice on the edge of tears, me trying hard not to let it affect me, but with my voice catching with emotion. As much as I tried to tell myself that I wasn't in love with her there was obviously something very strong there.

We phoned Bullwood Hall, the jail she had failed to return to, but they said they had no vacancies and that she would have to hand herself in to Holloway. It gave us more time to be together, as we were already in North London.

Almost with an air of impending doom, I pulled up outside the gates of Holloway. I carried her bag of belongings, as she rang the gate bell. A large door swung open to reveal two serious-looking wardresses. There was no time now for lingering displays of affection. I placed her bag on the floor, gave Janice a quick kiss on the mouth and walked away without looking back.

As I drove back to the Scrubs' hostel, I reflected on the synchronicity in our lives. We were both children of the institution. It had denied us so much pleasure and caused us so much pain. But at least we had each other now. I hoped that thought would sustain Janice as it sustained me. As I lay in my hostel bed I thought of her. Just across London, I could picture her lying in her cell, thinking of me.

✳ ✳ ✳

Without the diversion of Janice in my life, I now concentrated exclusively on my work with Fred. It wasn't any less fraught, I courted death on an almost daily basis, but I didn't have the added irritation of Janice drawing attention to me.

Having said that, relations with Fred were becoming increasingly strained. Because Fatty was his contact, he began to act as if he was in charge. In one heated exchange I pointed out that I worked with him, not for him. He could have got someone else, but I did have some excellent contacts to sell to.

As luck would have it, 'sod's law' now came into play. With all my time free to concentrate on the Fatty connection, he suddenly got nicked. There was a big police raid on his garage and he and several of his workers were arrested. Fred huffed and puffed for a few days in a frenzy of paranoia, but there was no real connection to Fatty. It was some consolation, because we were both now out of work.

I returned to doing the daily rounds of my pals, looking for work. We hadn't exactly decided to call it a day, but after our argument I saw less and less of Fred. I wasn't exactly on the floor. I had no immediate work, but I did have about £20,000 behind me.

Every week, I went up to see Janice. Ian always came with me and passed her her little 'parcel'. It felt really strange visiting my girl in jail. I still visited quite a few pals, but now prison had become part of the family.

If anything, Janice had become more juvenile in prison. She would bounce on to the visit, wave to her pals on other tables, then wind herself around me and kiss. I didn't want to seem a prude, but I wasn't one for public displays of emotion. Again the age difference was a factor. Most of the other girls on the visit were clearly street girls. In my paranoia, I was sure they would think I was just a punter.

On the positive side, I had never seen Janice looking so healthy. My visits were reassuring for her and the little 'parcels' meant that, not only didn't she have to suffer the trials of withdrawal, she also had stuff to trade with. I only ever sent her Valium, Rohipnal and puff, but she got it virtually on a weekly basis.

Her letters and cards to me showed just how much of a little girl she still was. They were full of entreaties not to hurt her and were extensively embellished with kisses, love hearts and intertwined names. She emphasised how much she was looking forward to getting out.

That only brought home to me the responsibility of having a girlfriend. I would have to provide for her and wasn't at all settled myself yet. Also, I wasn't completely sure that I wanted to commit myself to her. At least I still had several weeks before she was due out.

I hadn't forgotten about my book deal, after all, I considered myself to be a writer first and foremost. However, it was something that was largely out of my control. I could only write the copy, it was in the hands of others to get it into print.

The publisher assured me though that we were only weeks away from publication. I had to choose a cover from six not particularly suitable photographs. The heavily tattooed con's arm handcuffed to that of a screw smacked of cliché, but at least it was self-explanatory.

Suddenly, it was my last day on the hostel. I cleaned out my locker in my room and left for the last time. There was no civic reception on the town hall steps, no pyrotechnic thunderstorm as the forces of good and evil battled for my soul, just a massive sense of anti-climax. The only clear feeling I could distinguish was that it had been a terrible waste of 24 years.

I badly needed a holiday, a clean break from the mean streets of Nineties London. For weeks, an old friend had been inviting me out to Spain. We had been prison comrades, but I hadn't seen him for 15 years. It was rumoured that he was doing well.

I couldn't go while I was on the hostel and, even now, I would need my probation officer's permission. I pitched a strong case, saying that if anyone needed a holiday, I did. He agreed to let me go.

·I had never been abroad before, so it was something of an adventure for me. Janice moaned that she wouldn't be able to see me for a while, but I countered that it would only be for two weeks. Further, it was a possible career opportunity for me. I just might find an important Spanish 'clue'.

I already had my passport, getting it in the early days of my home-leaves. Booking the flight was a major logistical nightmare for me, the furthest I'd been from home previously was Dublin. I set out for Gatwick with all the uncertainty of a cosmonaut on his first space mission. My pals reassured me that millions of people went to Spain every year.

I realised that because of the seriousness of my offence and also the criminal connections of some of my associates, the police could well be taking an interest in my movements. I might be able to give them the slip in Spain, but while I was in the terminal at Gatwick I would be fully under observation. The closed-circuit TV and armed police did wonders for my paranoia.

On the plane, I thought of JD and the last time I had seen him. He was a strange man, even by prison standards. John had been born deep in the Brazilian jungle of English evangelical parents. Their closeness to the great creator was no guarantee of an immaculate conception. The infant John was an absolute monster, a cleft palate the least of his afflictions.

Sixteen major operations later, the finished product was far from beautiful. Broad shoulders supported a massive, leonine head. Although his face was still out of proportion, the hare-lip was the sole remaining sign of his childhood truma.

His chosen profession had been armed robber and he had been

quite successful for one so young. But in the incestuous world of prison politics, he lacked the status he so badly desired. Friendship with me would enhance his standing.

But I was very much a loner; my world had been too filled with pain to share with anyone. I admired his principles and sympathised with his predicament, but restricted my involvement merely to sharing a tea-boat with him. He was grateful, though, and had never forgotten it.

At times he was a pain. Probably to compensate for the rejection his appearance inevitably brought, he was loud and often confrontational. The volume exaggerated the effect of the hare-lip. In full cry, his sentences were regularly interspersed with 'nuffs'. In the cruel world of prison his nickname was 'Nuff-Nuff' or 'The Lip'. I always called him JD.

I landed at Malaga with considerable trepidation. I was to meet JD in the bar area of the airport lounge. What if he wasn't there? It was easy enough for me to get lost in London nowadays.

I left the aircraft and walked the red marble corridors of Malaga airport. Suddenly, I felt completely different. The oppressive, depressive angst of England wasn't there any more. On a spiritual level, I felt my heart soar to the heavens. Perhaps it was England itself that was the problem. I had a good feeling about what was to come.

I collected my baggage and walked to the bar area. Immediately, I saw him. We shook hands and briefly hugged.

'Come on, mate, let's get out of here. There's too many eyes here.' The diction was less forceful, but the words were still distorted.

He was pleased to see me and the feeling was mutual. In the car, he explained that he had been living in Spain for several years. He provided large amounts of puff for several big firms, occasionally ferrying it up to Barcelona. He had several large homes and warehouses and an extensive team of workers.

You could see that he was quite proud of his achievements and, by criminal standards, it was certainly something to be proud of. He had even indulged his passion for motor racing and ran his own Formula Four racing team in England.

'I've put you in a nice little villa on your own, Norman,' he said as we neared Marbella. 'Let's drop your stuff off, then we'll go to my place.'

There was nothing 'little' about the villa, but it was certainly nice. Three floors of marble-floored rooms decorated in exquisite Spanish style was to be my home for the next two weeks.

We dropped off my cases and got back in the car. 'Take careful note of the route,' he said, 'you've got this car for the duration and you will be driving back here later.' Almost as an afterthought, he tossed an envelope into my lap. 'Here's two grand,' he said.

Thus far, it had all been like a dream. Spain seemed to be the land of opportunity. It had certainly been good to JD.

His home was a large, sprawling villa, sumptuously decorated and with an olympic-sized swimming pool. His wife was a pleasant-faced young Irish woman, their son carrying only a mild hare-lip as evidence of his genetic inheritance. The mother and father-in-law were of salt-of-the-earth Irish stock. I reflected that he had done well for himself.

Over the next few days, JD showed me around his set-up and introduced me to some of his workers. If the conditions of my life licence had allowed me to come and live in Spain, then that is what I would have done. However, JD indicated another alternative.

He said that he could always lay his hands on large quantities of puff at very reasonable prices. If I could arrange for people to come over and buy, he would put on £50 per key for me, paying me in puff that would go on the load. Back in England, this would more than double my return.

By coincidence, or, more likely, design on his part, Ivor came to Spain on holiday a few days later. He assured me that he had cars and drivers ready. We could start just as soon as we got back.

This put an entirely different complexion on things. I was now in the enviable position of having a small smuggling operation going. What's more, I was pivotal to the whole operation and couldn't be cut out.

The ensuing days were like life on a different planet. The sun and beautiful scenery stimulated my spirit. I concluded that Spain was an entirely more spiritual country than England. I resolved to spend as much time as I could there.

Janice wasn't forgotten. She was always in my thoughts and I didn't so much as look at another woman. Perhaps one of the reasons I feared her betrayal so much was that I would never have betrayed her.

I had special permission to phone her at Bullwood Hall. She managed to get permission to phone me on Ivor's mobile. It was only later that the significance of that would dawn on me.

Refreshed, nay spiritually rejuvenated, I returned to England. Within two weeks, Ivor and I had our first bit of transport home. All went very smoothly. There were no massive amounts involved. I collected mine and JD's shares, dropping his off to the racing team company. I was left with £10,500, not too bad for only two weeks' work and it was an ongoing proposition.

It was now close to Janice's homecoming and I was even more unsure of my feelings for her than before. Sometimes, she was so off her face on visits, I couldn't conceive of her getting her act together on the outside. However, in truth, there was little I could do about the situation. She was bang in love with me and, deny it as I may, I had strong feelings for her.

On my final visit out, she asked me to go and see her mother. She had told her about our relationship and her mother wanted to see me. It was something I really wasn't looking forward to. I was well aware that all Janice's previous boyfriends had been small-time junkie criminals. Fortunately, Janice's mother didn't know anything of my background. The down-side was the massive discrepancy in our ages.

I had become aware that Janice's relationship with her mother was pivotal to her feelings about herself. She felt that her mother didn't really care for her. She had never visited her in prison and had shown preferential treatment to her younger brothers. Therefore, it was very important to Janice that I create a good impression. With a new and responsible boyfriend, perhaps her mother would reassess her feelings for her and come to love her again.

A further problem was that not only was Janice's mother the same age as myself, she was also black. Janice's father had been white, but her mother was full-blooded West Indian, albeit from a thoroughly middle-class background. She was a fully trained private nurse and, I gathered, something of a snob.

I was very much a reverse racist as far as black people were concerned. I hated the idea that you could dislike someone merely because of the colour of their skin. Perhaps I found echoes in the notion that someone could hate me simply because of my criminality. It put me in the position that, however Janice's mother treated me, I would put up with it without complaint.

In the event, I handled the situation very well. Wearing a dark, pin-striped business suit and a collar and tie, I treated it like a business meeting.

Janice's mother was an attractive, well-dressed, professional woman in her early fifties. Her voice was cultured, with little trace of an accent. I could tell that she was immediately impressed with me. I reflected that all of my predecessors had been junkie yobbos.

It was all thoroughly civilised. Mrs Harris made tea and we drank it in a spotless, well-furnished lounge. Interaction was formal, bordering on the clinical. It was almost as if I was talking to a headmistress about one of her pupils. Mrs Harris emphasised how often Janice had let her down in the past.

For my part, I could only be honest and magnanimous.

'Mrs Harris, I only want the best for Janice. I realise there is a great discrepancy in our ages. For that reason perhaps we will never marry. I will be satisfied if I just give her back her life again.'

I meant every word and hoped I would be strong enough to step aside when the time came. Mrs Harris smiled and nodded. I concluded that the meeting had gone well.

It was only later, speaking to Janice on the phone, that I realised how well. Mrs Harris had given me the keys to her flat to pass on to Janice, so she could get in while she was at work at the hospital.

'My mum's never done that before,' she said suspiciously. 'What did you say to her?'

It occurred to me, that, on an intellectual level, I probably had more in common with Mrs Harris than with Janice. However, the former was quite cold and distant. My relationship with Janice was entirely more fiery and spiritual. And long may it be so, I concluded.

I still hadn't managed to get myself a flat. The council were unco-operative and I really didn't know how to go about getting one from the newspapers. More to the point, it was far more serious a step for me than Janice or anyone else realised. I now knew that I had this inordinate fear of living alone, or rather, of returning to an empty flat. Had I taken a flat with Janice and she had subsequently left me, the ensuing void in my life could well have irrevocably depressed me. As it was, I was comfortably in little boy mode, living with my mother. And don't think that this didn't seriously bother me.

If nothing else, it was reflected in my attitude to life. I could hardly be a mummy's boy. I had hit the street and embarked on suicide missions, so my bottle wasn't in question. Further, although I was no longer enslaved to 'the Beast', I had my gun and a Kevlar vest and woe betide anyone who challenged me.

On a bright, sunny day, I drove along the Southend Road to collect Janice from Bullwood Hall. As an avid observer of my own life I fully realised that all was pathos. It was just that I had no reference point to compare it with.

In the back of the car was a hamper containing a selection of foods, a bottle of champagne, some puff and a couple of Es. I had examined the map and envisaged a picnic in the surrounding woods. At some stage, I would break the bad news to Janice about the non-existent flat.

As it turned out, it was the first thing she asked me as she got in the car. Her disappointment was palpable. Her face dropped and it was obvious she felt betrayed. If I had had more experience of relationships, I would have realised that this was absolutely fundamental to our future.

I assured her I loved her and wanted to be with her. I explained that I didn't know how to go about getting a flat and that we could get one in the coming week. She didn't look convinced. When I suggested the picnic, she clearly regarded it as an excuse to get her in the woods and shag her. As we drove into the Essex forest, she sat sullenly beside me.

The picnic wasn't a success. A disinterested observer could have been forgiven for thinking that it was an eve of incarceration wake rather than a celebration of release. We drove back to London in strained silence.

We went to her mother's and Janice put her things in her room. We went on to Ian's. He was ecstatic to see her again, but from Jan's expression it was clear that she felt that we hadn't made any progress. We were still like two teenage lovers, both living with our parents, just meeting for dates.

By now I was about £62,000 strong and getting stronger by about £5,000 a week, thanks to the Spanish move with JD. Of all my driving passions, mystical or otherwise, the need to be a success was paramount. On the one hand, surviving 24 years in jail was something to be proud of; on the other, the waste of so many good years smacked of being a loser. I was well aware that, in the world I had come out to, money seemed to be everything. Also, I had heard so many tales of men who had come out, amassed a small fortune, then frittered it away. I was determined that wouldn't happen to me.

On the picnic, I had told Janice that I hadn't wasted my time while she was inside. Her ears pricked up when I mentioned the £62,000. However, when I explained that I wanted to build up a sum of capital to invest in moves and was going to hold £50,000 in reserve, she gave me a look of disbelief mixed with disgust.

She did seem somewhat mollified when I told her that I had obtained a supply of all the pills she needed. I had bought a parcel of hundreds of Valium, Rohipnal and others for only £100. She was disappointed that I hadn't brought them with me and annoyed when I said I would give her so many at a time on a daily basis. I emphasised that, otherwise, at the first weakness, she would swap the lot for crack. As we sat at Ian's, I gave her her first ration of pills.

Perhaps it reminded her of what I had said.

'I need a pipe,' said Janice in a tone that brooked no argument. She had the old driven look in her eyes, the crack persona had taken over again.

'I ain't buying you crack, Janice, I've told you before.' I was angry now, she was starting out right where she had left off. It vindicated my reluctance to get a flat with her.

'You're all bollocks, you, ya know. You say you're going to help me and you won't see me suffer. I'm virtually off the smack now. You don't realise what a feat that is for me. I intend to come off the crack, too, but I can't do it all at once.' Her voice trailed off in exasperation.

'Jan, I've got you pills, a fucking nine bar of puff, we'll have a flat very shortly, but I'm not ironing my dough out on crack. What's the bottom line with it? £100 a day? £200? It ain't as if it puts you in a good mood either, and it's fucking killing you. I ain't put myself on offer to get a lump of money together, just for you to waste it on crack.'

'Yeah, your fucking money,' she sneered.

'No, *our* money, Janice. I'm going to spend it on us. I lived like a monk while you were away. I wasn't out spending my money on birds.'

I had forgotten just how much that word was a provocation to her. Eyes flashing, she threw her head back.

'Oh, birds, eh? Yeah, I suppose you was fucking every old slag you could get your hands on, while I was being faithful to you in there.'

There was no arguing with her when she was in this mood, rationality was irrelevant. That made it all the more frustrating for me. The options were either to back down, or engage in a verbal slanging match. On this occasion, her first day out of jail, I chose the former.

It didn't calm her. In fact, it seemed to provoke her the more.

'Pah,' she exploded, jumping to her feet. She stormed from the room and I heard her slam the bathroom door.

I looked appealingly at Ian. He wasn't the sanest of authorities to appeal to, but he had known Janice longer than me and just might have some insight that I lacked.

'What's the fucking matter with her, Ian? I ain't so much as looked at another bird whilst she was inside. I've got a chunk of money together for us and still she's not satisfied.'

Ian pursed his lips and looked at the floor. I reflected that, when it came to wasting money on drugs, his sympathies would all be with Janice. Had it been up to him, the £62,000 would have gone on one enormous binge of drugs and booze.

'She don't believe it, Norm.'

The answer was ambiguous.

'What don't she believe, Ian?'

'She don't believe you're genuine. I know you mean what you say. I've known you for 20 years. Sometimes you drive me mad with all the discipline, you should relax a bit. But Janice doesn't know you yet. All her other boyfriends have lied and cheated her. I've told you what it's like out here. As far as she's concerned, you're too good to be true.'

'So what have you told her?' I asked accusingly.

'She don't listen to me. Janice doesn't listen to anyone. But I've told her to cherish you and you'll look after her.'

I heard the toilet flush, signalling that Janice was coming back. If she caught us talking about her it would provoke another paranoid outburst. Ian and I fell silent. Janice stormed back into the room. I reflected that she never entered a room casually.

'Are you going to run me over to Camden Town? I want to see Nigel,' she demanded.

Nigel was a sore point between us. He was a very wealthy property dealer in his late thirties, whom Janice had met while buying crack once. Because of his middle-class background, the dealers often ripped him off. Janice knew all the street dealers personally, she was a regular customer. She always got a good deal. Nigel would get her to buy for him. In return, Janice would smoke it with him for free. She emphasised that crack wasn't a solitary drug, users liked to smoke with someone. Understandably enough, I wasn't too pleased with the arrangement.

'Is that all that goes on?' I had challenged her once.

She had sat back, coolly looking at me. 'I've told you before. I'm with you. I won't go with any other geezers while I'm with you.'

It was as if it was all so very obvious and she was explaining it to a child. She was strangely calm, rational and convincing. Although I agonised over it, I did believe her. She often went into dangerously compromising situations, but was massively strong and manipulative around men, especially men like Nigel. And seeing as how I had refused to buy crack for her, and she couldn't give it up, it was a better solution than shop-lifting.

I drove her to Camden Town and waited while she fetched Nigel from his flat. She would tell him I was a minicab driver.

They were down immediately and climbed into the back. I glimpsed Nigel as he passed, the weak chin and pasty face, and resisted a powerful urge to jump out and smash him to pieces. I cursed for allowing myself to be drawn into these situations. But any relationship with Janice was filled with compromises. Unusually for me, I felt an air of inevitability and defeat settle over me.

We drove over to King's Cross. There was a hurried transaction in a darkened doorway and they got back in again. Within five minutes, we were back at the flat.

'Please wait, driver,' said Nigel as he got out. I stared grimly ahead, nearly choking with frustration.

It was 40 minutes before they reappeared. All the familiar jealousies battled for primacy in my mind. I watched their body language closely. He had his hand on Janice's shoulder as they walked towards me, but there was no proprietary cuddling or other familiarity. He patted her on the back as she got in.

'Thanks, Janice, it's nice to see you again. I hope you've got enough to keep you going.' Nigel turned to me. 'How much do I owe you, driver?'

I was temporarily lost for words. I had forgotten that I was supposed to be a minicab driver. I didn't want his money, but I would have to take something to keep up the pretence.

'Give me a tenner,' I growled.

'What?' said Nigel. Obviously, he had done this many times before and it was always more.

'Give me a tenner,' I said even more aggressively.

He looked worried now and hurriedly passed me a £10 note. However, there were many surly, unbalanced minicab drivers working around King's Cross. He quickly turned away.

'Bye, Janice,' he called out as I drove away.

'That was rude,' said Janice from the back.

I pulled into the kerb, slammed on the brakes and turned to face her.

''Ere, listen, you. Don't take the fucking piss out of me, OK? I ain't one of your usual crack-head, smack-head, scumbag, burglar boyfriends, you know. I've stood for that chinless prick borrowing my bird to score crack because she's hopelessly addicted to it. But I don't have to fucking like it.' I screamed the last sentence.

Janice sat silently in the back, suitably intimidated. It was always a constant war between us. I wasn't a man who threatened his girlfriends or otherwise abused them, but if I didn't regularly put her in her place, there was no bottom line with Janice.

We drove back to her mum's in silence. Janice got out and walked away without speaking. As I drove away, I was determined that I wouldn't see her again.

It was late morning when my phone rang. ''Allo,' she said in her familiar raggedly breathy, little-girl voice. It was sad, enquiring and vulnerable, all at the same time. It never failed to strike a chord in me.

I was angry, but found myself smiling in spite of myself. I reflected that our relationship was very similar to that of addict and drug. At some point of surfeit, we would hate and violently reject each other. By the following day, however, we would be missing each other, suffering withdrawal symptoms, if you like. The only cure was to be together.

I remembered what Janice had said about our being strong together. Even with my massive inexperience concerning relationships, I was aware that there was something intensely spiritual between us. We were both fatally flawed and deeply self-destructive, but there was an undeniably strong bond that neither of us could resist. In that sense, we were doomed to pursue it to the end.

'Do you want to see me?' I asked.

'What do you think?' she replied in a manner that said of course she did. I could imagine her smiling at the other end of the line.

'I'll pick you up at your mum's in two hours.' I was laughing openly now.

On the drive over, my mood became more sombre. I had hoped that Janice would emerge from jail a new woman, drug-free and well-balanced. I now had to come to terms with the inescapable fact that these flaws were an integral part of her character. My pride demanded that I do better. But another voice answered that I was a double killer fresh out of jail, who had shot to death one girlfriend when just 18 years old. This was hardly a pedigree that would appeal to most women.

Yet Janice accepted me without question. Further, she was an outlaw just like myself, with a wild and untameable spirit. Not least, she was a pretty, sexy mixed-race girl who was less than half my age. Lastly, we undoubtedly had strong feelings for each other. Perhaps it was a match made in heaven. I realised now that our relationship would always be tempestuous. I would have to hope that the good times outweighed the bad.

I rang the downstairs bell and Janice buzzed me up. I climbed to the top floor and entered her mother's flat for only the second time. Janice flung herself at me and hugged me to her. Something caused me to look up and I saw a young, mixed-race youth standing not a yard away.

Slightly embarrassed, I gently pushed Janice away, turning her towards the youth.

'Oh, Norman, this is Luke, my brother,' she said.

I knew that Janice had two younger brothers. This one had healthy, clean-cut good looks, with bright, intelligent eyes. I reflected that it must have been a relief for her mother to have at least one of her children who was drug-free.

Luke and I shook hands, but he seemed shy, or was it reserved? I reasoned that perhaps he was dubious about Janice's boyfriends; she hadn't chosen well in the past.

Janice led me into her room, which was small and quite cluttered.

'I'm the oldest child, you'd think my mum would give me the big bedroom, but she always treats Luke as the favourite,' she complained.

'Perhaps that's because he's here all the time and doesn't give her grief,' I said matter-of-factly. Janice shot me a steely look, but said nothing.

Surprisingly, she was almost ready. She sat before her dressing table, putting the final touches to her make-up. For the moment she had forgotten about me and was engrossed in the task. She looked remarkably relaxed and normal and beautiful. I found myself wishing that she was like this all the time.

'You're looking remarkably pretty today, madame,' I said, specifically emphasising the French form of madam. Janice looked at me quickly, searching for sarcasm, but I was smiling broadly. She smiled back and turned away shyly at the compliment. How I loved her at these little-girl moments.

Soon she was finished and bustled about looking for various items that were strewn about the room. She crammed them haphazardly into a purple bag. We shouted a 'Goodbye' to Luke and heard a muffled reply from his room. Then we set off for Ian's.

It was a beautiful sunny day.

'Let's go to the countryside,' I suggested.

Janice wrinkled her nose with uncertainty, then, as if realising there were no hidden threats, no dangers to a town girl like herself from such an unusual proposal, nodded in agreement.

Ian thought it was a good idea too. He scampered about his flat getting ready, with all the enthusiasm of a child promised a special treat. It was at times like these that I realised how much damage the prison had done to his mind. Finally, he was ready, but there was an essential ritual to carry out.

Janice got out a screwed-up piece of silver paper and unwrapped it carefully on a low table. Ian's full concentration was now entirely on the matter in hand. The silver paper was unfolded to reveal several large, off-white crumbs of crack.

'Nigel gave them to me last night,' said Janice by way of an unsolicited explanation.

'How much did he give you?' asked Ian.

'Mind your own business,' said Janice sharply. I mused on how selfish this crack seemed to make people. Ian had reasoned that if Janice still had some left from Nigel's gift of the night before, she must have had quite a large amount to start with. In that case, she was sharing only this small amount with him. He sat there sulkily, obviously put out, but not wishing to say more lest Janice deny him even this reduced share.

A home-made bottle-and-pen pipe appeared and the ritual began. Dozens of cheap plastic lighters were tried and discarded, before one could be found that worked. The 'rock' was set atop a small pile of ash that was heaped on the top of the pipe, then lit.

There was no immediately obvious ecstasy, in fact, from their pained expressions, one could have been forgiven for thinking that it was a thoroughly unpleasant experience. Then they both sat solemnly, almost grudgingly, as if cheated somehow.

They didn't seem so interested in the countryside trip now, but I pressed the matter. Ian suggested that we go to Hampstead Heath, near Jack Straw's Castle. It was only half-an-hour's drive away.

We pulled into a large, public car park that was almost empty on this weekday. I drove to the farthest corner before parking. Now it was my turn. I got out a small, factory-made hash pipe and a small piece of hash. Sliding down in my seat, I smoked two pipes. Ian, never one to be left out of anything involving drugs, asked for a go. Janice passed. I reflected that a cynic might well have accused me of a policy of 'If you can't beat them, join them.' However, it was a beautiful sunny day and the hash relaxed me. Further, it was awkward being the only straight head around most of the time. Lastly, I rationalised that what was all right for Bill Clinton was OK for me.

Janice and I strolled across the heath, Ian blithering along to the rear, a cross between an idiot child and a demented elderly parent. He kept making remarkable discoveries of completely mundane and commonplace things like daisies. He would insist on showing us the fine detail of individual petals, all the while marvelling at the ingenuity of the Great Creator.

Perhaps it was the writer in me, I couldn't help but take a step back from reality and observe the scene objectively. I reflected that this Great Creator must certainly have a sense of humour to have given me this present family.

Janice was quite relaxed, seeing as how she was in crack mode. Her smile was open and friendly, even if she was gripping my hand rather too tightly. We sat down in long grass by some bushes, not far from a refreshments kiosk. Ian was showing her the intracacies of a nettle as I headed towards the kiosk for some ices.

Out in the sunshine on the heath, with my girlfriend and an old pal, for a moment, life was almost idyllic. Gone was the normal, gut-wrenching worry about the future, about success. I realised that much of this feeling might be the hash, but resolved simply to enjoy it. Ian and Janice were talking earnestly as I returned with the ices.

The refreshments finished, Janice and I lay back in each other's arms. I felt the sun on my face, a cool breeze occasionally wafted over us. Nearby, Ian was snoring loudly. Bliss, sheer bliss.

Janice raised herself on one arm. 'You know,' she said smoothly, 'if we're going out together, you really ought to give me some money each day.'

Even in my 'out-of-it' state, the words lanced into my consciousness. An icy-cold shower of reality galvanised me from my dream, but I paused. Was it prison paranoia or was she really trying to graft me? Was it reasonable for a boyfriend to give a girlfriend daily house-keeping money nowadays?

But she had no house to keep. We weren't even living together yet. Had Ian put her up to it? I had seen them in earnest conversation as I returned with the ices.

I experienced a sudden sinking sensation in my stomach. Bitter disappointment flooded my brain. Life away from the cold loneliness of prison had been so nice, but what if it was all false? And when my money ran out, would Janice leave, too?

One small voice accused me of meanness, that I loved my money and the pursuit of success above everything. There was a niggling feeling of guilt, I was obsessed with success, but injured pride overruled it.

'I've told you before, Janice, I'm not going to pay you just to be with me. I'll pay for everything for us, but I'm not going to give you money. Anyway, you'd only spend it on crack.' I was angry now.

Surprisingly, Janice let the matter drop. But the damage had been done. The suspicion seethed there in my brain for the rest of the day. Remnants coloured my judgement for months to come.

* * *

Our flat was still a burning issue, but the coming weekend we were due to go down to Newhaven to stay with my old prison pal, Steve. Janice had listened in rapt attention as I told her how Steve, a 19-year-old biker, had been given life for killing another teenage biker. His then girlfriend, Mary, had waited faithfully for 16 years until he came home again. They now ran a guest-house together and were married.

The implication, of course, was that true, unselfish love could conquer all. But you could see that Janice was interested in meeting Steve and Mary. She seemed to like my friends. They were suitably off-the-wall, without being shot away into the bargain, like all of Janice's North London acquaintances.

Friday noon, we left London for the coast. I was looking forward to seeing Steve. He had been a close and trusted friend in prison. This would be the first time I would see him since college and town visits at Ford. Mary was delightfully friendly and caring, but seemed to have an inordinate interest in my personal life. It was all very innocent, almost motherly concern, and had become something of a joke. I knew she would be fascinated to meet Janice.

Janice, though, could be very paranoid and aggressive around other women. Also, she would get very off her face and upset people. Steve and Mary were both kindly, broad-minded people. I secretly cringed at the thought that Janice might make a scene.

Things didn't start too well at all. We were barely on the coast road when Janice suddenly decided she wanted to take an E. I had declared that I was bringing a couple of speed tablets and several Es with me, to take over the weekend. In fact, Janice was always more interested in what drugs we were taking with us than where we were going.

The problem was that I didn't want Janice on an E when she first met Steve and Mary. She had already gobbled several of her daily ration of pills and was wired, but relatively stable. But 'relatively stable' was only a comparative term when applied to Janice.

'Don't tell me when I can take my fucking drugs,' she shouted, at what was only the beginning of a previously mild disagreement.

'They're not your drugs, Janice,' I replied, quite reasonably.

This served only to provoke her further. Perhaps if I had thought about it, I might have realised that she was suffering in some way. The trouble was, Janice never whinged about anything, never complained that she was in pain. She was too brave for her own good. I once saw her take a tumble down a flight of basement steps and gash her leg. She got up and walked away without saying a word. Maybe she didn't want to admit a weakness, fearing that I would exploit it as power over her. She was fiercely independent.

'Powder-power cunt,' she screamed, face contorted. 'What, do you want me to beg? Is that it?' She turned towards me, aggressively.

I started to bite now. 'Don't fucking talk to me like that.' I turned towards her, too. 'Just look at you. Look at your face all contorted with hatred. Why are you so fucking nasty at times?'

'Oh, you aren't nasty, are you, you gangster cunt?' she came right back at me.

That stung. The reference to my background was uncalled for. Anyway, the term 'gangster' was an insult among my circle. It smacked of bullying and of cowardice.

'Why don't you fuck off?' I shouted back.

'You fuck off,' she screamed.

I turned towards her again, raging. 'Another word and I'll stop and put you out the car.'

I meant it at the time, but it certainly didn't have the effect I intended.

'Fuck you and your car.' Her voice was a ragged roar in the confined space. She grabbed the steering wheel and twisted it violently to the right. The car swerved towards the oncoming traffic.

We were travelling at about 70mph, any collision would be disastrous. In sheer desperation, with a strength born of fear, I wrenched the wheel free from her grasp and the car swerved back on to a straight course again.

The shock temporarily drove all anger from my mind. Whereas before I had felt hot, now I was stone cold. As the realisation of what we had so narrowly missed slowly dawned, though, it all came flooding back. Quickly, I pulled over to the side of the road.

Now it was time for my face to contort. With eyes bulging, I grabbed her by the shoulders.

'You ever do that again and I'll break your fucking neck.'

The volume alone should have been enough to intimidate her. She sat there, frightened now. She realised she had pushed me to the limit.

I prided myself on my self-control. Yet this girl had the ability to provoke me beyond measure. I guessed that it was because I had strong feelings for her. The recent incident had proved just how self-destructive she was. She could have killed us both. I was beginning to realise just how dangerous this relationship was becoming for me. We drove the rest of the way in silence.

We didn't go to the guest-house, which was in the centre of the town, but met Steve at his flat on the outskirts. It was to be ours for the weekend. If Steve was surprised in any way by Janice, he didn't show it.

'Hello, young lady, I'm very pleased to meet you,' he announced cheerily. 'Mary sends her apologies, she's got to work at the moment, but she'll see you when we go out tonight.'

Steve showed us into a two-bedroomed, ground-floor flat that was clean if unpretentious. 'Try not to disturb upstairs if you can help it,' he whispered in my ear conspiratorially as he left. 'He's the landlord.'

Janice and I unpacked, then, as it was several hours before Steve and Mary were due to collect us, we drove to the beach. It was stony, but clean and largely deserted.

We stripped to sunbathe. Janice lay in my arms on a large beach-towel. You could see she quite liked the idea of being on holiday, even if it was only Newhaven. It occurred to me that, under normal circumstances, namely when she wasn't with me, she would rarely leave North London. That was where the drugs she so badly needed were most readily available.

We were happy again. Suddenly, it was all worthwhile. We swam, dried ourselves, dressed, then strolled hand in hand through a shopping precinct.

We came to a point at which several paths crossed and I noticed an old lady staring intently at us. She came over.

'Do you know where Dolcis the shoe shop is?' she asked, addressing the question at me, but occasionally sneaking a glance at Janice.

As an active criminal I was constantly on my guard for the unusual. My liberty might depend on it. But surely I had nothing to fear on a weekend break in Newhaven? I confessed that I didn't know where Dolcis was, explaining that we were visitors. It then all became very clear.

Not at all put out that her quest for Dolcis would continue, she asked, 'Down here with your, er, daughter...?' Her question hung in the air.

The nosy old cow. So that was what it had all been about. She just had to know the nature of Janice's and my relationship. It was both a shock and a surprise to me. Perhaps I was too wrapped up in my own life ever to consider what other people were doing. Certainly, it took all my attention. But I honestly didn't give a damn what others were up to. This old lady must lead a very sad and empty life to be so fixated on the activities of others.

I remembered what Janice had said to me about us being so strong together and that others might feel intimidated by it and try to split us up. For a brief second I was angry. But what for? This sad old lady was to be pitied.

Leaning forward almost conspiratorially, with a smile fixed firmly on my face, I stared her directly in the eye.

'No, I'm down here with my girlfriend.' The emphasis was all on the last word.

The old lady backed away, then hurried off. Janice and I just smiled at each other, but didn't even bother to discuss the incident. I put my arm around her waist and hugged her closer, lest any others should wonder about the exact nature of our relationship.

* * *

Steve and Mary came round to pick us up at 7.00pm. We were to meet a friend of Steve's at Brighton, then go out on the town. We set off in two cars.

Steve's friend, Brian, lived in a big house on the outskirts of Brighton. He was a friendly, slightly chubby man in his early thirties who ran a small, but successful, local computer company. He and Steve had been friends since their school days.

I could tell that Steve had told him about me, the book and possibly some of my prison exploits. He greeted me with all the enthusiasm of a fan. He fussed around Janice, taking her coat, then introduced us to his girlfriend, a slim, dark-haired woman of a similar age to himself.

Janice seemed remarkably relaxed and friendly. Usually, by now she would have scowled at one of the women or taken offence at some mild joke that wasn't remotely directed at her. Much of it was due to Mary. She was short, shorter than Janice even, and far from attractive. However, she had the most wonderful temperament. She got on with everybody and had the knack of making everyone seem special to her. She hovered around Janice, making a fuss of her, much like an older sister.

The proposed plan for the evening was to eat at a good Chinese restaurant, the best in Brighton, Brian assured me, spend some time on the pier, then go to a nearby nightclub. Steve looked across at me for approval.

'Steve, it's great to be away from the madness of London,' I reassured him. 'I quite like Brighton. It's buzzy without being nasty and dangerous like some parts of London. I can relax down here.'

Janice, sat beside me, nodded in agreement. We all had a quick puff, even Mary who didn't usually indulge, then set off in two taxis for the restaurant.

By now, Janice was champing at the bit to take the speed tablets and the Es. I managed to convince her that she should at least eat her meal first, otherwise the pills would affect her appetite.

There was a small scowl, but the restaurant was so sumptuously decorated and the food so inviting, she realised she would be missing a considerable treat.

The food was good and we all relaxed in each other's company. The normally taciturn Janice was chatting quite animatedly to both

Mary and Brian's girlfriend. I was deep in conversation with Steve and Brian, but, from time to time, managed to catch snatches of Janice's conversation. There were references to 'hoisting', scoring 'rocks' down the Cross and the rigours of doing time in Holloway, all spoken about as if they were everyday occurrences for all young women. Mary and Brian's girlfriend nodded in unison, totally engrossed, but adding nothing to the conversation. No doubt they felt that Janice would find tales of housework and shopping at the supermarket less than gripping. I was sure that Janice didn't realise the effect she was having and was thankful that I wasn't a snob out to create an impression.

However, I did resolve to be careful where I took her in future. Should my book take off, I could see Janice creating havoc at some Mayfair cocktail party.

The meal finished, Janice and I took a speed tablet each. I had been warned that they were very strong and only to take half. Janice gave me a withering look of contempt, positively daring me to interfere with the dosage of her drugs, having already tampered with the timing. However, I did manage to delay the taking of the E until we got on to the pier.

I hadn't been on Brighton Pier for 25 years. Then, it had been all candy floss, hoopla and kiddies' rides. I did wonder out loud to Steve what we were going to do, apart from walking up and down it. 'There's some great rides, Norm,' he enthused.

I didn't ask him to explain, but I was puzzled. The rides I remembered were little cars, buses and fire engines that rotated slowly on a miniature merry-go-round and the dodgems. They weren't going to get me on those, even with the assistance of the speed tablet.

It was a balmy evening, with no trace of a breeze. We strolled the length of the pier, assailed on all sided by a riotous cacophany of sounds and colours. It was gaudy, tacky, intrusive and mercenary, all the things I remembered it to be. Holding hands, Janice and I were the archetypal couple, stall-holders calling out for me to impress my girlfriend and win her a prize.

Again, I reminded myself that I wasn't a snob, but why did I feel uncomfortable, almost embarrassed?

As we neared the far end of the pier, I heard Steve calling to me. He was standing with the others over by some kind of ride. There was a circular, metal-floored area, much like the one the dodgems ran on, surrounded by a multi-coloured wooden barrier. In the middle stood a thick, greasy steel post. Off this post radiated several steel arms, jointed at the middle. At the end of each arm was a two-seater 'car'. Clearly, the steel post would turn, the arms rotate and the 'cars' be sent spinning around the metal-floored area.

Steve and the others had already bought their tickets and were waving at us to join them. Janice was excitedly pushing me in their direction. A young crowd stood expectantly around the ride.

I wondered what all the fuss was about. I suddenly felt very conscious about my age. Did men of 50 go on kiddies' rides? And if they did, could they manage to retain any dignity? Feeling quite foolish, I bought two tickets.

A youth led Janice and I to a 'car'. We climbed in and a massively padded steel safety bar came down across our chests, effectively pinning us to the seat. I wouldn't be going anywhere until the ride was finished.

'Let's take that other E now,' shouted Janice excitedly in my ear. In the circumstances, I didn't fancy an argument. I reached awkwardly into my pocket, fished two out and we took them.

A blast of music announced the start of the ride. The central post turned, the hinged arm rotated and the 'car' glided smoothly across the floor, straight at the barrier and a sea of young faces. At the last moment, at the extremity of the arm, we abruptly changed direction to skim the perimeter of the barrier. Then, at a greater speed now, we skimmed across the area, straight at another part of the barrier.

Up until this point it had been much as I had expected. I sat there, arm protectively around Janice, with a foolish grin fixed to my face. Suddenly, that all changed.

As the 'car' reached the extremity of the arm once more it accelerated like a bullet, straight at the barrier. The sheer speed took my breath away and I couldn't help but fear we would crash into the barrier. The centrifugal force pinned me to the outside of the seat, Janice's weight against my ribs feeling more like twenty stone than just nine.

Then we were fired across the floor again and, had it not been for the retaining arm, we'd have both been flung from the 'car' to certain death. Instantly, I took the ride a whole lot more seriously.

Focusing all my attention, I braced my body one way, then the next, trying to counteract the twists and turns. Janice's weight against me was threatening to crack several ribs. With commendable self-control, I talked myself out of a rising sense of panic, rationalising that it was only the effects of the speed tablet.

Janice was totally oblivious to all this, whooping like a banshee next to me. Towards the end, I did start to enjoy it. Then it was over.

We walked to join Steve at the side. He was pointing at me and laughing fit to burst.

'You dirty bastard,' I said, laughing myself now.

'Kiddies' rides, eh? I knew you hadn't been on the rides for 20 stretch. Changed a bit, hasn't it, mate?' They were all laughing now.

We went on another ride that was something like a cake tin which spun at speed, the centrifugal force pinning you to the sides. Then the bottom slid away. Logic reassured me that it was safe, but, with a sheer drop of 50 feet between me and the ground, extreme vertigo was a logical response.

Normally, both speed and Es take a while to have an effect, especially after a big meal. However, all the shaking, twisting and turning I had been subjected to considerably hastened the process. Suddenly, I was absolutely gone. My brain was bombarded with a chaotic confusion of sights, sounds, colours, smells and strange feelings. I became oblivious to where I was, spiralling helplessly within my own bizarre universe. I felt elated, afraid, hot and cold, all at the same time. The rides would have been a significant experience on their own, but mediated through a pharmacopia of contending and conflicting chemicals, the effect was surreal in the extreme.

We went on one more ride, a row of seats that suddenly took off vertically before swooping downwards again, then we went in search of the nightclub. This was the bit I wasn't particularly looking forward to. I still hadn't got used to standing about in the semi-darkness, trying to talk to complete strangers over the top of loud music. Further, I hadn't danced for more than 20 years. Viewed from that perspective, dancing looked positively contrived and silly to me. Needless to say, you needed to relax to dance and I hadn't managed to achieve that state yet.

The Escape was a big club right on the sea-front. Fliers advertised a live band. I cringed at the thought that it might be a punk outfit. By a lucky coincidence, it was a soul band. I could remember dancing to that just before I was nicked.

Once again feeling quite out of place, I pushed through a crowd who were almost exclusively in their teens or early twenties. We all found a place right up in the corner, by the side of the band. I clutched Janice's hand tightly lest I be left standing on my own and feeling even more out of place.

I glanced at Steve and he looked quite self-conscious. Even he was twice the age of many of those there. But the music was very good. The lead singer, a woman, and the saxophonist were both black. The remaining three were all white. Yet they had a sound reminiscent of some of the great black soul bands of the Sixties. Or perhaps it was just the drugs.

Janice was jigging about next to me and suddenly it all came back. I used to dance regularly to soul and was good enough. I began to dance with Janice. She beamed with pleasure, this was the first time she had got me to dance. She was forever telling me that I had to learn to relax.

We twisted and spun and moved about each other, totally in thrall to the music. Janice moved off in one direction and I moved off after her, dancing all the time. She moved again and I followed. I was beginning to wonder why she didn't stay in one place. During the brief break between numbers she leaned close to me.

'Girls and fellas don't dance together all the time now, you know,' she said. 'You've got to circulate.'

Before I had time to answer, the band started up again and all further conversation became impossible. Janice danced away and I let her go, but, in truth, I was quite confused. Apart from the fact that I was a 50-year-old fella dancing amongst teenagers and needed her with me, we didn't know anyone down here, apart from Steve's crowd that is. I felt a familiar sinking sensation indicating that Janice was about to upset me again.

I made my way back to where Steve and the rest were and danced alongside them.

'Where's Janice?' Steve mouthed and mimed with his hands.

'Don't know,' I mouthed in return and saw unease register in Steve's face.

As I danced, I looked around the crowded room and, suddenly, I saw her. She was dancing with a young guy of about her own age. They seemed to be talking and I saw them both laugh.

Even through the swirling haze of the drugs, rage burst into my consciousness. Pride was undoubtedly a fault with me, but it had sustained me through over two decades in prison. I had walked with my head up through some of the most violent jails in the country. Occasionally, I had felt afraid, but I never backed down from any situation. It was clearly quite a juvenile outlook, but was the law of the particular jungle I had lived in. If someone challenged you or insulted you, then you did something about it.

But there had been no women in prison and not very much else to be possessive or territorial about. These were unfamiliar feelings of jealousy and affront I was experiencing. But it hurt and was embarrassing me in front of Steve and the others. What should I do?

I looked more closely at the young guy Janice was dancing with. He was slightly taller than I, but half-a-stone lighter. His slim arms and flat chest showed clearly though his shirt. By contrast, 10,000 hours pumping iron in the gym had moulded me into a mass of densely packed muscle. Insane circuit routines had raised my level of fitness to professional athlete standards. I was confident I could handle him in a punch-up.

Childishly, I ran through other options. What if he had mates with him? I didn't have a blade with me, but perhaps I could find some weapon behind the bar. Whatever level they wanted to take it to, I would go one higher. I was 18 again and the homicidal, self-destructiveness coursed through my veins.

But underneath all the uproar of the rage, a small, insistent voice kept calling to me. 'So what?' it said. 'The fella doesn't know you, doesn't even know Janice is with you, so how is it his fault? If anything, it's Janice's fault and, ultimately, your own fault for choosing her.'

I turned away, in control now, but determined that I was finished with Janice. I would put up with a lot of things from her, but I wouldn't stand for her being unfaithful.

I felt a tap on my shoulder and a hand on my arm. I turned and it was Janice. 'I've been trying to get us some more pills,' she hollered.

I didn't want any more pills, I had already had too much, but too much was never enough for Janice.

'These young geezers are as silly as bollocks down here. I'd have their money if I wanted it, but I can't seem to find any pills.' Then she was gone again.

I stayed with Steve and the others, dancing, drinking soft drinks and talking when we were able. After about an hour, Steve signalled that he had had enough. The others were ready to leave, too. We headed towards the door.

'What about Janice?' Steve hollered in my ear.

'Fuck her,' I shouted over my shoulder. Out of the corner of my eye

I saw him turn and go over to where Janice was, deep in conversation with another young fella. I carried on out the door and stood waiting with Mary, Brian and his girl. Suddenly, Steve appeared with Janice close behind him. I still ignored her.

In a group, we walked to a nearby taxi rank. Steve got in a taxi with Janice and I, the others followed on behind in another. We all got out at Brian's house and went inside.

The lounge was very big and I sat in an armchair in the far corner. Steve and Mary cuddled together on a sofa. Brian put on some music, then sat close to his girlfriend. Janice was slumped in a chair just by the door.

I felt embarrassed that the evening was ending this way. I didn't want to seem ungrateful for their hospitality. But the incident with Janice had really upset me. She didn't seem too pleased herself. She lounged in the chair, nodding, as if in imminent danger of falling asleep.

Suddenly, she got up, walked right across the room and draped herself across my lap, arms around my neck, like some giant pussy cat.

'Aahh,' went Mary.

Aahh indeed, I thought. The others were all smiling now and I felt myself begin to smile sheepishly, too. I suppose honour was satisfied, it was Janice's way of saying sorry. Brian stood up.

'You and Janice are welcome to stay the night here, Norm, there's plenty of spare blankets and pillows, only Steve and Mary have already got the spare room.'

'No, that will be great, Brian. I don't want to be any inconvenience, but I don't fancy driving back tonight.'

We said our goodnights and everyone went off to their rooms, leaving me to make a bed up on the floor for Janice and me. By now, though, she was almost completely unconscious.

I lowered her to the floor and managed to get her under the covers. Her head thumped heavily on to the pillow. Now I was concerned.

'Janice, Janice, what's the matter?'

I raised her head with one hand, lightly slapping her face with the other.

'I think that last fella gave me a dodgy pill,' she slurred.

'How do you feel? Tell me what you feel,' I insisted.

Her head lolled from side to side, her eyelids flickering. I repeated the question again.

'I've never felt like this before,' she mumbled. 'I'm so out of it.'

Janice never whinged, exaggerated or complained. If she was saying that she had never felt so out of it before, then she was indeed severely under the influence of something. I wondered what that last pill she had been given had contained.

She was sound asleep beside me now, but her breathing was so shallow I could hardly hear it. I felt for the pulse in the side of her neck, it seemed both weak and irregular. I was dead tired myself. It had been a long day, what with the drive down and the exhausting evening. I felt an overwhelming urge just to roll over and go to sleep. It would be so easy. All I would have to do was close my eyes.

But I was concerned for this girl lying next to me. Anger still burned in me for the way she had behaved at the dance. She lived so wildly, so self-destructively, she would deserve anything she got. But I was beginning to understand this sad spirit. Life had hurt her so deeply she tried to blot it out. When others drank or took drugs they sought Nirvana, Janice sought oblivion.

I reached a decision. I got up and went into the kitchen. I took a pint beer glass from the side and filled it with cold water. I returned to Janice.

'Come on now, up you get', I encouraged, trying to lift her into a sitting position. Janice gave a deep moan and opened her eyes.

'Whas marrer?' she mumbled.

'Come on, I must have your attention,' I continued, gently shaking her. Finally, she opened her eyes fully.

'Janice, I want you to drink this water. It will dilute whatever it is you've taken. Now you must do it, then I'll let you sleep.'

There was some complaining, but slowly, gradually, sip by sip I got her to drink the full pint. She was more awake now.

'Right, up you come, on your feet.' Lifting under her arms, I raised her, awkwardly, to her feet.

'What ya doing? Let me sleep,' she pleaded.

'After you've walked some of this off, Janice,' I coaxed. 'Let's just walk up and down for a little while to get that water circulating, then we'll lie down and have a nice sleep.'

So, at 2.00am, dead tired and in a strange house in a strange town, I walked this crazy girl up and down Brian's lounge. I didn't bother to ask myself how I had got into this particular situation, they seemed to seek me out, or rather, I sought them. Instead, I just kept walking.

We walked for half-an-hour, then we lay down. Janice fell asleep immediately. Again I listened to her breathing and felt her pulse. Both were still weak. I dared not fall asleep yet.

I propped myself up on one arm, curling the other around her neck, my finger on her carotid artery. Through the fingertip I felt the rhythmic beat of her pulse. It was quite hypnotic and I felt myself falling asleep, but my head slipped off my arm, waking me. I propped myself up again.

Eventually, dawn's early light filtered through the curtains. Janice slept soundly beside me, I hadn't slept a wink. I looked at her, so helpless and so vulnerable lying there. Something in me went out to her. For all the bluster and bravado, she desperately needed someone to look after her. I had probably saved her life that night, although she was blissfully unaware of it. No matter. For I, who had taken two lives, perhaps it had been a chance to put one back. Whatever else, I felt that something had irrevocably changed between us.

I roused her with difficulty, told Steve we were leaving and drove back to Newhaven. Like two sleep-walkers, Janice and I stumbled through the flat, casting our clothes aside as we went. We climbed into bed, nestling together. Immediately, I fell into a deep sleep.

I woke very late in the afternoon. Janice was still asleep. She spent an inordinate amount of time unconscious. I was sure that, had it been an Olympic discipline, Janice could have slept for England.

I didn't bother to wake her, we weren't due to go anywhere until later that evening. Jim and Julie were expecting us in Brighton. Both were very broad-minded and liked a drug themselves. The potential for Janice to embarrass me was minimal.

If I had expected heartfelt thanks from Janice when she woke, then I would have been disappointed. I explained what had happened, the extreme drowsiness, the pint of water and the walking up and down.

'I thought my legs felt tired,' she said surlily.

I wasn't going to let her get away with the dance-hall incident though. 'Right, Janice, I'll put up with quite a few things from you because of the drugs, but I ain't going to stand for you fucking about with other geezers. Do you understand?'

'I wasn't fucking about with other geezers. You're so fucking old-fashioned. What do you want me to do? Stand right next to you all evening? Well, that ain't me. I'm with you. Don't you understand?'

'So why did you keep fucking off and talking to those young fellas?'

'To graft them for their pills, that's why. Some of these Brighton geezers are so stupid, if you chat to them for a while, they think you're going to stay with them for the evening, and they'll share whatever they've got with you. Then I tell them to fuck off.'

'Did it ever occur to you that I don't want my bird grafting other geezers for their pills? I'll give you any pills you need.'

'But I ain't "your bird",' she was shouting now. 'I'm *with* you, but you don't *own* me. Look, you're a thief and I'm a thief, yeah? I don't tell you when to graft and you don't tell me, OK?'

This concise definition of the criminal division of labour temporarily confused me. Debating with Janice was a positive minefield of *non sequiturs*. What possible connection was there between stealing for a living and my girl flirting with other fellas and making me look foolish?

'Janice, Janice,' I said wearily, 'let's just come to this agreement, eh? When we're thieving, we're thieving. But when we're out socially, please humour this silly old fucker by not grafting anyone for anything. Just ask me for it, OK?'

'Yeah, that's OK,' she said, sticking her chin out in a determined pose. I suddenly realised that I might have just made a rod for my own back. I had given her a licence to ask me for whatever drugs she required, under threat that, if I didn't give them to her, she would graft them from some fella.

That evening, we drove to Brighton. Jim and Julie were both from the East End and no strangers to drugs and druggies. Neither were what you would call druggies themselves, but both had significant coke habits and Julie liked a drink as well. They often rowed quite ferociously, so wouldn't be put out by any friction between Janice and me.

In the event, it all went very well. I gave Janice, Julie and Jim an E, but just had a puff myself. For someone who prided himself on being relatively drug-free, weekends with Janice were turning into binges. We went to a pub, then returned to their flat to listen to some music. Janice got very drunk.

It was an enjoyable evening though. I had been close pals with Jim in jail and it was good to see him in conditions of freedom. Julie pulled me aside just before we left.

'She's all right,' she nodded in Janice's direction, 'but don't give her all your money,' she said pointedly.

I thought that over as we drove back to Newhaven. Julie was as street-wise as any East End girl, so perhaps she ought to know.

Maybe it was just a bit of jealousy, I had been warned that women were often bitchy. And how could she know that about Janice in just one meeting? However, it made me even more paranoid where Janice and money were concerned.

As we neared Newhaven, we started to argue. It was over something so trivial that I couldn't even remember it afterwards. Soon we were shouting at each other. At some stage, I told Janice to fuck off back to London. She screamed for me to let her out of the car so she could go.

It was 2.00am as we pulled up outside Steve's flat, on a dark and deserted coast road just outside Newhaven. Nothing stirred. The silence was so intense it almost hummed.

Inside the car, I had fallen silent just before getting within earshot of Steve's landlord. These were the situations that Janice enjoyed. There was always a bottom line with me. She just didn't give a damn.

She climbed halfway out of the car and continued to berate me loudly. Luckily, the car was between her and the houses, across the road was the sea. Still, her voice screeched over the hedgerows, in painful counterpoint to the gentle hissing of the waves.

I ran around the car and tried to force her back inside. 'Steve's landlord, Janice. For fuck's sake, think of Steve's landlord.'

'Fuck Steve's landlord,' she roared, trying to get out of the car. I pushed her back down and she forced herself up again. Suddenly, with all my force, I pushed her downwards and sideways, into the car.

Unfortunately, she managed to force herself up again. With a resounding thud, Janice's head hit the top of the door arch. There was dead silence. Janice crumpled into her seat, hands clutched to her head. I was instantly remorseful.

'Oh, sorry, Janice, I didn't mean to do that. Are you OK?'

Quiet now, head held in her hands, she slowly climbed out of the car. With one hand on her arm, I helped her out.

Almost bent double, she placed both feet on the road. then slowly straightened up.

'YOU FUCKING CUNT.'

The roar was so loud and close I momentarily froze. 'Hit a woman, would you, you gangster cunt?' Her voice broke off in a ragged scream.

For a brief second I considered running away. My next thought was to knock her out or otherwise stifle her in some way. In the event, I just stood there pleading, 'Janice, please, Janice.'

She stormed away from the car, and headed off along the coast road. But I couldn't let her go. It was pitch black, without a soul about. She would be in less danger than on the darkened streets of her native North London, but she was a town girl. What if she decided to leave the road and head across the fields? What about the animals? I reflected that I would feel sorry for any cow or horse who came across Janice in her present mood. However, I ran after her.

As I caught her up, she turned and began screaming again. It occurred to me that, should anyone phone the police, as a lifer out on parole I might have some explaining to do in pursuit of a screaming girl at 2.00am on a dark country road. I let her go again.

Like some bizarre game of follow-my-leader, I pursued Janice at a distance of about 30 feet. I speeded up in an attempt to speak to her again.

'FUCK OFF,' she roared.

At that moment, a local taxi came along. She flagged it down, told the driver to take her to London and climbed in. I watched as it drove away.

I felt thoroughly deflated as I walked back to the flat. What a way for the weekend to finish. What would I tell Steve and Mary in the morning? I let myself in and stood by the bed we had shared, thinking I would be alone tonight. That old feeling of intense loneliness came rushing back. I feared I would never escape it.

Suddenly, there was a sharp rapping at the window. It made me jump and I rushed to pull the curtain back. Through the glass I saw Janice.

'Open the fucking door then,' I heard her shout.

My thoughts firmly with the landlord, I ran to the front door and let her in.

'He won't take me. I'll have to go in the morning,' she shouted as she stormed past me.

Behind her, standing on the path was a portly, middle-aged man who was obviously the taxi driver. He looked at me sympathetically and held out both hands in a wordless gesture that spoke volumes.

'What do I owe you, mate?' I asked.

'Naw, that's all right, mate. Take it easy, eh.' With that, he turned and was gone. He seemed to be an experienced man, obviously far more experienced than me. Perhaps he'd had similar experiences with women himself, I thought to myself.

There was a sudden thud from behind, that brought me out of my reverie. It reminded me that Godzilla was still loose in the flat. I closed the door quickly and ran back inside. I resolved to say nothing. That way I couldn't provoke her.

Janice had a way of storming about a flat without actually doing anything. As she stormed about in pursuit of nothing, I undressed and climbed into bed. I heard her grunt deeply. If I had been expecting her to climb in next to me, then I was to be disappointed. She flounced past, into the spare bedroom and slammed the door behind her.

'Goodnight,' I said in a tiny voice she couldn't have heard and reached across and switched off the light.

Almost immediately, the door flew open again. As a reflex, I automatically cringed. Perhaps she was going to attack me with something. Janice wasn't to be underestimated when in a rage. I wouldn't have put it past her to stab me.

Instead, she breezed past into the bathroom. I heard running water and the sound of gargling. Then she was off again, past the bed, through the door and SLAM.

'Goodnight,' I called out more loudly. There was dead silence. That's it for the night, I thought and settled down to sleep.

A couple of minutes passed. The door flew open again and Janice sped by, this time into the kitchen. I heard her rummaging about in the fridge. Safe beneath the covers, I felt a smile spread across my face. It was all becoming quite funny.

This time, I managed to get my 'Goodnight' out before she slammed the door. 'Hmpff,' was her only reply.

A good ten minutes passed and I was convinced that it really was it for the night, when the door flew open again. From under the covers, I heard a body rustle by. Suddenly, the covers flew back exposing my naked back and legs to a cold blast.

'Too fucking cold in there,' I heard her say as she climbed in next to me.

With the greatest of self-control I managed to stop myself from laughing. Instead, I lay there mildly shaking with mirth and hoping she would think I was shivering. After a while, I felt her snuggle up next to me. Later, I turned and cuddled her.

* * *

The following morning, all was forgotten until I realised my phone was missing. Now it was my turn to curse and rage about the flat. I was obsessive about my phone. It was for 'work' and therefore all-important. There were people whose numbers I didn't have, who only phoned me. Now I would lose contact with them.

I verbally volleyed Janice, saying that all she ever did was cause me grief. I told her how generally useless she was and that no fella in his right mind would ever stand for her. The phone was the final straw. She could fuck off back to her mother's.

She suffered all this in silence. She seemed to know when she had gone too far with me. We packed and went out to the car. To my surprise, there was a note attached to the windscreen saying that my phone had been found and was at the local police station. I guessed I must have left it on the roof as I remonstrated with Janice the night before.

On the one hand I was pleased I hadn't lost the phone, on the other I didn't much like the idea of the police having it. There were apocryphal tales amongst the criminal fraternity of the police tapping phones. I would just have to be very careful what I said on it in future.

I asked directions, then drove to the local police station. Although I was fully alert for any suspicious signs, I reclaimed my phone easily enough. The station sergeant seemed thoroughly disinterested in the whole procedure.

We drove round to say goodbye to Steve and Mary, then set off for London like two monks from a silent order. I got out at her mother's to give her her bag from the boot. An icy 'Thank you' were the only words she had spoken the whole journey.

It was late the following afternoon that she phoned me. Her ''Allo,' sounded even more plaintive than usual, but perhaps I was missing her. Life with Janice was unrelenting turmoil, but life without her was a return to that intolerable wasteland of loneliness. It was as if I was trapped, maybe even doomed.

Perhaps the trauma of the weekend had touched a nerve somewhere deep inside her, but when I saw Janice at her mother's, she was serious, bordering on the profound. As we sat in her bedroom, she told me details of her life. Of how her mother had never really shown her any love, always favouring her two younger brothers.

Her father had been white and the editor of a prestigious national newspaper. Janice had been deeply upset when her mother separated from him and forced him from the family home. Barely a year later, with Janice just 15, he died. It had devastated her.

Storey, her 15-year-old boyfriend, was already on heroin. It didn't take much to involve Janice. Soon, she was addicted to smack, too. Storey was a typical North London low-life, petty-thieving to fund his habit. He took Janice with him on burglaries and encouraged her to shoplift. At around this time, she was raped, but she passed over the incident so rapidly I could tell she didn't want to talk about it.

Inevitably, she and Storey were arrested. Her horrified mother showed little sympathy and less support. Still only 15, Janice found herself in Holloway. It was a nightmare world full of bigger, older girls. Bullying and drugs were commonplace. Janice tasted the loneliness of the prison cell.

When she came out, she was trapped by her addiction. She returned to thieving with Storey. Her mother's solution was to lock her in her room for long periods. Often she would escape by climbing 50 feet down a drainpipe. Other prison sentences followed.

The tale didn't just pour out like some cathartic release. Rather, I prised nuggets of detail from her over a period of hours. It was interspersed with details from my own life, so there was some degree of mutual exchange. It was all part of the getting-to-know-each-other stage of any relationship. If it had come at a relatively late stage in our relationship, it just went to show how secretive Janice was about her personal life. As if any detail could be used by an enemy against her. She had spent years constructing the mask of the tough exterior.

'I'm "clucking", Norman, I need some gear,' she said suddenly. It was as if she had said too much, told me too much about herself. 'There's some friends of mine near the Angel I can get some off.'

Other than the months when I visited her inside, I had been with Janice for a total of about a month now. In all that time, I had met very few of what Janice described as 'her friends' and then only in passing.

Ken and Emma lived with their daughter in a chaotically untidy one-bedroom council flat near The Angel. At 40, he was a good twenty years older than Emma, but long-term heroin addiction had aged him beyond his years. He had the typical washed-out, unshaven, scruffy look of the terminal smack-head.

Emma was quite plump, well-nourished even, but it was only her youth that made her seem less of a hopeless case than Ken. She, too, was seedy and unkempt. Heroin inevitably made people selfish, but there was something innately greedy and self-indulgent about her, as if she would yield to her desires unconditionally.

I didn't think about other girls while I was with Janice, but I found Emma quite sexy, although her sexuality was undoubtedly subordinated to the heroin. Janice had previously shared a flat with her and had told me that Emma liked sex.

The tragedy was the child. She had the most delightful blue eyes and an angelic, trusting face. At only two she was thankfully too young to understand the nightmare she was a part of. The flat was a veritable minefield of dangers for her. Her parents were oblivious to everything that didn't concern heroin.

They made us welcome enough, Ken trying to forge a bond with me as an older man with a young girlfriend. I was sure that any similarity between us began and ended there, but I was civil enough, if quite guarded. I would have been paranoid around them anyway, but something Janice had said before we arrived kept running through my mind. She had asked me to watch her bag if she had to leave the room. I wondered what kind of friends these could be that they would steal from her. It was just another insight into the hostile, uncaring world that Janice lived in. No wonder she was paranoid about me at times.

The transaction done, I watched as the three of them chased lines of smack across tin foil. As usual, I sat well back in a corner to avoid the fumes. I couldn't help but reflect on the futility of addiction. Why would any sovereign individual voluntarily surrender a part of themselves into a virtual slavery? The answer, of course, was to escape the awfulness of reality. My retort to that was, focus all your energies and talent and try to change that reality.

The inescapable logic of that argument would have been wasted on the three of them. With my help, though, Janice could be saved. I would take her away from this squalid world of the doomed. All the while, blissfully unaware, the child played in the corner of the room.

After we left, Janice said that she would like to see my mum, so we drove over. Mum made her a cup of tea, the only time I ever saw her drink tea, and they settled down to chat together.

Again, I stepped back from the scene and tried to analyse the reality. On the face of it, it was merely a son who had brought his girlfriend round to see his elderly mother. Underneath, I knew I was failing my mother. She had supported me all those years I had been inside and only wanted to see me find some happiness.

But I could no more help the way I was than I could stop

breathing. We were all spirits, temporarily trapped in a corporeal world. I knew myself to be a powerful, untamed spirit, albeit one at war with its own dark side. I was driven by ambition, tormented by a feeling of destiny. I just couldn't live the life my mother wanted for me.

Of late, I had been deliberately distant, rude even. As if trying to distance myself emotionally from her should I be nicked again or otherwise self-destruct. I had caused her so much pain I couldn't bear to cause her any more. But at the moment, all seemed fine. She smiled across at me, then turned her attention back to Janice. If Janice was to be my chosen partner, then my mother would play her usual supportive role.

We stopped at a wine bar on our way back to North London. We were both well-groomed enough to fit in, but I felt little in common with the professional types who thronged it. I knew I was at least their equal in intelligence and probably earned more from my criminal pursuits, too. Admittedly, they didn't live under the constant threat of imminent arrest, of disaster, but they weren't free. They were slaves to their jobs and spent their lives in spiritual subservience to their bosses.

Whatever I was, I was a free spirit. Though just out of prison and having to report occasionally to a probation officer, I came and went as I pleased. No one told me what to do or when to do it. I had no dress code I had to adhere to, or behaviour code either. I had the stimulation, the excitement of living by my wits. The only stimulation or excitement they would find was in a line of coke at the weekend or in some illicit sexual liaison.

Last but not least, I was a writer, the oldest, most honourable of the arts. I was a commentator on an age, offering an unusual perspective, mediated through a unique vision. Although I hadn't yet received what I felt to be the acclaim I deserved, I was just starting out and already I had attracted significant plaudits from those who could be expected to know.

My past would always overshadow my work for some, others would be put off by my anti-establishment stance, but fuck 'em. It wasn't me who created this chaotically unfair world, I just had to find my way in it and make the best sense out of it as I could. Melodramatic as it might sound to some strait-laced, lesser spirit, I would embrace the role of writer–outlaw. The flawed and fiery spirit that was Janice would be a suitable partner. If I went down to a dusty death, then so be it. Rather, to live heroically for a day, than to survive for a lifetime, emasculated by the constraints of a soulless society.

* * *

That evening, as we sat in her bedroom, I decided to approach Janice's problem from another direction. I had been focusing almost exclusively on her drug addiction and that wasn't the cause of the problem, only its symptom.

I had always been interested in psychology; half of the units that comprised my Open University Honours degree were psychology-based. I often joked that I was now half a psychologist. Having said that, psychologists are only human 'mirrors', who reflect back the twisted reality that patients present to them. I had been interviewed by scores of psychologists in prison and had come to the conclusion that a natural insight into the human condition was more use than any formal training. I thought I could help Janice.

We had the flat to ourselves, both Luke and her mother were out. As we lounged on her bed, listening to music, we had a puff. Soon, the hash had changed our perception. I floated in and out of different realities, Janice's face relaxed into the beautiful, caring visage peculiar to her 'good' persona.

I had talked with her before about the two distinct personae or personalities that seemed to make up her consciousness. The first persona, which I called Janice 1, was that of a delightful, mystical girl, generous, caring, mature, wise even. I told her I loved Janice 1.

The second persona, the one I called Janice 2, was altogether different. She was nasty, selfish, driven, unreasonable and uncaring. She was like a need personified, that would seek fulfilment whatever the cost to others — in short, a drugs persona. At a spiritual level, she was cold, almost to the point of being evil. Physically, her general tension caused her to clench her jaw, changing the whole look of her face; her body would collapse into a defensive, curled-up position. I told her I hated Janice 2 and would do away with her if I could.

Unaware of my ruminations, Janice sat there, completely relaxed now. I smiled at her and the mystical woman that was Janice 1 smiled back. I must help this woman.

'Janice, I know what your problem is.'

Her expression changed not one iota. Her lips smiled, her face smiled, her eyes smiled and, behind her eyes, she rested secure in the knowledge that, whatever this man sitting opposite her knew, it couldn't be her most sacred secret.

'When your father died,' I continued, 'it deeply hurt you, didn't it?'

Her lips still smiled, her face still smiled, but her eyes had stopped smiling. They had become focused, wary, hard, implying whatever he knows, this is too close for comfort.

'And it hurt you so much,' I pressed on to my conclusion now, 'that you swore you'd never let anyone get close to you again.'

Her lips had stopped smiling now and so had her face, but the most amazing transformation was in her eyes. Although I go back over the memory a thousand times, it is difficult to describe. It was as if her normal eyes had been painted on to two circular pieces of black metal, with the iris, the colours, the whites all clearly visible. In an instant, the metal discs had flipped over, revealing the matt black colour of their metal base. There was something inhuman about them and their bottomless darkness.

At the same time, her head reared back on her neck, like a snake about to strike. Her face contorted into something completely unnatural and she clenched her hands into fists.

'You fucking cunt.' Her voice was somewhere between a rising growl and a shriek, as she drew each word out to twice its normal length. 'Don't you fuck with my head.' The rest was a torrent of the foulest abuse, like some form of verbal bile that she vomited at me.

I was stunned into immobility, by both the speed of the reaction and its extreme form. At a later date, following subsequent events, it would have frightened me terribly. Protected by my blissful innocence, I was merely shocked.

I tried to calm her, but every entreaty was met by violent reaction. If we had been anywhere else, no doubt she would have stormed from the room, but this was her bedroom, the *sanctum sanctorum* into which she retreated from the world.

Two hours it took for her to be calm again. Two hours of long, cold silences interspersed with meaningless chatter. It had taught me a lesson. I wouldn't try psychological analysis with her again.

The following day Janice put me right on the spot. She said that her mother was going to throw her out of her flat and she had nowhere else to go. We would have to get a flat together immediately. I suspected a plot between them. They both had a vested interest, Janice to be in a flat with me and her mother to get her out of her house. However, as I was due to collect Janice and her belongings that same day, I was presented with something of a *fait accompli*.

I agonised over what to do. I really didn't know how to go about getting a flat. All I'd ever done in the past was to ask the wing Senior Officer for a cell change. I feared that any prospective landlord would want to see a bank statement and references. The former would show no regular income (I kept all my criminal income in cash), the latter no previous abode.

The money wasn't really the problem — I had all of £70,000 in cash around me now. However, my natural caution and, I must confess, a degree of meanness, baulked at the idea of paying out the £300 or so each week, that running a home would entail. Further, I didn't want to be left in a flat on my own should Janice decide to storm out.

Surprisingly, a solution was supplied by Ian. Charlotte, the sharp-faced young woman with two children who often came round Ian's to do crack, had just vacated a council flat with her boyfriend. As Charlotte told it, the boyfriend had smashed the flat up in a fit of jealous rage, breaking fittings and smearing the walls with paint. Charlotte and the two children had been immediately rehoused in a hostel, but she still had the keys to the flat. The bad news was that it was right in the heart of Stoke Newington's crack city.

Together with Ian and Charlotte, Janice and I drove round to see it. It was quite a large two-bedroomed flat on the second floor. The myriad unsavoury types lurking in doorways and alleys attested to the fact that it was crack city, but that didn't particularly bother me. They had been at the bottom of the pecking order in prison. If they hadn't bothered me in there, I certainly wouldn't give a damn about them out here.

Once we had thrown out the worst of the broken furniture and cleaned up the paint smears, the place looked quite habitable if not exactly homely. The bed was a problem though. The mattress had been slashed from top to bottom.

'I'm not sleeping on the floor,' Janice complained. 'You'll have to get a new mattress.'

We left Ian in the flat, Charlotte went off to collect the children, and we drove to the Caledonian Road. It felt strange to be shopping with Janice for our home. It made us more of a proper couple now. We chose a mattress and several other things we would need. I paid cash on the strict understanding that everything would be delivered the same day.

When we got back to the flat, Ian had been joined by Judy and Georgie. They gathered round Janice in sisterly solidarity as she showed them around. It wasn't so much a celebration of a place to live — Georgie was homeless, although Judy had a dilapidated council flat — more of who she would be living with. Both of them had suffered from violent, selfish, drug-raddled boyfriends. By comparison, I was quite a catch for Janice. I was always clean and smartly dressed. I also was comparatively well-off. Over and above all those things, though, I loved Janice and treated her well.

Despite a couple of snide remarks about a 'fucking squat', I could see that Janice was quite pleased with the situation. At least I had made the commitment to live with her. She emphasised that this place would only be a temporary measure and made me promise to start looking for a proper flat immediately.

Suddenly, there was a knock at the door. The mattress had arrived, together with the other things we had ordered. I left Janice and the others to unwrap and arrange the items while I slipped out. I came back with a dozen cans of beer, a couple of bottles of wine and some cigarettes. It wouldn't be much of a house-warming, because it wasn't much of a house. But it was a start. I would test out my relationship with Janice here and, if it worked out, get a more permanent place with her.

Later, after all the others had left, Janice and I undressed for bed. This would be my first night ever in a flat of my own with a girlfriend. It had been a long time coming, at 50 years of age. I looked at Janice across the bed. 'Just like playing grown-ups, eh, Jan?' She missed the point entirely.

'I am a grown-up,' she said sulkily.

LIFE
AFTER LIFE
viva espana

For some time I had been meaning to go down to Portsmouth to visit an old friend of mine called Ambrose. Ambrose was in his sixties and quite seriously overweight, But he had been a good thief in his time as well as a loyal friend. He lived with his wife of 40 years in a big house outside Portsmouth. I briefed him about Janice, but he was extremely broad-minded. He had always had several young birds on the side himself.

We drove down on the Friday evening. Janice had been making a special effort to stay off smack and had promised me she would never touch it again. In return, I got her a constant supply of Methadone, all the other pills she needed, puff, cigarettes and the occasional E.

We stopped at a motorway service station. I waited in the car while Jancie went to the toilet. She was gone all of half-an-hour. When she returned, she was pasty white and sweating, the usual signs that she had just done smack. I was immediately very angry, accusing her of lying to me and betraying my trust. She insisted that she had never tried to give up everything for anyone, but she was trying to do just that for me. I suppose I didn't appreciate what an effort she was making. I sulked for the rest of the journey.

As I had expected, Ambrose's house was both large and well-furnished. His wife Joy had been an attractive woman in her day, but now, in her late fifties, was more interested in her gambling than her looks. Always a country girl, she was studiously polite to Janice, but it was obvious that she was puzzled by her. Although there was the age difference, of course, there was absolutely no point at which their interests coincided.

We went out for a meal together, and then on to Bingo. I wasn't at all sure how Janice would handle this less-than-young-and-trendy pastime — heaven knows, I had trouble handling it myself. Ambrose smiled sheepishly, as if it was an indulgence of his wife's that he suffered for the sake of harmony. Joy was set for the evening. After about an hour, Ambrose left her to it and took Janice and me on to a casino.

You could see that Janice liked the casino. It fitted in more with her idealised view of herself. I doubted that she had ever been in one before. She was fascinated by the roulette. Ambrose gave her £50 and she enjoyed herself for 20 minutes before losing it all. When we returned to Ambrose's house, Joy was already in bed. Ambrose showed us to our room.

Like the rest of the house, our bedroom was exquisitely furnished. Joy's feminine touch was much in evidence in the bedding and drapes. Our bed was a confection of various silks. On each side of our pillows were twin toy gorillas dressed in clothes. Perhaps it was the finery of the surroundings. Janice refused to make love saying that it wasn't proper in someone else's house.

Saturday saw Ambrose give us a guided tour of Portsmouth town centre. In the evening we went for a meal with him, then on to a club. You could see that his heart wasn't really in it. He was just going though the motions. In his sixties now, clubs were a thing of the past.

Early Sunday morning saw Janice and I walking along country lanes together. We tarried in a village churchyard bathed in bright sunlight. It was beautiful, both peaceful and idyllic. We were quiet and thoughtful, as if measuring our town-fired relationship against this bucolic alternative.

We had lunch with Ambrose, his wife and four friends, both couples, in a swish country restaurant. You could tell it was an important social occasion in their country calendar, everyone was dressed to the nines. The two couples were both from professional backgrounds. Everyone, apart from Janice, was over 50.

The talk was all of house prices, designer labels and local fêtes. Janice was soon out of her depth. Her erratic interjections were completely out of context. You could tell the two couples were both confused and embarrassed. Ambrose and I carried on as if nothing was untoward. Janice was oblivious to the impact of her remarks anyway. It was all quite amusing.

The drive back took us up the M3. As we neared London, Janice complained of wanting to go to the toilet, emphasising that it was a genuine call of nature. In suburban Teddington, there was nowhere suitable to stop, though. Suddenly, we were at the traffic lights at Mortlake. I was in a dilemma.

'There is a place on the left, Jan,' I said.

'Well, that will do, I'm bursting,' she replied.

We drove into one of the enormous cemeteries in the area. I knew there was a toilet just inside the gate.

I parked in the drive and walked towards a rustically inspired toilet building that was surrounded by the most beautiful flowers.

'I must tell you, Janice,' I said grim-faced, 'Susan's buried here.'

Perhaps I was too honest for my own good, but I didn't want to keep anything from her. Anyway, she knew about Susan, the girlfriend I had shot to death when we were both 18. I wondered how appropriate it was to take one's present girlfriend to the graveyard where a previous one I had killed lay. I reflected that my life was so strange anyway, this latest bizarre interlude would make little difference.

I finished first, as boys do, and waited outside for Janice. She walked quickly down the path and stopped where the profusion of flowers were thickest. She began to pick some. I watched in silence, puzzled.

She picked about a dozen then walked across to me. 'Come on then, I want to put these on Susan's grave,' she said breezily as if it was the most natural thing in the world.

My normally rumbustious spirit was already cowed, as it usually was in this graveyard. The place stood as a constant rebuke to my continuing existence. Humility, remorse and deep sadness possessed me while I was here, and often long after I had left.

Janice sensed my anguish and was gentle with me. At times she seemed so wise.

'Come on, Norman, now I'm here I might as well pay my respects.'

Like a child with a guilty secret, I led her along the paths between the graves.

We reached the row where Susan lay and continued along it.

'Here it is,' I said with downcast eyes, stopping right on it.

Janice pushed me roughly aside. 'Don't you know it's not right to stand on someone's grave?' she said accusingly.

I was in no mood to argue. I stood there, head bowed, shoulders slumped, hands together prayer-like, not at all the arrogant street warrior I so fancied myself to be. Tears welled in my eyes and a deep, deep sense of shame overwhelmed me in the presence of the evidence of my mortal sin.

Janice was oblivious to my condition. She had taken her shoes off and stood before me, on the edge of the grave.

'Oh, she's inviting me closer,' said Janice, as if it was the most commonplace thing in the world to be in communication with spirits. Hardly daring to breathe, I watched her walk on to Susan's grave and sit down.

What would they talk of, my murdered girlfriend and this living one? Could Susan find it in her heart to say anything kind about me? She couldn't deny that I had loved her, but would that mitigate my selfish act that had denied her life?

Whatever it was that passed between them, Janice kept it to herself.

'She liked me,' was all she would say. In the circumstances, I could only consider that I had got off lightly.

*　*　*

When I had gone to Spain the first time, I had promised Janice that I would take her, too, when she got out. It just so happened that my smuggling operation with JD had reached a stage where a trip to see him was necessary. I phoned to say that I would be bringing my girlfriend with me. Ever the gentleman, JD assured me that he would make the appropriate arrangements.

Although she tried to pretend otherwise, Janice was quite excited at the prospect of going to Spain. Other than a trip to St Lucia when she was seven, she hadn't been abroad since.

We already had her passport; I had taken her to get it several weeks earlier. It only served to wind her up. A constant refrain had been, 'I don't know why you bothered to get my fucking passport, you obviously don't intend to take me anywhere.'

I took her shopping to get her the beachwear she would need. We made a small parcel up of the various pills she would need to sustain her for two weeks in a foreign country. I warned her that I could get her tons of puff and keys of coke, but that a single Valium tablet might be beyond me.

On the eve of the flight, we went to bed early and got up even earlier. I was a stickler for detail when it came to logistics, erring heavily on the side of caution. We drove to Gatwick and got there four hours early. Our flight was at 2.00pm.

I could have handled it. Janice found the confines of an airport lounge to much to bear. We ate breakfast and shopped and ate and drank some more, but there was still two hours left before departure. I had made the mistake of telling her that I was taking some Es with me. With the intolerable torture of another 120 minutes stretching out in front of her, Janice demanded that she be allowed to take one.

It was one of those situations where she knew she held all the cards. I really didn't need a scene at Gatwick, especially in view of the nature of the trip. I gave her the E and soon regretted it.

I regularly mused about what any police observation teams made of my actions. I already stood out, a 50-year-old man with a foxy, 23-year-old mixed-race girl. Now, this foxy girl was bopping alongside of me to music no one else could hear. Short of hanging a sign around my neck saying, 'Look, we're drug smugglers,' I could hardly do worse.

The flight was uneventful, other than just before landing, when Janice became terribly paranoid.

'I want to phone my mum,' she insisted. 'I could disappear over here. Your friends could murder me.'

At the time, it didn't make any sense. She was with me and I would protect her from Armageddon itself. However, in view of what was to transpire later, it made a kind of sense.

I pointed out that there were no phones on the plane and that we would call her mum at Malaga Airport. This served to calm her. I put it all down to the after-effects of the E, combined with the unusual experience of air travel.

We landed at Malaga, passed through Customs, collected our baggage and were met by the car hire lady in the arrivals hall. She escorted us to our car and saw us off. We suddenly realised that we hadn't phoned Janice's mum. Janice flew off the handle.

I couldn't understand what all the fuss was about. Janice was completely safe with me; my friends, who would meet us, were wealthy and influential in Spain. In short, she had nothing to worry about. Rationality and logic weren't Janice's long suits though.

She became increasingly distraught the further we drove along the *autovia*. I was suddenly in the presence of a full-blown Janice 2. I had an ominous feeling about the imminent meeting with JD.

'Janice, for fuck's sake, please calm down,' I entreated. 'Very shortly, we're going to meet my pal John and his father-in-law. John's the one who has set up this Spanish coup for me. It's the only way I'm getting any money at the moment. If you fuck it up by upsetting him, you'll ruin me. Is that what you want to do, ruin me?' I was upset myself now.

'I want to phone my mum,' shouted Janice. 'I don't trust your gangster pals.'

'Janice,' I pleaded. 'Can't you see that, if my pal sees me with a completely unreliable and crazy bird, he'll think my judgement's gone to pieces. He could well stop dealing with me.'

'I don't give a fuck,' screamed Janice in a familiar refrain.

Clearly, I had to do something. It didn't seem to matter what I did for this girl, she always insisted on embarrassing me at the most crucial moments. If she fucked things up for me with JD, I'd have nothing else going for me. I would end up skint. Then I'd lose her anyway. Drastic measures were called for.

'You listen to me, you cunt,' I screamed at the top of my voice, my face contorting demonically, 'if you don't shut up right now, I'll pull over, strangle ya, and bury you at the side of the fucking road.'

The sheer intensity of my emotion temporarily cowed her. I didn't mean it, but I certainly felt it at that moment. It was a convincing performance.

She cowered to one side of the passenger seat, peering at my contorted face, her shock tinged with fear.

'You really are a nutter, aren't you?' It was part question, part statement of fact.

'Yeah, you're fucking right,' I continued in the same vein. It seemed to be working and I had no other strategy. 'I could make you disappear over here dead easily, Janice. So shut your fucking mouth. OK?' We drove the rest of the way in silence.

We met JD and his father-in-law near the bullring above Puerto Banus. I got out quickly.

'John, my girl's very upset. She's not used to travelling and the flight has made her ill. Also she's missing her mother badly. We need to get to a phone.'

JD was hospitality personified. 'OK, come on. Come on, young lady. There's a phone just over here. You'll be talking to your mum in two seconds.' He waved Janice towards a bank of phones by the side of the road.

Janice climbed out of the car very warily. Whether it was JD's strange diction, courtesy of his hare-lip, or my previous threat to do her in should she misbehave, I couldn't tell. But she still managed to behave in a thoroughly surly fashion. As JD held a Spanish phone card out to her, she unceremoniously snatched it out of his hand. With an audible 'Humpff' she marched over to the phones. I hurried across to join her.

The phone call to her mother was unremarkable, save for Janice's bad humour. As she returned to the car, JD was clearly puzzled. He would have rather died than be rude to a woman, especially my woman. Yet he could tell that Janice was annoyed with everything, including him.

John and his father-in-law drove off, with Janice and myself following. He took us to the house I had stayed in previously. As he showed us in I excused Janice, saying that she wasn't herself and needed to sleep. As it was now evening, it would be best if we saw them tomorrow. Looking less than convinced, they left us.

When she examined the house, the marble floors, en suite bathrooms and sumptuous furnishings, Janice seemed to relax. Clearly, she had never been in such luxury before. In the fading light, I showed her the communal swimming pool, the putting greens and the gardens. The evening air was thick with the smell of flowers giving off their scent. It was a heady musk that I always found romantic. It served to soothe Janice's savage breast, too. Soon, we were billing and cooing on the veranda, like any loving couple.

When Janice awoke the following morning, she explored the villa. Clearly, she had never been in anything like it before. With something approaching a scowl on her face, she went from room to room, opening drawers and peering into closets as if daring it all not to be real. The clincher was the garden. She hadn't had time to take it all in the previous evening, what with the travelling and the arguing, but in the clear light of day the natural beauty of the Spanish countryside was breath-taking.

I watched out of the corner of my eye as she walked across the veranda and on to the neatly mown lawn. The sun was shining with such brightness and the air was so clear, every detail stood out in stark relief. The palm trees with their long green fronds looked like they had just been transplanted from some desert kingdom. Exotic flowers, quite unlike any English flowers, blossomed in wild profusion in carefully tended beds. The water of the pool was an improbably deep shade of blue, but the light still pierced to the bottom revealing every detail of the tiles. A ring of immaculate, white-painted villas surrounded the area, like fairytale homes in a fairytale land.

For someone who had only seen the slums and mean streets of North London, it must have been stunning, overwhelming. Janice stood for quite a while, turning her head slowly one way and then the other, taking it all in.

'It's nice here, innit?' she said as she came back into the villa. It was a masterpiece of understatement. Janice was never too generous with praise, no doubt through the bitter experience of having so many treats turn to ashes in her mouth.

'Yeah, Jan, I thought you'd like it.' I walked across and put my arm around her. 'We're going to be happy here for a while, eh?'

Unfortunately, love was a form of war for Janice, the two principals forever contending for supremacy. I had learned to be wary of being too loving, too caring towards her, lest she take it as a kind of weakness. Then she would become totally unreasonable, seeing just how far she could go. I suppose it was another example of her self-destructiveness. As if she couldn't believe that someone could truly love her or, in fact, that she was truly lovable. Like a child with a favourite toy, she would test it to destruction. Then, when it finally broke, she would blame it on the weakness of the toy. I wasn't to be disappointed.

'Yeah, well, I'm just out here as smother, I suppose,' she said breaking away from me.

'What the fuck do you mean, Janice?' The exasperation was plain in my voice, although I knew exactly what she meant.

'Well, you and your mates and what you're up to,' she replied.

'Janice, we're out here on holiday. We're going to go to the beach, eat in nice restaurants, drink in bars, see the sights, all the things that people do when they're on holiday.'

'Yeah, but you'll still see your mate.'

'Of course I will. This is his villa we're staying in. He's an old friend.'

'There'll still be business.' Janice wasn't going to let it go.

'No, nothing will go on. There will be no drugs moved about or anything like that. There are a couple of things I've got to discuss with him, but that will take about half-an-hour.'

'Yeah business,' she said with finality, as if proving her point. 'If I'm working, I should be paid.'

This old, familiar refrain caused a rush of sheer frustration to my brain. It was like dealing with an ungrateful child. For a second, I felt like running across the room and shaking her violently. But I would never hit her. I would never add to the sum total of pain and suffering that her life had been.

'Janice,' I was nodding my head slowly as if acknowledging that I was on to her, 'don't take the piss. Most of the "chaps" I know take their bird with them on holiday. Sometimes they talk a bit of business. It doesn't involve the bird and they certainly don't pay them. Anyway, I'm paying for everything as it is. Whatever you want, just ask me. Is there anything you want that I haven't given you so far?'

She screwed up her face sulkily. 'We've only just got here.'

I smiled indulgently. 'Well, if you see anything you want, just let me know, eh?'

About noon, we drove over to JD's villa. I had cautioned Janice about misbehaving, but that was really to defeat the object of the exercise. If she knew it was a situation where I couldn't afford a scene, she would push things to the limits. If it hadn't been so damn serious with regard to my future prospects, I suppose it would have been quite funny.

If Janice had been impressed by our villa, then JD's positively took her breath away. The enormous rooms, the marble floors, the richly embroidered drapes all attested to a standard of living that she had only dreamed about. She walked about like a fan on a film set.

There was only JD and his father-in-law, Jack, in residence, the rest of the family having gone back to Ireland. JD was uncomfortable with women, probably due to embarrassment over his affliction, and he compensated by being overly formal and polite. Jack was in his late fifties and was of solid, Irish, working-class stock. He was simple, proud, loyal, salt-of-the-earth Irish, in fact. Nothing in his experience would have prepared him for someone like Janice. I would have to be permanently on my guard. One outrage from Janice would deeply insult and embarrass the pair of them.

In the event, it all went quite well. In such a formal setting as tea and biscuits in someone's lounge, the scope for outrageous behaviour was minimal. Janice made a couple of remarks totally unconnected with the conversation, the odd reply to a question that made no sense

169

and had one fit of pique with me.

Polite he may have been, but stupid he wasn't. JD got it very quickly. He was originally from North London himself, so had seen enough druggie girls in his time. He smiled knowingly at me when Janice wasn't looking once, and I realised that he understood.

That first meeting out of the way, Janice and I really were on holiday. I had mentioned to JD a possible coup involving two brothers I knew who lived in Portugal and he was going to come back to me on it. Other than that, the rest of the two weeks were completely free.

Janice and I spent long days at the beach, swimming, sunbathing or just sleeping off the effects of too much puff and wine. In the evenings we would make the rounds of the bars and discos of Marbella and Puerto Banus. JD would appear from time to time, usually around our villa. But he wasn't one for socialising in the bars and discos, sensibly preferring to keep a low profile.

At the end of the first week, JD came back to me on the Portuguese coup. The two brothers I knew had said that they could supply puff at £600 per key up in Lisbon. This was an attractive proposition for two reasons. Firstly, the current price along the coast was between £650 and £700 per key. Secondly, there would then be an extra charge to move it up country to the north of Spain from where most of the transport back to England originated. So, starting off in Lisbon, you were already some of the way there.

The problem for me was that I would have to go up to Lisbon personally to negotiate the deal. The brothers wouldn't meet a stranger and it wasn't sound business policy for me to put people together without my being there. That was a sure way to get left out of a deal.

Obviously, I couldn't take Janice with me, for so many reasons it just didn't bear thinking about. I would drive straight up there and straight back, so I should only be gone for a day. I asked JD and Jack to keep her entertained as best they could. They didn't look too enthusiastic about it.

Needless to say, Janice took the news very badly.

'Oh, that's it,' she cried, 'I knew I was only smother.'

I explained how important it was to me — nay, us — and promised to make it up to her. If anything came of the trip, I would buy her something nice, anything she wanted.

She pricked up her ears at this. 'Anything?' she demanded.

'Yeah, within reason. Anything,' I countered.

'You didn't say anything about "within reason",' she shouted.

'OK, OK,' I conceded, 'but only if you behave yourself while I'm gone.'

'Anything?' she insisted stubbornly. I reflected that no United Nations diplomat ever negotiated as doggedly as Janice. I agreed.

I dropped Janice off at JD's before I left. As I drove away, three very glum faces stared after me. On the positive side, this Portuguese move would put me in a strong position with JD. So let him put up with Janice for a while and see what I had to contend with.

In truth, I was looking forward to the journey. For someone not long out of prison, it was like some great adventure. I had planned my route out in advance with a map. Whereas previously they had only been names on a page, now they would become real towns and cities for me.

I was also looking forward to seeing Gino again. He was the brother I had been closest to in jail. He was an interesting guy. Originally from Sicily, he had lived in Mozambique until the civil war, then moved to Lisbon. He had been sentenced for a big coke operation in London involving millions. He was both loyal and honourable, with exquisite Old World manners. I counted him as a good friend.

The diesel-powered hire-car I was driving was only a production model family saloon, but it would cruise at around 100mph. I would take the *autovia* coast road to Cadiz, the motorway to Seville, then punch north-westwards to Lisbon. It was the long way to go, but was quite straightforward. I didn't want to get lost in the Spanish hinterland.

With the sea on my left, I sped along the coast. As I pushed north, through picture-postcard Spanish towns and villages, the terrain was much more mountainous and the temperature rose appreciably. I was struck by the primal beauty of the peaks, the valleys, the streams and the general wildness of the terrain. I reflected that it must have been like this since prehistoric times.

The sheer spirituality of my surroundings gave me the time and space to consider my place in the grand scheme of things. This frantic journey, Janice waiting impatiently for my return, what would they mean in 100 years' time? We humans are so bound up in our lives, so driven, that we invariably miss the important things. I thanked God that I had found my spiritual side. Hopefully, it would express itself in my writing. For only art could justify man's existence, art and perhaps great contributions to the general well-being. The latter, however, were so often exploited or abused. But for an epitaph, one could ask no more than to leave an enduring image, one mediated through one's unique consciousness.

On a rocky, mountainous road, I passed from Spain into Portugal. There was a cursory Customs check, then I was on my way again. The massive, modern bridge over a vast chasm literally took my breath away. Art could express itself in architecture, too, I thought. Then I was in Lisbon.

It was a city of great extremes. One moment you would be passing an ultra-modern sky-scraper, the next a shanty town nestling in its shadow. I found the main avenue I had been directed to, then phoned Gino.

He arrived within ten minutes. It was nine years since I had last seen him, yet he had changed little. Slightly fatter, with a touch of grey in his dark hair, but the smile, the enthusiasm, the general demeanour were still the same.

He was so pleased to see me. He hugged me, asked how I was and enquired after my mother. On a more serious note, he explained that times were hard for him at the moment. He had lost everything when they deported him from England after his sentence. He hoped we could do some business. Or rather, that I could do some business with his friend, for that was who I was due to meet.

It was the first disappointment. I had thought that I would just meet with Gino, sit down in a bar for half-an-hour to agree the broad detail, exchange codes and phone numbers, then be on my way back.

Gino smiled politely, indulgently, explaining that that wasn't the way things were done in Portugal. His friend, quite a young guy really, was a very important man in the local organisation. He was very wealthy, influential and stylish and was looking forward to meeting this Englishman whom his friend Gino had told him so much about. He wanted to take me out on the town.

Inwardly I cringed. That would have been all very well if I had been expecting it. I was a stickler for protocol myself. I would have brought smart clothes and booked into a hotel. As it was, I had spent the past nine hours in a car and was sweaty and unshaven. Apart from a clean shirt on a hanger, my toiletry bag and a towel, I had just what I stood up in.

I explained the situation to Gino. He looked uncomfortable. I felt terribly embarrassed that I had put him, a man so proper in his manners, in this position. Once again I cursed Janice. Her demands on me consistently caused me to cut corners. I realised that, all the time I was with her, she would be a considerable handicap on my being successful at anything.

I was soon to discover that Gino's embarrassment wasn't only to do with any discomfiture his friend might feel at my less-than-respectful, shabby appearance.

'Norman, you can come to my house to wash, shave and change, but you must forgive my circumstances. I am very poor at the moment.' Gino lowered his head in embarrassment.

In my mind, I dismissed his apology. He didn't have to stand on ceremony for me. I might have £80,000 around me, but the flat back in Stoke Newington wasn't exactly a palace. I was sure that Gino's humble abode would be perfectly acceptable.

I bought a change of underwear and some socks in a store, then followed Gino's absolute banger of a car and parked in the shadow of a modern skyscraper. I suppose the car should have warned me what to expect.

I followed Gino around the corner of the building. One moment I was in the twentieth century, the next in the early nineteenth. Spread out in front of me was a chaotic tangle of corrugated tin, pieces of boarding in various colours, plastic sheeting, breeze blocks and the occasional bit of badly pointed brickwork. It was a veritable shanty-town of small-village proportions.

From an outsider's perspective, it all looked like one, homogenous whole. But the discerning observer could see that, although one dwelling was never completely detached from another, discrete homes did exist. Between these stretched lines of electric cable, the sole testament to the fact that we were, indeed, in the twentieth century.

I suddenly felt an insane urge to run through the alleyways yelling, 'Planning permission, planning permission,' but I was sure that the residents wouldn't have seen the joke. Instead, I stayed silent.

Gino led me to a corrugated tin door hinged on a scaffold pole and I followed him in. There were several rooms, most with bare earth floors, but some covered with lino. The inside of the wood and tin walls had been lined with coloured plastic sheeting and, in some places, wallpaper. The furniture was a hotchpotch of mismatched pieces of varying antiquity. Around one table I saw four different chairs.

Gino pulled back a curtain to reveal a small room inside which sat a South American Indian-looking woman with an infant at her breast.

'Norman, this is my second wife,' he intoned solemnly. The woman said something to me in a language that was as unfamiliar to me as it was unintelligible. I'm sure my reply of, 'I'm very pleased to meet you,' was as equally unintelligible to her. The infant, who had its mouth full at the time, said nothing.

Secretly, I marvelled at a life which stubbornly insisted on imitating art at the slightest opportunity. Here was I thinking I was going to Lisbon to do a major drugs deal with the local mafia, but instead, I was in a *National Geographic* travelogue, set in a South American shanty town.

Gino led me to another room which must have been the bathroom, except that there was no bath. Instead, in one corner, stood a porcelain shower base above which hung a metal shower-head connected to a piece of hose-pipe. Around the whole contraption was wrapped a large sheet of plastic. At this stage, Gino left me.

'And I thought Parkhurst was a piss-hole,' I muttered under my breath. Figuratively I shrugged. I had overcome worse hurdles than this. Anyhow, I would only have to put up with it for 20 minutes. Poor old Gino spent his entire life here.

Soon I was showered and shaved. With my clean shirt on I looked reasonably presentable. However, now we were early. So Gino and I repaired to a local bar and discussed our recent pasts.

Compared to Gino, I had been spectacularly successful. His story was one long catalogue of doom and gloom. Failed business ventures, divorce and deaths littered a tale that was a virtuoso performance of rotten luck. But at some stage, a surfeit of tragedy in one man's life becomes funny. I changed the subject before I laughed.

Finally, it was time to leave. Gino drove us to a nearby restaurant, where we waited for his friend to arrive. Within ten minutes, a tall, slightly swarthy man in his late twenties walked in. He was slim, handsome, stylishly dressed and carried himself with an air of confidence. I refected that he wouldn't have looked out of place in the King's Road.

Smiling broadly, he came over to us. I stood as Gino made the introductions. The first problem became immediately apparent. Jojo, for that was his name, spoke only Portuguese; I, of course, spoke only English. So, with Gino interpreting, we sat, ate and attempted to socialise.

The second problem was that Jojo wanted to take me out club-running, or whatever the Portuguese equivalent was. I asked Gino respectfully to apologise on my behalf and tell Jojo that I was already dead tired after a nine-hour drive up here, my fiancée was awaiting me back in Marbella and, after my meeting with him, I would have a nine-hour drive back.

To his credit, Jojo understood. However, he had just come from the hospital, in fact, where his wife was having a baby. He was in the mood to celebrate. He suggested that we talk business, have a quick drink in a nightclub, then, he insisted, I stay in a hotel as a guest of his overnight, because he wouldn't allow me to drive all the way back that same night. I could hardly refuse and, in truth, could not have managed the drive back without some sleep.

We concluded our business, had a drink in a nightclub that you could have found in any European capital and left for the hotel. Jojo had an expensive American sports car and seemed intent on killing us all or, at least, frightening us half to death. I suppose he thought that if he couldn't show me that he drank and womanised like a London playboy, he'd show me that he drove like one.

The hotel was small, but luxurious. They took me up to a well-appointed room. In truth, I was so tired by now I could have slept in Gino's bathroom. I was dying for them both to go, but there seemed to be some final ritual that had to be played out. Jojo was muttering surreptitiously to Gino in the doorway. Gino turned.

'Norman, Jojo asks if you would like a woman?' he said, slightly embarrassed.

It was late, I was tired, and there had been some difficulty with translation during the evening, so I was about to ask, 'What for?'

Seeing my hesitation, Gino felt the need to elaborate. 'A beautiful young woman.' He held out both hands expressively at about breast height.

Now it was my turn to be embarrassed. I had never been with a prostitute in my life. It wasn't prudery. Ethically, I felt it just wasn't right. Or rather, just wasn't right for me and my particular value-system. What others did was up to them.

Over and above that, though, I wouldn't cheat on Janice. That was another of my old-fashioned values. I firmly believed that, if you were in a relationship, you didn't cheat. I realised that I did love Janice now and to be unfaithful would hurt her if she found out. I didn't intend to start living a lie with her.

'Please thank Jojo for his kindness,' I said with what must have been an embarrassed look on my face in any language, 'but I have my fiancée waiting for me in Marbella.'

If Gino looked puzzled by my answer, it was nothing to the effect the translation had on Jojo. He jabbered something rapidly at Gino, obviously thinking I hadn't understood properly. I stood there musing that now my life had turned into a Peter Sellers sketch.

'Jojo says that he has a wife himself, he saw her in the hospital tonight, yet a beautiful woman waits for him downstairs,' explained Gino.

I looked directly at Jojo and smiled at him as internationally as I could. 'Please thank him,' I said turning to Gino, 'but I can't cheat on my fiancée.'

Gino translated and a look of sheer incomprehension registered on Jojo's face. With a shrug, he called out something that I took to be the Portuguese equivalent of 'Goodnight' and left. Gino said 'Goodnight' in English and followed him.

As I lay in bed, I wondered if I could have handled it differently. Perhaps, according to Portuguese custom, to refuse the offer of a brass is a grievous insult. Maybe I had now mortally offended Jojo. I could imagine him sitting next to Gino in the car saying, 'What's the matter, our Portuguese brasses not good enough for him?'

Perhaps, to avoid offence, I should have accepted. Then, just lain next to her and slept. However, should the young lady then have told Jojo what had happened, namely nothing, he would think I was queer. It did occur to me that he was probably thinking that right now anyway.

'Oh Janice,' I mused aloud, 'you do get me into some situations.' This only served to set me thinking of her raging in JD's villa, cursing my late arrival. Only sheer exhaustion saved me. I fell asleep.

I woke early, showered, dressed and left the room. By coincidence, I met Jojo on the stairs. He was just coming in. With him was an extremely beautiful young woman. Long dark hair framed a perfect face. She had the figure of a model and was dressed immaculately. She could have been a film star.

Jojo waved and gave me a look that might have said, 'Well, I did ask you.' I waved back and was out the door.

As I was already late, I decided to take a short-cut back. Or, at least, that's what it looked like on the map. In the event, I got lost in the mountains east of Seville. Finally, I found myself on the world's most dangerous mountain road, barely two car-widths wide, with a sheer drop, first on one side then on the other, as it twisted and turned through the mountains.

I was tired and angry and not at all tuned into the aesthetics of the mountain passes. However, I turned one sharp bend, swooping down into a rocky gorge spanned by a narrow bridge, with two derelict villas in its lee. Figuratively, I gasped. It was a place of incredible natural beauty. The image stuck in my mind like a striking photograph. I made a mental note of its location, intending to revisit it at some later date.

I arrived at JD's villa just after 6.00pm, I had been driving for ten hours. JD, Jack and Janice met me at the door. I could tell it hadn't been an enjoyable experience for any of them. I told JD I would brief him about the meeting in the morning and left with Janice.

Janice started as soon as she got in the car. I let the tirade wash over me like the surf washing over a rock. The image appealed to me. I sat there silent and rock-like as Janice 'surfed' all over me. In the event, Janice found my silence even more provocative than words. She spun in her seat as if to punch me or grab the wheel. I immediately abandoned my rock-like stance.

'Janice, I couldn't get away.'

'You said you'd be back in a day,' she countered.

'After the meeting, the fella insisted I stay the night in a hotel.'

'And you let him talk you into it?'

'It wasn't a case of him talking me into it, it was all about good manners.'

'And what about the bad manners of leaving me roasting in that fucking villa,' she screamed.

'I'm sure JD did everything he could to make you feel at home.'

'He's a fucking muppet.'

'Don't say that, Janice. He's a nice fella and he's my mate.'

'You promised you'd be back,' she moaned, returning to her original theme. 'You don't give a fuck how you upset me.'

Exasperated now, I fired the last shot in my armoury. 'Janice, they even offered me a brass and I refused because of you.' It was like pouring petrol on flames.

'A brass, a brass,' she screamed, as if she'd been stabbed. 'Oh, that's it. There's a fucking brass involved. No wonder you're late.'

'Janice, I refused it.'

'Bollocks!' she said shortly. 'You expect me to believe that? Fuck off. That's it. We're finished. Don't even speak to me.'

We drove the rest of the way in silence. The silence continued in the villa for the rest of the evening. When it came to bedtime, I asked her if she was sleeping with me. I always barricaded the door when staying in unfamiliar houses and slept with a dagger by the bed. She didn't answer. I entered the bedroom, undressed, then called out to her again.

'Janice, if you don't come in now, you're out for the night 'cause I'm barricading the door.' There was no reply again. I guessed she would sleep in one of the other bedrooms.

I got into bed and settled down to sleep. All was quiet, except, for a short time, I heard a rustling outside the first-storey window, as if something was shaking the vine-covered trellis. Then it stopped. I settled down to sleep again when, suddenly, there was a sharp rapping on the door.

'Open the fucking door then,' I heard Janice call out from the other side. I got out and let her in. She climbed into bed without saying a word. Needless to say, there was no love-making that night.

The following morning, she happened to mention that she had tried to climb up the vines and into the room. I mused on what might have happened had she succeeded. In my sleepy state, I could well have run her through with the dagger. I wondered how I would have explained that to JD.

JD arrived soon after and I briefed him on the meeting. I then told Janice that, as a treat, I was taking her up into the mountains for a picnic. From the sneer on her face, I could tell she wasn't impressed. In her book, treats involved drugs and clubs and parties. Her next look said that she would humour me, although I would have to prepare the picnic.

Janice was sitting stiffly next to me, listening to the radio, as we reached the mountain road below Ronda. The view was so breath-taking that it started to affect her, as I had known it would. If you could just get her away from the drugs and streets of North London long enough, there was a deeply spiritual side to her. She raised her head and was soon peering eagerly all about her. She started to enjoy herself.

We drove beyond Ronda and the countryside flattened out again. We decided to dispense with the picnic and stopped at a road-side restaurant.

Afterwards, I pressed on to the Jerez road. I was studying the map carefully now, looking for the 'C'-class road that would take me up to Coripe. Once on it, I relived the nightmare journey back from Portugal.

For a while, I thought I was on the wrong road. Then, suddenly, rounding a bend, the gorge and the bridge were below us. I parked by the side of the road and we got out.

The place was wild and deserted and magnificent. It was only a rough, concrete bridge, but overshadowed by the towering cliffs it seemed to share their majesty. Below, a turgid stream trickled and gurgled past reed-clogged banks.

There was a rough pathway that led down from the side of the bridge to the stream. In an open space stood the two derelict villas. Their insides were completely gutted, including the floors. Golden-hued sunbeams danced between the shadows.

I suddenly realised that we had been there for all of twenty minutes and had hardly spoken a word. But it was beyond words. So mesmerising was the effect that it spoke directly to the soul. In the presence of the divine only silence is appropriate.

Quite involuntarily, we turned to each other and held hands. We walked between the ruins, the golden sunlight reflecting off the walls and colouring our skins. I took Janice in my arms and kissed her. She responded and clung to me. She looked questioningly into my eyes as if to ask if I felt the same thing, too.

And I did. This is what I had been searching for. A moment of utter bliss in an enchanted place, with the woman I loved, who loved me in return. All the pain of the prison years fell away and the loneliness was but a distant memory.

I had brought a camera. We posed beside the bridge, the stream and the ruined villas. We found an old tunnel that carried a dirt road up to Coripe before the bridge was built and photographed each other next to that.

As we headed home, we realised that it had been a magic day, one that had strengthened our love for each other. It would stay in our hearts for a long time. I knew there would be troubles to come. I hoped the memory of this day would help us overcome them.

* * *

As we neared the end of our second week, the prospect of returning to England loomed over us like an ominous, black cloud. For all practical purposes, I could have lived in Spain, just popping back to England occasionally to sort out the finances of my smuggling operation. I knew plenty of others who did it.

The move would have suited Janice, too. Away from the mean streets of North London she hadn't once expressed any interest in either crack or smack. Admittedly, she'd had Methadone tablets and her usual pharmacopia of other prescription drugs. Then there had been the occasional E, buttressed by heavy, daily puffing and drinking. Janice could puff beyond a point at which the average person would fall over, but remain relatively unaffected.

Strangely, she wasn't a great drinker, although she had been caning it a bit while in Spain. As she rarely complained about withdrawal pains, I guessed she was overdoing the drinking to compensate for the lack of crack and smack.

In truth, I was quite pleased with the way things were going with her, drug-wise. Even I, with all my awesome self-discipline, realised that no one could come off everything all at once. I would never have told her how well she was doing, that would only have triggered off some outrageous demand for several Es or an equivalent, but quietly, privately, I felt we were getting somewhere.

At some stage, I would take her to the gym with me, but it was far too early for that. Any suggestion was met with such a withering look of utter contempt, that I didn't mention it again. However, if I didn't train regularly myself, I experienced feelings of extreme guilt. I'd convince myself that my life in general and my body in particular was falling to pieces. In England, I trained every day. As a concession to being on holiday, I ran about three times a week and went to the gym twice.

The gym I used was next to the bullring above Puerto Banus. Very few English used it, which was a bonus because I wasn't exactly trying to advertise my presence in Spain. There were all the usual posers and people fighting a losing battle, but I always focused and ignored everyone when I was working out anyway.

It was late morning and I had left Janice in bed. The sun was strong and bright as I strode across the Plaza towards the gym. Even behind the sunglasses, my eyes narrowed in the unrelenting glare.

I passed a restaurant and was aware of people sitting at tables outside. Suddenly, a large man stood up and walked towards me, arms outstretched.

'Norman, Norman, fancy seeing you here.'

Even with watering eyes I recognised him immediately. It had been ten years earlier at The Verne. Ambrose from Portsmouth had asked me to look out for a friend of his who would be arriving. The friend turned out to be this very same Ron, who was standing before me now.

As it had turned out, we became good friends. Ron was both interesting and amusing. In his early thirties then, he'd had an irrepressibly mischievous nature. This, more than anything, had drawn him into crime. First, he had amassed a small fortune running a porn cinema in Soho. No mean feat for a country boy from Hampshire new to London. Then he had started smuggling cannabis, which was the reason he did his five years.

He was a big, barrel-chested man, with a schoolboy's quiff of jet-black hair above a plump, pleasant face that was always laughing. Not that he didn't care about the dangers of his chosen professions. It was as if he just couldn't help but get involved, and hoped for the best. The last time I had seen him was just before he had absconded from the prison farm party. I guessed he must still be on the run.

Ron led me over to a table where four other men of varying ages sat. They were all English and, on first impressions, didn't seem particularly 'criminal' to me. There was none of the tell-tale hardness of manner or clipped slang; in fact they all spoke with quite well-to-do accents.

Ron introduced me and said that they were his 'crew'. The term had a multitude of meanings and I didn't particularly want to go into details in the circumstances. I told him I was on my way to have a work-out. He said they had just got there and would wait.

An hour later, after a rushed work-out, I rejoined them. Ron came in my car and I followed the others in their late-model Range Rover. We pulled up at a large house just off the main road through central Marbella. Even from beyond the high walls you could tell it was a substantial house. Parked outside and in the drive were two more late-model jeeps and a BMW, all signs that, whoever the owner was, he was doing well.

Ron led me inside and I could tell he was enjoying himself now. He wasn't a boastful man, but in view of what Ambrose must have told him about me, no doubt he felt he should establish his credentials. I was duly impressed and listened carefully. I had come to Spain originally to look for 'clues'. The more I found the better.

In the privacy of his house, Ron introduced me to his crew and that's exactly what they were. All four of them were expert seamen. None of them had ever been in trouble with the police, a fact that I had already picked up on. Yet Ron had them sailing vast quantities of Moroccan cannabis all over the place. It soon became apparent that he never sailed with them, remaining safely in his house.

I didn't smile openly, but I was amused. Ron, the arch manipulator, had recruited his own band of tame drug-smugglers who did all the dirty and dangerous work. That was why he had picked straight-goers. Proper criminals would never have stood for it. As soon as he got me on my own, he admitted as much and laughed out loud. It was a concession that he would never try to deal with me in the same way, as well as an acknowledgement that, no doubt, I had already worked the situation out for myself.

I didn't tell him about my little operation and I had no immediate plans to start shipping large amounts of puff by boat, but it was a valuable clue. Success in the criminal world, like success in any other world, is all about networking. Perhaps I could find someone who was interested in a shipping move, then get in the middle of the deal.

Ron bemoaned his luck that he had met me on virtually the last day of my holiday. I had lied, I still had three days to go, but I didn't want him to meet Janice at that stage. He made me promise that I would tell him when I'd next be in Spain, we exchanged numbers and I left.

* * *

The closer it got to our departure, the grumpier Janice seemed to get. It was almost as if she begrudged having let her guard down and enjoyed herself. She was preparing herself for English mode and all the rucking and rowing that involved. There were a couple of remarks in the vein of 'Call this a fucking holiday?' and 'I can't wait to get back and see my mum,' but I knew she would miss Spain.

JD waved us goodbye as we drove off to the airport. He had come with me on my previous trip, but I guessed he wouldn't be sorry to see the back of Janice. However, he was earning well out of my smuggling operation and you could tell that that was his main consideration.

Janice was particularly irksome in the check-in queue. She wouldn't stand close by me like other couples were doing after an enjoyable holiday. Then she wandered off for quite a while as I got ever closer to the check-in desk. Finally, when she did rejoin me, she smiled at a group of four young fellas in such a way that they smiled back, probably thinking I was her dad.

It was all done to annoy me, and she succeeded admirably. She knew I was always anxious anyway at airports and that, in such a public setting, I could hardly do anything about it. Instead, we just snapped and growled at each other beneath an outward guise of pleasantness.

Matters hardly improved on the plane. Barely had she sat down than she demanded a drink. I pointed out that drinks weren't served until later, which she took as if I had personally refused her. Then she started an elbow fight over the arm of the seat, viciously brushing me aside. The skirmishing escalated into minor fisticuffs, to the growing alarm of a middle-aged woman in the aisle seat. I conceded defeat and we sat simmering in an angry silence for the rest of the flight.

Stoke Newington had never looked so mean and inhospitable. Our flat was still secure, probably because it looked like there was nothing in it worth stealing. After the marble floors and exotic drapes of Spain it all seemed thoroughly tawdry and depressing.

Hardly had we got in the door than Janice said that she was off out looking for a pipe. Just being back had reminded her of her crack habit.

'You stay out all night and you can fuck off permanently,' I yelled at her retreating back.

'Bollocks, don't tell me what to do,' she shouted over her shoulder.

'I mean it,' I roared in return. 'You just see if I don't.' Spain and the romantic day in the mountains seemed a lifetime away. In the event, she was back in under two hours. However, the crack persona was firmly in place. It was Janice 2 who climbed into bed with me.

The following day wasn't exactly a coming-home party, but seeing as how I was virtually the only one who wasn't permanently poverty-stricken, Ian and the 'street people' descended on us in force. Charlotte, Judy and Georgie marvelled at Janice's suntan, a holiday in Spain being beyond their wildest dreams. Ian emphasised how well we both looked by constantly slapping us both on the back. Clearly, a celebration was called for. They were a cheap night out, though. Three cans of strong lager each and they were well away.

With drink, Ian regressed totally to prison mode. All the pain and suffering returned to such an extent that it drove him to act it out. It was always the same, some terrible punch-up where he had sustained considerable damage before beating or, at least, containing his opponent.

He had been a good amateur boxer and a dangerous street-fighter, despite his small size. An unquenchable spirit allied with blind, Scots courage had seen him through many a battle with bigger men.

Now he swayed on his feet in the middle of my front room, arms held high in boxing pose to protect his head. Invariably, someone would have punched him first. He reeled, face contorted in mock agony, but beneath all the lines, scars and straggly grey hair it looked more than real.

'Crash,' he'd roar, 'I smashed him with a right hook.' With his left he parried his unseen opponent's counter. And so it would continue, Ian bemoaning his agony to the brink of defeat, when, suddenly, a ferocious punch would lay his tormentor out.

I had tried to stop him before, castigating him for living in the past. I had put it behind me, so must he. However, it was a form of catharsis for him, a release. Afterwards, he would be quite spent and lapse, maudlin, into the drink.

In due course, the drink took effect and Ian sat down again. Now it was Janice's turn to hold forth, albeit less demonstrably, about the holiday. For someone who had spent a lot of the time out there complaining, she certainly had happy memories of the place. The girls sat in rapt attention as she told them of the delights of the villa, the mountains and the beaches, all a million light years away from Stoke Newington.

However, she couldn't resist having a couple of digs. She told them of how I had left her to go to Portugal. When she mentioned that there had been a brass involved, all the girls nodded in sisterly solidarity and looked sideways at me to gauge my reaction. I explained my version, but none of them seemed to believe that I had refused the offer.

Janice then launched into a spirited rendition of the volley she had given me on my return, neatly segueing into the elbow fight on the plane. Suddenly, I felt like a cad. Luckily, the situation was saved by Charlotte.

'You know, I can see what's going to happen,' she interjected, as if she had just had some amazing insight. 'You do row a bit, you two. I think you will have a big row and break up. Then you will get back together again for good.'

Janice gave her a withering stare. But perhaps it was more than that, because its effect on Charlotte was remarkable. She recoiled as if struck physically, and positively cringed.

'What did you do, Janice? What did you do?' she cried, fear registering strongly on her face. 'Stop it. Don't do that to me.'

For the rest of us it was as if we were missing something. Her reaction seemed wholly out of proportion to Janice's action. However, it must have seemed real for Charlotte, because, for the rest of the evening, she sat cowed in her chair, trying to maintain as much distance between herself and Janice as she could.

After they all left, I asked Janice about the incident.

'Oh, I'm a witch,' she remarked off-handedly. She had never made any similar remarks before, so I took it to be humorous and let it go.

Janice got up to go to the toilet and I went into the kitchen to prepare some food. When I returned, she was on the sofa, turning her handbag out.

'Norman?' The voice was small, questioning and hesitant. I looked over at her. Still she hesitated. This was quite unusual. Janice was usually forceful in most things. Suddenly, as if coming to a decision, she stuck her chin out. 'Have you taken something from my bag?' Still the line of questioning was unsure, hesitant.

I understood immediately. Smiling pleasantly, I leaned forward. 'I beg your pardon?'

'Have you taken something from my bag?' She was sullen, almost crestfallen now.

Still smiling pleasantly, patience personified, I looked her straight in the eye. 'Janice. Do you mean, have I stolen something from your bag?'

She dropped her eyes and looked away. 'Well, there's something missing.'

'Jan, just look at me, will you.' She looked up. 'You really don't know me at all, do you? I suppose I should be insulted that you could suggest such a thing, but it's so impossible that I just can't take it seriously. Janice, I would cut my fucking hand off before I stole anything from you.'

She looked guilty now. 'I'm sorry,' she conceded.

'Jan, I understand something of the world you live in and of some of the fellas you've been with, but you've got to start to trust me. We're both helping each other in various ways. We *are* good for each other.' I sat down next to her and she cuddled up to me.

'I know.' She said it almost grudgingly, but it was a major

admission on her part. She started to massage my neck.

'I do love you, little girl.' I nuzzled her face with mine.

She pulled away in mild annoyance. 'Don't call me "little girl", I'm 23 years old and a woman.'

'Yeah, I know.' I pulled her close and nuzzled her again. 'But the drugs and the prison have kept a lot of the little girl in you.'

'What about you, then?' she countered. 'You've still got a lot of growing up to do. If I'm a little girl, you're a little boy.'

I was laughing now, she had a point. 'OK, then. This little boy and this little girl will help each other grow up. Yeah?'

'Yeah,' she replied, laughing herself. I felt it was a milestone in our relationship.

* * *

'Castles in Spain, castles in Spain', how apt the image seemed. We had been back in England barely two days, yet Spain and Spanish dreams seemed as remote as Mars. The environment seemed to affect our attitudes, too. Janice was firmly in 'crack city' mode.

We both still had to do what we had to do to get by. For me, this meant picking up money and dropping it off and generally ducking and diving in the constant pursuit of new 'clues'. For Janice, it meant filling in the time when I was gone, usually by going 'hoisting' with Judy or one of the other girls. Proceeds would always be spent on crack, which inevitably led to arguments. Not between Janice and I, though, as I had grudgingly come to accept that, in her own words, she was a thief, too. If I went out and did my thing, then she felt free to do hers. By the same token, she would be free to spend the proceeds as she wished.

Often, when I returned there would be tension between Janice and Judy, or Georgie or Charlotte. It was always the same. One or the other hadn't had their fair share of 'the pipe'. It was all beyond rationality anyway. On the one occasion I had tried to mediate, I found myself caught up in a circular argument that had no beginning or end, or even a point of exit. I solved that particular disagreement by suddenly roaring, 'For fuck's sake, shut up, the lot of you.' I never interfered again.

In view of the fact that I spent a lot of my time driving about the same 'manor' that Janice went 'hoisting' on, it was amazing that I never saw her. However, she did have a favourite boast that she was invisible on the 'manor' and that, should she ever run away from me, I would never be able to find her. There was an extensive warren of flats, squats, pubs and alleyways where she would sell her stolen gear or score the drugs she needed.

It was late afternoon on a sunny September day. I had left early and was now inching my way through the thick traffic of the Euston Road on the way back to our flat. At King's Cross the road opened out and the traffic flowed more freely. I swept through at speed on my way up to the Angel.

Almost as a reflex, I glanced at the ruck of people who forever gathered on the corner opposite the station. At some time or other, most of the 'street people' of North London would visit the area to score. Suddenly, out of the corner of my eye, I saw a bushy black head of hair startlingly reminiscent of Janice.

I felt my heart jump in my chest as a terrible empty feeling overwhelmed me. Janice had never admitted that she had hustled around the Cross to get money for drugs and it was a subject that was guaranteed to send her into a towering rage should I even hint at it. Most of the girls admitted to 'clipping' punters when they were desperate. All Janice admitted to was going to the Cross to score.

I drove another 100 yards and parked in a side street. With my heart pounding I ran around the block so that I came down towards the corner from the opposite direction. As I drew near to the group, I stayed close to the shop fronts, finally stopping in the doorway of a derelict shop.

Secretly, I examined the group. There were about 20 of them, mostly men, ranging from their late teens to their early sixties. Most looked thoroughly unkempt. The five girls were all in their early twenties and stood in two groups. The first group of two were laughing with the men. The second group stood off to one side, talking amongst themselves. Janice was in this second group.

I observed them more closely. There was a black girl and a mixed-race girl slightly darker than Janice. There was nothing remarkable about their dress, it wasn't particularly revealing. Occasionally, the men would call over to them and they would reply. But there was no undue familiarity.

I supposed I watched for about 20 minutes, all the time feeling more self-conscious. I was too well-dressed for the area and the 'street people' were always on the look-out for police. At last, I walked over to Janice's group.

The surprise on her face was a picture to behold. At first, she stared closely at me as if not believing that I could be there. But as undeniable recognition dawned, you could see her mind racing for an explanation.

'I hope you're not doing what I think you're doing,' I said in a reasonable tone that belied my underlying turmoil.

'No, I'm not,' replied Janice sharply, but defensively. 'I'm just down here seeing a couple of my friends.' She gestured to the two girls with her. They looked at me curiously, smiled, then nodded. I guessed that Janice must have spoken about me. I nodded back.

'Coming home, then?' my question hung in the air.

'I was just leaving anyway.' She said a quick goodbye to the two girls then came to me and grabbed my arm. The gesture of solidarity soothed me somewhat, but I was still upset. I saved it until we were in the car though.

'Janice, if I thought for one moment that you were brassing ...'

'Oh that's it, oh that's it, you see me down the Cross and you automatically think I'm brassing,' she broke in. 'I've told you before, I don't do that. How fucking dare you accuse me of it either.'

Her anger seemed so spontaneous and genuine I paused.

'Loads of people go down the Cross for all sorts of reasons,' she continued. 'Half of North London go down there.'

'Yeah, well, do me a favour, will you? Don't you go down there. I don't want my bird hanging around King's Cross with all them fucking low-lifes, OK?'

Janice remained sullenly quiet.

'OK?' I repeated forcefully.

'OK,' she replied quietly.

'Look, Jan, it isn't much to ask, is it?'

'OK, OK,' she replied more forcefully now, 'you don't have to keep on. I won't go down there again.'

It was enough to set the mood for the evening. I was angry, she was sullen. It was Friday and we were due to go out. Tom had invited me to a rave over at Heston. Janice had been invited to a party in Islington. Janice had already managed to antagonise Tom and they were uncomfortable around each other. I knew that Janice's party would involve people drawn from her circle of smack-head, crack-head friends. The outcome was inevitable.

After several particularly loud vollies of 'Fuck you, then', we both went our separate ways to the different functions. Mine was the moral victory, though. I managed to dress quickly and left first, slamming the door loudly behind me. I heard a muffled cry of 'Bollocks' as I descended the stairs.

The meeting place was the Park Lane Hilton. At times it amazed me how varied my life had become. With Jess, I frequented the restaurants and private clubs of daytime Soho; with Nick and Tom I went to the best nightclubs and hotels; with Janice I was restricted to the bars and dives of North London. It wasn't that I didn't want to take her to the other places. It was just that she always misbehaved and caused a scene. Further, she had antagonised all my friends.

Following the weekend with Ambrose in Portsmouth, he had phoned me and emphasised how much he had enjoyed my visit, then, his voice thick with embarrassment, explained that, while I was always welcome, his wife wouldn't have Janice in the house again.

One evening, Jess had invited Janice and me round to his place for a meal. Although she wasn't blatantly rude, Janice managed to antagonise both of Jess's four-year-old boys to such an extent that his wife, Laura, had to put them to bed early. Janice then regaled Laura with stories of drug-taking in Holloway, including one particularly detailed account of smoking heroin.

The following day, Jess made an issue of the heroin story. He said that, while I was his closest pal and was always welcome in his house, he wouldn't have a smack-head like Janice near his kids. I personally thought the explanation smacked of hypocrisy. After all, he had a major coke problem of his own. In the event, the outcome was that I saw less and less of him, as I was nearly always with Janice.

As I arrived at the Hilton, Tom and his crowd greeted me warmly. All were expensively dressed, the girls wearing particularly stylish creations. After the low-life atmosphere of the Cross, it was uplifting. We had a quick drink in one of the hotel bars, then jumped into three cars for the trip over to Heston.

It was the first proper rave I had been to. Several thousand people had gathered outside a private leisure centre. It soon became apparent to me that I was by far the oldest person there. I could have done with Janice being with me and began to miss her. But the anger was still fresh in my memory and I quickly dismissed the thought.

Half-an-hour and a couple of Es later, I was in the thick of it. Bodies writhed, lights flashed and deafening music washed over the throng. As I looked around me, flashes of objectivity interspersed the controlled insanity of the E buzz. The scene from *Apocalypse Now*, the fire-base under attack at night, came back to me. The world I had come out to wasn't exactly in the throes of the 'last days of Rome', but there was definitely an air of psychedelic chaos.

At about 2.00am, we exited into the cool of the night. Echoes of the madness still sounded in my head. Tom's group milled around as they worked out the logistics of the next move. They were very sophisticated in the sense that the evening invariably ended with lots of drugs in a hotel room and group sex. I was far too shy and inhibited for that and, despite my argument with Janice, I still wouldn't cheat on her. I drove home alone.

As I neared our flat, I realised I missed her. I wondered how her party had turned out and where she was. I regretted not going with her. As I let myself in, I felt all the old loneliness come flooding back.

To my surprise, she was already home and in bed. I undressed quietly and slipped in beside her. She immediately snuggled up close to me and I realised that she must have been lying there awake. I reflected on what a state of war a relationship was, two spirits in constant turmoil. A great, warm feeling overwhelmed me and I drew her close. For this night we would be safe, cocooned in our love for each other.

* * *

Although it was a constant refrain from Janice that she was a thief as well as I, I was so caught up with the major problems surrounding my own criminal pursuits that I paid little attention to hers. Occasionally, in the evenings, she would tell me of incidents in which she had been chased out of shops, or had even been caught and chastised before being released. I couldn't stop her from what she was doing and I could hardly go with her. So I just ignored it and hoped for the best. After all, shoplifting was a relatively minor offence. If the worst came to the worst, I could always go and bail her out.

In the event, that was exactly what happened. I was driving along one afternoon having left Janice a couple of hours earlier, when suddenly my phone rang.

'Could I speak to Norman Parker, please,' said a rather official-sounding male voice.

'Norman Parker speaking,' I replied warily.

'Oh, Mr Parker, this is Sergeant Jones at New North Road Police station. We have a Ms Janice Harris in custody here and she is asking to speak to you. Will you take the call?'

I said I would and Janice came on the phone. I wasn't too pleased that she had given my number to a policeman, but I didn't make an issue of it. It seemed that she had been arrested for shoplifting earlier and she wanted me to come along and bail her out.

It seemed both strange and ironic walking into a police station to bail someone out, something I had never done before. From the Desk Sergeant's attitude I was sure they knew who I was. I didn't know the procedure, but to my surprise I wasn't asked to sign anything. I just showed them proof of my identity and was allowed to leave with Janice.

Janice said that she had posted her own bail, which, if I had thought about it carefully, seemed quite unlikely. However, I didn't know the procedure for petty offences and I trusted Janice implicitly when it came to dealing with the police. A possible future problem was that she said she was due in court the following morning, but wasn't going. I could hardly make her. A warrant for her arrest would be issued and she would be officially 'on the run'. So I now had a fugitive girlfriend to add to all my other worries.

Gradually, as the novelty of living with Janice wore off, I began to realise things about myself that I had never noticed before. Living alone in a cell for 23 years had made me extremely self-orientated, maybe even selfish. I didn't have to consider anyone else. If I wanted the radio on, then I would turn it on. The more alienated I became from others over the years, the less I considered their individual needs.

Then there was my ambition and blind pursuit of excellence. It had been said of me that I didn't suffer fools gladly. That was another way of saying that I was both arrogant and intolerant. Needless to say, Janice's chaotic lifestyle didn't sit easily with mine. Whereas I was fastidiously neat and tidy and well-organised, she was exactly the opposite. It was the source of countless arguments.

One morning, about two weeks after we had moved in, I was in the bathroom shaving. Janice was still in bed. As I finished, I pulled the plug out to empty the hand-basin. The water refused to run away. I reached under the sink for a plunger and pumped it up and down several times. Slowly, the water level fell until only a drop remained. I continued to pump the plunger up and down.

Now there was little water left in the sink, a strange sight met my eyes. Every time I pumped the plunger upwards, a dozen tiny white things appeared from the plug-hole only to disappear again as gravity pulled them downwards. I looked closer. There were dozens of little cotton-bud sticks down the sink. Obviously, Janice had been putting them down there. Anyone with a modicum of intelligence could have foreseen that the sticks were too long to go round the bend of the pipe and would block the sink.

It was early, I had a potential suicide run coming up later that day and I was tense, and it was the latest in a long line of petty frustrations.

'JANICE!!' I roared at the top of my voice. 'Janice, come here.'

Half-a-minute passed before she appeared, bleary-eyed, in the bathroom.

'What's that?' I demanded, pointing at several cotton-bud sticks that protruded from the plug-hole.

'How the fuck do I know?' she replied angrily, hardly bothering to look.

'They're cotton-buds and you've put them down the sink.'

'So?' she retorted aggressively.

'So you've blocked the sink up, you fucking moron,' I screamed.

'Is that what you've got me out of bed for?' she said, turning away.

I wouldn't let it go and followed her. 'Haven't you got any pride?' I demanded. 'Is that how you live?'

'Yeah, yeah yeah,' she called over her shoulder as she climbed back into bed.

'You're a fucking disgrace, Janice.'

'Yeah, so are you.'

'You never do any washing or cleaning or cooking. I don't know why I fucking bother with you. I could hardly do any worse.'

'Well, fuck off then. You won't find any other young bird to stand for you,' she retorted.

'Yeah, well, anyone would be better than you, you're fucking useless.'

'Piss off. You're lucky to have me,' she snarled.

'Lucky? Fucking lucky? I could go down King's Cross and have you any time I liked for fifty quid.'

Janice sat bolt upright in the bed. 'Ooh, ooh, you can be really wicked, can't you?' The tone was more hurt than angry now.

In my rage, I ignored it. 'That's right. Serves you right for being so fucking useless.' I turned and stormed out of the room.

About an hour passed and my anger had subsided. There hadn't been a sound from the bedroom. I called out to Janice a couple of times, but there was no reply. Thinking she had fallen asleep again, I walked into the bedroom.

She was lying half in and half out of the bed, her bushy, black head nearly touching the floor. I rushed over and lifted her on to the bed. Her arms flopped, rag-doll-like across her body.

'Janice, Janice, what's the matter?' My tone was urgent as I shook her gently.

Her eyes rolled in her head as she tried to focus on me. I noticed that her face was wet with tears.

'Useless. I'm useless,' she mumbled in a voice so slurred I could barely understand it.

Concerned now, I pulled her close to me. 'Jan. What have you done? What have you done?'

'Useless. I'm useless,' she slurred again.

I looked at the small table beside the bed and noticed that the box she kept her supply of pills in was empty. I had given her a week's supply only the previous evening.

'Jan. Have you taken all those tablets?'

There was no reply.

'Jan, Jan, speak to me. Have you taken all those tablets?'

'Yeah, I'm useless, useless,' was the barely coherent reply.

Coming to a decision, I rushed over to the wardrobe. I grabbed a pair of her jeans and a jumper. Talking to her all the time, I managed to get her dressed. Getting her to walk was more difficult, but with my arm around her waist I managed to get her down to the car.

The nearest casualty department was at Archway. Traffic was light and within 20 minutes she was being examined by a nurse. I described the type of pills she might have taken. The nurse didn't seem over-concerned. She put Janice in a bed and told me that she would probably sleep for several hours.

I sat for a while by Janice's motionless form. With my hand on her head, I watched the rhythmic rise and fall of her breathing. There was little I could do now but wait. Suddenly, I remembered that I hadn't seen my mother for several days. One drawback of being with Janice was that I saw less and less of my mother.

Janice wouldn't wake up for several hours, the nurse had said so. That would give me the opportunity to drive across London to see my mother. Giving Janice a light kiss on her cheek, I left and drove away.

I returned four hours later. There was another patient in the bed where Janice had been. I found the nurse who had tended to her earlier. Her replies to my questions were brusque to the point of rudeness. She assumed that Janice must have left of her own accord an hour or so earlier, but her anger seemed out of proportion to a patient who had merely discharged herself. I asked if Janice had misbehaved.

'I don't know about that,' said the nurse as she walked away, 'but what I do know is that my handbag disappeared at about the same time as she did.'

LIFE
AFTER LIFE

**from hero
to heroin**

My relationship with Tom was first and foremost a business one. Although he was extremely intelligent, he was far too drug-raddled and shot away for me to be able to relate to him in any meaningful way on a personal level. Whereas I was into strength and self-control in all their various forms, Tom was completely the opposite. I thought I understood his problem. By seeking oblivion, he sought to escape the tyranny of mundane, boring existence. I too sought to escape this tyranny, but whereas Tom did it by figuratively burying his head in the sand of drugs, I remained stone cold sober and totally focused to be better able physically to alter my reality. In short, I wanted to become rich and successful in order to create my personal ideal world.

Apart from his phenomenally varied circle of friends and contacts, Tom was something of an electronics genius. For some time now he had been experimenting with a machine that could tap into the electronic transfer of money between financial institutions. It was all way beyond me. I had missed the electronic age to such an extent that the working of the home video recorder was a complete mystery to me.

Merely to divert electronic funds, however, would bring us no benefit whatsoever. We had to find a bank to which we could divert them, then get that bank to pay us out in cash. This meant having an account that allowed the holder to take a very large sum out in cash, seconds after it had arrived. Needless to say, such an arrangement was extremely difficult to come by.

And even when we had found someone with just such an arrangement, the problems didn't end there. It was one thing to send them the money and entirely another to get them to hand over our share after they had drawn it out. Tales abounded of people who had beaten the system only to be 'knocked' when it came to the share-out. That was where I came in. My reputation, and that of some of my closest friends, among the criminal fraternity was such that I had a better chance than most of being paid out.

Tom had been talking to a couple of Greek guys who said they had the appropriate facility to draw out a large sum in cash. I remained in the background during these negotiations. Finally, after several false starts, Tom tapped into the system and diverted £105,000 to the Greek's account. Or so he thought.

There was an immediate problem. The Greeks said that the money had not landed in the account. As we had no access to their receiving bank, we couldn't confirm this one way or the other. However, Tom did have a contact in the sending bank. The latter was adamant that the money had actually been sent and confirmed that there was now a full-scale investigation going on.

I was now in a considerable dilemma. On the one hand I had agreed to act as 'security' on the deal. On the other, Tom was such an irresponsible druggie, not to mention a consummate liar, that I wasn't at all sure the money had actually been sent. Getting money off someone who owes you is one thing; demanding it off someone who doesn't is another entirely.

However, the least I could do was to confront the Greeks. They immediately passed responsibilty on to someone they called 'Bud the Yank'. In due course, I met Bud. To my surprise, I knew him from Ford. He was an elderly, loud-mouthed Yank whose Brooklyn accent could be heard all over the jail. There was some talk that he had been around mob figures back in the States. This didn't really concern me, as he was now a long way from home and mob help. However, what did concern me was that he was a close, personal friend of Johnny Cotton, the oldest and most powerful of the Cotton brothers.

I went to see Boy-Boy, who took me to see his close friend Perry Cotton.

'Put one in the American cunt,' said Perry on hearing of the problem. Boy-Boy advised caution. He told me that Perry and Johnny, although brothers, didn't get along. If I went and shot the

Yank, there would undoubtedly be a serious comeback from Johnny. However, Johnny had the reputation of being an honourable man. Boy-Boy said that I should go and see him.

It took another three days before I got to see Johnny, three days of being handed from one associate to another. Finally, we met in a pub near the Angel.

Johnny was in his late thirties, immaculately dressed and with Burt Reynold's good looks. He was cool to the point of being unfriendly. There was a dilemma here for him. He had to be loyal to his friend, Bud, but he also had to be honourable over the deal. He listened in silence as I explained my side of it. At the end, his sole concession was that he would speak to Bud and tell him to sort it out.

In the circumstances, there was little more that I could do. Other friends of mine advised that I had taken a considerable chance even to challenge Johnny over it; their gang had been responsible for more than a dozen murders in recent years. All self-destructiveness aside, I would just have to hope for the best.

The best turned out to be that Bud gave us £16,000 over the next month. It wasn't the £30,000 we should have received, but, at least we now knew the system worked.

Although I didn't tell Janice every detail of my criminal activities, I did keep her broadly informed. I trusted her not to inform on me to the police, she was far too anti-authority for that. Further, it served to remind her not to do something outrageous that might compromise me. Lastly, being around me a large part of the time, it was impossible to hide certain things from her anyway.

I always had to be very careful with large sums of money, though. Janice had never had more than £500 at any one time in all her life. I regularly came home with £10,000 in cash. I knew that Janice 1 would never run off with it, because she wouldn't want to be away from me for more than a day. Janice 2 was a different matter entirely. For that drugs persona, £10,000 would represent an orgy of drug-taking, an orgy that would probably kill her. I always hid large sums from both Janices.

One Sunday, I had been out on a run to collect and deliver money. I had driven a couple of hundred miles, through the Midlands and Bedfordshire before finally returning to London. The darkness of early evening was falling as I climbed the stairs to our flat, my inside pockets stuffed with over £10,000 in cash.

The flat was silent and in darkness as I let myself in. I remembered wondering where Janice might be. As I passed the lounge, on my way to the bedroom, a movement caught my eye. There, in the semi-darkness of the lounge, facing me, stood Janice. She was fully dressed, her top-coat buttoned, ready to go out.

Suddenly, there was a movement behind her. Another figure stepped out to one side. It was a dapper, middle-aged black guy, whom I seemed to recognise from somewhere. He was slightly shorter than me, with a round, pleasant face and a bald head. His immaculate brown raincoat was fully buttoned and dark grey, well-pressed trousers were suspended above shiny black shoes. He looked uncomfortable.

I stared questioningly at Janice, who also looked put out. A couple of seconds passed.

'Well?' I finally said.

'Well what?' Janice countered.

'What's happening?' I asked, looking her firmly in the eye, the familiar rage rising in my chest.

The black guy looked even more uncomfortable now, obviously thinking I deserved an explanation as to why he was in my flat, with my girl, and all in the semi-darkness.

Janice was acting very strangely. She seemed both distant and hostile. She was obviously annoyed that I had been away all day.

'This is Buck,' she finally said, almost as an afterthought. She made a gesture with her hand towards the black guy.

He stepped forward. 'We were at Gartree together, Norman,' he offered. His eyes had trouble holding mine.

I quickly weighed him up, but couldn't remember him. I was in battle-mode now and the only consideration was whether I could handle him. Unless he had some hidden weapon, I was confident I could. I ignored him and continued to focus on Janice.

'What are you doing?' I continued.

'Well, I ain't sitting around here all day waiting for you,' she countered. 'I'm going out.'

'Where you going?' I asked more sweetly than I felt.

'You can drop me over my mum's,' she replied.

It had been a long day for me and I still had the £10,000 to put away. I didn't fancy arguing with her and it seemed that she was firmly in Janice 2 mode. Perhaps the best solution was for me to do as she asked.

'Could you drop me off too?' piped up Buck, sheepishly.

In silence, the three of us left the flat and descended to the street. I unlocked the car and Janice climbed in next to me, while Buck clambered into the back. As I went through the ritual of fastening my seat-belt and starting the car, my mind seethed in a tempest of rage and jealousy. Was Janice having it with this guy?

'Where do you want dropping?' I called over my shoulder to Buck in the back.

'Newington Green,' came the reply.

'Drop me at Newington Green, too,' interjected Janice suddenly.

A sheet of blinding, white rage passed before my eyes and I gasped involuntarily. In one irresistible movement, I swivelled in my seat and punched Janice full in the face. As she covered up, I rained more blows on her head and arms.

Far from being intimidated, it served to provoke her.

'You cunt, you cowardly gangster cunt,' she screamed. 'Hit a fucking woman, would ya?'

In the back, Buck was decidedly panicky. 'Please, please, you two. Please.'

'What the fuck's going on, Janice?' I demanded.

'Nothing,' she screamed back at me. 'We're going to do some rocks."

If the explanation was meant to mollify, it failed. Incandescent rage still seethed in me.

'You can come round, too, Norman,' offered Buck.

I had never hit Janice before and was already cursing myself for doing so. But it had been largely involuntary. Jealousy and rage had overwhelmed me. I had released 'the Beast'. Almost as if in a dream, I drove off towards Newington Green.

Buck directed me up a street. We parked and got out. I followed him and Janice into an untidy, basement flat. Still my mind seethed. As Janice and Buck settled down to carry out the ritual of piping rocks, a kaleidoscope of violent images flashed before my eyes. It had been many years since I had felt like this, years when 'the Beast' was young and uncontrollable.

The violence was totally focused on Janice. It was beyond rationality. I scanned the room for a weapon. Mercifully, there was nothing.

Janice was sitting in a chair, making a pipe out of a plastic bottle. As my rage erupted, I smashed her in the side of her face with my forearm. She fell to one side, but was instantly on her feet.

'Cunt, cunt,' she screamed, flailing at me with her arms. Strangely, her aggression served to curb mine.

Buck jumped to his feet and tried to get between us.

'For fuck's sake, please, please. She's only a little girl, Norman.'

His implied reproach and Janice's continuing attack calmed me. Now, I just wanted to get away.

'I'll get you, you cunt. I know people round here. They'll do you,' Janice screamed after me as I climbed the stairs to the street. For someone who fancied himself to be tough enough, it was something of an ignominious retreat. I drove off into the night like a coward.

With Janice's words echoing in my mind, I decided not to stay at the flat that night. I drove back to my mother's flat. She was already in bed, but got up as she heard me come in. She could see I was distraught and asked me what was the matter. It all poured out of me. It was as if I was a teenager again, telling my mum my troubles. I instantly regretted it, realising it would cause her to take sides between Janice and me.

The following morning, my regrets were even more intense. By hitting Janice, I had done the very thing that I had always swore I wouldn't. I had always emphasised to her that I would never add to the sum total of the misery that her life was. In turn, she had emphasised that the one thing she would never forgive me was if I hit her.

I drove over to the flat, but it was deserted. All day I scoured her usual haunts on the manor, but no one had seen her. At tea-time I waited outside her mother's flat as she returned from work. She greeted me sourly, evidence that Janice had already told her.

I was constantly amazed at how cold Janice's mother seemed towards her daughter, but perhaps she had just given up after so many years of pain and let-downs. She explained that Janice lived her own life and she didn't even take notice of her comings and goings now. She finished by saying she was sure the day would come when the police would tell her Janice was dead.

That sad note served to send me out into the night like some marauding spirit in search of my soul-mate. Loving Janice was such agony, like an addiction itself. But my spirit was irrevocably intertwined with hers now. I couldn't conceive of living without her. I would shrivel and die, just as a plant would die if the sun disappeared from its sky.

Suddenly, my phone rang. Janice's ''Ello,' was even more plaintive than usual. I felt tears spring to my eyes.

'Jan, where are you? Please don't ring off,' I pleaded.

'I don't want you to hit me again.' Her voice was small and sad.

I screwed up my face as a wave of shame and regret washed over me.

'Jan, I'm so sorry,' I was on the verge of tears myself. 'I swear I'll never hit you again. I couldn't help it I was so jealous. I thought you was having it with Buck.'

'I've told you before,' she said in the tones you would use to speak to a child, 'if I'm with you, I won't cheat on you. I've known Buck for years. We often pipe together.'

'Please meet me, Jan,' my voice trailed off.

Even in her present sorry state, love was still a form of war for Janice. She realised that she held all the cards. For once, she could feel wronged and righteously indignant.

'No, not tonight, Norman,' she said quite formally. 'I'll phone you tomorrow.' With that, she hung up.

As sad as I was, her call had cheered me up. I realised that there was a chance of reconciliation. Whatever the conditions, I would have to accept them. The awful realisation that I couldn't live without her was upon me. It wasn't just the fact that I was in love with her that bound me. For the first time in my life, it seemed that I had found someone who loved me, too. Only that could make all the years of loneliness go away.

She phoned me about noon the following day and I drove over to meet her at the flat. She was surprisingly subdued. I had expected her to rail at me and that I would have to calm her. Instead, little-girl-like, she told me that it wasn't right that I should hit her. In a quiet, passive way, she seemed outraged that I should have done so. I realised that she had come to trust me, and that was why it had come as such a shock.

It occurred to me that, in some ways, I was both father and lover to her. Her father had been such a strong influence in her life and she missed him so much. Much to my shame, I confess I exploited this factor. In truth, I was terrified of losing her. While reassuring her that I really did love her, I also added that I was sure her father would have approved of someone like me to look after her. This seemed to convince her, although she seemed to stare into my eyes for a long time, trying to determine the veracity of my words.

'If you ever hit me again, Norman, I will definitely leave you for good,' she cautioned finally.

I hugged her to me. 'I swear I won't hit you again,' I reassured.

As part of our new understanding, I promised to get us a proper flat. It still seemed like a complicated process to me and the fact that we weren't married only seemed to compound the difficulty. I felt like a child imitating a man.

This time we wanted a flat away from drugs and drug-dealers on every corner. I thought that if it was near my mother's flat, we could pop in more often. I finally found a clean, one-bedroom flat out at Carshalton. It was on the first floor of a semi-detached house that stood in a quiet square surrounding a village green. Other than for the residents, there was no through traffic. It was idyllicly and refreshingly rural compared to North London.

I only took Janice to see the outside, I didn't want her with me when I met the landlord. Even at her best, she was still decidedly 'off the wall'. I told him that my wife would be joining me later.

I falsified some references, paid the deposit and arranged a date to move in. Janice was delighted and told everyone, including her mother. The latter seemed pleased that Janice would now be living some distance away.

'At least you won't drive me mad all the time now,' she rejoined. It served to drive the smile off Janice's face as she turned thoughtful.

Ian and all the 'street people' were significantly more emotional.

'We'll never see you, all the way over there,' moaned Ian.

'Yeah,' chorused Judy and Georgie.

'Don't worry, we'll be round almost every day,' I reassured them. 'It's best for Janice. She must get away from all the drugs.'

Janice nodded wisely, the girls didn't. You could tell from their expressions that the last thing they wanted was to be away from the drugs. In fact, that only served to remind them of their need.

'We must have a party before you go,' said Judy defiantly.

Janice continued to nod, even more vigourously, but the wisdom had disappeared from her expression.

'Come on, Norm, we must have a going away party,' she entreated.

Normally, I would have put my foot down, but, in view of our recent argument, I let it go.

'OK,' I agreed, 'but I've got to go and get a van to move our stuff.' I gave Janice £50 and left.

I returned with a big, white Transit van an hour later. The party was in full swing. Music blared as about a dozen 'street people' sat around the coffee table in our lounge. A few of them I had never seen before. A couple I recognised as local, street-corner 'rock' dealers.

Under normal circumstances I would have thrown them out. but, with luck, soon we would never see them again. They looked up warily as I entered, but relaxed when I ignored them.

Ian and Janice called noisily for me to join them. I kissed Janice ostentatiously, just to let the rock-heads know she was my girl, then literally dragged Ian away to help me load the van.

Within the hour, we were finished. All our belongings were jammed inside the van. I returned to the party only to find that Janice 1 had left and Janice 2 was firmly in residence. Stone cold sober, I tried to negotiate with this dark spirit.

Janice just wasn't having it. Her jaw was set in the determined manner that said she wasn't going anywhere and was only intent on piping. Arguing only brought a bad-tempered response.

I felt both angry and betrayed. She was so unreasonable and so regularly let me down. Apart from that, she constantly embarrassed me in front of people.

'Come on, Janice,' I cajoled. 'The van's loaded and it will take us an hour-and-a-half to get to Carshalton.'

'Fuck Carshalton,' replied Janice shortly. The 'street people' dropped their eyes and lapsed into silence.

'What do you mean, "Fuck Carshalton" ?' I demanded.

'What do I want to go over there for? This is where I live. Near my mum,' she answered.

My rational mind baulked. I thought back to earlier that day, when Janice and I had stood in the newly-decorated and carpeted flat at Carshalton and enthused over moving in. She had taken my mother from room to room, detailing where she would put things and talking of what else she would have to buy. What had happened to that? She had expressed absolutely no reservations about the move. Now, she didn't want to go at all.

My frustration soared off the scale. What was I supposed to do with this girl? She was so unreasonable. I realised it was all part and parcel of her drug problem, but that didn't make it any easier for me to live with.

'Janice,' I said gruffly, 'either get in the van or I'm leaving without you.' The 'street people' suddenly became intensely interested in the pattern of the faded carpet we were leaving behind. Not one pair of eyes met mine.

'Fuck off,' she retorted, then drew heavily on a bottle-pipe.

'Aah, fuck ya,' I said, then turning to Ian, 'Come on, Ian.' He followed me out of the flat. As we reached street level, I noticed that one of the 'street people' had followed us. He was a wizened, half-caste guy of about 40, whom I recalled seeing dealing on street corners.

'Norman, Norman,' he called after me. I stopped and he caught up with us. 'Look, respect Norman, but I have known Janice for years,' he continued. 'Janice is a little crack girl. Get a bag of rocks and she will do whatever you ask her to.'

He spoke as one man to another, as if offering practical advice for an awkward problem. No doubt he thought he was doing me a favour. Unfortunately, I was far too angry to reciprocate.

'Look, mate,' I shouted. 'I don't want Janice to do what I want just for some rocks. I want her to do it because she loves me."

The rock-head cringed, held up his palms to placate me and backed away. Ian and I climbed into the van and drove off.

The following morning I awoke in the new flat. There was still a lot of stuff in boxes, so I spent a couple of hours unpacking and laying things out. I finished, made some breakfast, then sat in front of the TV to eat it. The meal over, I was immediately restless. I realised that I didn't like being in a flat on my own. It smacked of all the years I had been in a cell on my own. As much as I hated to admit weakness, this was the only tangible way that prison had damaged me. Being on my own brought all the years of solitude rushing back.

I drove over to my mother's and spent a hour with her. Then I drove over to the old flat. The door was locked. I unlocked it and went in. It was deserted, with no sign of recent occupancy.

When I arived at Ian's, Georgie, Judy and Charlie were all there. They thanked me for the party the night before. They commiserated about Janice, but none of them had seen her. At tea-time, I phoned her mum, but she hadn't seen her either.

It was dark when I set out for my mother's flat. I drove past the old flat, just for one last check. When I put the key in the lock, it wouldn't turn. The catch was down from inside, so someone was in.

I took a step back and kicked the door violently with the flat of my foot. It sprang open to reveal a darkened hallway. The electric had been turned off, so I moved from room to room in darkness. In the lounge, by the reflected street-light from the window, I determined an uneven lump on the old sofa I had left behind. I stopped.

I felt the hairs rise along the back of my neck and I was a boy again, bunking in the pictures to watch a horror film. A sense of *déjà vu* enveloped me as I held my breath in anticipation of the figure rising from the sofa, its fangs gleaming in the half-light.

It was all completely irrational, but I did feel it. I approached the lump and saw it was Janice, fully dressed in her buttoned-up top-coat. I reflected on the state of her mind that she could sleep alone in a derelict flat in such a run-down area. Such a lost and disposessed spirit. In some ways just like that vampire figure, doomed to roam the earth in a painful existence, without the warmth of love. But I would save her from such a sad and dismal end. I understood her loneliness and sense of alienation. I had also lived in a world devoid of love and compassion.

I shook her gently and she came slowly awake. There was still something unearthly about the situation and I was nervy.

'Are you OK, Jan?' I asked unevenly.

With some effort, she sat upright and I realised that she was still groggy from the drugs. From her passivity, I gathered that Janice 2 had gone.

'Jan, it's cold here. Come back to our flat with me,' I entreated.

She dozed beside me all the way to Carshalton. With her arm around my shoulder and supporting her around the waist, I half carried her up the stairs. To mumbles of disapproval, I undressed her and put her in bed. I undressed and climbed in next to her. I hugged her close and willed with all my being for her to be strong and try to fight her addiction. Tears welled up in my eyes as I warmed her with my love. She was oblivious to it all. She grunted deeply and turned on her side. I would get no sense from her until she had had a deep, deep sleep.

* * *

At first, life in our new flat was relatively blissful. Janice seemed genuinely pleased to be away from North London and the drugs. We dropped in at my mum's every day and they seemed to grow closer.

'Your mum treats me as if she was my own mum,' said Janice after we left one evening, the second time she had made that remark.

We explored the local area, the parks and the shops, just like any other couple. Shopping at the supermarket was problematic though. It wasn't that we couldn't afford things, we wandered from aisle to aisle throwing everything we remotely fancied into the trolley. Janice, however, became increasingly surly and difficult. When I asked her what the matter was, she ignored me. Finally, she let it out.

'Fucking waste of money,' she growled.

I thought she meant that we were buying things we would never use, but it was more fundamental than that. It seemed that Janice had a real problem with actually paying for things in a shop. She didn't mind occasionally paying for small things, but when it came to regularly handing over cash for purchased goods, she positively baulked at the idea.

I pointed out that it wasn't so much that I could well afford to pay for everything, it was more that I was on 'life licence'. That meant that I could be recalled to prison for even the most minor offence. So, in those circumstances, shoplifting became a very serious offence for me.

In the event, we compromised. Upon entering the supermarket, I would take a trolley and Janice a basket. We would then go our separate ways. Janice always wore the same green coat with long baggy sleeves. She only went for high-value stuff, like perfumes and toiletries. Initially, she would put them ostentatiously into her basket. At some stage, she would transfer them to the sleeves of her coat. We would meet up at the check-out.

This was always a trying time for me. She would tip a few things from her basket into my trolley, then stand next to me. Sometimes she was a bit dozy from the medication she was taking. I always feared her suddenly forgetting and dropping her arm. I could imagine all the toothpastes and deodorants cascading out in front on the startled check-out assistant. Relief only came when we were safely in our car.

For someone who had spent so much of his life in solitude, it was absolutely amazing to have another spirit around me all the time. I positively buzzed from being close to her. In her own way, Janice reciprocated. I could tell that she wasn't used to showing her true feelings. If I asked her if she loved me, I would get an almost grudging 'I'm here with you, ain't I?' back. Yet, in more intimate moments, she would pull me close and entreat, 'Please don't hurt me,' in her little-girl voice. Very occasionally, the tough exterior would crumple completely and, as if she had the weight of the whole world on her shoulders, she would ask, 'Why is the world so wicked?'

Sexually, we were very compatible, although it was a subject she was touchy about and I had to be careful not to be crude or over-forceful. She told me I was highly sexed, which was probably just as well, for she certainly was.

I liked nothing better than to get into bed first and watch her bustle about in her body-stocking, her bushy Afro framing her perfect pretty face. I would think how lucky I was that, in a few moments, she would be climbing into bed with me to make love.

Unfortunately, though, I was a confirmed pessimist. Experience had taught me that, at some stage, it would all go wrong. I had truly lost everything I had ever loved. So, as much as I exulted in Janice's company, I didn't enjoy it as much as I should have. There was always this small voice reminding me that it wouldn't last.

Then there were the arguments. I suppose it was inevitable that two people like us, with our peculiar outlooks and painful experiences, should clash at times. But it was more basic than that. It was almost as if our powerful personal chemistry built up to a point where there would be the inevitable explosion. It went in three-day cycles.

On the first day, we would desperately need each other and cling together like lost souls. By the second, we would be stronger and more confident. Our individual arrogance and wilfulness would grow to the point where we would shine together. But by the evening of the third day, the electricity had built up until it was virtually intolerable. Then, we would spit and snarl at each other like beasts in the primal swamp, until there would be a final, cataclysmic explosion and we would just have to get away from each other.

After a day or so, we would need to be together and it would start all over again. For someone as rational as myself, it was extremely frustrating. However, I realised that it was also completely beyond my control.

By now *Parkhurst Tales* was close to its publication date and there was the inevitable media interest. My first TV interview was on *GMTV*. I approached it with quiet confidence. I reasoned that, having coped with a lifetime in jail, anything else would be easy by comparison. Strangely enough, my time spent in solitary would help me. Then, I had articulated my thoughts, or rather, talked to myself. Sometimes I would have far-ranging discussions on diverse subjects. I would converse with experts and world leaders. It all served to help me formulate my thoughts before I opened my mouth, a useful skill for TV.

I arrived at the studio early. I had left Janice in bed as I didn't want the distraction of wondering what she was up to whilst I was on camera. Up close, Lorraine Kelley looked more homely and friendly than on the screen. She did her best to put me at my ease, but I was keen to take advantage of this opportunity. I had already realised that it didn't matter how good a writer you were, if you were an unknown author and no one got to hear about your book, it wouldn't sell. A writer also had to be a self-publicist.

It started off well enough and I was soon quite relaxed. The questions were light and trivial, the replies unlikely to outrage anyone. Suddenly, she asked me about the Home Secretary's latest penal initiative. I paused for a millisecond as contending answers fought for primacy.

I had only contempt for Michael Howard, both as a politician and as a Home Secretary. I found his pronouncements to be purely 'political'; that is, designed to elicit maximum voter response from the public. In purely penal terms, they were nonsense. He had stifled all serious political debate on crime and the criminal justice system. Every politician walked in fear lest they be seen to be 'soft' on crime.

But could I say that on national TV? I could imagine the impact on any watching Home Office officials. For two decades I had plagued them whilst in jails then, just when they thought they had heard the last from me, I popped up on their TV screens to condemn them.

Further, the 'establishment' often closed ranks. By attacking them would I exclude myself from further TV appearances?

The alternative, though, was unacceptable. How could I praise something I felt to be so very wrong? What would my friends and former prison comrades think at such a sell-out?

'In purely penological terms, the Home Secretary's latest initiative is complete nonsense,' I began. 'However, next month is the Tory Party Conference. Michael Howard will stand up in front of the blue-rinse ladies waving hand-cuffs and the right-wing political Neanderthals calling for the reintroduction of capital punishment and get a standing ovation for being tough on law and order. He will hope it will strike a resonance amongst a public traumatised by the fear of crime and so increase the Tory vote. That's where it all makes sense,' I concluded.

For a split second, Lorraine Kelley paused. Her eyes spoke to mine saying, 'Well, aren't you just a clever sod. Here was I expecting a lumpen convict's view, when you suddenly hit me with a politically sophisticated and extremely virulent attack on the Home Secretary.' It was surprise more than annoyance, though, and she continued seamlessly. She thanked me warmly afterwards.

I don't know what I was expecting from the launch of my book, but, in the event, it was all very much of an anti-climax. There was no particular day set aside for a launch party, nor even a press conference. In fact, the book actually came out two weeks before it was announced to the media. I did a couple of interviews for national newspapers and two radio stations talked to me live on air over my phone. A clear pattern soon emerged. The main news interest was that I was a murderer who had written a book, rather than that I was a writer who was once a murderer. My feelings were too well protected to be hurt, but at times I had to remind myself that I had done something positive. (Like all new publications, a copy of *Parkhurst Tales* had been placed in the British Library.)

My publisher reassured me that advance orders were good and would continue to build, but then fate took a hand. The headlines in all the tabloids screamed that three lifers had escaped from Parkhurst and were loose in the surrounding countryside. Police swarmed all over the Isle of Wight, questions were asked in the House and the prison Governor was forced to resign. The prisoners were quickly recaptured, but the hue and cry in the media continued unabated.

It was early evening as I drove home to Carshalton with Janice. My publisher had told me earlier that day that Radio Four wanted to do a 'down the line' interview with me. I stopped at an isolated phone box and made the call.

The interview was both long and far-ranging. It dealt with my imprisonment, prison conditions, penal policy and general criminal justice issues. Finally, I was asked for my comments on the recent Parkhurst escape, especially as there were passages in my book describing how previous escape attempts had been made.

Almost as an afterthought, the producer asked if there had been a copy of *Parkhurst Tales* in the jail and whether the three escapees might have read it and picked up some useful pointers. I said that I had sent a copy in to an old friend a week or so earlier and that it was customary to pass books around in jail. It was entirely possible that one or more of the fugitives had read it. With that, the interview ended and I was told that excerpts would be broadcast the following morning. I went home, turned my phone off and went to bed.

The next morning, I turned my phone on at 9.00am and it rang immediately. My mother sounded flustered to the point of panic. She told me that her phone had been ringing since early that morning and that every newspaper, radio and TV station wanted to talk to me. It was headline news that the Parkhurst escapers might have been assisted by hints in my book.

For the rest of the day, my phone never stopped ringing. I had to restrict the duration of the calls lest my battery ran out. Various news organisations arranged to visit me at Carshalton. At times, the quiet suburban square was thronged with vans and cars bristling with communications antennae.

In the circumstances, Janice was very good about it all. As I did TV and radio interviews in the lounge, the front garden and the square, she stayed in the bedroom. Which was probably just as well as she was now officially wanted for the shoplifting offence. The neighbours looked on in amazement and I realised that any hope of my remaining anonymous had disappeared.

There were still two further TV interviews to do though. We drove into London and Janice sat quietly in a waiting room as I performed in the studio. The high point of the day was my reading excerpts from *Parkhurst Tales* on the *Nine O'Clock News*.

As I lay in bed that night, I reminisced on a day that had been unusual by any standards, but was just another day for me. I had handled it well enough, but then dramas and crises were daily occurrences for me. By comparison, appearing on national TV was a piece of cake.

* * *

Slowly, over a period of weeks, Janice and I gradually fell into a rough pattern of living that, although far from blissful, was as near to that state as our two lives were likely to get. Regular rows sent us both home to our respective mothers for a day or so at a time. My mum still made a fuss of Janice, though, and Janice's mum still treated me with extreme courtesy.

For quite a while I had been working on Janice to try to get her to come to the gym with me. I emphasised that merely the effort of going would help to strengthen her will-power.

'I know, I know,' she would respond aggressively, 'I used to go to the gym in jail.' I knew that was a different matter entirely. Often, prisoners would go to the gym just as an excuse to get out of a workshop for a couple of hours. It wasn't necessarily serious, dedicated training.

For the year that I had been home, I had been using the YMCA gym at Putney. It was well equipped, with a good selection of both free weights and exercise machines. I always went at about 9.00am when it was relatively empty. There would be about a dozen regulars, mostly women ranging from their teens to middle thirties. All seemed to suffer from the same problem of fat bums and fleshy thighs.

I knew I would have a problem mixing in, having been so stand-offish and insular in jail. The fact that they were mostly women and, as it turned out, quite cliquey as well, didn't help matters. I solved the problem in my own inimitable way. I totally ignored everybody, except for a couple of the instructors.

I would walk in, focus on the work-out in hand, then lose myself in a world of sweat and pain. As I passed among them from machine to machine, I would occasionally hear them gossiping about trivia from their social lives. I guessed they might wonder about me. I was sure at least one must have seen me on TV or noticed a reference to my writing in the papers. That would serve to alert them all. In the circumstances, I could well understand that some of them might want to avoid me. In that respect, I made it easy for both them and myself. I never so much as acknowledged one of them.

It must have caused quite a stir amongst them, the first morning I walked in with Janice. Her petite figure was tightly encased in a knee-length, grey singlet, her hair held up in bunches with elastic bands and new white socks and trainers on her feet. I gave her a minimum of instruction, Janice never liked to be lectured on anything, and set her free.

I got on with my usual work-out, watching her all the while out of the corner of my eye as she moved from machine to machine. Unlike myself, Janice was a master of the art of social interaction. Soon, she was chatting animatedly with several of the women. I had severely cautioned her about telling them anything of our private business, pointing out that I didn't want to have to leave the gym because of any outrage Janice had caused. The one subject that was bound to be broached was touched on very quickly. Several of the women asked Janice what her relationship to me was. 'I told 'em you were my fella,' said Janice perkily afterwards. I had to smile. That would give them something to talk about.

To my surprise, Janice quite took to the gym at first. My only gripe was that she took such a long time to sauna, shower and dress afterwards. Often, I would have to wait for 40 minutes after I had finished in the men's changing room. Eventually, I took to sending someone in to hurry her up. On a couple of occasions, they came out to tell me that she was fast asleep in the sauna and they had had trouble rousing her. She was still desperately groggy when she finally came out. I recognised the tell-tale signs. After a massive argument, she confessed she'd been smoking smack in the toilet before going into the sauna.

It wasn't exactly what I had had in mind when I had first taken her to the gym. I realised that, at some stage during the day, she would have to have her usual dose of heroin. It just didn't occur to me that she would choose the women's changing room and the period after her work-out to do it.

Needless to say, I was outraged. I pointed out the repercussions, both for me as well as herself, should she get caught. Apart from that, it was contrary to the whole ethos of going to the gym.

'I just wanted to relax after a hard work-out and the sauna seemed like a suitable place,' she countered, quite miffed.

'Just wait until we get home, Janice,' I thundered.

'OK, OK, there's just no pleasing some people,' she replied, as if it was me who was being unreasonable.

I cursed myself for my naïveté in thinking that the gym was one place where the scope for her to get into trouble was minimal.

Where Janice was concerned, naïveté could be fatal.

* * *

For several weeks, Janice had been asking me to take her to visit her brother Mark in Highpoint Prison. At 21, he was the middle child between Janice and Luke. In view of the tenuous and sometimes acrimonious nature of her relationships with her mother and Luke, I always bent over backwards to support Janice regarding her family.

Over a period of months, I had steadily built up an uneasy relationship with Luke. At 19, he was still quite immature and, no doubt, he had painful memories of some of Janice's less salubrious boyfriends. Further, as Janice regularly borrowed or stole things from his room, his relationship with her was often tempestuous. Perhaps he viewed me as the ally of his most persistent tormentor. But we were never relaxed together.

Luke was his mother's pride and joy. A quiet, handsome, light-skinned youth, he didn't share either Janice's or Mark's criminality, something of a relief for Mrs Harris. Neither Luke nor his mother ever visited Janice or Mark when they were in prison.

Mark was six months from finishing a four-year sentence for a relatively minor robbery. It was drug-related in so far as Mark needed money to buy drugs. He too had a 'smack' and 'crack' habit.I feared the worst. Janice told me that she was closest to Mark, so I would have to try to get on with him. I carefully folded up a £50 note to pass to him. That should start me off on the right foot.

The day before the visit, I got the map out to plan the journey. Highpoint was near Newmarket, so I would have to go up the M11 and turn off at the A11 junction. As I followed the A11 on the map, I suddenly recognised familiar territory. At a roundabout where I would turn right for Highpoint, Wandlebury lay barely a mile to the left.

What a coincidence that a place so mystically memorable for me should lie on my route. Immediately, a plan formed. Now that I felt myself to be irrevocably bound in love to Janice, I sought for some way to bind her irrevocably to me. Her telling me that she loved me wasn't enough. I wanted something infinitely stronger.

I had baulked at using 'crack' to bind her to me, yet I confess I felt a twinge of guilt as I made my preparations. My chosen method would draw from no earthly pharmacopia. I would make Janice eternally mine by magic.

At mid-morning one Wednesday, we set out for Highpoint. It was a clear, bright day and the fields and streams either side of the M11 were a welcome relief to the satanic mills of the metropolis. I surveyed a landscape that could have changed little since pagan times and tried to connect with some underlying spiritual current. I didn't actually feel any connection, but I did feel elated in anticipation of what was to come.

I saw the sign for Wandlebury as I turned right at the roundabout. I mentioned to Janice that I wanted to stop off there briefly on the way back. She was humming softly to a tune on the radio and absent-mindedly nodded her head. I had to repeat myself to catch her full attention.

Half-an-hour later, we arrived at Highpoint. I had never been there before, but the campus-style accommodation and high fences were no different to scores of similar, low-security jails.

After passing through all the usual checks, we were shown into a large room with about 80 tables laid out in six parallel lines. As we sat at a table waiting for Mark, barely half-a-dozen other visitors came to sit at other tables.

Mark was the first to come in. He was quite short and slim, but much darker than Janice. He had a round, boyish face with neatly-combed, greasy black hair that curved round in a fringe across his forehead. He wasn't exactly scowling, but he did have something of a peeved expression on his face. The charitable side of my nature rationalised that perhaps, like most drug abusers in prison, he was suffering permanent withdrawal symptoms.

He seemed friendly enough. He was of an age when young men are terrified of showing any weakness, so I could expect some front to be kept up. Luckily, there were a couple of copies of my book in the jail and he was definitely impressed by that. If he had any qualms about a 50-year-old double killer going out with his 23-year-old sister, he kept them to himself.

He gave Janice a perfunctory embrace, sat down quickly then shook my hand across the table. Initial shyness quickly gave way to inquisitiveness. He asked me about my time inside and soon the talk was all of crime. I regularly tried to steer the conversation back to Janice and his family, but he was more concerned whether I knew various people he was acquainted with.

When Janice mentioned that she had a £50 note for him, she instantly grabbed his attention. As soon as she had passed it over though, he returned to discussing crime. Whether my presence inhibited more intimate exchanges between Mark and his sister, I couldn't tell. However, the restrained embrace for Janice at the end completed a thoroughly understated performance of fraternal devotion. As we left, I resigned myself to the fact that maybe they were an unemotional family.

Within minutes of driving out of the prison car park, Janice fell soundly asleep. Whether she had been drained by the visit or had merely achieved some form of stasis between the uppers and downers she took that had resulted in unconsciousness, I couldn't tell. I mused that some of the longest, trouble-free periods we spent together were when she was asleep.

As I reached the roundabout and headed for Wandlebury, I shook Janice gently. She didn't stir. I drove through the gates and parked with Janice still fast asleep. Now, I shook her more energetically. Still she hardly stirred.

'Come on, Janice, we're at Wandlebury. There's something I want to show you,' I cajoled.

Her head lolled drunkenly as I pulled her upright in her seat.

'Oh leave me, leave me,' she pleaded, 'I really am so tired.'

I got out and went round to Janice's side of the car. I opened her door and shook her again. 'Come on, Janice. This is for me. I'm always doing things that you want. How about doing something for me?'

Slowly, drowsily, she lowered her feet to the dust of the car park and tried to stand. I caught her as her legs buckled beneath her.

'Strange. That's strange,' she muttered, 'I just haven't got any energy. My legs don't seem to work.'

I wouldn't be denied, though. Supporting her around the waist, I slowly walked her towards the spot where Lethbridge's figures lay. She stumbled along like some arthritic 80-year-old. My stubbornness blinded me to the signs that hindsight would later reveal.

By the time we reached the circle of shallow indentations, she was more awake.

'Come on, Janice, just sit on the edge of this dip with me.'

We sat on the rim of the bottom-most indentation. Above us was the brow of the hill and the Roman ruins, below lay the fir tree line.

'What are we doing?' asked Janice as she suddenly realised that she was now sitting in the middle of a field on an exposed hillside on a not-particularly-warm day.

'I'm going to do some magic, Jan. I'm going to make our love so strong that it will never break.'

I took a small, bright coin from my pocket and showed it to her. 'That's silver, Jan. Give me a couple of strands of your hair.'

I separated two strands of her hair and pulled. It was thick and strong and broke with difficulty.

'Ow, that fucking hurt,' she shouted.

'OK, Jan, I'm sorry. I'm going to do the same to myself now." I pulled two strands from my own hair. 'Look now, Jan.' I held up the silver coin and wound both sets of strands around it.

'Let's kiss the coin to bless our union, Jan.'

I held the coin to her lips and she kissed it. I kissed it myself, and then, bending over, I pushed the coin into the earth of the indentation. Holding her hand tightly, I tried to commune with Gog, Magog or whatever pagan force that had been worshipped here in ancient times. I begged God to bind this girl to me in love so that I would never lose her.

There was no clap of thunder or blinding insight. Instead, Janice fidgeted next to me.

'I'm cold,' she announced, in a tone that intimated that she had had quite enough of this for one day.

'Just one more thing, Jan.' I remembered her remarks when stepping on Susan's grave. 'What do you feel here?'

Janice lowered her stockinged feet into the indentation until they touched bottom. She quickly pulled them up again. 'Oooh, I don't like it,' she complained. 'Something scrabbled at the soles of my feet. Something nasty happened here.'

It wasn't enough to upset her though and she quickly forgot it. So did I. I could only focus on the fact that I had achieved what I had set out to do. For that reason alone, it was a memorable day for me.

Pagan rituals notwithstanding, I still said my prayers every morning. In the confusing, pain-filled world of freedom, I found that it made me strong and gave me direction.

In a small flat, it was something that was difficult to hide from Janice and I had no desire to do so. She watched suspiciously as I knelt down with my prayer book, a pink kappel on my head and a tasselled prayer shawl about my neck. When she asked what I was doing, I explained that I felt that it positively charged my soul and made me a better person. I explained that I also prayed for her.

'As long as it's not evil,' she said, still suspicious.

'Janice, I'm Jewish. This is how Jews pray,' the exasperation was clear in my voice.

'That's why you're so careful with money then,' she remarked sarcastically.

It struck a nerve. 'Fuck me, Janice, I get you whatever you want. You don't go short of anything — Methadone, Rohipnal, Valium, puff, Es, whatever. It's just that I absolutely refuse to buy you crack or smack. And it's got nothing to do with the fact that I'm Jewish and say my prayers.'

'Well, I don't like it,' she announced with finality.

In time, she got used to it and, on a couple of occasions, actually knelt and prayed with me. But she was never comfortable with it and I always had to talk her into it.

If the ritual at Wandlebury had been intended to strengthen our relationship, there was no immediate evidence of it. In fact, on the contrary, things got decidedly worse. Increasingly, Janice felt the yearning for North London and the drugs, and perhaps her mother. 'What are we stuck out here for?' was a constant refrain.

It wasn't as if we didn't still spend a lot of time in North London. It was a rare day that we didn't drive over to see Ian, Janice's mum, Judy or Ken and Emma. There were still regular missions in search of the illicit drugs Janice needed.

But the 'crack' beast seemed to be increasingly upon her. When in its thrall, she was impossible to deal with. It was, quite literally, like dealing with another person; one who was dark and vicious and quite evil. In the end, all I could do was to let her go. She would disappear into the warren that was Hackney and Islington and I would await her return. Often it would be in the early hours. My phone would ring and I would drive to pick her up somewhere. Then we would return to our flat for a couple of days' peace until the 'crack' demon appeared again.

Perhaps I should have bought a large quantity of coke and washed it up into 'crack', then given Janice a measured dose each day. But there was no such thing as a 'measured' dose with 'crack'. Whenever I watched Janice, Ian and the other 'street people' do 'crack', they did everything that was available, There was never so much as a crumb left. Further, merely knowing that 'crack' was available and to hand would have impelled Janice to ask for it all the time. Then, instead of driving Janice 2 away, I would have had her for my constant companion.

∗   ∗   ∗

Despite the constant pressure of being around Janice, the drugs and the dramas, my health continued to improve. Workouts in the gym had now returned to pre-illness standards. I wasn't running again yet, but virtually all the stiffness had gone from my knees. The sole residual symptom was a tendency to doze off after I had eaten 'problem' foods.

I explained the situation to Janice, but she wasn't having any of it. To her paranoid mind, falling asleep from eating, say, chocolate, was an unlikely explanation. She accused me of 'gauching', falling asleep after taking certain drugs, namely heroin. I was sure she didn't acually believe that I was on heroin, and her concern wasn't that I might be taking it, rather that I wasn't sharing it with her. 'Fucking allergy,' she would mutter in disbelief.

If I had had any doubts myself, they were soon dispelled by one particular incident. My little red Vauxall Nova had been a reliable car for me, despite disparaging remarks by Janice about it being 'only a little run-around'. It had literally taken me all over the country, some days covering hundreds of miles. This particular morning I was driving along Blackwell Road in South London on my way over to pick Janice up from her mother's. Although it could be a busy road carrying buses and other heavy traffic, this morning it was quite clear. I day-dreamed as I drove.

Suddenly, there was a loud bang and the car shook violently. I gasped as I opened my eyes to realise that I had collided with a parked car and was now speeding towards the pavement. I stamped on the brake as hard as I could as a wooden bollard rushed to meet me. I hit it head on, tearing it halfway from its mooring in the pavement and came to an abrupt halt.

I immediately realised that I must have fallen asleep at the wheel. I was completely unhurt, but the immediate problem was the crowd that was gathering around the car. I wondered how much they had seen.

As soon as I climbed out and they saw that I was OK, the onlookers dispersed. In typical London fashion, everyone assumed that it was nothing to do with them. As I looked at the uprooted bollard and the smashed-in bonnet of my written-off car, I realised just how lucky I had been. The road had curved round to the left. It was a miracle I had hit a parked car on the left and not crossed the road and collided with something head on.

I managed to push my car into the curb, phoned the AA and the police, then went to look at the parked car. The damage was surprisingly slight. I rang a few door bells until I located the owner, then we swapped details.

The police arrived and seemed quite uninterested. I told them that a young black kid with a baseball cap on back to front had run out in front of me chasing a ball, then run off after he had seen the accident. The police nodded knowingly. This was South London. They knew all about young black kids with reversed baseball caps. They didn't even remark on the uprooted bollard. When I told them the AA was on its way, they drove off.

My next problem was that now I didn't have a car. The following day I met Johnny Morris and we went to a car-dealer pal of his. I paid

£3,500 for a clean-looking white Ford Sierra that was a distinct improvement on the Nova. Other pals of mine said that I had paid about £1,000 too much, but at least I had transport again. Further, there would be no more snide remarks from Janice about 'little run-arounds'.

✻　✻　✻

As neither Janice or I worked at regular jobs, weekends made very little difference to us. Admittedly, there were a lot more people about in the shops, streets and parks, and the prevailing atmosphere was more 'family orientated', but as neither of us spent weekends with family, it was largely situation normal.

This particular Sunday I was quite relieved that I had something to do. I had to pick some money up in the Midlands, drop part of it off in Hertford, then bring the rest home. Janice was still in bed when I left at 10.00am.

It was late afternoon when I returned to Carshalton. The quiet square was just as deserted as on weekdays. I let myself into our silent flat.

As I reached the top of the stairs the heat hit me. Its source was the kitchen. I rushed in to see every one of the electric hobs of the cooker glowing red hot. On each stood a pot or pan.

I couldn't tell how long it had been like that, but it was obvious that within minutes the whole lot would burst into flames. I snatched glowing pots from hobs and switched the stove off. Then I went in search of Janice.

I didn't have to look far. She was unconscious, rather than asleep, on the sofa in the lounge. Music tapes lay strewn across the carpet, around the silent music centre. Whatever she had taken, she had taken a lot of it. It took me a while to rouse her.

There was no explanation about the cooker and no apology. She seemed blissfully unconcerned that she had been within minutes of setting the flat on fire and possibly burning to death. 'I got fed up waiting for ya,' was all I could get out of her.

I hadn't been out on a suicide mission, but ferrying around large sums of illicit money can be stressful. After spending all day trying not to attract attention to myself, I didn't need to come home and be beset by fire engines and police cars.

Janice couldn't have cared less. In truth, she could hardly stand.

'Take me home to my mum,' demanded Janice 2. Like the replay of a boring holiday movie, she packed her bags, loaded them into the Sierra and I dropped her off at her mum's.

The following day was unusual in that I didn't hear from her at all. She had phoned me at least once virtually every day since we had met. When I phoned her mum late that evening, she was non-committal to the point of rudeness. After one recent violent argument, Janice had told her mother that I had been in prison for murder. After that, her attitude to me had changed completely.

When I hadn't heard a thing by the following day, I went round to her mum's. Both Luke and Mrs Harris were adamant that Janice had left home some time in the early hours of the previous day. She had taken a suitcase full of clothes with her and said that she wouldn't be back.

Now I was seriously concerned. Of late, she had been getting worse and worse, harder to get on with and more self-destructive. It seemed like Janice 2 was taking over completely.

I did the rounds of all our mutual friends, but no one had seen her. I remembered her threat that, if she ever decided to leave me, I would never find her. Having spent so much time with her over the past six months, though, at least I had an idea where to start looking.

First, I picked Ian up. In his demented state I never really knew where I stood with him nowadays. He didn't show much sympathy when I told him that Janice had run away. Perhaps he still hadn't forgiven me for taking her away from him.

The obvious place to look for Janice was at King's Cross. At some time or other she would have to go there to score the drugs she needed. Failing that, as it was a congregating point for most of the 'street people' of North London, someone might have seen her in their travels.

The problem was that strangers asking questions weren't welcome at the Cross. There could be trouble with dealers, brasses or their minders. We would need a bit of help. We went round and picked Davy up. The three of us had stood together in some of the toughest jails in the country. We shouldn't have too much trouble at the Cross.

'Fuck me, Norm,' said Davy when I first asked, 'people will think I'm looking for a brass, and a right cheap one at that.'

'You know I wouldn't ask,' I entreated, 'but I'm desperate to find her. She's acting really strange, getting worse and worse. I'm afraid that if I don't find her, something will happen to her.'

So morning, noon and night for a week, the three of us scoured King's Cross for any sign of Janice. Needless to say, the regulars were suspicious and only slightly imtimidated. These were people who lied as a matter of course. They probably thought I was a punter whom Janice had ripped off.

Between us, Ian and I managed to find a couple of girls who we knew through Janice. I left them a phone number and the promise of a reward should they find her for me. On a couple of occasions, people said that we had just missed her. It was all very frustrating, but at least we knew she was still in the area.

As loyal as he was to me, Davy was becoming tired of the search. 'It's what they do these birds, duck and dive,' he said. 'If they don't want to be found, they won't be. And there's another thing, Norm. Don't think that this area isn't closely watched by Old Bill. They'll know by now that we've been looking for someone. And when they punch us up on the computer and find out who we are, all the alarm bells will start ringing. We've got to leave it out, mate. Otherwise we'll be nicked for something.'

He was right, of course. We stopped searching as a team, but I was like a ghost, haunting the places where Janice and I had been. I would set out first thing and drive round and round North London, dropping in on people and places, then doubling back later to see if Janice had been there in the meantime.

I still continued to do radio and the occasional TV interview. I managed a professional enough performance and no one could tell that anything was amiss, but my heart wasn't in it. As much as I wanted to be a successful and famous writer, it all meant nothing if Janice wasn't by my side to share it. Once again, the world was a cold and lonely place for me. Life had no meaning without Janice.

It was more than halfway through December. Janice had been missing for almost three weeks now, but I couldn't accept that I would never see her again. Her mother and Luke were no help. She had often gone missing for months in the past and they had no idea where she was or any real desire to find her for that matter.

Christmas was always a hard time for me. Loneliness and unhappiness seemed particularly onerous at a time when everyone was supposed to be happy. I was determined not to spend Christmas in England. I phoned JD and Ron in Spain and told them I would be over for the holiday, then booked my flight for the 23rd.

That evening, Ian told me that Janice had been seen earlier that day in a nearby street with a local girl. We drove round to the house. The girl was non-committal, but said she would pass on a message if she saw Janice. I left her with a written note.

At about midnight, my phone rang. The little-girl voice seemed even more strained and plaintive than usual. My heart leapt into my mouth and I was terrified that she'd ring off.

'Please don't ring off, Jan,' I begged.

'What do you want?' her voice was slurred and unsteady.

'I must see you, Jan. Just meet me. Please.'

'It's no good, Norman. I've tried to change, but I can't. I'll just drag you down.'

'I don't care, Jan. I just want to be with you. I've missed you so much. Have you missed me?'

There was a pause. 'Yes,' she said, then another pause, then, 'of course I have.'

'So meet me, then. Come and meet me.'

'Not tonight, Norman. I'll meet you tomorrow.' There was a resigned tone to her voice.

'Come to Ian's. What time will you come?'

'I'll see you there at four.'

'Don't let me down Jan. Please be there.'

'I'll be there. I've said I will, haven't I?' and with that she rang off.

For a second it was like a lifeline being cut. For as long as the call had lasted, my spirit had been in contact with hers. Now she was lost to me again. But at least I had the consolation that I had found her and that I would see her tomorrow. That night I slept more soundly than I had since she had left.

The following day I was at Ian's well before midday. I wasn't going to take the chance that Janice would forget the time and come early. Word had gone around that Janice was coming back and everyone was there. I pointed out quite forcefully that Janice didn't need a welcoming committee and that I wanted our reunion to be private and personal. Everyone except Charlie took the hint and left. I sat down with him and Ian to wait.

Just before 4.00pm, I heard the gate rattle, announcing that someone was at the door. I ran along the passage like a child to a much-awaited treat. The door stood already ajar and through the gate I could see Janice standing there. She looked so painfully thin. I had never seen her so pale and drawn. The whole shape of her face had changed, her cheeks drawn in, reminiscent of pictures of concentration camp victims. She was wearing an unfamiliar camouflage pattern army-style jacket and through its thin material I could see her bony arms.

I fumbled on the floor for the key and quickly opened the gate.

I pulled her inside and into my arms. Like someone who had been chilled to the bone for a long time, I hugged her tightly and warmed my spirit with hers. We clung together as if magnetised, an aura of love, warmth and caring binding us together. We had always known the bond between us was strong, now the heat and energy we generated between us was almost tangible.

'I've missed you so much, Jan,' I moaned, my whole body shaking with tearless sobs.

'And I've missed you too.' She sniffed as tears coursed down her face.

'Why did you go, Jan? Why?'

She was sobbing uncontrollably now and I tried to kiss the tears from her cheeks.

'I didn't want to keep on hurting you. I've tried to give up everything for you, but I can't, I just can't.'

She broke off as she buried her face in my chest. 'I've gone back on heroin, injecting, to try to blot the memory of you out.' She continued to hide her face from me.

'Oh, Jan, Jan. It's OK now. We've got each other and that's all that matters. We'll heal you again. Make you well again.'

I led her along the passage and into the front bedroom where we had first made love. We sat on the edge of the bed, still clinging to each other, like two young siblings long separated but now reunited.

Quietly, almost unobtrusively, Ian and Charlie slipped into the room and sat on chairs at the foot of the bed. Even the normally rumbustious Charlie was cowed into silence by the warmth and energy that Janice and I continued to generate.

'Look at the two of you,' muttered Ian *sotto voce*, eyes wide with amazement. 'You're lighting up the room.'

It was a very strange moment. The four of us sat there in total silence, unmoving. I couldn't have let go of Janice if my life had depended upon it. Ian and Charlie seemed content to sit there and bask in the warmth of the love that Janice and I shared.

Suddenly, I wanted to take her home to our flat. Ian and Charlie hugged her and told her it was great to see her back. We said our goodbyes and got in the car and set off for Carshalton. It was so good to be going home with her. I had stayed at my mother's since she had left.

As we drove, Janice told me of the past three weeks. Of stealing to get money for her heroin, then sleeping on sofas in friends' flats. She burst into tears again and as the sobs subsided blurted out that she had been raped.

An insane rage flared in my brain, but I had the presence of mind to control it. The more fuss I made about it, the more damage I would do to Janice. I must play it down, tell her it made no difference to me and that she should try to forget about it as much as she could.

She told me of Rudy, a big, black guy who hung around the girls at the Cross. Janice had thought that he was a friend, but one evening at his flat he had grabbed hold of her.

'He was just too strong for me,' she sobbed. 'He held me down ...' she broke off as she was overcome again.

'OK, Jan, OK. It's all over now. Let's just get you well again. The important thing as that we are back together. When the time is right, I'll find the fucker. We'll see how he performs with a grown man.'

For the rest of the journey I talked of the things that had happened since she had been away. How Ian, Davy and I had scoured the Cross for her.

'Oh, I heard you were looking for me,' she interjected, 'lots of people told me. But, as I told you before, if I don't want to be found, I won't be.'

I tried to keep the conversation going. I didn't want her dwelling on the rape incident. As we pulled into the green square bordering our flat, she visibly seemed to relax.

The flat was just as we had left it. Janice poked around to see what clothes of hers were still there. She mentioned that she had a suitcase full of clothes that she had left round a friends which we would have to pick up later. It was only 7.00pm, but it was already dark. 'Shall we go to be early, Jan. I just want to hold you.'

She turned and smiled at me weakly. 'Yes, I'd like that, but first there's something I must do.'

She rummaged around in her handbag. Finding what she was looking for she faced me, but with lowered eyes.

'It's best that you don't see this, Norman. I know how you hate it. But I must have this one last hit. Now that I've got a regular supply of pills again, I can stop injecting.'

I started towards her, but stopped quite involuntarily as I saw the syringe she was holding in her hand. As tough as I thought myself to be and despite the many terrible things I had seen in jail, I had a very powerful aversion to needles piercing flesh.

'OK, Jan, you do whatever you have to do,' I said, turning away from her. 'I love you, little girl.'

I heard her grunt a reply behind me and guessed she was engrossed in preparing the hit. I physically cringed as I thought of her sticking the needle into her flesh without an anaesthetic. I had nightmare visions of the syringe being torn from her arm, ripping open the vein. I closed my eyes tightly, but still the vision wouldn't go away.

I must have stood like that for over five minutes. There was dead silence, except for Janice's laboured breathing in the background.

'Are you OK, Jan?' I called out quietly. There was no reply. I turned slowly. She was half-standing, half-sitting, one buttock resting on a small table. Her eyes were closed as her head lolled on her chest. Her face was pasty white with small beads of sweat on her forehead. Her right arm was extended in front of her, its back resting on her thigh. From the joint where forearm met upper arm, a syringe hung from her flesh, its point embedded in the vein.

I stared, fascinated and horrified both at the same time; fascinated that such a relatively small thing should have such power over her and horrified that she should violate her body in such an obscene way. I wanted to run across and gather her in my arms, but was repelled by the needle and feared to dislodge it.

It seemed quite a while before she opened her eyes again and I realised that she had been totally oblivious to my presence. Such was the power of this drug. I cursed its existence, then cursed myself for not understanding the hold it had over Janice. She had been torn between satisfying her appetite and doing what I wanted. I would try to understand in the future.

Janice eased the syringe from her arm, took a small bottle of disinfectant from her bag and some cotton wool and dabbed at the small incision that remained. She fixed a small plaster over it and started to undress. I undressed, too, and we climbed into bed together. I decided against making love to her this night, content just to lay in her arms. With the rape still fresh in her memory I didn't want to do anything that might remind her of it.

As we snuggled down together, a feeling of great peace came over me. Time seemed to stand still and I was content, oh, so content. Of all the places in the universe, this was where I wanted to be and was where I was meant to be. The devil take tomorrow. For this moment in time, everything was as it should be.

LIFE
AFTER LIFE

**love's
labour lost**

If only you could stay in bed, lying next to the person you loved, for the rest of your life. The thought had the transient beauty of a snowflake. Its romantic appeal faded with the rising of the sun and would melt as surely as that crystallised drop of water. Harsh realities intruded. In barely two days' time, I was booked to fly to Spain. I wouldn't go without Janice and it would be difficult to get a flight this late. There was a lot of running about to do.

Leaving Janice to sleep, I rose, shaved, bathed and started to prepare breakfast. Janice declined breakfast, as I knew she would. However, I managed to force some toast and fruit juice down her.

As I roused her, I was relieved to see that Janice 2 was nowhere in evidence. The smack seemed to have subdued every facet of her personality. She was passive and permanently sleepy. I realised that it would be late morning before she'd be ready to go out.

After a lot of phoning around, I managed to find a flight for her that was on the same day as mine, from the same airport, only two hours later. I didn't like the idea of leaving her behind at Gatwick, even for two hours. There were too many things that could go wrong. She wasn't used to flying, and there was always the possibility that she would miss her flight.

We spent the next 48 hours running around frantically, collecting her ticket, the rest of her clothes, a fresh supply of all the pills she would need and saying goodbye to her mother, my mother and various friends.

We arrived at Gatwick early. Hundreds of families milled around, all with the same goal as Janice and me, to get away from England for Christmas.

With both sets of luggage on a trolley, I pushed through the throng to stand in the check-in queue for my flight. Immediately, Janice was restless. She insisted on going for a walk. I insisted that she stayed with me until I had checked in, then we both could go for a walk. But there was no reasoning with her. It wasn't Janice 2, but she was in a particularly stubborn and unreasonable frame of mind.

'Don't leave me standing here with your luggage after I've checked mine in,' I shouted at her receding back.

'I'll be back in time,' she called over her shoulder.

With a mounting feeling of frustration and rage, I worked my way to the front of the queue. Still Janice hadn't reappeared. I checked my bags in, then stood in the middle of the section with Janice's bags at my feet. Another half-an-hour passed and still there was no sign of her.

What had happened to her? What could I do? Ever mindful of the fact that there was still a warrant out for her over the shoplifting charge, I was loath to page her over the tannoy. I had intended to slip out of Gatwick with a minimum of fuss.

Raging to the point of actually muttering to myself, I went in search of her. Pushing the baggage trolley in front of me, I went up in the lift to the retail floor and made two complete circuits, looking into every shop and restaurant. Still there was no sign of her. I began to wonder if she had been arrested and taken into custody.

'Fuck it. Fuck it,' I said out loud to myself, causing several passers by to look at me curiously. Why did she do this to me? Why did she always cause me so much grief and upset me? Was it really too much to ask for your girlfriend to stick with you in the airport until you could get on your flight. Especially as we had the added problem of boarding two separate flights.

Coming to a decision, I started to make my way to the left luggage counter. I couldn't take her luggage with me and I was damned if I was going to miss my flight, too, and be stuck in England for Christmas. Perhaps I could pretend that we had never met up again. If only I could wipe all traces of this girl from my memory.

Suddenly, over all the background din, I could hear something, something that was tugging at my attention. I listened more carefully. I heard a distorted voice from the tannoy mention my name and something to do with the information desk. Desperately, I searched the overhead signs, then hurried towards the information desk. As I got closer I could see Janice standing next to it.

'Where the fuck did you get to?' I exploded. 'I've got about five minutes before I have to board my flight.'

Unusually, Janice looked flustered, without a ready answer to hand. However, there was no time to argue. Her flight was from the other terminal, a short train ride away. I had intended to go over with her and sit her in the appropriate departure lounge. There would be no time for that now. All I could do was to point her in the right direction.

I forced £100 and her ticket into her hand and propelled her towards the rail-link corridor.

'Jan, all you've got to do is get on the plane. I'll be waiting for you at the other end. OK?'

'OK,' she answered as if it was all an insult to her intelligence. I gave her a quick kiss on the lips and literally sprinted away. As I sat sweaty and agitated in my seat under the curious gaze of my fellow passengers, I found myself wondering what the chances were of Janice getting to Malaga. A multitude of possible pitfalls rose before me, like spectres on an old battlefield. With the greatest of difficulty I swept them away and tried to relax for the flight.

Less than three hours later, I was sitting in the cafeteria at Malaga airport watching the arrivals board. I had collected the keys of the hire car earlier and noted its position in the car park. I looked for Janice's flight, checking that it hadn't been delayed. It would be at least two hours before she arrived. I sat, partially obscured by a pillar, secretly observing the other travellers. Again, I didn't want to advertise my presence in Spain.

Ten minutes before her flight was due to land, I took up a prominent position at the front of the barrier in the arrivals lounge. If she crawled out on her stomach, Indian fashion, she still wouldn't be able to slip by me unobserved. I waited.

The board duly announced that the flight had landed and I stared eagerly at the doorway through which the passengers would come. They arrived, firstly in dribs and drabs, then in a torrential flood of bodies. My neck stretched and my head rotated as I peered amongst moving groups of people. There was no sign of Janice.

I reasoned that she was sure to be last. I waited for individual stragglers. Still no Janice. The doorway to the baggage reclaim remained shut, no one else came through. My spirits plunged as I resigned myself to the fact that she had missed her flight.

Well, planes weren't like buses, she couldn't be on the next one. JD was waiting for me at his villa. I would phone Gatwick from there. Miserable and deflated, I drove along the *autovia* towards Marbella.

JD had all his family over from Ireland for the holiday. His wife, mother and father-in-law and young son all gathered around to welcome me. It seemed uncharitable to be miserable in the circumstances. When they enquired about Janice I brushed over it as if it was just a temporary hitch. However, I noticed JD's concerned expression in the background.

He got me on my own and I explained what had happened. He handed me his unregistered mobile to phone Gatwick. I spoke to several departments and they all claimed ignorance of Janice. I finally spoke to the airport police. They sounded wary and suspicious and told me to call back in the morning.

The following morning they put me straight through to a senior officer. After confirming my identity he told me that Janice had been arrested for shoplifting the previous afternoon. He sounded almost as surprised as I was. With closed-circuit TV covering virtually every inch and regular patrols of armed police, one would have thought that Gatwick was the last place that anyone would go shoplifting.

The next bit surprised me even more. He went on to inform me that Janice had been bailed and would be travelling on to Malaga that day. He even gave me the flight number.

I tried to figure it out. Shoplifting was only a minor offence and I knew that offenders regularly got bail. But what of the outstanding warrant? Perhaps it hadn't got into the national computer for some reason. Similar mistakes were commonplace. As for the new flight, perhaps she had paid for it out of the money I had given her. I suppose that, as a so-called professional criminal, I should have known better. But I couldn't think of any other explanation and, as long as Janice arrived, I didn't really care how she did it.

Again, I waited for the designated flight and again she wasn't on it. When I got through to the senior officer again he seemed flustered. He could give me no explanation as to why she had missed her flight again, but assured me she would be arriving on another one. He gave me the new flight number.

When she didn't arrive on this one either, I didn't know what to do. If I hadn't been talking to a senior police officer at Gatwick I would have thought that someone was winding me up. Perhaps it was the Janice effect. Only she could miss three flights in a row.

I drove back to Marbella and JD. Seeing how upset I was, he commiserated. However, he had some imminent business to attend to and had to leave. I drove off with him.

As we sped along I looked at the azure sea, the lush shades of green of the vegetation and the reds and the browns of the earth and mountains, all brought into perfect focus by the bright, strong sunlight. How was it possible to be so miserable in such a paradise?

Suddenly, JD's mobile rang. Intent on other things, I absent-mindedly noticed him answer it. He screwed up his face in puzzlement and held the receiver at arm's length as he stared at it with exaggerated curiosity.

'It's for you,' he said as he handed it to me.

With JD's permission, I had given Janice his number for use in an emergency. No doubt this was just such an emergency.

''Allo,' the childlike voice said.

'Is that you, Jan?' I queried. 'Where are you?'

'Hang on a minute,' she replied, 'I'm using some geezer's phone. I'll ask him where we are.'

Suddenly, another voice came on the line, male and English, with a London accent.

''Allo, mate, your girl's in a cab outside Eagles bar above Puerto Banus. Do you know it?'

Of course I knew it, it used to be Freddy Foreman's bar several years ago when most of the 'chaps' in Spain used it. But there were several surprises here. Firstly, Janice was in Spain, so she had caught a flight at last. Secondly, the Eagles bar was barely 200 yards from the small villa JD had got me, a place I had never stayed before. Still the coincidences eluded me, and the alternative was unacceptable.

'Tell her to stay there, mate,' I said to the English voice and 'I'll be there in ten minutes. I turned to JD. 'Janice is outside the Eagles bar, John.'

'How the fuck did she get there?' His expression was pensive. 'And who was that other person you were talking to?'

'Janice stopped some English fella and borrowed his phone,' I explained.

'Very strange, very strange, Norm,' said JD shaking his head. 'There ain't that many English guys with mobiles out here right now and the "chaps" don't let people use their phones.'

'You don't know Janice, mate. She's very persuasive. Let's go and pick her up before she disappears again.'

In less than ten minutes we were outside Eagles. Janice was leaning against the side of a Spanish taxi; there was no sign of the English fella with the phone. I jumped out and hugged her to me. Christmas would be OK now that Santa had sent me my present.

I paid the Spanish taxi driver and Janice came with JD and I. He dropped us at the villa then went on his way. As she unpacked, I asked Janice about what had happened at Gatwick. She said that, after she was bailed, she had phoned Nigel to come and pick her up. The pair of them had got off their faces, that was why she missed the other flights. I assumed that Nigel must have paid for them.

Looking back now on that last holiday in Spain, it was as if we somehow knew that it was our final time there together. Christmas Day we spent with JD and his family, but mainly we stayed on our own, savouring each other's company. We buzzed around the flat, went for long walks together and sat for hours on the beach. At times, I caught Janice looking at me wistfully, her painfully thin face with just a ghost of a smile at the corners of her mouth. She looked sad almost, but stressed that she was quite happy. She was unusually clingy, cuddling me for hours and stroking my hair and my neck and telling me she loved me. I knew something was bothering her underneath, but I thought it was the fear of getting back on heroin when we returned to England.

With a TV appearance scheduled for 5 January I could hardly extend our holiday and all return flights seemed to be booked for the first week of the New Year. I decided to travel back on the 30th on my original ticket. Janice was on a flight that left two hours later. I would get JD to come to the airport with us to make sure she got on her flight.

I thought little of it when I was allocated a seat right at the front for my return flight, although the nearer we got to Gatwick, the more uneasy I began to feel. Janice had attracted a lot of attention to us both when she was arrested for shoplifting.

The plane landed, and as soon as the door opened, three police officers entered. A male and female officer, both armed, remained by the door, while the third officer with a dog walked the length of the plane. I did catch the female officer surreptitiously looking at me, but, as paranoid as I usually was, I shrugged it off. It couldn't have anything to do with me. After all, I had only been away for a

Christmas break.

Coming through Customs, though, I was led aside into a room and given a thorough strip search. I didn't bother to complain, or even to ask what it was all about. They wouldn't have told me anyway and all I would have succeeded in doing was to attract more attention to myself. I exited into the arrivals lounge and settled down to wait for Janice.

With a growing sense of *déjà vu*, I checked the flight number against the arrival time, saw that the plane had landed and watched the passengers stream into the arrivals area. There was no sign of Janice.

The information desk said they couldn't help me and wouldn't even confirm that she had been on the flight. It was only after a long and acrimonious shouting match on one of the 'help' phones that airport security admitted that they had taken a Janice Harris into custody and that she would be appearing at Highbury Magistrates Court the following morning charged with shoplifting. There was nothing I could do but go home and wait.

I was at the Magistrates' Court early and was comforted by the thought that at least I would see Janice. I had strong doubts about whether they would let me take her home. This was her second shoplifting offence within a month and she hadn't shown up at court for the last one. Then there was the problem of whether they would allow me to stand bail for her. I was hardly anyone's idea of a fit and proper person. I was still on life licence for murder.

In the event, everything went remarkably smoothly. The magistrate was pleasantness personified. She smiled at Janice and nodded approvingly when I said that she was living with me at the Carshalton address. Janice was bailed to that address and I was informed that it was my duty to see that she appeared at court on the appropriate day. I left with her, thinking that we had definitely got away with something. Perhaps the magistrate was feeling magnanimous because it was New Year's Eve.

That evening, we celebrated with Ian. I had been invited to several New Year parties, but the invitations hadn't included Janice. We ushered in the New Year in an Islington pub — Ian was like some inebriated village idiot, leering lopsidedly at any woman whose eye he could catch. I was blissfully happy, though — Janice and I were together again.

* * *

If I had thought that the Gatwick experience had taught Janice a lesson, or would subdue her for a while, I was to be disappointed. Perhaps it was the 'England Factor'. Within hours of being back in her native North London she was as boisterous as ever. On the positive side, I was pleased that her spirit was strong again after the debilitating effects of the smack. Further, she had started to put on weight and was not nearly as gaunt as before. The downside was that, with the resurgent spirit, came the arguments.

The TV programme was scheduled for a Sunday. It was called *It's Your Shout* and the format was one of a mock trial. It was to be filmed in the old, disused Nottingham Assize Court. I was to be the mock defendant, make-believe lawyers would prosecute and defend me before a mock jury of local dignitaries. My fee was a nominal £100, but the real benefit was that I was to be captioned as NORMAN PARKER — AUTHOR— *PARKHURST TALES*. It all helped to sell more books as well as raising my media profile. Something could come of it.

Janice didn't seem to resent my media appearances, in fact, I think, secretly, she was quite proud of them. However, that was absolutely no guarantee that she wouldn't misbehave when one was imminent. It was another one of those situations where she felt she held all the cards.

Arguments were inevitably about money, that I should regularly give her sizeable sums. If I asked her what it was she needed, what she wanted me to buy for her, she had no answer. I bought her the majority of the stuff she asked for. If I had given her money, that would have been the last I would have seen of her for a couple of days. The sole beneficiary would have been some North London crack dealer.

As we sped up the motorway, the old familiar argument flared again. Soon, we were shouting at each other angrily. We drove the rest of the way in silence. As we parked in Nottingham, she leaped from the car and stormed off.

I could hardly let her go. She was a long way from home in a strange city and I had a TV programme to prepare for in a couple of hours. I ran after her.

Lunch in an expensive reataurant seemed to placate her for a while. We were both smartly dressed and Janice liked set-piece, formal occasions. She had no more idea than me about what wine to order, but it was quite amusing to watch her agonising over the wine list like some society lady.

Afterwards, we strolled through an extensive shopping precinct. It was very modern and much cleaner than anything you could have found in London. Although many of the shops were open, Sunday afternoon trade seemed sparse, with very few people on the streets.

'We'll have to be getting back to the car in a minute, Jan,' I suddenly said, checking my watch. 'I want to get to the TV studio in plenty of time.' It was an innocuous enough remark, but it seemed to provoke her.

'Yeah, well, it's all right for you, Mr TV Personality, but I've got my own career to think about.' She snatched her hand free from mine. 'All I'm doing is wasting time around you. I should be out fucking grafting.' With that, she stormed off.

I followed her along a narrow street, almost running to keep up. 'Jan, don't be stupid. What are you going to do?'

'You'll see,' she threatened.

At that point, the narrow street opened out into a wide square. Right opposite was a large department store. Clothes, furnishings and household goods filled the brightly lit windows. Before I could do anything, she hurried across the square and into the store.

I paced up and down outside, wondering what to do. At any second I expected to hear a rumpus from inside the store. I wondered how the Sunday-sleepy store staff would deal with the vengeful Janice, she who had pillaged the length and breadth of Islington.

Also, I would have to consider my own position. All loyalty aside, should she be nicked for shoplifting, they might think that I was an accomplice, waiting outside. There was little I could do for her anyway, just pacing up and down. I retreated to a bench 20 feet away and sat unobtrusively watching the store entrance through which she had disappeared.

There were very few people walking by and, from what I could see through the shop windows, very few people in the store either. Janice would stick out like a sore thumb. A feeling of impending doom swept over me. There would be no bail this time.

Suddenly, I saw the familiar bushy-haired figure in the shop window. My heart leapt. She disappeared, then reappeared again in the shop doorway, her arms full of clothes. She swept out into the street.

The surprise, the sheer cheek of it caused me to jump to my feet. At any second, I expected a hue and cry to start. With the few passers-by looking at her in amazement but not quite knowing what was going on, I hurried across.

Walking quickly past her, I muttered out of the corner of my mouth, 'Jan, just follow on behind me. If I bump into any Old Bill I'll show out and you can dump the gear in a shop doorway.'

I continued walking, not daring to look back. I cursed Janice and myself for involving me in this.

I walked through the narrow streets in the direction of the car. There had been no plan, I hadn't expected her to do this. It was all I could think of in the circumstances.

From time to time I looked surreptitiously over my shoulder and cringed. It was ridiculous. She had a small mountain of clothes piled up in her arms. She could barely see over it. And sticking out here and there was the occasional hanger and price tag.

Those few passers-by we did encounter stared as she passed. However, she was so brazen about it, I suppose that no one could quite believe that anything illegal was going on. Had we bumped into any patrolling policeman, we would have been immediately nicked.

Eventually we reached the car park. I have never been so relieved to see my car. I opened the boot and she slung the lot in. She started to sort through it, but I pushed her away and slammed it shut.

'For fuck's sake, get in the car,' I growled.

Tutting loudly, she flounced along the side, opened the passenger door, climbed in and slammed it loudly.

'That's it, Jan,' I called out as I climbed in next to her, 'try to attract as much attention as possible.'

Trying not to hurry, I reversed out of my parking space and drove slowly out of the car park. As we got half a street away, I felt as if a great weight had lifted from my shoulders. Suddenly, I began to laugh. A giggle at first, but then full-blooded, hearty laughter. Janice looked at me curiously, then began to laugh, too.

'You cunt, you utter cunt,' I managed to get out, tears of mirth streaming down my face.

'What?' said Janice, between howls.

'You fucking know,' I replied. 'I've got you, you know. You're trying to kill me by giving me a heart-attack, aren't you?'

Her laughter was the only reply.

We drove for a while in silence, occasionally suppressing

giggles. We arrived at the old court house and I parked nearby.

'You'll have to behave yourself now, Jan, this is important to me.'

'OK,' she replied, the buzz of the recent shoplifting seemed to have taken all the contrariness out of her.

I found the producer and he showed us into the courtroom. The carved stone, dark-stained woodwork and brass fittings were from a bygone era. It was like stepping back into the past.

Janice was given a seat at the back of the court and I was now free to concentrate on the task in hand. The producer introduced me to both prosecuting and defending counsel, local solicitors who were dressed for the part. On the bench, the 'Judge' was a bewigged and begowned retired circuit judge. He nodded to me gravely as I was seated in the dock.

The three-man jury were still taking their seats. As they sat, they were introduced one by one. The former Chief Constable attempted a smile, but only produced a grimace. The local Tory MP smiled broadly and waggled his hand as if greeting a rally of electors. The local stipendiary magistrate stared at me sternly.

For a second, I had to remind myself that I wasn't on trial for real. It wasn't that they were consummate actors, more that they had all reverted to a role they knew so well. I stole a glance at Janice sitting at the back of the courtroom and inwardly cringed. I thought of the pile of stolen clothes in the boot of my car, just outside in the car park. None of those present would have been at all amused. Once again, I reflected on how often my life imitated art.

The subject of the debate was murder and the death penalty. In the circumstances I was an ideal defendant. Special TV lights came on, temporarily blinding everyone, then the cameras began to roll. I immediately focused all my attention on the proceedings. If I was to give a good account of myself, I would have to follow all the arguments carefully and be ready to put my own case.

Probably because of the moderating effect of the TV cameras, I got off quite lightly. Everybody was bending over backwards to appear nice and polite. The Tory MP made the obligatory law and order oration and the Chief Constable delivered a spirited defence of the status quo. As the sole representative of the forces of darkness I had to be both erudite and reasonable. I succeeded well enough to be congratulated by the producer afterwards.

Later, as I drove back to London with Janice snoozing quietly beside me, I couldn't help but ruminate on how events inevitably conspired to make my life complicated. Sometimes I wondered where it would all end. I was well aware that happy endings were mostly for fairytales. For the present, I would settle for happy middle bits.

* * *

With Janice's 24th birthday approaching on the 28th of the month, I was desperately searching for a way to make it a special occasion. We had argued so often of late, I hoped that some grandiose but sincere gesture might convince her that I loved her. Both Ian and Judy had told me that she often asked them if they thought I really loved her.

Perhaps I could come up with something that would settle her incessant paranoia, because that's what I increasingly felt it to be. In the face of so much deviousness, subterfuge and downright nastiness, she had retreated into a world where she trusted nothing and no one.

As the birthday got nearer, I did drop a hint that it might be a good idea if we got engaged. Even though she was still grumpy over an earlier perceived slight, I could tell that the idea appealed to her. She looked quickly at me to try to discern if I really meant it.

In private, my mum didn't like the idea at all. She was growing increasingly concerned that Janice would get me nicked again. Further, as I invariably returned home to her when Janice and I fell out, she could see just how unhappy Janice was making me. In truth, I did have strong doubts myself, but what could I do? As destructive as our relationship was, we were hopelessly in love with each other. We would have to see it through to the end, whatever that might be.

On balance, the move to Carshalton had been a mistake. Physical distance from drugs bore no relationship to Janice's desire for them. All it really meant was that we spent hours travelling backwards and forwards to North London.

If I had thought that being part of a semi-rural community would soothe Janice's savage breast, then I had been dreaming. Our neighbours in the little square ignored us to a man, woman and child. Whether it was the TV cameras which alerted them to who I was, or Janice's regular foul-mouthed rants, I couldn't tell. I didn't go out of my way to speak to anyone, but whenever Janice and I walked down the street everyone suddenly seemed to be intent on some aspect of a bush or flower bed. Consequently, I tried to be as considerate and polite as I possibly could, but all to no avail.

We had had a comparatively quiet evening by our standards. We had arrived home just after 6.00pm, cooked a meal and settled down to watch TV. At about 8.00pm Janice started to become restless. I could actually see Janice 2 begin to appear, small facets of her character niggling and probing at mine.

At first I ignored it, but it was an insidious pressure. Minor complaints and insults to begin with, then, when that got no reaction, major slurs over things she knew I was touchy about. Resist it as I might, I could feel myself rising to the bait. It was the kind of antagonism that inevitably provoked a response.

When it came, it was all the more forceful for having been held back. Soon we were shouting at each other again. I watched her face distort as she became this other person I so despised. She turned away from me to get some clothes from a cupboard and, figuratively, I raised my hands to throttle her.

It was at rare times like these that I realised just how far I had come, how much I had 'the Beast' under control. Whereas before I would have been aware of this dark, powerful force straining to be released and I would long to indulge it, now I knew I was almost incapable of taking a life. I had already seriously compromised my immortal soul, there would be no further evil acts from me.

However, I did wish harm on this dark persona before me. I did act out in my mind the doing away of it. And perhaps as highly attuned a spirit as Janice's might have felt it. She gave me a withering look as she turned.

It was the same old refrain. We were finished and she wanted to go back to her mother's. Wholeheartedly, as never before, I wanted the same thing. We snarled at each other as she packed her bags.

The little green square was silent, deserted and in darkness as we left. Janice just couldn't resist it.

'YOU GANGSTER CUNT. YOU FUCKING MURDERER,' she roared as she struggled up the path to the car.

I physically cringed. 'For fuck's sake, Janice, turn it in.'

'Bollocks!' she screamed raggedly. 'Everyone should know what you're like.'

It continued in the car in the same vein, but the situation was far more private. I could do something here to protect myself. I didn't want to slap her, but she was completely out of control. If I let her go on she just might grab the wheel again.

'Listen you, ya cunt, just fucking shut up,' I screamed at this stranger sitting beside me. It was enough to give her pause. She lapsed into an angry silence.

At the bottom of Nightingale Lane a completely different voice spoke to me.

'Norman, Norman, please hold me.' The tone was that of a child pleading for a parent's understanding. I turned to look at her and the hard visage of Janice 2 had dissolved and in its place was the soft, mystical, pretty face of this girl I loved so deeply. She sat on the edge of the seat, hugging herself with her arms, looking for all the world like the loneliest soul in all Christendom.

As angry as I still was, I turned into a side street and stopped the car. I turned to face her.

'Janice,' I said firmly but gently, 'you can't just misbehave one minute and expect to be forgiven the next. I never know where I stand with you.'

The implied rebuke instigated another transformation.

'Oooh,' she said like a long, drawn-out sigh, 'I shouldn't have done that. You'll think you've got me.'

I shook my head in weary disbelief. 'Why is it always a war with you, Janice? Why is it always about who's in control and who's not?' I started the car and turned back into Nightingale Lane again.

Several minutes passed and I was intent on negotiating the traffic islands in the road. Suddenly, there was a stinging blow to the side of my face and I felt hands snatch at the wheel.

There was traffic speeding towards me, any crash would be disastrous. An icy sensation gripped my stomach. I twisted the wheel to straighten it again and, steering with one hand, grabbed Janice by the face with the other. I don't know how I did it, but I managed to turn into a side street and stop.

Now I turned on Janice with a vengeance. In truth, fear still gripped me from the near miss, adrenalin still coursed through my veins. I grabbed Janice's face with my other hand and squeezed, forcing her head back against the window. Intimidated now, she shrank in her seat, eyes wide with fear.

'You fucking idiot.' My angry words were a throaty growl. 'I've fucking had it with you. It just gets worse and worse. Just fuck off out of my life. Let me get you back to your mum's.'

She flinched as each angry word struck her like a stone. Suddenly she looked so small and childlike. Whatever I was going to do next, I certainly wasn't going to hit her. I let go of her face.

Quietly, slowly, she opened the door and climbed out of the car.

'Where are you going now?' The words were barely out of my mouth when a shriek cut me off.

'YOU FUCKING CUNT.'

Even though I was still inside the car the sheer volume made me jump. 'HIT A FUCKING WOMAN, WOULD YA?'

Janice ran to the front of the car and tore at a windscreen wiper. She wrenched it backwards and forwards until, suddenly, it came away in her hand. She began to beat at the car with it, all the time screaming at the top of her voice, 'GANGSTER CUNT, FUCKING HIT A WOMAN, EH!'

Alarmed now, I jumped out. This was rapidly becoming a public incident that could be fraught with danger for me. From the things she was shouting, I was sure that it was for the benefit of an audience. Although it was a quiet side street, I was sure there must be some people about.

Sure enough, in a nearby garden two middle-aged women gossiped over a fence. Or rather, they had been. Now their attention was firmly riveted on Janice. I would have to be very careful what I did.

'Janice, Janice.' I held my arms out in supplication. Out of the corner of one eye, I was trying to watch the women. As I got close, she ran at me and began to beat me with the wiper. I managed to take the blows on my arms, but her anger gave her extra strength. Each blow stung. I realised that if she hit me across the face she could well open me up. I had to get the wiper away from her.

Blocking a blow with my arm, I grabbed her wrist and stepped in close. She kicked me and, moving her face close to mine, tried to bite me. Holding her at arm's length, still with one eye on the two women, I tore the wiper from her grasp.

Frustrated now, she attacked me even more fiercely. She kicked at my legs, trying to position herself to hit my groin. Her arms lashed my shoulders and arms. All the time she screamed abuse at the top of her voice, her face twisted into a demonic mask that bore no relationship to her normal face. It was like being beset by a demon.

More residents were coming out of their houses now, windows were opening and people looking out. A small crowd had gathered at the end of the street. I suddenly became aware that it was I who now held the wiper in my hand. Some newcomer might well think that I was attacking Janice with it.

I turned to the crowd and held out my arms in mute appeal. A stinging blow struck me to the side of the face. In her demented state Janice wasn't holding back at all. I hurried to the back of the car, opened the boot, threw the wiper in, then slammed it shut. I would need both hands to defend myself. Janice continued to kick me.

'Get my stuff out of the car, you cunt,' she screamed. 'Get it out.'

'OK, Jan. For fuck's sake calm down,' I pleaded quietly.

'Calm down! Calm down, you gangster cunt,' she roared, 'you haven't seen anything yet.'

I unloaded several bags from the car and placed them on the pavement. All the time, she kicked and struck at me, screaming abuse. One well-aimed blow caught me full on the nose. The pain temporarily stopped me in my tracks.

My reaction was quite involuntary. I grabbed her by the throat and screwed up my face in rage. At the last moment, I remembered the crowd. I sneaked a quick look at them. They were about 20 strong now, and I noticed several black people amongst them. Janice was clearly a mixed-race girl. Equally clearly, I was an older white guy. I would have to be very careful here. The sympathy wouldn't be at all on my side.

Suddenly, Janice broke away from me. With one final baleful glare, she turned and stormed off. She rounded the corner of the street and disappeared from sight.

On my own now, I considered my options. Simple self-preservation and good common sense demanded that I jump in my car and drive off immediately. But that would mean leaving all Janice's belongings at the side of the road. Left unattended, they would soon disappear. Perhaps I should put them back in the car. I wondered where she had gone. A few of the crowd began to drift away, but the majority of them remained, observing me carefully, as if wondering what I would do next.

As I pondered this next move, it suddenly became quite academic. Janice came back around the corner. She seemed calmer now and was quite silent. She moved towards me purposefully, but with no haste. I examined her face, but her expression was non-committal. Her eyes were bright like two shiny black buttons.

She held her arms down by her side in an unthreatening manner and, as she drew close, smiled a charmless smile at me.

But something was not quite right. You don't spend 24 years surviving in prison without developing a sixth sense for danger. Without changing my demeanour in the slightest, I went on full alert.

The attack was sly and quite vicious. She moved her body between us, shielding her right hand from me. Suddenly, her arm arched over as she slashed at me. In my heightened state I saw every detail clearly. In her hand she held a plastic phone card with one corner sharpened. It was an old trick, but very effective. If she caught my face, she would cut me badly.

At the last moment, I tilted my head towards my shoulder and tried to sway out of range. The sharpened plastic caught my head, the top of my ear and my shoulder in its downward arc. I felt a sharp, stinging sensation in my ear.

I grabbed her wrist and wrestled the card from her hand. It fell to the floor. She began to scream and curse again. I released my grip and went to step back.

As I paused, Janice suddenly broke away from me. She tore at the wiper on the back window and wrenched it free. She made as if to hit me with it.

This wiper was fully twice as big as the front one. A blow from it could seriously injure me. I had to get it away from her. Again I moved in close and wrested it from her. She clung to me as I held it up at arm's length, kicking me and trying to reach it.

Suddenly, a police Panda car screeched around the corner and pulled up sharply. The single uniformed officer jumped out. I gaped in amazement. There were very few black officers in the Met. It was just my luck to get one all to myself.

He was very young, barely in his twenties, and of African extraction rather than West Indian. He took one look at the little mixed-race girl struggling with the burly middle-aged man and acted.

'You there. Put that wiper down right now,' he shouted.

I looked at him, then at the wiper I held in my hand. All the while, Janice was trying to position herself to kick me in the groin.

'But I've just taken it off her,' I shouted in reply. The situation had suddenly become extremely serious. Many lifers had been sent back to prison for several years for incidents similar to this.

'Put it down NOW,' the officer shouted, advancing towards me.

I managed to push Janice away for a second, opened the boot and I slung the wiper inside. As I slammed it I took a stinging kick to the ankle. Janice beat at me with her arms.

'Gangster cunt. Murderer,' she screamed.

By now the officer was upon us. As he forced his way between us, I stepped quickly back. This was the first good thing to come out of his arrival. Let him deal with Janice.

She still tried to get at me, aiming kicks and blows around the policeman.

'Now then. Now then,' he sounded surprised as he pushed her away from me.

But Janice was completely out of control. Her sole intent was to injure me. She began to flail at the policeman with her arms and legs. Suddenly, he was having to defend himself, just as I had been.

I didn't feel any satisfaction, but I was relieved that he would now realise exactly what I had been trying to deal with. Namely, that I wasn't the one who was being violent. By now, I had reluctantly come to accept that I would probably end up at the police station over this incident.

Left to his own devices, with no crowd watching, the officer could have handled Janice quite easily. But he had exactly the problem I had had. He couldn't hit her, but tried to parry her blows. As he held her off with one hand, he took his radio out with the other and spoke into it. Then he forced Janice back against the Panda car and held her there.

I waited. The crowd waited. The people hanging out of their windows waited. Janice and the officer waited. Everyone was wondering what would happen next, except perhaps the officer.

I had temporarily forgotten that I was in South London. I had seen the officer call for assistance on his radio. I should have known what would come next.

The sirens were a wall of discordant sound that drew inexorably closer. Into the narrow side street sped two large Transit vans, closely followed by three police cars. All screeched to a halt in the best traditions of the TV cop shows. The policemen didn't so much as get out, rather, the cars and vans disgorged their contents. Suddenly, there were 30 uniformed officers milling about in the street. More cars and vans continued to arrive.

If I had had any doubt previously, I now realised that I was in very serious trouble indeed. With a sinking feeling in my stomach, I imagined myself in a cell in the police station, awaiting my transfer back to prison. Of all the dangerous situations I had come through unscathed, how ironic that a domestic dispute with Janice should get me locked up again. I could see my TV and writing career lying in ruins.

The mob of officers swarmed around the black officer and Janice. I continued to stand over by my car. I watched, but couldn't hear, as he explained to them what had happened. Subconsciously, I noted the fact that every one of the new officers were white. Whatever had been said, a couple began to smirk.

Leaving Janice behind, the black officer came over to me.

'She says that you threatened to kill her,' he said, as if it was the most serious thing he had ever heard. 'Did you threaten to kill her?'

'No I didn't,' I replied earnestly. 'She's my girlfriend. We were just having an argument.'

'Well, she says that you threatened to kill her. I think I'm going to have to charge you,' he announced with an air of finality.

There was a shout from the group of officers with Janice.

'Just a minute,' said the black officer to me. He returned to the group. Within seconds he was back. 'It's OK, she's withdrawn the charges ...' He paused as a second shout came from the group. He returned to them. There was a hurried exchange, then he came back.

'It seems that she wants to press charges.' He didn't seem quite so sure of himself now. 'I'm charging you with threatening to kill your girlfriend. Please get in the van.' He took me by the arm and led me over to a nearby Transit. I climbed inside and sat on a seat.

I could see Janice through the open door, still surrounded by the other officers. Catching her eye, I shouted across, 'Do you really want to do this to me, Janice?' I stared straight at her. She looked away quickly. I saw her say something to one of the officers. He called to the black officer, who hurried across. I saw a heated argument break out.

By now, some of the other officers were laughing openly. They seemed to be enjoying the discomfiture of this rookie black copper. I smiled weakly at them and shook my head in solidarity.

'For fuck's sake, fellas,' I entreated, 'you can see what she's like. She's a nutty little druggie girl.'

A tall, tough-looking officer suddenly beckoned me over. 'Do yourself a favour, mate. Get in your car and fuck off,' he said gruffly.

'Thanks, mate,' I called over my shoulder. I jumped in my car and drove off. In my rear-view mirror I could see the police, the cars, the crowd and Janice's bags, still on the pavement. I felt an overwhelming sense of relief.

I wasn't completely out of trouble, though. What if Janice still made a formal complaint? I would need an independent witness just to be on the safe side.

Roehampton Hospital was on my way home. I called in at the casualty department and explained what had happened to a nurse. I didn't require any treatment for my injuries, but I wanted her to check them and make an official record of them.

I had bled quite heavily from the cut on my ear. The nurse cleaned and dressed it, then examined the bruises on my arms and legs. I was covered with large red and blue welts. She commiserated with me. I wasn't making a meal out of it, but I did feel quite sorry for myself. I wondered what my pals in the nick would think if they could see me now and flushed with embarrassment.

I had decided that this was the final straw as far as Janice and I were concerned. However, I could see her turning up at the Carshalton flat. There could be another serious incident with the police being called. I would have to try to protect myself.

One of the conditions of Janice's bail was that she had to report to the local police station once a week. I drove to the station and told the desk officer that, as of now, I was no longer responsible for Janice and didn't want her to be bailed to my address.

It seemed far from straightforward, though. He made one phone call, then another. Then he disappeared for ten minutes. He returned to tell me that he couldn't do anything. I told him of the earlier incident at Nightingale Lane. Still, he refused.

On the drive to the Carshalton flat, I consoled myself with the thought that Janice wouldn't be a problem for me tonight. I hoped she hadn't been nicked for assaulting the black copper. I wondered how she would get home to her mother's with all her bags. Perhaps the police would drop her off.

It was 11.30pm when I turned into the square where the flat was. I braked abruptly. The flat was ablaze with light, music blared from the open windows. Janice was obviously in residence. But how? My detour to the police station had taken barely 20 minutes. Someone must have driven her straight to the flat.

It must have been the police. Janice hadn't had the money for a taxi. I wondered how she had managed to talk them into that. Anyhow, it was largely irrelevant. What was very relevant was how I was going to deal with Janice should she still be in demon mode. The recent incident had shaken me up quite badly.

Perhaps the police were trying to provoke me. They must have known I was 'active'. And I had said several unflattering things about them on TV and radio. My heavy-duty record couldn't have helped either. Maybe they wanted me on a GBH charge over Janice. Or even, her on one over me. Well, two could play at that game. I would do this by the book.

The desk sergeant was surprised to see me again so soon. He listened attentively as I described finding Janice in my flat. He didn't bat an eyelid when I told him that I was on 'life licence', which only confirmed what I had already suspected. That he knew already. I told him that I couldn't afford any violent confrontation whatsoever and asked for one of his officers to accompany me back to my flat, just to ensure that there wasn't going to be any trouble.

He listened to all this impassively, made a phone call and disappeared for ten minutes again. Then came back and told me that there was nothing he could do. I realised I was on my own.

'Well, just make sure you make a record of my request then,' I demanded. I watched as he wrote it in the occurrence book.

So what did I do now? If I drove over and stayed with my mum, would Janice show up there and make a scene? There was nothing else for it, I would have to confront Janice in our flat.

I parked a couple of streets away and crept into the square like a thief. The flat was now in complete darkness and was as silent as the grave. The image troubled me. Our relationship seemed doomed and I could well see it being the death of one or the other of us. In truth, I had plumbed such depths of despair of late, I felt that I wouldn't care if it was me. There seemed no other way out and, at least, the torment would be over.

I had never been a burglar. I had quickly graduated to bank robbery, cutting out whole areas of intermediate crime. At this moment I regretted I had never developed burgling skills.

I gently pushed the key into the front door lock and turned it slowly. Hardly daring to breathe, I eased it open, then pulled it to behind me. Should I lock it? That might make a noise and, should Janice come at me with a knife (there were several in the kitchen), I might want to flee into the street.

Again I wondered what my prison pals would think if they could see me now. However, it wasn't a joking matter. Janice in demented mode made for a very dangerous adversary indeed. How did you stop someone totally committed to stabbing you, who had no regard for their own safety?

I inched up the stairs, pausing on each step to listen for the slightest sound or movement. There were twenty steps and it took me all of ten minutes to climb them. I peered into every dark shadow to make sure that Janice wasn't poised to leap out on me. Now I stood outside the bedroom door barely daring to breathe.

This was the hard bit. She could be behind the bedroom door. I cringed in anticipation of the blood-curdling scream and the searing pain of the blade.

Taking a step backwards, I took a deep breath and launched myself at the door. I ran into the room and stopped dead. Janice was asleep in our bed.

There was no sense of anti-climax or even a feeling of relief. At any moment she might rise from the covers, knife in hand. I edged closer.

I needn't have worried, she was sound asleep. Whatever she had taken, it had knocked her out completely. I shook her gently for fully 20 seconds. Finally, one eye opened lazily.

'What?' she mumbled.

'Are you all right?' My question was largely superfluous, but I couldn't think of anything else to say.

'Let me sleep,' she mumbled again, closing the eye.

I went downstairs again and closed the front door. I stood by the bed watching her closely as I undressed. She wasn't faking it, she really was sound asleep. I reasoned that, as tired as I was, I would wake before her. There was little danger of her stabbing me to death in the night. The morning would be another matter entirely. With that thought on my mind, I drifted off to sleep.

The morning saw us both very subdued. We both realised how close Janice had come to destroying me. She wasn't apologetic and I wasn't sulking, but we treated each other with exaggerated politeness.

The atmosphere during the drive over to her mother's was frosty. We made small talk, but there was none of the usual passion. That evening, I was due to appear on a TV programme in Bristol. As I kissed her goodbye, I promised to see her the following day.

The Bristol programme would be a good opportunity for me. *Late and Live* was their Friday night flagship programme. It was a current affairs chat show, complete with live audience.

I drove down to Bristol, checked into the hotel where they had made a reservation for me and phoned the studio to confirm the time they would expect me. I had a couple of hours to spare. I would use it to put the events of the previous evening out of my mind and to try to focus on the job in hand.

I arrived at the studio early and was introduced to all the staff. It wasn't easy being a guest murderer, but I was nothing if not insular. It was all a challenge and I was sure I was equal to it.

The studio itself was quite intimidating. The audience of about 150 sat in tiered ranks. Directly in front of them would sit the night's guests.

A largely unknown Liverpool drag comedian called Lily Savage was on first and received a warm reception. I couldn't take too much encouragement from that. The worst Lily had ever done was murder a few jokes.

Next up was some local singing talent and they received rousing cheers. Ken Livingstone and Sir Rhodes Boyson were the guests before me. At opposite ends of the political spectrum, they ensured a lively debate. Again, there was thunderous applause.Now it was my turn.

I had been taken to sit in darkness, on a raised chair directly behind those occupied by Ken Livingstone and Sir Rhodes Boyson. As they vacated their seats, a spot-light came on fixing me firmly in its glare. Serried ranks of curious faces stared down at me.

The presenter introduced me. He made much of *Parkhurst Tales*, which he described as a 'bestseller'. There were no gasps when he told of the murder conviction and 24 years in prison, but I could discern a definite change of mood. He went on to describe me as an expert on Criminal Justice issues, which, in view of his previous remark, sounded quite ironic. He began to ask me questions about current criminal issues.

I was dressed very smartly in dark blue evening suit, with white shirt and dark tie. I had always been quite articulate. My answers were concise and well thought out. In situations like these, appearance was everything. If I had come along dressed like a yobbo and talked like a dimwit, I would have lost before I started.

There were clearly two contrasting shades of opinion. The first held that, providing that I was contrite and had learned from my mistakes, my achievements should be applauded and my opinions given a hearing. The second was wholly condemnatory. It held that a murderer was a murderer and could never be forgiven. Anything I achieved should receive no praise whatsoever. My opinion was of no consequence and I shouldn't be given a platform to air it.

'It sounds like you've learned your lesson,' said a man at the back. 'So long as you're trying to do good, you've got my blessing.'

'I'm not a bad person,' said an elderly Welsh lady at the front, 'but

I'd take you out and hang you personally.'

The argument raged back and forth, supporters and detractors swapping insults across the studio.

'Just a minute,' my voice lanced into the hubbub. The audience fell silent. 'Just tell me something. When this Home Secretary speaks about prison conditions, do you believe him?' I demanded of no one in particular.

'No,' answered several disembodied voices.

'When the Prison Officers' Association speaks about prison conditions, do you believe them?'

Again the voices answered, 'No.'

'And when the *Sun* newspaper tells you about prison conditions, do you believe it?'

This time there was a chorus of noes.

I paused. 'Well, then,' I said to the pregnant hush, 'don't you think it's about time you listened to someone who's actually been there? Someone like me.'

For a brief second there was silence. Suddenly there was a loud chorus of 'Yes' followed by a smattering of applause. The applause grew and grew until it seemed that most of the audience was applauding. It was a turning point. After that, I could hardly do any wrong.

Afterwards, with the cameras off, some of the audience came down to meet me. Among them was the elderly Welsh lady. In view of her earlier remark, I kept a wary eye on her. Suddenly, she pushed through the throng.

'Do you feel remorse?' she demanded of me apocalyptically.

'Every day of my life,' I replied seamlessly, looking her straight in the eye.

'Well, God bless you, then,' she smiled and reached to shake my hand.

The producer was ecstatic.

'You were great,' she enthused. 'You could be the next McVicar.'

This was something of a backhanded compliment for me. Many criminals of my acquaintance did not like him. I smiled and let it pass.

As I lay in my hotel bed, I mused on the thought that I could handle a hostile TV audience with comparative ease, yet a relationship with my diminutive, young girlfriend was beyond me. Perhaps I should be thankful that there was only one Janice. An audience-full would be a daunting prospect indeed.

✳　✳　✳

I took my time driving back the following day. I was in no hurry to meet Janice again. I tried to rationalise this ridiculous situation I had got myself into, but it was beyond rationality. Perhaps it had everything to do with the 24 years I had just spent in jail. I had plumbed such depths of loneliness, become so estranged from the rest of the human race, maybe I desperately needed another spirit to cling to. I knew that when I lay in bed with her and held her close, it all became worthwhile. I hated myself for such weakness, because in virtually every other way I was so strong.

I picked Janice up from her mother's early on Saturday evening. It was already dark and a chill wind swept the streets of North London. I tried to muster some enthusiasm for a Saturday night out on the town with my girl.

'What we doing?' demanded Janice as we drove.

What indeed! There were several things going on that night, events in clubs, parties, which involved friends of mine. I would have been more than welcome, but not Janice. I could have taken her, but the initial bad atmosphere would soon have escalated into something more substantial. Janice could cause an outrage with minimal provocation.

'I've got some Es,' I offered, 'but it's a bit early yet. Maybe we should go to the pictures first.'

Janice wrinkled her nose in mild disapproval.

'Well have you got a better idea?' I asked pleasantly.

'Let's take the Es first,' she suggested.

'What, then go to the pictures?' I sounded doubtful.

'Yeah,' she nodded as if trying to convince herself.

I wasn't in a mood to argue. I couldn't handle another traumatic confrontation. It would be nice just to have a pleasant night out for once with no dramas. I would agree to anything within reason.

We took the Es and went to the cinema near Islington Green. *Interview with the Vampire* was showing. It was hardly suitable for an E buzz, but neither was sitting in a cinema anyway. With an E you needed movement and music.

The buzz was already starting as we settled into our seats, drinks and sweets in our laps. I took a deep breath as my nostrils flared, I experienced the first feelings of elation. But it jarred with the tone of the film. Already some poor soul was being lured to an inevitable death at the hands of a vampire. I mused on the values of a culture that could be entertained by such a death, even if the vampire was Tom Cruise.

Janice must have been experiencing similar feelings, although perhaps not in so deeply philosophical a vein. She suddenly rose to her feet and started to leave. I stood and followed her. The brightness of the foyer seemed positively dazzling after the gloom inside.

I didn't make an issue of the fact that she had left without even consulting me. Only a fragile peace existed between us and I didn't want to be left alone, distressed and angry in the emotional turmoil of an E buzz.

'Where now?' I asked deadpan.

'I don't know,' Janice countered. In the event, we settled for a drink. Neither of us were drinkers or even pub people, but we had a couple of hours to kill. A meal was out, the E having supressed our appetite for food.

It was still a bit early, but at 10.00pm we drove over to Camden. The Black Cap was a gay pub that stood in the main High Street. Its disco bar was frequented by an extremely varied clientele. Men danced with men, women with women, there were also straight couples, too. There were people of all ages, cultures and creeds. Dress was casual and never pretentious. The music was wicked, the dancing uninhibited. I liked its anonymity. No one took the slightest notice of the middle-aged white guy dancing with the little mixed-race girl.

We took another E each, danced and stopped occasionally to sip our soft drinks. Janice was enjoying herself. Her face was wet with sweat and she smiled constantly. When resting, she cuddled up close to me.

We left at about 2.00am and drove the short distance to Ian's. This was usually a busy time for the 'street people', with Ian's flat a hive of activity. I had some reservations about whether the surroundings would invoke the 'crack beast' in Janice, but the euphoria of the E overrode my fears.

Ian's flat was in darkness; we guessed he was already in bed. To wake him would have initiated a mission to find an illicit off-licence to buy him cans of beer. We crept away and drove home.

We lay in bed watching a late-night movie, eating sweets and sipping soft drinks. With Janice snuggled up next to me it was great fun. I realised that I had missed out on so much that others took for granted. For 24 years I had been locked in on my own at 9.00pm; by 10.00pm I was usually asleep. There was something delightfully illicit about staying up late and watching a movie, and to do it with my girlfriend lying by my side was Nirvana indeed.

We rose late on Sunday afternoon and lazed about for a couple of hours. Then we drove over to Ian's, stopping briefly at Janice's mum's. Later, we were due to see Tom.

There had been a drastic turn in his fortunes of late and decidedly for the worse. It had been inevitable really. Crime was a serious business. To keep getting off your face all the time could only lead to disaster.

There had been a botched operation to smuggle Es from Holland. It was wholly Tom's work, I only heard about it after it had gone wrong. The courier, a mutual friend of ours, had been nicked on a coach returning with 40,000 Es. Somebody whom Tom had confided in was a police informer, so it had to be assumed that Tom's name had been mentioned, too.

To add insult to injury, he had just fallen out with a close friend who had been virtually supporting him. Tom excelled in his role as court jester, organiser of wild parties and procurer of sexy girls. Danny fancied himself as something of a playboy and liked to have Tom around to supplement his social circle. Tom couldn't help but take the piss though. At times his mercenary nature became painfully apparent. Then so-called friends would turn on him.

Danny was the brother of my pal Boy-Boy. Whilst being nowhere near as dangerous, he was still quite capable of extreme violence. Smarting from one of Tom's latest liberties, he put out a £1,000 reward for anyone who would tell him where Tom was. Such was the nature of Tom's circle, that former friends were now looking for him to turn him in to Danny for the reward.

At that time, Tom was living in a run-down council flat in a tower block just off Camden High Street. When he did venture out, he did his best to disguise himself with a baseball cap pulled down tightly around his ears. He had grown the beginnings of a scruffy beard. However, he had Elaine, his latest girlfriend with him, which largely defeated the object of the exercise. Elaine was a statuesque blonde with the sort of striking good looks that inevitably drew admiring stares. And as she revelled in the attention, there was no chance of her dressing down just for Tom.

I found it all quite amusing. Tom's principles weren't such that he would have been considered an honourable man by the 'chaps' and I had no strong personal ties to him. However, we were collaborating on a project involving his machine and a proposed electronic transfer of funds. Enlightened self-interest demanded that I did something.

One word to Boy-Boy was enough to get Danny off Tom's back. Perhaps by way of gratitude, Janice was now no longer *persona non grata*. Ergo our impending visit to Tom and Elaine.

Janice wasn't known for caring about creating a good impression, so she couldn't have felt under any pressure. However, somewhere between her mum's and Tom's flat, she must have taken a large dose of something. Suddenly, she was completely off her face; unsteady on her feet, paranoid, unpredictable and hyperactive.

Tom opened the door and was nearly bowled off his feet as she swept into the flat like 'Hurricane Janice'. Tom explained, *sotto voce*, that Elaine wasn't feeling very well and was lying down. This didn't deter Janice in the slightest.

'I'll sort her out,' she announced and stormed into the bedroom, sat herself on the edge of the bed and earnestly engaged Elaine in conversation.

Tom looked at me in an unspoken appeal for help. It was beyond me. I just shrugged and we both went into the lounge, leaving the girls to it.

It was a good 20 minutes before Janice joined us. The three of us talked for a while and then Tom got up to go and see how Elaine was. When he returned he motioned me into the kitchen. Usually the master of every situation, now he struggled for words, embarrassment plain on his face.

'Look, Norm, I don't want to cause any trouble,' he whispered, 'but Elaine says that Janice has just stolen some of her clothes.'

For a second I just closed my eyes and stood there, saying nothing. 'How does Elaine know?' I asked finally.

'She watched her do it,' he replied, incredulity in his voice. 'Janice just went to a drawer in the wardrobe and helped herself to some of Elaine's best underwear. She's very upset.'

What could I say? It would be hard to imagine a greater insult to one's hosts than one's girlfriend stealing from their home. Did Janice do it deliberately to embarrass me, I wondered? Perhaps, by isolating me from everyone else, she hoped to keep me for herself. There didn't seem to be any other logical explanation. However, logic played little part in Janice's thinking. Especially when Janice 2 was in control.

I must have looked quite deflated and not a little embarrassed. Tom put one hand on my arm.

'Don't worry about it, Norm. It's not really important. But Elaine would like her clothes back if you could get them for her.'

Janice sat there so out of it that she was unaware of our conversation. Gently, I brought her out of her reverie. I didn't want a scene in the flat. However, underneath I was seething. It started in the lift.

'Have you taken some of Elaine's clothes?' I demanded with no preliminaries whatsoever.

'No, I fucking haven't,' replied Janice forcefully.

'Well, Elaine says you have,' I continued.

'She's a fucking liar. Just because she's a blonde bimbo. I suppose you fucking fancy her.'

This complete *non sequitur* indicated a degree of desperation. I feared the worst.

'Well, when we get downstairs then, we'll have a look in your bag then, won't we?'

The rest of the descent passed in silence.

There were some children playing in the lobby as we reached the ground floor. I decided to postpone the search until we reached the car.

'Take me home to my mum's,' demanded Janice as I unlocked the car doors.

The 20-minute journey passed in complete silence.

'I'm still looking in your bag,' I announced as we pulled up outside her mum's.

'Trust you to take her word,' shouted Janice. 'Just because she's a white bird, eh?'

I looked at her sharply. 'You've got no cause to say that, Janice. Your colour has never made the slightest difference to me. I've always loved you just as you are. It's a liberty that you should say that.'

'Well, she's a white bird.'

'That's got nothing to do with it.' I picked up her bag. Tom had told me that the underwear was red, with white frilly lace edging. Definitely Elaine, but not at all Janice. Sure enough, it was at the bottom of the bag. I took it out.

As soon as she saw it, Janice started screaming abuse.

'You fucking cunt,' she roared. Suddenly, she punched me full in the face and made to get out of the car. In pain and rage, I leaned across and pushed her. She stumbled and fell to the pavement. I tossed her bag out after her.

'Cunt, fucking cunt,' screamed Janice. She began to kick the side of the car. The engine was still running. I put it into gear quickly and pulled away. A torrent of abuse helped me on my way.

I told myself that that was definitely it. We just couldn't go on like this. However much it hurt me, I would have to stay away from her. In time, I'd get over it.

Suddenly, my phone rang. 'Norman, come back here this minute,' the angry voice demanded.

'Fuck off, Janice,' I shouted at the phone and rang off. Seconds later it rang again.

'Norman, please come back,' her voice was pleading now.

But I was still raging. 'Just fuck off my phone, Janice,' I roared and switched the phone off.

Fully expecting her to come after me, I drove to the Carshalton flat. I'd rather she created a scene there than at my mother's. Further, if she rang my mother's, she would tell her I wasn't there. With my mobile switched off, she wouldn't be able to contact me at Carshalton.

I undressed quickly and switched off the light. If she did arrive perhaps I could pretend I wasn't in. It was a vain hope, but it was all I could think of in the circumstances. I lay there, savouring the silence of the surroundings. At some stage, I must have fallen asleep.

Monday morning, I started out as I meant to carry on under my new régime sans Janice. I went to the gym early, then drove to my mother's for breakfast. By 9.15am I was off in the car, visiting various friends, following up 'clues'.

I tried not to think about Janice, what she was doing, where she might be. I regularly examined my feelings for her, dreading the onset of the deep yearning I felt must inevitably come. Today, however, I really did feel different. Rationality dictated that I must end this relationship that was bringing us both such pain and putting me in so much danger. And, for the moment, rationality ruled, untrammelled by the vagaries of unpredictable emotion. It was early days yet, though.

At about 5.00pm, I called in at my publishers to deliver a synopsis of my next book. I had already written the 400-page manuscript of *The Goldfish Bowl* while at Ford. Under my new régime, I would start to edit it, something I could never find the time to do while around Janice.

Ironically, the publisher's offices were in a seedy side street near King's Cross. As I swept past the junction where I had seen Janice before, I stared straight ahead.

I spent a couple of hours with an old friend in the East End, then drove home to my mother's, arriving just before 9.00pm. I got out *The Goldfish Bowl* manuscript and sat down at my word-processor. Soon I was walking the landings of Kingston Prison again and renewing acquaintanceships with old comrades. Still I felt positive and strong, with no desire to phone Janice or seek her out.

At about 11.00pm, my mother went to bed. I wished her goodnight absentmindedly, still deeply engrossed in my work. I would continue as long as I could concentrate. It gave me something to focus on and was an important part of my new future.

Whereas *Parkhurst Tales* had been short stories, *The Goldfish Bowl* was a full-length story. If I was to establish a reputation as a writer, this would be the book to do it. In my heart, this was still my most important goal. If I was to make anything of myself, to turn all the years of failure into something like success, it would only be through my writing. I had lost sight of that since I had been with Janice.

I worked on, engrossed, and lost all track of time, the silence of the night interrupted only by the quiet 'clack' of the word-processor keys.

Suddenly, I was aware of a strange sensation. It was a cold, uneasy feeling, not so much in the back of my neck, but rather in the back of my mind. A 'spooky' sensation, as if something was behind me.

I consciously ignored it, refused to acknowledge it. I was a creature of the real, corporeal world and master of any situation I had ever encountered. I had never found the slightest evidence of a spirit world entering this world and dismissed it out of hand. It would be a weakness to turn and look behind me. Especially as I was sure that nothing was there.

I carried on working, but the sensation was now very strong. It bore into the back of my consciousness so coldly, so intrusively that I could hardly resist it. Barely controlling a shudder, I spun in my seat and looked behind me. The room was empty, there was nothing there. Slightly embarrassed, I continued to work.

Again, I lost track of time. I 'clacked' away at the keys as the night-time silence spun out seamlessly.

Suddenly, a loud buzzing sound rent the air. The entry-phone screeched its raspberry rasp, announcing the arrival of a visitor downstairs. I jumped to my feet and, as I ran into the hall, glanced quickly at my watch. It was just after 2.00am. Who could it be at this time in the morning?

'Janice', the word I had been avoiding all day leaped into my consciousness. It could only be Janice.

The buzzer was so loud and insistent, I feared it would wake my mother and, perhaps, the neighbours. Frantically, I snatched the phone off its mounting and fumbled at the controls. I was still unfamiliar with its workings, not knowing which was the 'entry' button and which was the 'speak'. I pressed both repeatedly and heard a metallic 'click'. I went to stand by the front door, face up close to it, peering through the tiny spy-hole.

I heard the lift doors open. Through the fish-eye of the spy-hole two elongated, black figures hove into view. Policemen. Two policemen. My heart skipped a beat. What did they want at 2.00am? It must be serious. All thoughts of Janice disappeared as concerns for personal survival took over.

I ran back into the lounge to fetch the front door keys. The bell rang once as I pulled the door open. Two tall, young coppers stood in the doorway, hats in their hands.

'Excuse me,' said the one with the short cropped, blond hair, 'are you Norman Harris?'

My mind was racing ahead of his words.

'No, I'm Norman Parker, Janice Harris is my girlfriend.'

The slip was almost Freudian. In my heart I must have felt that Janice and I were still together, would always be together.

'May we come in?' he continued.

I led the way into the lounge, the second copper closing the front door behind him. I tried to assess their manner, their attitude. It didn't seem particularly threatening or oppressive. However, my pulse was still racing.

'So you know a Miss Janice Harris?' The blond copper was still doing all the talking.

'Yes, as I said, she's my girlfriend.'

So this was about Janice. Immediate fears for my personal safety began to subside. They were instantly replaced by concerns for Janice.

'I'm afraid there's been an accident.' The young copper's expression was more serious now.

My mind processed his words frantically, spun them around and analysed them for every nuance of meaning. 'Janice'. 'An Accident'. An image sprung up of Janice crossing the road in her own inimitable fashion, virtually oblivious to oncoming traffic as if positively daring them not to stop for her. A thousand times I had warned her to be more careful. She had always dismissed my caution out of hand, a reflection of how self-destructive she could be.

But this couldn't be serious. She had just been knocked over and was now lying in a hospital somewhere with broken bones. We were so close, so mystically, spiritually close, that if anything really serious had happened I would surely have 'felt' it.

'There has been an accident at a railway station. I'm afraid Janice is dead,' the blond policeman announced with finality.

A blinding sheet of pure white light passed before my eyes. Quite involuntarily I plunged my face into my hands and spun across the room.

'Noooo ...' My cry was a long, tormented, drawn-out moan.

I couldn't remember the last time I had cried, it had been so long ago. Certainly, I had never shed a tear in jail. For all the things that had been done to me, for all the pain, rage and frustration I had suffered, I would never have shown such weakness. I had prided myself on the fact that there was nothing the 'screws' could do to make me cry, I was beyond tears.

They came in floods now. I fell sideways into an armchair and wept uncontrollably. Janice, my Janice, dead and gone. It was too cruel. Life that had been so cruel to me already, that had taken from me everything I had ever loved, had now taken the one spirit that could have saved me. I couldn't comprehend it. I wouldn't comprehend it.

The blond copper moved to console me, placing a hand on my shoulder.

'Where ... where did it happen?' I managed to stammer through my tears.

He avoided my question. 'The facts aren't entirely clear yet. We're still making enquiries. What we would like you to do, though, is to come with us and break the news to Janice's mother.'

In my distressed state, the illogical nature of his request escaped me.

'I must put some shoes and a jacket on first,' I replied, my mind grasping at this diversion as a welcome, if temporary, respite from the awful reality of life without Janice. As long as I was in motion, doing something, I wouldn't have time to think about it. Further, to see Mrs Harris would bring me spiritually closer to Janice. There was no other way I could be close to her now.

Suddenly, the door to the lounge swung open and my mother shuffled in. She looked first at the policemen and then at me through shocked, sleep-dazed eyes.

'What's going on?' Her voice was thin and reedy and filled with concern.

'Oh, Mum ... Mum,' I cried as I rushed towards her. 'Janice is dead, she's dead, killed in a train accident.'

Her face, already a waxy pallor, blanched deeper as her mouth fell open with shock. Her hand flew to her mouth as she mouthed a wordless, 'Oh.'

'I've got to go over to North London to tell Mrs Harris.' My words were interspersed with sobs, as I struggled to pull my jacket on.

She held out her hand as if to question me more, but I wouldn't be delayed.

'I'll see you when I get back,' I called over my shoulder, the two coppers following in my wake.

Their patrol car was downstairs in the car park. I climbed in the back and we set off. As we passed through the now deserted streets of the familiar route to North London, old memories of similar journeys with Janice flooded back. I cried bitterly. In truth, I hadn't stopped since first being told the news. Now new paroxysms of grief wracked my body.

I was aware of the coppers observing me curiously in the rear-view mirror, but I was beyond caring. Their opinion, or anyone else's, was completely irrelevant to me. Had I been in full view of everyone who had ever known me, I still couldn't have controlled myself.

The journey began to take on a dream-like quality now, separate scenes appearing before my eyes as if unconnected. I was at the entrance to Janice's mother's block. I was ringing the door to her flat. I was in the hallway with Mrs Harris before me, Luke standing off to one side, the policemen behind me. All the while I still cried.

Mrs Harris seemed strangely unmoved. As I blurted out that Janice was dead, killed in a train crash, she stood there, her face grim, but largely impassive. Luke seemed similarly impassive. As distressed as I was, I was aware that it was a bizarre performance. As if the other actors in the piece were refusing to play their roles. Perhaps Mrs Harris was still cold with me following Janice telling her of my murder conviction. Maybe she thought that, somehow, this outcome was all my fault.

There was an awkward silence as the five of us stood there in the hallway. I don't remember saying goodnight. Then we were back in the patrol car, on the return journey to Wimbledon.

It was just after 5.00am as the two coppers dropped me off at my mum's flat. She had gone back to bed and I decided not to disturb her. I was dead tired myself, emotionally and physically exhausted. I desperately needed a couple of hours' sleep.

My mum woke me when she got up at 9.00am. As I swam up to consciousness, a myriad images of the night before assailed me. I examined them carefully to make sure they were real. The deep, aching emptiness inside me bore testimony to their substance.

In that twilight world of consciousness, before my emotions had fully kicked in, I examined my feelings. Gone was the incredible pressure of a doomed relationship. Gone was the terrible yearning for Janice, the wanting to be with her. Gone were the feelings of self-destructiveness. A fledgling feeling of guilt flitted through my mind as I came to the realisation that there was a positive side to what had happened, that I was free of Janice and the servitude that loving her entailed.

The nascent feeling existed but for a micro-second, evaporating in the face of the more awful reality. I was alone again. Like a surging, icy-black tide, the loneliness washed over me, overwhelmed me. Deeper than 24 years of solitude, more acute than the isolation of solitary confinement, I would find no peace now, no contentment, this side of the grave. Unable to resist it, I cried again.

As I came more fully awake, another thought evolved. Objectively, I examined the proposition. It was God's punishment on me. This was my comeuppance for that evil deed I had committed 24 years ago. With exquisite skill and blinding insight, he had designed a punishment that would humble a man so arrogant in his infinite strength and his unlimited ability to survive almost anything.

He had struck at my Achilles heel, the one area where I was vulnerable, my loneliness. He had given me a soul-mate, someone who had rolled back the feeling of isolation to lead me back into the human race again. Now she was gone. A soundless scream echoed through my soul. I was in my castle again, drawbridge raised, standing on the ramparts, observing that great body of the human race that, once more, I was no longer a part of.

Suddenly, I felt incredibly old. Like some 1,000-year-old spirit who roamed the earth, taking no solace from life, yet not ready for death. I must complete my mission, whatever that might be. I felt that I still had something to do, then perhaps I could rest. In the meantime I could only face the future with resignation.

I became aware that my mother was sitting in a chair, regarding me. Her face still had that waxy quality I had noticed earlier. Her hair was wild and uncombed. She seemed smaller, shrunken even. She had visibly aged. I became concerned.

'Are you OK?' I asked.

'What happened last night?' she queried weakly as she shook slightly.

I started to tell her what the police had told me about the accident.

'No, no,' she interrupted impatiently. 'What happened when you got to Mrs Harris's?'

I described what had happened, and she listened intently.

'Now you listen to me,' she leaned forward to give greater emphasis to her words. 'Mrs Harris was expecting you.' She waved me silent as I made to interrupt. 'Just after you left, Mrs Harris phoned. She said the police had been to tell her about Janice. She wanted to warn you that they were on their way over to see you.'

I was still too upset to be stunned by anything, but it did make me pause. So what had been the intent of that charade of taking me over to tell Mrs Harris something she already knew?

It was Norman the Murderer again. That could be the only explanation. The police had known about my previous convictions and put two and two together to get five. I was suspected of involvement in Janice's death.

In all my pain, I was beyond anger or even resentment. Perhaps this, too, was part of my punishment. All the more ironic in that I had saved Janice's life on several occasions, loved her with a passion and was incapable of harming her. Mentally, I shrugged it off.

Mum was talking again, but I was only half-listening. I caught something about Janice being in her room last night. 'What are you saying?' I demanded, my attention fully on her.

Mum was shaking visibly now, as silent tears ran down her face. I took her hand to calm her. 'OK, love, OK, just take it easy,' I consoled.

My mother had never been over-religious or superstitious. She said her prayers every night, but had always been quite pragmatic and down-to-earth. Although 84 now, her mind was still clear and sharp. She had never imagined anything before. The tale she told, however, was unbelievable. I sat transfixed, in utter silence, until she was done.

'I saw Janice in my room last night,' she began. 'I was just getting ready for bed, sitting on the side of the bed about to get in. Suddenly, I couldn't move a muscle and felt icy cold. At first, I thought I was having a heart-attack. I tried to call out to you, but I couldn't.' Her voice broke as the trauma of the memory was upon her again.

'OK, love, OK,' I comforted.

She paused to control herself. 'Then, I managed to move my fingers, then my hands. I got into bed. As soon as I lay down, it seemed like I was 6ft above the bed in some kind of cloud, looking down on myself. It frightened the life out of me, I can tell you.' Her shoulders shook again and she wiped her eyes before continuing.

'Suddenly, Janice was beside me, floating in the cloud. I've never seen her look so well. Her hair was nice, she was smiling happily. I never saw her look so happy before. She took me by the hand and asked me to come with her. We were flying over fields and streams. Suddenly, I remembered you.' She paused again and took a sip of the tea she had beside her.

'I said, "I've got to go back and look after the boy," ' she continued. ' "There's some money in the flower pot he doesn't know about." Janice was annoyed. "You worry too much about him," she said, "but if you want to go back, go back then." Then, she was gone and I was back lying in my bed again, paralysed with fear. I lay there, unable to move, until I heard the noise of you and the police.'

I felt an icy chill run right down my spine and I suppressed a shiver. As much as I didn't believe in that sort of thing, there was an uncanny ring of truth to my mother's tale. For certain, she believed it and I had never known her to lie, fantasise or invent things before.

Suddenly, I remembered the strange sensation I had experienced myself, the feeling that there was something behind me as I worked at my word processor. Now I thought more carefully about it, there was definitely something more than cold, evil even, about it.

I questioned my mother carefully. I made her go over her story again and again. Each time she repeated every detail the same way as before.

I was a rational man, a child of the scientific age. Mine had been the first generation to study physics and chemistry at school. There was a clearly established methodology to research, to the determining of facts. Yet my mother was a sane and rational person, was I to dismiss her testimony out of hand just because it didn't fit neatly within the parameters of what science accepted as proven fact?

And what of my own experience? The more I examined it, the clearer was my memory of an evil presence. Perhaps whatever had manifested itself in my mother's room had also come next door to me.

There was a further consideration. This wasn't just some academic debate about the existence or otherwise of the spiritual world. Whatever my mother had experienced, the shock had nearly killed her. She sat before me pale and shaking, a shadow of her former self. Overnight, she had aged ten years. We would have to be very careful that some further shock didn't finish her off competely.

And what of myself? If there had been a visitation by this baleful spirit, what had been its true intent? It could only be some manifestation of Janice 2, the dark side of the Janice I loved so dearly. I was sure the latter had loved me in return and would never have done anything to harm me.

Yet this manifestation had nearly frightened my mother to death. Where was it taking her when it led her by the hand through the clouds? What would have happened if she hadn't remembered me and decided to return? Would I have awoken in the morning to find that I had lost my girlfriend and my mother on the same day?

I felt suddenly afraid. Within the space of 24 hours my world had changed completely. The parameters of reality had been pushed back so that now spirits, demons and ghosts could walk in places formerly reserved for the corporeal. I had never feared anything previously, because I had no fear of death itself. My self-destructiveness had been firmly founded on my unhappiness. But all previous threats had been from living, corporeal enemies. How did one fight a spirit?

I comforted my mother as best I could, but there was something I had to do. My grief was too strong for me just to sit in one place. I had to find out the full circumstances of Janice's death. I had to go to the place where she died. I had to see her body. This was the only way I could think of to get close to her. Previously, there was always somewhere I could go to find her. Where do you go to find someone when they have entered the spirit world?

I phoned Mrs Harris. She had already left for work, Luke answered the phone. We both wanted to know more, the police had told him very little, too. He mentioned that the place Janice had died was called Torrington. We decided that we should go there.

I drove over and picked him up. He was clearly distressed over Janice's death; his eyes were red-rimmed from crying. His grief was a catalyst for mine. Soon I was sobbing again. We made for a strange pair as we drove in search of Torrington, first one of us breaking down, then the other.

I questioned him about what he knew. It transpired he knew little more than I did. The British Transport Police, for that is who the policemen were, had been very vague. His mother had told him of seeing Janice late Sunday evening, but there was little more. I resolved to ask her when next we met.

Torrington was little more than a village that lay to the north of London, just the other side of Harlow. It was firmly in the commuter belt with regular, fast trains connecting it to the metropolis. We stopped in the High Street to buy flowers. The young shop assistant seemed embarrassed by our tear-stained faces.

In the bright sunlight of late morning, Torrington Station looked peaceful and idyllic. A narrow lane wound its way down to a level crossing and passed right through. A country pub stood close by, surrounded on all sides by rolling fields. Old barges gently wallowed at their moorings in a slow-moving stream.

If this was the last place that Janice had seen while alive, then at least she had died in beautiful surroundings. If her spirit now wandered the fields and hedgerows of Torrington, it was far better than to be forever doomed to haunt the mean streets of her native North London. That was little consolation to me, though.

The station itself was identical to hundreds of other suburban stations. Two platforms, bare except for ticket vending machines, sloped at one end towards the crossing, at the other into wild countryside. The single ticket office stood shuttered and deserted. A sole traveller sat in a glass shelter.

We wandered the length of both platforms, looking for some evidence of the accident. Nothing seemed untoward. We descended to the crossing, again nothing seemed out of place. But it was peaceful here, away from the concrete and steel of the station itself. This would be a fitting place to place our flowers.

Luke and I stood in silence, our heads bowed, two small heaps of blooms at our feet. For a short while, we were both lost to this world as we walked again with Janice in our memories. Perhaps Luke recalled earlier times, before his sister had become enslaved to heroin. I had only known this latter sister, but still, I recalled the happy times.

The moment passed, we had paid our respects and couldn't stand here for ever. Even so, my leaving smacked of betrayal, as if I was deserting her. For a long while we drove in silence. It was strangely comforting being close to Luke, as if I was also close to Janice.

Suddenly, my reverie was broken as my phone rang. It was a young woman's voice, soft, with the slightest trace of a West Country accent. She introduced herself as Anna and said she was a contributing writer for a parole magazine. She had seen me on the *Late and Live* programme and had got my number from the producer. She wondered if she could interview me for the magazine.

I hadn't given up on my media career, but my world was too dark and pain-filled at the moment to think about anything except Janice. In truth, I was surviving from minute to minute. Anna was persistent, though. More than that, she was downright suggestive. Unless I was completely mistaken, she was looking for more than just an interview.

I still considered myself to be bound to Janice. To contemplate another liaison so soon would be a betrayal of our love for each other, though, Heaven knows, I could have done with the company just to drive the loneliness away. I put her off, telling her to phone me later in the week.

Luke had the address of the British Transport Police at Whitechapel, so our mission wasn't over yet. Perhaps they would have more information for us. I headed towards the East End.

The Transport Police seemed very guarded. A harassed-looking middle-aged man in civilian clothes took us into an interview room. His sad face with its flabby jowls and the large paunch that hung out the front of his trousers seemed more in keeping with some backroom storeman than a policeman, but he was probably more the former than the latter. This was the place where the belongings of victims of accidents ended up.

He told us that Torrington Station had been closed for several hours after the accident and that enquiries were still continuing. At that moment, all he could tell us was that Janice was struck by the 5.10pm through train to Bishops Stortford and died instantly. He showed us a large, clear plastic bag containing her belongings, but said that he would have to keep them until after the inquest.

Suddenly, from inside a locked drawer, he produced a smaller, clear-plastic bag. Inside were some sheets of paper, an exercise book and a smaller, red book that I instantly recognised. It was Janice's address book.

'We haven't reached any definite conclusions yet,' said the sad-faced man, 'but these could possibly be suicide notes. They were found in her bag.'

He handed me the three sheets of paper. With Luke looking over my shoulder, I spread them out on the table in front of me.

The writing, in pencil, was sprawled out, child-like, across the exercise book-size pages. I recognised Janice's writing, but it was untidy even by her standards. I guessed that she must have been very off her face when she had written it.

The first was addressed to Luke. It was short, just six lines, and was both rambling and maudlin. It assured him that she loved him and regretted that she hadn't been able to say goodbye. In sum, its meaning was ambiguous.

'Dear Mark, little brother that I love so much,' began the second, 'I've tried to survive out here, I really fucking have, but I can't.'

She went on to tell of how she had tried to come off the drugs which she knew were killing her, but had failed. She asked him to tell their mother she loved her and to look after her.

'Got to go, Love Janice,' she signed off.

The writing was barely decipherable and the tears that wet my eyes made it all the more difficult, but the meaning was clear. Janice was saying a final goodbye. I moved on to the third note.

'My Dearest Darling,' it began and my heart leapt in my chest as a coldness filled my stomach. Who was this addressed to? Janice had never used such emotional, gushing words to me. Why hadn't it begun, 'Dear Norman' with a name like the two other notes? Her life with me had been filled with so many lies, so much subterfuge, was I to be betrayed by Janice even in death? Was this a farewell note to some other boyfriend whom I had been unaware of, the one she had truly loved?

I tried to prepare myself, to steel myself for this final irony. It had all been a lie. She had never loved me, only used me. I had been a 'punter' all along. My periods of happiness with her had been an illusion, or rather self-delusion. I cursed this life of utter, unrelenting misery that I had been forced to bear.

Nervous now, I followed the words on the page, ever more conscious of Luke reading next to me. How humiliating, that he should witness this final embarrassment. Not only no final word for me, but instead a lover's farewell to her true love. I read the words again. 'My Dearest Darling, sorry I had to leave without saying goodbye. We shared some good times together. I tried to change for you, but I just couldn't. I will love you for ever. Bye now, Janice.'

My mind was a whirlpool of conflicting emotions. If this note was to me, why hadn't she put my name on it. The other two notes had been addressed to someone. As I wrestled with the conundrum, I was aware of the sad-faced man speaking again.

'There are a couple of unfinished notes in the exercise book, copies of these, we think,' he said, handing me the yellow school book. Sure enough, amongst pages of doodles and childish drawings there were badly scrawled copies of the notes to Luke and Mark, but nothing else.

The mystery consumed me now as an obsession. I must find out who the third note was meant for. I reached for Janice's red-covered address book.

'Can I make a note of some of these numbers, I want to inform her friends of what has happened?' I asked.

'Sad Face' nodded approval. I quickly copied the 20 or so names and numbers on to a sheet of paper he gave me, before he changed his mind.

I finished and bent down to look at the large plastic bag on the floor.

Staring through the plastic, I recognised the familiar handbag that she had rummaged in so often, looking for the latest thing she had misplaced. I recalled my chastising her that she should be more careful and put things in their proper place. So frustrating then, but what would I give to be able to do the same now?

'Sad Face' reminded us that we could have all of Janice's things after the inquest and showed us to the door. As I stood blinking in the bright sunlight, I wondered what I would do next. If only I could keep in motion, be on some sort of quest in search of Janice, I could keep the despair at bay.

I drove Luke to his mother's and stood for a while in Janice's room. It was just too painful, though, to be so close to her things, in so familiar a place, yet to be so far away from her. 'Little girl, little girl,' I moaned and cried again. I reflected that, for a supposed tough guy, tears were becoming a habit with me.

I heard the street door open and the familiar sound of Mrs Harris's voice. I came out of Janice's room to meet her in the hall. If she was surprised to see me, she hid it well. It occurred to me that she was hiding all her feelings well. She looked sad and stressed, but far less emotional than either Luke or myself.

She led me into the lounge and questioned me about the events of the day. I told her of Torrington and the visit to the Transport Police at Whitechapel. I skipped over mention of the notes. I had been so concerned over to whom the third note had been addressed that I hadn't noticed that there was no note addressed to Mrs Harris.

I asked her how she was. With a deep sigh, she said that she was all right, then paused. I saw something pass behind her eyes, a shadow of a memory that had temporarily distracted her attention. When she looked at me again, she regarded me more carefully.

'In many ways, you didn't know the real Janice, Norman. I lost that one many years ago. She was such a beautiful child. Good at her studies, her dancing lessons. Always laughing.'

She paused briefly as she walked with this Janice again, embraced her in her memory, then pushed her away as the remembering became too painful. I reflected that perhaps she had had to protect herself over the years, to harden her heart. That was why she seemed so cold and distant to Janice. But she was speaking again. 'You only saw the Janice on the drugs. I didn't know that Janice or the things that she did.'

An image flitted through my mind of Janice hustling at King's Cross and I wondered if Mrs Harris knew or suspected that.

'In some ways, my Janice died several years ago.'

There was a long pause.

I broke it by asking about the last time she had seen Janice. She said it had been late on Sunday night. Janice had come in and was raging about an argument she had just had with me. Mrs Harris had watched as she had twice phoned me until I switched my phone off. Inwardly, I cringed with guilt.

Then Janice had asked her to drive her over to Carshalton. She had refused. She had asked her for the money for a taxi. Again, she had refused. Later, she had heard Janice phoning someone and agreeing to meet them. She had packed a bag and left just after midnight.

So Janice had tried to get to me that Sunday night. The thought warmed me, reassured me somewhat, but what of the third note? Who was 'My Dearest Darling'? That would be my quest, before the search for Janice's spirit. For why would I search for her spirit if she had truly loved another?

I went round to Ian's. He would have to be told, as would the rest of Janice's friends, such as they were. They wouldn't find out from her family, who had always been totally divorced from this side of Janice's life.

As damaged as he was, I knew it would hit Ian hard.

'No,' he shouted loudly and jumped to his feet, his face contorted in mental anguish. 'How? How?' he demanded, pacing the floor with a restless energy that prevented him from standing still.

I told him what I knew and had trouble convincing him it was true. No, I hadn't seen the body myself yet, but the police had told me and Janice's mother and brother. He saw my own grief and reluctantly came to accept it, but still the questions came. What was she doing at Torrington? (Where was the place, anyway?) Was it really suicide? He didn't want to believe it. It meant we had all failed her.

Suddenly, Judy arrived, closely followed by Charlie. Together, we commiserated with each other and shared our grief. Somehow it made it a bit easier, but mine was the greatest loss. There was a strong element of 'there but for the grace of God go I' in the reflections of Judy and Charlie. Their first reaction had been fear, a fear that had shown clearly in their eyes.

After they had left, Ian and I talked for hours. We shared memories and I felt the spirit of Janice with us. We were the two people she had been closest to while alive. Perhaps this was the way to invoke her presence now, to be in the company of those who had known and cared for her.

It was late in the evening when I arrived at my mother's. This would be home to me again now; I couldn't stay at the Carshalton flat where I had been with Janice.

Further, the darkness brought fear now, the fear of the unknown. The reign of the night heralded the coming of the spirit world. The vengeful spirit of Janice 2 could be abroad again. My mother and I would huddle together for strength and solidarity. She still looked shocked and frail. For the next couple of nights, I would sleep on the floor of her room.

Strange, I know. Irrational, even and something I would have scoffed at barely 48 hours earlier. But what had happened to us the previous evening was beyond conventional rationality. For the time being, we would have to make it up as we went along and do whatever felt right.

LIFE AFTER LIFE

As much as Janice's death had affected me, and at virtually every level it had devastated me, its effects on my mother were far more visible. There were no tears or deep moods of depression, but she had visibly aged and her life-force seemed weaker, as if she had been spiritually wounded. I would have to watch her carefully, lest there be another death for me to deal with.

I couldn't sit indoors with her, though. If I had been a restless spirit before, I was now a driven, possessed one. My only salvation was to be in pursuit of some goal, to be in motion on some quest. That way I didn't have to sit still and think.

I phoned some friends and told them the news. They phoned others and soon I was besieged with invitations to come round so they could commiserate. They might not have approved of Janice, but they could sympathise with my grief.

Jess was a rock. We met in Soho and toured the usual bars and restaurants.

'Oh, mate, mate,' he said, 'you could have done without that. You haven't had much luck in your life, have you?'

It was a rhetorical question that didn't require an answer, but I reflected that the answer would have to be a resounding 'No'. I told him about all the events surrounding Janice's death, including my mother's spiritual visitor in her bedroom.

In the face of any threat, even a spiritual one, Jess inevitably reverted to 'Jock fighting mode'.

'Well if Janice 2 comes anywhere near me, I'll soon tell her to fuck off,' he roared.

It wasn't really what I wanted to hear, but he was sympathetic and supportive in every other way. He kept me with him all day, even taking me home with him to have dinner with his wife and children.

Nick's reaction was in character. His relations with women were so many, so varied and so superficial, his thoughts immediately turned to a replacement.

'That's no good, mate. We'll have to get you out with a few tarts and get it off your mind,' he enthused. No doubt he meant well, but he wouldn't have understood that I was still very much in love with Janice and to form a relationship with anyone else at the moment was the furthest thing from my mind.

Boy-Boy's reaction was entirely predictable. He explored various conspiracy theories as to who could be behind it.

'Just say the word and I'll have him ironed out,' he whispered conspiratorially. I suppose I should have been grateful, but the thought of being the cause of another death, the bringing of grief to some other loved one, filled me with so much pain I had to get away.

For all his selfishness, Tom was more considerate. He told me that Elaine couldn't even face me at the moment, she was too upset. All the more because Janice stealing her clothes had sparked the argument between us. He placed his hand on my shouder and looked at me closely, as if trying to gauge my mental state and to predict what my reaction might be.

'Norm,' he began gingerly, and I looked up to see his worried expression. 'I don't mean to be inconsiderate, really I don't. You're my mate. But, in some ways, it could be for the best. Me and Elaine have been talking. There was nothing you could do for Janice, Norm. She was too far gone. You did more for her than anyone else ever did. I don't know any of my friends who would have taken Janice on and did for her what you did.'

He paused, still looking for my reaction. I was listening intently. Tom was far more wise in the ways of the world than me. Maybe he could impart some nugget of wisdom about Janice.

'She was killing you, Norm,' he continued. 'Everyone noticed the difference in you. If she hadn't got you nicked, she could easily have been the death of you. She won't be suffering any more. Perhaps it's all for the best. You won't see it like that right now, but maybe in time you will.'

There was a strong element of truth in what he said, but I wasn't ready to hear it. I was still very much in love with that idealised picture of Janice I held in my memory. Further, if she had committed suicide so shortly after I had finished with her, then, obviously, I was responsible for her death. So, to the guilt I already carried over my two victims, I now had to add the guilt of causing Janice's death. It would be uncharitable to denigrate her memory in the slightest.

Ivor and Bessie sounded grief-stricken.

'Are you sure you're OK?' he demanded. 'Come up here for the weekend and get away from it all,' he offered. It sounded like a good idea. Every time I phoned someone or they phoned me, I relived the tragedy. I promised I would come up to stay as soon as I could get away.

But first, I had to solve the riddle of the third note. I wondered how well I had really known Janice. My personal recollections couldn't be trusted. I would have to go in search of the real Janice. I could only do that now by asking her friends and those who had known her.

Ian seemed guarded. 'She never really spoke too much to me about it, but I'm sure she cared for you,' he offered without meeting my gaze. I wondered if he was still trying to punish me for taking Janice away from him.

'Of course she loved you, Norm,' said Judy emphatically.

In a landscape so blighted with indifference she could relate strongly to the idea of two people who cared for each other.

'Often she would ask me, "Do you think he loves me? Do you think he fucking loves me?"'

Judy found herself smiling as she imitated Janice's 'little-girl' voice. I smiled too, but screwed up my eyes tightly as I felt them redden and verge on tears.

'You could tell she loved you by the way she used to look at you,' said Charlotte in a considered manner. She had less reason to praise Janice than anyone, she hadn't liked her at all. But all women's hearts are touched by love, especially tragic love. 'If ever you were talking to anyone except her, she'd watch you like a hawk. Especially if you were talking to a bird. It was a mixture of pride and jealousy. And love, of course.'

Emma had known her longer and more intimately than anyone. They had been friends since their schooldays and had shared a flat in their teens.

'Janice wasn't nearly so tough as she made out to be,' she confided. 'Underneath, she was just a frightened little girl, but she had to put a front on to survive in some of the places she went. I know for a fact that she loved you, Norman, because she told me so, over and over again. She said that no one had ever done for her what you had.'

'So why didn't she tell me, Emma?'

'Because she was frightened to show her true feelings. She'd been hurt so many times before. She thought that, if she told you she loved you, you'd take her for granted and think you had her.'

'But what about that third note, Em, why didn't she address it to me?'

'I don't know. Who could know, the state her mind must have been in? All I do know is that there wasn't anyone else it could have been to. I would have known, she told me everything.'

'What about Storey?' I asked. Storey was her ex-longtime boyfriend who was still in prison.

'Pah!' exploded Emma. 'Janice hated Storey. He was the one who originally got her on "smack" when they were kids. Come to think of it, that's just reminded me. A couple of weeks back Janice said to me, "Em, I've been in love with two men and one boy. Norman will be my last love." '

I suppose I should have been reassured, but Janice had made disparaging remarks about all her friends and acquaintances. She told me that she didn't trust any of them. So would she have told them if she was having a secret affair, especially if they could use it as a weapon by telling me?

And what of the malicious intent of the Janice spirit in my mother's room? It could have been Janice 2 of course, but, if not, they were hardly the actions of someone who loved me. I would keep on looking in my search for the truth.

Suddenly, I remembered the phone numbers I had copied from her address book. Perhaps the answer lay there. I would phone them one by one, saying I was just a friend of Janice's and passing on the awful news.

I realised that the likelihood was that they would be dealers and fellow thieves. Any response to someone they didn't know would inevitably be cautious. For the most part, they were women's names. I began to work my way through the list.

Often, there was no immediate recognition. I was asked to

describe this Janice and then they would recognise someone they had known only casually. Not once was there the strong reaction you would expect from one friend learning about the death of another.

I had saved the men's names for last. Of the six, the first four remained unmoved and said they barely knew her. Only Nigel and Derek remained.

Nigel? The full, formal form of the name was rarely used amongst 'street people'. Usually it was Nige. The only 'Nigel' I had heard Janice refer to was the rich property dealer whom she occasionally smoked crack with. I rang the mobile number.

'Hello, I'm a friend of Janice Harris,' I said to the male voice that answered. 'I found your number in her address book and I'm just ringing round to let everyone know that, unfortunately, Janice was killed in a train accident at Torrington on Monday evening.'

There was a dead silence, and for a second I thought the line had gone dead.

'Hello, you still there?' I asked.

Still there was no reply.

'Hello, hello?' I continued.

'Yes, yes.' The voice was strange, wary, surprised. 'Look, this has been a great shock to me. Can you give me five minutes to collect my thoughts? This has been a great shock.' This time the line did go dead.

Well, I had finally got a reaction out of someone. The picture I had been building up was of a girl who had very few friends indeed. It brought back something Emma had said to me about junkies not having any real friends. Janice's world was beginning to look quite bleak.

I waited a good 20 minutes before I phoned Nigel again. This time he seemed more composed, but was still wary. He asked me who I was and I didn't feel inclined to lie. At the mention of my name, he lapsed into silence again.

'Janice talked about you to me,' he said finally. 'We were up all night, talking,' he added almost as an afterthought.

I was on it in a flash. 'When did you last see her then, Nigel?' My question was as calm and unthreatening as I could manage.

'Well, Janice stayed at my place at Torrington Sunday night and stayed over the following day. We went for a drink in the pub by the station about 4.00pm.' Nigel paused as if considering what to say next, as if reluctant to commit himself.

'To be honest, we had a bit of an argument in the pub,' he

continued. 'I left her in the pub car park at about a quarter to five.'

My mind was racing so fast I could hardly think. So with this particular phone call I had struck gold. Not only was this Nigel a friend, he had actually been with Janice on her last day alive. Jealous thoughts writhed together and I felt deflated. So perhaps this was the 'My Dearest Darling' of the third note. Maybe Nigel was the one who she would 'love for ever'. A sense of betrayal spread through me like an Ecstasy come-down.

I recalled a conversation I had had with Janice a couple of months previously. She had asked if I minded if she went and found Nigel to smoke some 'rocks' with him. I had made some disparaging remark about him being a 'fucking crackhead' and coupled it with a threat to go round and beat him up.

'Don't you dare,' said Janice with as much righteous indignation as I had ever heard her muster. 'Nigel has been a good friend to me when I've been in trouble. He sent me things when I was in prison.'

My heart sank. I now had my prime suspect. I could hardly ask him if he had been having a secret affair with Janice behind my back, though. And even if I did ask him, could I trust his answer? No, the truth of the matter would have to come from another source.

Nigel asked me for more details of the accident and I told him what I knew, without mentioning the 'suicide' notes. He requested that I keep him informed about Janice's funeral. We agreed to keep in touch.

That left just one more phone number in the address book. As I dialled Derek's number, I recognised a local area code.

'Hackney Police Station,' said the clipped, efficient-sounding voice that answered. Almost as a reflex, I hung up. I checked the number again. Perhaps I had pressed the wrong button. I dialled again.

'Hackney Police Station,' said the forceful female voice. I hesitated, temporarily confused, as the shadow of a suspicion began to dawn. 'Hello, hello?' the voice interrupted my train of thought.

'Er, could I speak to Derek, please?'

I went through the motions, feeling that I was obviously wasting my time. How could 'Derek' live in a police station?

'I'm sorry, Derek isn't on duty at the moment, could I take a message?' The voice had changed from forceful to guarded but encouraging. Helpful even.

'No, that's OK, I'll call back.' It was my turn to be guarded.

'Do you want to leave a name?' cajoled the voice.

'No thanks, I'll phone later.' I hung up.

If my mind had raced following the 'Nigel' phone call, it was now in utter turmoil. Paranoia flared as self-preservation took over. Coldly, precisely, I advanced through the logical steps of the argument. I had been to that particular police station. It was a large block of a building, with scores of staff. I had got through to the main desk at the station, yet the desk officer had immediately known who 'Derek' was. She had said that he wasn't on duty, so he must be a policeman of some kind. She had then tried to get me to leave a name.

I had never been an informant or knowingly associated with informants, but I knew something of how the system worked. Every police station had officers who worked with their particular informants, usually on a first name basis. If someone phoned and asked to speak to one of these officers, they would be treated with courtesy and be encouraged. After all, it might be an important tip-off.

Mentally, I pushed my idealised picture of Janice away from me and examined it. Where initially there had been concern over romantic betrayal, there was now something far more fundamental. Janice had the number of a policeman who handled informants in her address book, did this make her an informer? And, more to my immediate concern, had she been informing on me?

I dismissed it out of hand. Quite simply, if Janice had wanted to bring me down, she could have done so on scores of occasions. She had known when I was ferrying drugs or large sums of money around. There had been occasions when I had had my gun on or around me. One phone call could have got me severely nicked. No, Janice hadn't been informing on me.

However, there was another possibility. The police could have thought she was. It was common knowledge that the police regularly tried to get information from 'street people'. Especially when they were druggies who were in and out of the nick all the time. Deals were done, favours returned.

Further, I was a tempting target for them. Fresh out of jail after 24 years, mixing with active criminals and suspected of being active myself, they must have looked at me. When they noticed this little druggie, street girl around me, did they think that this would be the way to get to me? They would certainly have tried. They would also have had ample opportunity. Janice had been in and out of custody several times. As the realisation hit me, I felt the cold hand of fear brush my heart.

Perhaps she had played them along. Perhaps she had secretly agreed to inform on me in return for some help, but never delivered. Suddenly, it all began to fall into place.

I drove straight round to Ian's. He was the only one I felt I could talk to about it. He was immediately indignant and dismissed it out of hand.

'Janice wasn't a grass,' he exploded. 'She hated Old Bill. And she would never have done anything to harm you. She loved you,' he said emphatically.

'Ian, I really don't want to believe it, but certain things make sense now.'

'What things?' he demanded.

'Well, that time the copper phoned me on my phone from the nick and told me that Janice had been nicked for shoplifting. I'd told her never to give my number to anyone, especially a copper. Then, as soon as I showed up at the nick, they let her out on her own bail. She's fucked off so many times, she must be the world's worst bail risk. It was as if they were just checking that she really did know me.'

'Norman, she was in the nick. How else was she gonna get in touch with you?' There was exasperation in his voice now. 'And as for the bail, it was only a shoplifting charge. The nicks are bursting at their seams. Murder charges are getting bail. That wasn't a surprise.'

'That's only a part of the picture.' I was firmly on the defensive now. In truth, I didn't really believe it myself. In some ways I was just thinking aloud, testing the theory out on Ian. 'What about the trip to Spain then?'

'What about it?' he demanded.

'Don't you think it funny that, even though she had recently jumped bail on one shoplifting charge, they immediately gave her bail again for shoplifting at Gatwick?'

'Don't I remember you saying that you thought that perhaps it hadn't gone down on her record yet?' Ian countered. 'And anyway, it was only shoplifting again.'

'What about the new tickets she must have needed to miss two further flights and get on the third?' I felt like a prosecutor putting his case.

Ian shook his head. 'Didn't you say she was with Nigel after they let her out? Maybe he bought them for her.'

'OK, OK, well how do you explain her turning up in Spain just a couple of hundred yards from where I was staying? And who was the English geezer whose mobile she used to call me?'

Ian thought for a few seconds. 'I don't know,' he conceded. 'But I'll tell you what I do know. They nicked her quick enough when she got back to England,' he added with vigour.

'But they let her out again and bailed her to my Carshalton address. Wait a minute. Wait a minute.' I held up my hand to stop Ian interrupting. 'Yeah, it definitely makes sense. That black copper could have nicked me for threatening to kill my girlfriend, but suddenly they let me go. Did they look me up on the computer and see that there was an ongoing operation involving me and Janice? And how did Janice get back to Carshalton so quickly if the Old Bill didn't take her? Do they do that, Old Bill? Ferry people and their luggage all over London, especially when they've just assaulted a copper? No, mate. There was something very strange about that night. It was as if they wanted her back next to me.'

'I'm still not having it that Janice was a grass,' insisted Ian.

'I'm not saying she was, mate,' I countered. 'I think she was playing them along. She was due in court shortly over the two hoisting charges. I'll bet they were putting pressure on her over that.'

It was the word 'pressure' that did it, that made me examine recent events anew. Yes, Janice had seemed under more pressure than normal over the past couple of months. Perhaps that was why she had run away from me and disappeared. Maybe the police had put pressure on her to give me up and she wouldn't. Perhaps they had threatened to hammer her with a bigger jail sentence when she appeared in court.

'Perhaps' followed 'perhaps' in irresistible sequence, the one leading inexorably on to the next. Finally, I had to confront that last awful 'perhaps'. Perhaps, in the shadow of a jail sentence; under pressure from the police to inform on her boyfriend and recently ditched by that boyfriend, the last love of her life, she had jumped in front of a train!

How sad. How fucking sad. I could imagine her poor tormented mind, not knowing which way to turn, seeking a hiding place in the drug-induced stupor. Until, finally, there was nowhere left to hide.

I had failed her. I had promised always to be there for her. To protect her from the world, the oh-so-wicked world that had hurt her so much. It was the final straw. She really did love me and without me she just couldn't go on. Of course I was 'My Dearest Darling', how could I have doubted it?

And with that knowledge came the realisation of what I had lost. What a truly horrible world this was. It seemed that you had to snatch brief moments of happiness where you could, just to survive the grinding pressure of everyday life. I had found some of those moments with Janice, but now she was gone. The space she left in my life yawned like a gaping pit.

Jess's words came back to me, 'You haven't had much luck, mate.' No indeed, I hadn't. It seemed as if I was cursed. Cursed never to find happiness for more than a brief interlude.

That realisation brought on a kind of cold rage in me, a rage against life, my life. I just didn't care any more, there was nothing left to strive for. Just as I had been passing time in prison, wishing the days, weeks, months and years away, that was exactly how I was living now. My innate self-destructiveness had moved into a new phase. Like some dark force that drew me inevitably downwards, I yearned for it to be over, to be with Janice again.

The incident with Janice 2 had made me aware of a whole new world, a world beyond this one. A spirit world where the dead continued to exist as sentient beings. Because that world had never touched me before, I had rejected its existence. I could ignore it no longer.

* * *

I had been shaving in the bathroom when the house phone rang. As I hurried to answer it, I glanced at the lounge clock. It was just after 8.00am. I wondered who it could be, calling me so early.

'Norman, Norman, she came for me, mate.'

The voice was ragged, frantic, bordering on hysteria. It was clearly male, but I didn't recognise it.

'Who's that?' I asked.

'It's me, Jess.' The voice was still throaty and breathless. 'It was Janice, she came for me.'

The words registered, but they made no sense.

'What the fuck you talking about, Jess?' I demanded.

'Norman, it was Janice. She came to me while I was asleep and tried to get me. I swear it, I fucking swear it.' His voice was more steady now, but he was still highly agitated.

Just for a second it seemed quite funny, like something from the

B-movie science-fiction films. 'It tried to get me,' screamed a victim who had narrowly escaped. But this was Jess — strong, down-to-earth, Scots street-tough Jess who just didn't believe in this sort of thing. Jess, who only a couple of days earlier had declared that he would soon send the spirit of Janice packing should it ever turn up at his house. So, what had happened to bring about such a dramatic change? Whatever it was, it must have been quite extreme and convincing.

'OK, Jess, take it easy,' I consoled. 'Just let me get dressed and I'll be right over.' This seemed to calm him somewhat, but he did exhort me to hurry.

With my mother still trying to get over her own recent spiritual experience, I thought it best not to mention this latest one involving Jess. I dressed quickly and left, telling her that I was going to visit a friend.

Jess met me at the front door as I came up the path to his house. Hurriedly, he ushered me inside. His wife, Laura, was feeding the two children in the lounge. She had her usual harassed look that came from trying to cope with two infant sons and the running of a house, but there was also something more.

Jess waved me into the kitchen. He followed and shut the door behind him.

'It was definitely Janice,' he began with absolutely no preliminaries. 'I recognised her quite clearly. I was lying in bed asleep with Colin, when she came to me. She tried to drag me away. It was Colin who saved me. If I hadn't had my arm around the bairn, been close to him, I'm sure I would have gone.'

Even though he was relatively calm now, his eyes were still wild and fearful. Whatever he had experienced, it had been very real for him. And perhaps it *was* real. My mother said that she had experienced the same thing. I had experienced a 'ghostly' presence. Were we to deny the evidence of our senses?

'Are you sure she was trying to hurt you?' I asked. 'Did she say anything?' Jess furrowed his brow as he examined the recent experience more closely. 'She didn't say a word, but I definitely felt that she meant me harm. I think she was annoyed that I had said bad things about her to you.'

I didn't smile, but inwardly I experienced a warm feeling. So not only did Janice still exist as some kind of disembodied but sentient entity, she cared that someone had been running her down to me.

Therefore, she cared about what I thought of her. Which could only mean that she still cared for me.

Suddenly, I felt quite reassured and not nearly so alone. Janice, who I loved so much and missed so deeply, still loved me. I wanted to get close to this spirit. I no longer feared it. Why would Janice, who loved me so much in life, want to harm me in death?

However, that didn't mean that there wasn't a spiritual entity that was the embodiment of Janice 2. Perhaps, just as the two personae had inhabited the same body in life, so they would be intertwined as spirits in death.

I examined the notion more closely. I couldn't escape the feeling that it all had something to do with Wandlebury and the lovers' pact I had made with Janice. I remembered how she had hardly been able to walk to the site of the carved figures. As if her very body was refusing to carry her there. Janice had been very sensitive to spiritual things. Deep down she would have felt that I was leading her into something harmful. It was only my stubborness that had forced the issue.

Then, when I had asked her what she felt there, she had recoiled and said that something nasty had happened there. A terrible suspicion began to grow in me.

What if there were powerful spiritual forces that existed in this world, albeit tangentially? What if it were possible to tap into them by invocation? Perhaps, when I had made that pact with Janice, I invoked some powerful dark spirit that attached itself to her. Or rather, to her dark side, to Janice 2. Maybe it had empowered Janice 2, because, virtually from that point on, Janice 2 came to control Janice more and more, until, finally, it destroyed her in front of the train.

Nonsense, absolute and complete nonsense, I felt the rational side of my mind say. What concrete proof was there? But we had gone beyond the merely corporeal now. Certain things had happened that had stretched the boundaries of that finite universe I had known before. And why should I be surprised? Wasn't I the mystical warrior, complete with my carefully constructed talisman, who had gone searching in the world for mysteries?

There was also the unanswered question of why it hadn't affected me. If the lovers' pact had attached this negative force to Janice, why hadn't it adversely affected me?

I felt I knew the answer. In many ways I was quite unique.

Undoubtedly, I had a very powerful dark side, one that had a hand in my past crimes. But I had controlled it, had caged 'the Beast'. Many years of prayer, positive thinking and deeds had positively charged my 'good' side, so that now my heart was clear. When this empowered 'good' side was complemented by my controlled dark side, it made for a very powerful spirit indeed. Nothing could touch me.

Suddenly, my mission became clearer. Events were undoubtedly still unfolding. Somehow, I would pursue this dark spirit Janice 2 and destroy it. Just as, in life, I had tried to protect my Janice from it, so in death I would do the same.

For the moment, though, my ministrations had to be in the corporeal world. A still-shocked Jess stood before me in his kitchen. I could hardly explain to him my theory about spiritual possession. I would just have to calm him.

'Jess, I think it's over now. I told you about how something visited my mum. Well, nothing has happened since. Perhaps it's the first flurry of a restless spirit, then things settle down.'

Jess didn't look convinced, but there was little more I could do and he knew it. 'I'll never say anything bad about her again,' he said with feeling, as if he was trying to convince any spirit that might be listening.

I left Jess and made my way over to North London and Ian. I felt myself drawn to him and Janice's 'street people' friends, as if by being close to them I could get close to her. I was just turning into his street as my mobile rang.

The voice asked for me, then introduced himself as Detective Sergeant Ford from the coroner's office. The police rank put me immediately on my guard, especially in view of the recent interest in me and my activities.

He was a genial soul, though, both kind and considerate of my feelings. He explained that his role was to gather whatever evidence he could for the inquest. He said he realised that I would still be very upset by what had happened and he apologised for having to ask me questions at this time.

As wary as I was, there was something about this man. It was a warmth, a genuineness that came through his words and touched me. I felt I could trust him. We talked for a long time. It transpired that he was the same age as me. He explained that he had never done criminal work with the police, having spent his whole career with the coroner's office. It was as if he was reassuring me that he wasn't tainted by that mutual antagonism that exists between policemen and criminals like myself.

There were several things about Janice's death that concerned him. He asked if I could come by to see him, but warned that he was based at Hertford. I assured him that I was as keen to find out every detail of Janice's death as he was. I arranged to see him the following day.

When I arrived at Ian's quite a crowd had gathered. There was no doubt that Janice's death had shocked everyone deeply, and these were people who were no strangers to sudden deaths. Hardly a week passed than someone they knew, however remotely, died of an overdose or somesuch. This was much closer to home, though, and, what made it that much more poignant was that they had all observed the tempestuous course of our love affair. To the women it was almost like the death of love itself. Their own hopes of finding someone who would care for them seemed doomed.

As I arrived there was a flurry of activity. Judy, Georgie, Charlotte and Emma all jumped up and crowded around me. Ian and Charlie called greetings and motioned me to sit down. Several voices questioned me at once about whether I had found out anything more. I told them of the impending meeting with the coroner.

'Do any of you know a Nigel Hampton?' I asked suddenly. 'It seems Janice was smoking "rocks" with him just before she died.'

'I know him,' said Georgie immediately. 'He's always down the Cross buying "rocks". That's where Janice met him.'

'Yeah, I think Janice has known him for quite a while,' I added.

Perhaps it was the look on my face or even my tone. 'Here, don't think for one minute that there was anything between him and Janice,' interceded Emma. 'Janice used to talk to me about him. All he was to her was somewhere to go to smoke for free. You're not into piping, Norman, so you wouldn't really appreciate just what a big thing that was. Most people have to go out and rob or hustle when they want a "rock".'

'I've smoked with him lots of times,' added Georgie. 'He's a bit of a weird geezer. Very posh. He buys loads of "rocks". If he tries to buy them himself he always gets ripped off, so he gets one of us girls to buy them for him. That's how Janice got to know him.'

I felt mollified, reassured. I had already come to accept that this Nigel wasn't the one for whom the third note was intended, but it was nice to have it confirmed.

'Buy us a drink, Norm.' Ian's voice interrupted my thoughts. Some of the others looked at me expectantly. I could see this turning into an extended wake, but so what? If I had failed Janice, by not getting her what she needed, I would try not to fail her friends.

Twenty minutes later they were all sitting in a circle drinking cans of lager. The talk was all of Janice, her exploits and some of the things she said. It was strangely comforting for me. As if as long as I and her friends got together to talk about her she would live on. The problem was that, at some stage, I would have to leave, then that Janice would die again.

The following morning saw me in Hertford, looking for the local police station. I had never been there before, but it was only a small country town and everything was well signposted. Soon I was at the reception of a large modern block that housed several services, including the police.

I gave my name and asked for Detective Sergeant Ford. Barely two minutes later I was joined by an avuncular-looking man in civilian clothes. He was balding like myself, but, although of a similar age, the years had not been so kind. He had the jowly, sad look that 'Sad Face' at Whitechapel had worn. He also had the paunch. I reflected that similar jobs must lead to similar physiognomies.

His personal manner was as friendly as his telephone manner. He introduced himself, insisting I call him John, and led me upstairs to his office. He asked me how I was feeling as he bustled about making me a cup of tea. By the time it was ready, I was completely at my ease.

He explained that his sole function was to gather evidence for the inquest and, in that regard, he was completely impartial. He remarked that this seemed to be a particularly tragic case and offered his sincere condolences. He asked me how much I knew.

I told him what the two policemen who had come to my mum's flat had told me. I related an account of my visit to Torrington with Luke, and the subsequent encounter with 'Sad Face' at Whitechapel. Sergeant Ford listened intently, occasionally nodding at a particularly relevant point, then making a short note on a pad in front of him.

The retelling of the story brought the inevitable tears to my eyes. I wondered how long it would take before this extreme emotional reaction passed. I sipped at my tea as displacement activity while I fought to regain control. John Ford diplomatically stared at his notes.

When I mentioned Nigel Hampton and his leaving Janice at the pub car park, he sat bolt upright, his eyes widening with surprise. He began to question me closely. I was instantly on my guard. I wasn't a grass. I didn't want to get someone into trouble unnecessarily. Janice had said that Nigel had been a friend to her, so she would hardly thank me if I compromised him in any way. Not with regard to her death, of course. I was sure it was suicide, caused because I had finished with her when I should have been more supportive. I wasn't going to try to shirk responsibility for that. So telling the police that Nigel was smoking 'crack' with Janice just before she died was hardly relevant.

Sergeant Ford's expression had changed now and he was looking at me quite sternly. It was reflected in his voice.

'Norman, I'm going to be very frank with you. We're extremely concerned about the role that Nigel Hampton might have played in Janice's death.'

If he had expected me to show surprise, he would have been disappointed with my reaction. I knew he was on the wrong track.

Sergeant Ford leaned forward conspiratorially.

'Norman, I'm going to tell you some things in the strictest confidence. If you repeat them, I'll deny I ever said them.'

I nodded my agreement.

'The police have been interested in Nigel Hampton for quite some time now. We know all about his trips to King's Cross to buy crack and the girls he smokes it with. It's out of character for a man of his background. He's a very wealthy landowner. In fact, he owns a land bank, which makes him a multi-millionaire.'

He paused and for a moment I thought that that was it, but he was considering what to say next. Coming to a decision, he spoke.

'About four months ago, he was driving home in his Range Rover with his two five-year-old daughters sitting next to him. This is the statement of the driver who was travelling behind him.'

He picked a sheaf of paper from the top of a pile and turned them towards me. I saw the legend 'witness statement' at the top of the first page, followed by lines of typing.

'The witness said that he saw the Range Rover suddenly swerve and hit the central barrier. It bounced off, turned over, rolled several times across the carriageway, then came to rest on its side on top of some railings at the side of the road.' He paused for effect, looking up to make sure I had noted this dramatic development. He continued.

'The witness pulled up and ran over. Nigel Hampton was standing next to the overturned car. One of his daughters was standing with him, in shock. The other was dead, impaled upon the railings.' Again he paused and regarded me.

'The witness asked him if he was all right. Hampton started to walk away, saying that he had to get away for a while. The witness said that he shouldn't do that, at which point Hampton ran off and disappeared into the surrounding fields. The police didn't find him until eight hours later.'

It certainly was an unusual story, horrific even. It began to germinate a seed of doubt deep in my mind, but I terminated the fledgling growth. So, Nigel Hampton was the sort of father who would run off and leave one daughter dead and one in shock, just to save himself from being nicked for driving under the influence of cocaine. What relevance did that have to Janice dying in front of a train? I would embrace my martyrdom like a Stoic. I killed Janice. I rejected her and she threw herself under a train.

Sergeant Ford seemed frustrated by my lack of reaction. 'Needless to say, the police are really out to get him over this,' he emphasised.

'Were there any witnesses to Janice's death?' I asked, changing the subject.

Sergeant Ford took a deep breath, then, as if changing to another tack, picked up another sheaf of papers and read from them.

'The incident happened at 5.10pm. It's January and was just starting to get dark, but you could see clearly from one end of the platform to the other. There was one man waiting on the platform on the other side, but he saw nothing. Drivers of cars waiting at the level crossing saw nothing. The station master in the ticket office was unsighted.'

He paused for the details to sink in, then fixed me with a piercing gaze.

'You might find this next bit upsetting, Norman. I must also add that, if this was suicide, it's one of the most unusual suicides I have ever investigated. And I've investigated a few over the past 20 years.'

He looked at his papers again.

'Janice was struck by the London to Bishops Stortford through train. The driver didn't see a thing. That's because Janice went head first into the side of the first carriage. She was killed instantly. Her head hit the steel plate above the wheels and was knocked clean off. Her body fell downwards and was dragged 50 yards along the track.'

As he spoke, I thankfully seized on his words about her being killed instantly and offered up a silent prayer. At least she hadn't suffered.

'Initial reports indicate that she had a phenomenally high level of cocaine in her blood and some alcohol. The local publican has said that Janice and Nigel Hampton were in his pub, but left around 4.30pm. They had been arguing. We have a statement from a local shopkeeper saying that Janice came into her shop at about noon, severely under the influence of something. She could hardly stand and had a large amount of money in her hand, which she dropped on the floor. The shopkeeper helped her pick it up. Janice said something like, "He doesn't deserve to have it."

'We have a statement from Nigel Hampton, made in the presence of his solicitor. He admits that Janice had been with him since the previous evening. He said that she stole some money from him, but he got it back. He admits to arguing with her in the pub. He says he took her to the station, where he left her. He didn't see her again.'

As he finished reading, he looked at me intently.

'You see, Norman, there are several unusual things here. Nigel Hampton told you he left Janice in the pub car park. He told us he left her at the station. If Janice was going to London, as she must have been, why was she on the Bishops Stortford side of the station? The only part of Janice's body that was struck by the side of the train was her head. The other injuries were caused by her being dragged along. Therefore, if she committed suicide, she must have jumped head-first into the side of the train. I've never heard of that before. Everyone always jumps in front of the train.'

He paused yet again, gauging the effect of his words on me. Prison had taught me to hide my feelings well. I had been absorbing every detail and mulling them over. My criminal mind synthesised the details and conceptualised various scenarios. Yes, there was something very strange here. But perhaps it was 'mystical' strange rather than 'criminal' strange. I just couldn't accept that, with all the other tragedy and bad luck I had had in my life, I could be so unlucky as to have someone push my Janice under a train.

'I suppose you know that he's smoked crack with Janice on several occasions before,' I offered.

'Yes,' said Ford, encouraged. 'Janice has been seen in Torrington before and Nigel Hampton has been seen at King's Cross. He was actually nicked there, buying drugs.'

'Are there any photos of the accident?' I asked. I had said 'accident' unconsciously.

'Yes, but you don't want to see them, Norman.'

'I feel like I must see them. I must know every detail,' I replied. In truth, I was still punishing myself. Why shouldn't I be confronted with the evidence of my deed?

Slowly, reluctantly, Sergeant Ford pulled a sheaf of several large colour photographs from under the papers. He handed them to me.

Mentally I cringed, preparing myself for what I was about to see. Would she be recognisable as a person? Would the wheels have chopped her up? Steeling myself, I stared at the first photo.

It was of a white-painted picket fence that ran along the back of the platform. Against it were several cycles. In the foreground a steel stanchion rose from the concrete platform. The fence, the bikes, the stanchion were all splattered with large gobs of blood.

The second photo was a continuation of the first, more white fence and more blood.

I stared at the third photo, trying to make out what it was. A trainer lay at the side of the track and, next to it, a sports bag from which it had tumbled.

The fourth photo was also of the side of the track, but further along. A plastic carrier bag lay on its side, clothes spilling out on to the gravel of the track bed.

There was an uncanny symmetry to the fifth photo. Dark-stained sleepers marched in parallel to the middle distance, framed by gleaming steel rails. Right in the middle was Janice's red shoulder bag.

I remembered Sergeant Ford's words. Janice's body had been dragged 50 yards. These were the things she must have dropped on the way. I prepared myself for what must inevitably come next.

It was clearly recognisable as a body and largely undamaged. My first reaction was one of outraged decency. Most of her clothes had been torn off. Her naked form seemed almost pornographic lying there in public view, the arms and legs splayed out as if she were running. There was a deep, red cut across one thigh.

The body lay right in the middle of the track with the legs in the foreground. From that angle you could hardly notice that the head was missing. Again I uttered a silent prayer that the damage hadn't been more gross. I stared at the photo for several seconds.

'You'll have noticed the bags.'

Sergeant Ford's voice cut into my thoughts. 'They're on the track, so Janice must have been carrying them when she went into the side of the train. That makes it even more unusual. Just think about it.

Who would jump head-first into the side of a train, carrying a sports bag in one hand, a carrier bag in the other and with a shoulder bag around their neck?'

I did think about it. I could imagine Janice standing on the platform on unsteady legs, clutching her bags. Perhaps she had just overbalanced and fell. But would that have carried her head first into the steel plate above the wheels? Sergeant Ford seemed adamant that she had been propelled into the side of the train.

I had had enough for the afternoon, though. It was as if grief and horror had overloaded my brain. I longed to get outside in the fresh air. I yearned to jump in my car and speed along the country lanes. I had to get away and I needed to be in motion.

I made my excuses and John Ford said that he understood.

'If there's anything I can do for you, Norman, it will be my pleasure,' he offered. I reflected that I had been lucky to have him to deal with. The afternoon's experience had definitely helped me.

He walked me down to reception and I hurried across to the car park. I didn't know he was watching me, but I felt his eyes on me as I drove away. I powered up through the gears and soon the tyres were singing on the road. As I raced back to London, I wondered where my mission would lead me next.

*　*　*

When Anna rang me late Thursday afternoon, I couldn't remember who she was. The events of the past week had been so traumatic, I had completely forgotten this Bristol woman who had seen me on TV and wanted to interview me.

I didn't fancy it at all. With what would have been Janice's birthday coming up on Saturday, I wanted to spend the day quietly mourning for the girl I had lost barely five days earlier. It would be tantamount to sacrilege to spend the day with another woman.

Anna was adamant, though, and very determined. She made it very clear that she was intent on something more than an interview, too. Still I demurred, saying I had another engagement. Finally, she said that she had already bought her ticket, so would have to come up anyway and have a look at London.

Wrapped up in my own sadness, I didn't want to be the cause of anyone else's if I could possibly help it. I agreed to meet her. I told myself I would just do a quick interview over lunch and send her on her way.

In truth, my mind was filled with my plans for Friday. It was an essential part of my continuing mission. I had planned to give Janice an engagement ring on her birthday. I could no longer give it to her personally, but I could give it to her ceremonially, to her spirit.

I still had the engagement ring I had given Susan over 30 years earlier. I didn't know if it was bad luck to give one girl's engagement ring to another, but it was my dearest possession. It was also quite beautiful. It had been an antique when first I had bought it. The thick gold band was heavily carved with country scenes.

I would spend Friday evening in our Carshalton flat. Her birthday would officially begin at midnight. I would lay out a birthday card to Janice together with the ring. Some might think it an empty gesture, but to me it was my commitment to her. If I couldn't be engaged to her in life, then I would be in death.

I told my mother what I intended to do. She looked puzzled and not a little frightened. I reassured her that no harm could come of it and I would only be gone for the night.

I arrived at the flat early Friday evening. I wanted to settle in, to give the place a lived-in feeling. I had hardly been there of late, just one fleeting visit to pick up some clothes. To be honest, following the ghostly visitation in my mother's room, I felt distinctly uneasy in the flat. The slightest unusual sound would have severely scared me. I had had to screw up my courage just to be there this evening.

As darkness fell, I moved all the things I would need for the night into the bedroom. This was where Janice and I had spent many of our best times, lying in bed cuddling or watching TV together. As I made one journey from the kitchen to the bedroom, I trod on a loose floorboard that creaked audibly. It was straight out of the 'Hammer Hall of Horrors'. I suppressed a shiver. I distinctly remember thinking that I would hate to hear that in the night.

By 9.00pm I was propped up in bed, reading. A birthday card stood open on the top of the TV, 'To my darling Janice' it was inscribed. In the crease between the pages lay the gold engagement ring.

The darker it got, the quieter it got. Soon the little square and its environs positively hummed in its stillness. I turned off the TV and returned to reading, but I couldn't concentrate. I was wound tight as a spring, secretly listening for every sound as the clock crept closer to midnight.

There were two clocks in the room. The one on top of the TV was right to the second, the one on the table next to the bed was five minutes fast. At ten to twelve I focused on my book with considerable determination and must have lost myself in the pages.

Creak ... creak, the two sounds lanced through the stillness. It was the sound of the loose board out on the landing, but improbably loud. It shattered the silence and galvanised me into sitting bolt upright in bed. I lay there, stiff as a board, every muscle paralysed with fear.

I stared at the door in abject terror and was sure that, should it begin to open, I would die from shock. I glanced quickly at the clock on the TV. It was exactly midnight. I swivelled my head to glance at the one on the bedside table. It said five past twelve. This served to unnerve me further, if that was possible. I returned to staring at the door.

I must have lain like that for ages. I mused that this must be how a rabbit feels in the face of the fox. Quite literally, I was paralysed with fear. I had never felt anything remotely like it in my life before. Any pre-planning would have been entirely superfluous. I simply wouldn't have been able to do anything.

For six hours I lay there, until dawn's early light began to filter through the curtains. Over and over again, I tried to rationalise what had happened. Repeatedly, I examined the experience in my mind. The sounds of the floorboard had been too loud, too distinct for me to have imagined them. And even if it was just some vagary of the building, a floorboard shifting due to heat changes in the night, why had it happened precisely at midnight?

There was no rational, scientific explanation. If I had needed any further convincing following the episode in my mother's bedroom, this was surely it. I now had no doubt that there truly was a spirit world and, moreover, one that could intrude into our corporeal one. It was a thoroughly chastened mystical warrior who left the flat that morning on the next leg of his spiritual mission.

✳ ✳ ✳

At just after noon, I was waiting by the entrance of platform 5 at Paddington. A hot bath, shave and change of clothes had done nothing for my state of mind. I was tired, stressed and not at all looking forward to my imminent meeting with Anna.

I had my strategy planned out. I would be formally polite, take her to lunch, give her a quick interview (if I could keep my eyes open long enough), then put her back on a train.

The train from Bristol duly arrived and disgorged a bustling throng of travellers. I had no idea what she looked like, but, if I stood in a prominent position, no doubt she would find me.

The first rush had started to clear, when I noticed a young woman with a small child hurrying towards me. Next to her was a stocky man in his late twenties, carrying a small suitcase. Suddenly, they stopped, the woman handed the child to the man and took the case in return. They kissed briefly, then the man and child followed the stream of passengers, while the woman walked directly towards me.

She was about 25 and decidedly attractive. Short black hair framed a pretty, smiling face. A smart brown suit couldn't disguise a figure that was both full and in proportion. Her eyes sparkled with a bright intelligence.

'Hello, I'm Anna,' she said in a soft, rich voice with just a trace of the West Country at its margins. She kissed me on the cheek and I kissed her in return.

I was agreeably surprised. This wasn't going to be as embarrassing as I had expected. I took her case from her and headed towards where I had parked my car.

Conversation flowed easily considering the circumstances. She was aware that she was meeting a double killer for the first time, yet she was completely at her ease. In fact, she was acting as if she knew me, all on the basis of seeing me on TV for half-an-hour.

I asked who the man and child where.

'Oh, that's my husband, he's looking after our daughter for the weekend. We do our own thing,' she answered dismissively.

I asked her where she was staying and what her plans for the weekend were.

'Oh, I thought I was staying with you,' she replied, looking me straight in the eye. Her answer was brutally unambiguous, even for someone as naïve in women's ways as me. I headed for a hotel.

Events now seemed to have taken on a life of their own, with me almost as an observer. I really didn't know what I intended to do. It was Janice's birthday, if only she had survived the extra five days to see it. Today we would have been celebrating both that and our engagement. Was I now going to mark this occasion by shagging some gangster groupie who had seen me on the telly?

I walked into the hotel room and searched in the darkness for the light switch. Behind me I heard Anna close the door. As I turned, she was on me.

In truth, it startled me. I had had too many surprises in conditions of darkness of late. I didn't exactly jump, but my overstretched nerves gave me a nasty jolt. As Anna wrestled passionately with me in the gloom, I found myself sneaking a look at her face in the shaft of daylight from the window. I don't know what I expected to see — fangs perhaps? But the parameters of my universe had seemed so fluid of late, I felt that anything was possible.

Doing a wrestler's waltz, we manoeuvred towards the bed. The suitcase and various articles of our clothing lay in our wake. The problem for me was that sex was the last thing on my mind. The trauma of the past week, coupled with the decidedly unsexy nature of the encounter combined to prevent me from getting a hard-on. I realised that there was no way I would be able to fuck Anna at the moment.

I prised her from me and turned on the light. Already her make-up was smeared and runny and her face wet with sweat. Her eyes, wide with expectation, turned to surprise. I sat her on the bed.

'Anna.' My voice was surprisingly steady. 'There's something I must tell you.' I told her of Janice's death just five days earlier, the fact that today would have been her birthday, the encounter with the coroner and my sleepless night. I neglected to mention the reason for the latter.

She was immediately sympathetic. No doubt my performance was sincere enough to convince her I was telling the truth. She cradled me in her arms and hugged me.

'What do you want to do?' she asked.

I realised that she was a nice person, genuinely warm and caring. I didn't want to be alone this coming night. I could do worse than spend it with her.

'First, I'd like to sleep for a bit. Then, perhaps, we could go out for the evening, if that's all right with you.'

She nodded her approval. We both undressed, climbed into bed and, within a very short time, I fell into a deep sleep.

It was early evening when I awoke. I felt both rested and refreshed. Anna was already awake beside me. We cuddled briefly and I felt myself respond. This time I made love to her.

I was wondering what to do for the evening. I considered the possibility of calling Tom and Elaine. I checked at the thought that

Tom was still in hiding and was reluctant to go out much. That triggered the suspicion in me.

Was this Anna really who she said she was? How had she got my number? Would the producer have given it out to a stranger over the phone? I should have checked it out. I was well aware that I had been a suspect in Janice's death. Would the police have gone to the extent of slipping a woman into me to see if I made any incriminating admissions? I knew they had done it in cases in the past.

I mentioned it to Tom. When I told him that we had had full sex he said that he doubted she was a policewoman, unless she took her job very seriously. He suggested we all go to the pictures together.

The four of us met up, had a drink, then went to the West End to a cinema. *True Romance* was a violent love story that struck a chord in me. Clarence and Alabama seemed equally as doomed as Janice and I had been, yet their love had conquered all. Perhaps I was just unlucky.

We returned to Tom's flat and had a puff. It was early in the morning when Anna and I returned to the hotel room. Again, we made love. As she lay in my arms and I drifted off to sleep, I was grateful for her company this night.

It was late afternoon on Sunday when I put her back on the train. There was no sign of her husband or child. We kissed quite passionately and said that we had both enjoyed ourselves. There was no arrangement to meet again. As she walked away and was suddenly gone, it was like the end of a dream sequence. Not that I snapped out of it, rather that I began to wonder if what had gone before was real. Was it really a case of some young woman seeing me on the telly and wanting to shag me? Or was it, in fact, a rather sophisticated undercover police operation?

Whatever it was, it had hardly done me any harm. If nothing else, it had got me through what had promised to be one of the loneliest nights of my life. I would always be grateful to Anna for that. Shaking my head at all the unusual intrusions into my life of late, I turned and walked away.

* * *

Initially, Janice's death seemed to bring me closer to her mother. I would find excuses to pop over to her flat to discuss the funeral and the imminent inquest. On many matters Mrs Harris indicated that she would leave decisions to me, almost as if this final shock had been all too much and anything to do with her daughter was too painful to contemplate. On one matter she was adamant, though. She rejected the suicide theory out of hand. She was sure that Janice had died in an accident.

It was something I wasn't going to argue about with her. Obviously, if Janice had committed suicide there was the implication that her mother had failed her, especially as she hadn't left a note for her. No doubt Mrs Harris was dealing with this as best she could.

Over the following weeks, though, her attitude gradually changed. As she got in touch with various members of her extended family, individuals who had seen very little of Janice incidentally, she began to exert greater control. She was always very conscious of appearances. This was reflected in the fact that she could never bring herself to visit either Janice or Mark in jail. It was as if she had suddenly realised that the funeral would be a very public and formal family gathering, one, moreover, at which she would be expected to play the leading role.

She began not to return my calls and was short with me when I phoned. Arrangements, which previously I had been making, were taken out of my hands and I wasn't informed of her decisions. It was only through talking to Luke that I managed to find out the date of the funeral. It was as if the daughter she had virtually rebuffed in life had been claimed by her in death.

* * *

With *Parkhurst Tales* selling well now, I began to receive regular requests to appear on radio and TV. Criminal justice issues were always topical and, no doubt, I was articulate enough to give a reasonable account of my point of view. However, I didn't kid myself about the real reasons behind my appeal. For a large section of the media, and the general public for that matter, I would always be 'Norman the Murderer' rather than 'Norman the Author'. It seemed that they needed a hate figure to rail at, almost like the symbolic burning of a witch to defeat evil.

The irony was that if they had taken the trouble to listen to what I was saying, it wasn't too far from their own position. *Parkhurst Tales* was a cautionary tale. Its message was that, should any young man want to be a gangster, he had better be ready to spend a large part of his life in jail. And all for no purpose.

A few days after the episode with Anna, I went up to Manchester to take part in a TV programme about the life sentence. At least, that was what I was told. I booked into my hotel and walked the short distance to the studio.

The programme was a major disappointment. The dozen participants fell into two distinct groups. The first were all relatives of people who had been murdered and they looked suitably wounded and angry. The second group was a mixed bag of psychiatrists, churchmen, probation officers and welfare workers who held generally 'liberal' views about the life sentence, in so far as they didn't believe in the death penalty or that life should mean life in all cases. Needless to say, I fell into this latter group.

To my surprise, the programme opened with a two-minute clip about Myra Hindley, hardly a typical 'lifer'. Then the presenter came directly to the invited guests for their views on the life sentence in general. In effect, anyone who held even mildly liberal views was placed in the invidious position of virtually appearing to defend Myra Hindley and her prospects for release. The two positions weren't mutually exclusive. It was quite possible to believe that Hindley was an evil cow, while supporting the proposition that some lifers could safely be let out.

The debate quickly grew acrimonious, with the relatives of victims understandably emotional. Soon they were shouting abuse at people they perceived to be defenders of child-killers. Meaningful debate rapidly descended into farce.

After the programme, I cornered the producer. I said I never would have appeared if I had known that Hindley was in the programme. The producer was unrepentant and seemed quite pleased with herself, arguing that it was good TV. It was a useful lesson for me. It taught me that I should be less trusting of the media in future.

I was still upset as I drove back to London the following morning. I wasn't claiming to be an angel, but at least I was on their side now. In similar situations in the past I had turned to Janice for comfort. Apart from the odd blast from Janice 2, she was never judgemental about me. However, where could I go to find her now?

Inevitably, I found myself heading towards Torrington. I don't know what I expected to find there. Perhaps some comfort from being at the place where she had passed from this world into the next.

It was mid-morning by the time I arrived. The ticket office was closed and, other than a single traveller on each side, the platforms were deserted. Even so, I felt very conspicuous as I closely examined the scene anew.

Now that I had seen Sergeant Ford's photographs, I could better piece together what had happened. I stood before the white picket fence, obviously well-cleaned since the incident. I tried to work out where Janice had gone into the train for the fence to have been splattered as it was in the photos.

I walked the edge of the platform, staring carefully at the track, trying to discern where the sports bag had been, where the carrier bag, the shoulder bag and, finally, where Janice's body had ended up. It was difficult, there was no trace of anything untoward now. There had clearly been a massive clean-up operation.

I returned to stand before the picket fence. Then moved on to lean against the stanchion, the one that had also been splattered with blood in the foreground of the photo. An idea struck me. Suddenly, I was in criminal mode. I was with Janice and intended to push her in front of the train. It would be no problem getting her to go wherever I wanted her to. She was so out of it, she could hardly stand.

I looked around me. Just along from the stanchion seemed a perfect spot. The platform sloped downwards here, so that we would be below the line of sight of anyone standing on either platform. Behind me and to one side was obscured by the picket fence and the superstructure of the steel staircase that went up and over the track. Immediately to my right, a wooden shed shielded me from the view of car-drivers waiting this side of the track. On the other side, the road curved obliquely so that for any driver to see me he would have to swivel his gaze through 90 degrees and peer beneath the staircase.

Suddenly, my thoughts were disturbed by the clanging of a bell. Across the track I saw the red-and-white-painted boom lower to prevent cars from approaching the level crossing. I guessed that the other boom had been lowered this side, but it was obscured by the shed. I awaited the arrival of the train.

There was a roar in the distance, but it was difficult to tell from what direction it was coming. From the lowered point of the sloping platform I had a limited view of the track towards Bishops Stortford, which was also partially obscured by the ticket office. To my right, the shed blocked out everything except a part of the level crossing.

The wall of sound drew closer. With an ear-splitting shriek it was suddenly upon me. The very air seemed to vibrate as an impressionist blur of train-carriage grey thundered through the station from my right.

It was the Bishops Stortford train. The same one that had killed Janice. Well, not perhaps the actual train, but a sister train. Almost too quickly for the brain to assimilate, as it had appeared, so it was gone again. All that remained was the receding howl of tortured steel and an imprecise memory of carriages flashing by.

It was literally breath-taking, a thunderous assault on the senses and it was over in seconds. If Nigel Hampton had intended to push Janice in front of the train, no wonder he had misjudged it. Unsighted, the train would have been on him and gone almost before he could react.

Instinctively, I had stepped back as the train came through. In the bright, morning sunlight something glinted, causing me to look down. The source was in a long crack where one section of sloping concrete platform met the next. It was something small, bright and silvery, like a crumpled piece of silver paper. I bent to pick it up.

The crack was a good inch deep and clogged with the detritus of windblown rubbish. Awkwardly, I manoeuvred my thumb and index finger to try to gain purchase on the object. Twice it slipped before I was able to pull it clear. As it came into view I gasped. It was Janice's silver ring, the one she always wore on her right hand.

With hands shaking, I peered closely at it to make sure. It was bent out of shape, the back forced inwards from the impact of the train as it had knocked it from her hand. There was black train paint in two smears across the elongated points of the front. But it was definitely her ring, I had seen it a thousand times.

How amazing. How incredibly, unbelievably amazing. It was ten days since the incident. Sergeant Ford had said that the station had been sealed off and a major 'scene of crime' search had taken place. Yet no one had found Janice's ring nestling in the crack in the platform.

I found myself smiling. A great, warm feeling spread through my body and I knew, I just knew. This was a gift from Janice. She had given her ring to me from beyond the grave as a keepsake of her love.

I drove home and examined photos of Janice just to make sure. The silver ring in the photos was identical to the one I had found. I took an old silver chain and threaded it through the ring. From now on, I would always wear it around my neck. It would protect me on my mission to destroy Janice 2.

The following day I was due to visit Ivor and Bessie. On the way through North London, I popped in to see Ian. I hadn't seen him for a couple of days, since before the meeting with Sergeant Ford, in fact. Normally quite lethargic, he jumped to his feet as I entered.

'Norm, Norm, I dreamed about Janice.'

His voice was strained and urgent as he grabbed me by the arms. I stared into the raddled face of my old friend and tried to determine his mental state. The combination of drink, drugs and the dementia had reduced him to a shadow of his former self. I only saw the man I used to know through brief windows of lucidity now.

He was sincere enough, though. He explained how he had been sleeping when he had seen the figure of Janice from behind. She was wearing the long, green coat she had on when she was killed. Suddenly, from out of nowhere, a foot had appeared and kicked her in the back, propelling her forwards into darkness. Then he had woken up, fearful and sweating.

On its own it was nothing, merely the rantings of a demented man. But taken in concert with all that had gone before, perhaps it had meaning. I told Ian about the meeting with Sergeant Ford and of finding Janice's ring at Torrington. As I journeyed north to see Ivor, it was a very troubled man I left behind me.

Ivor, Bessie and the children were sympathy personified. It was good to get away from London, but the flat where I had stayed with Janice brought back memories that tormented me. For a long while I just stood in the kitchen, staring at that spot in the yard where she had crouched, crying. In my thoughts, I cradled her in my arms again and tried to relive the moment.

By coincidence, or so she said, Bessie was due to see a psychic later that day. She saw her on a regular basis and swore she had learned important things in the past. She invited me to accompany her and Ivor.

The psychic looked just about as unmystical as it was possible to be. An overweight, dowdy woman in her mid-thirties, her thick, Black Country accent made most of her pronunciations as indecipherable as those of Nostradamus. Bessie had told me that she came from gypsy stock. The grimy, run-down house, in a terrace of similar dwellings, seemed a million miles away from a gypsy caravan and life on the open road.

Bessie and Ivor both had sessions with her alone, then it was my turn. Barely two weeks previously I would have dismissed the possibility of just such an encounter out of hand. Now I approached it with some trepidation.

Mavis, for that was her name, listened carefully as I detailed the events of the previous fortnight. I handed her Janice's ring. She turned it over in her fingers, briefly closing her eyes.

'I can't feel anyone around, can you?' she intoned in what passed for English in her neck of the woods. The word 'incongruous' sprang to mind and defeated 'strange' in a brief battle of semantics. I mused that, as a writer, I would never have dared to place such words in her mouth. She gave me back the ring.

'There is one thing ...' She paused midway through the sentence and closed her eyes again. 'You'll be coming into a large sum of money shortly ...' She stopped abruptly, opened her eyes and, all at once, seemed embarrassed. She visibly struggled for words. At last, with a self-conscious attempt at a smile, she got it out. 'Ooh, but you won't be getting it legally.'

It was the closest she had got in the ten minutes I had been with her. I hadn't told her I was a thief and it wasn't that obvious in my manner. However, I certainly expected to get large sums in the immediate future.

LIFE AFTER LIFE

Although I had never so much as thought about another woman while Janice was alive, now she was gone there was a yawning gap in my life. Whereas before I had tolerated the loneliness, treated it as an integral part of my life, now I knew there was something better. I yearned to warm my spirit with the presence of another.

I suppose it was to be expected that Judy and I would drift together. She had been a good friend to both Janice and myself. But I didn't intend to move into my flat with her. The memories of Janice were too strong and I had abandoned it to move back in with my mother. However, occasionally I did stay there with her. At other times, I stayed at her flat near Ian's.

There were several marked similarities between Janice and Judy, but also several differences. Both were black girls, but whereas Janice was of mixed race with light skin, Judy was much darker. She was also several years older and was statuesque to Janice's petite build.

Probably her best feature was her face. Long, black hair framed beautiful features, set off by perfect teeth. Like Janice, she had a fiery temper and could be a nuisance when drunk. When upset, her eyes would flash fire, reflecting a definite degree of madness.

The source of the instability lay in her youth. Whereas Janice had been raped at 15, Judy had been sexually abused at an even earlier age. Its legacy was a drink problem designed to block out the memory. Janice had enjoyed sex, but to Judy it was more of a duty, to be endured rather than enjoyed, lest she experience those feelings of guilt she still carried from the earlier incident.

As with Janice, Judy had a fearsome crack habit, but that was the only drug that possessed her. She funded her habit through shoplifting, but was nowhere near as professional as Janice.

I immediately experienced two severe problems with the relationship. First, I had just been through a love affair with a girlfriend possessed by crack and couldn't face the trauma of another one. Secondly, Judy wasn't Janice. There was no passion, no spark and we didn't share the magnetism.

In truth, I was still very much in love with Janice. The relationship wasn't helped by an incident early on.

One Saturday, after a night out together, Judy and I returned to my flat at Carshalton. We went to bed, made love, then I fell asleep.

The following morning Judy seemed somewhat subdued, but, like Janice, she was subject to extreme mood swings so I thought nothing of it. We were together all day and slept at her flat that night.

It was as I was making love to her that I first noticed her crying. 'Judy, what's the matter?'

I lay beside her, cradling her head in my arms. Beside me, she buried her face in the pillow, sobbing bitterly.

'Judy, please, Judy, tell me what's up. Is it something I've done?'

There had been a couple of arguments when I had refused to buy her 'crack'. Still sobbing, she shook her head.

'So tell me what it is. Please.' I cajoled as if coaxing an answer from a child. She turned to face me. Her eyes were wet with tears, but there was something more. She looked about her quickly, fearfully and pulled me closer as if to reassure herself that she was safe.

'Last night, Norman. Last night ...' Her voice faltered with fear and she dissolved into floods of tears again.

A familiar suspicion dawned and I felt the familiar cold hand clutch at my heart.

'What happened, Judy? Please tell me,' I pressed.

'It was after you fell asleep. There were footsteps on the stairs. All night long I heard footsteps running up and down the stairs. It was Janice. I know it was. She doesn't want me to be with you.' Again she cried.

Over the next hour I went through her account in minute detail. There was only one set of stairs, the one inside my flat. So the noise couldn't have come from another part of the house. She was convinced it was real. She had lain awake all night, stiff with fear. I knew the feeling myself.

Strangely, I felt comforted rather than threatened. Whatever it was, I hadn't heard a thing. It seemed that I was being haunted by a jealous spirit, one that clearly loved me. Equally clearly, it was an unquiet spirit, one that wouldn't rest. Perhaps it was trying to tell me something. As I continued on my mission I could only hope that it would be revealed.

$$* \quad * \quad *$$

Most weekends now, I tried to get away from London. Weekdays were spent ricocheting around from friend to friend, constantly in motion lest I stood still long enough to think. It was a constant pressure that demanded some respite.

This particular weekend, I went down to visit Ambrose. On the Saturday evening we went out on the town, but it was all half-hearted stuff. Both of us were just going though the motions. With his wife involved in a late-night card game, Ambrose and I returned to the house to puff and talk about old times. We laughed about old characters, old villains whom we hadn't seen for years. We retold old prison stories, ones we both knew by heart. We both studiously avoided talking about Janice.

When we finally repaired to bed, Ambrose put me in the guest room I had shared with Janice. I lay in the centre of the double bed, the twin toy gorillas either side of my pillow. Now my thoughts inevitably returned to Janice.

Through the effects of the puff, I felt that all my senses were highly attuned to my surroundings. There was absolutely no physical evidence of Janice's presence, but I did feel her close. Perhaps it was wishful thinking. My eyes wet with tears, I eventually fell asleep.

As I drifted up to consciousness, I knew that something had woken me. Equally surely, I knew that it was something to do with Janice. I was still in that twilight state somewhere between waking and sleep. I realised that I had better pull myself together quickly, lest whatever it was ended before I could fully witness it.

There was a vibration in the bed next to me, just beyond my right leg. 'Compute, compute,' I ordered myself mentally. 'Push through the fog. What exactly is it that you feel?'

I stretched out my right hand and placed it on the spot next to my leg. Immediately, I felt the sheet vibrate beneath my hand. I examined the feeling more closely. It wasn't a bouncing-up-and-down vibration, rather, it was as if it was coming from below the sheet and tended to pull my hand down into it.

I wasn't at all frightened, in fact, I felt myself smile. My Janice was near again. As I turned to look to my right, something white and diaphanous, like the sheerest silk scarf, flashed downwards and out of sight. I was aware of a tiny, tinkling sound like 1,000 fairy bells. It was coming from the top of the dressing table next to the bed. Dozens of small make-up bottles were gently vibrating together.

This all happened in the space of a few seconds. As I came fully awake, everything stopped. But I knew what I had experienced. I fell asleep again, comfortable in the knowledge that, somehow, Janice had managed to bridge the gap between the next world and this one.

∗ ∗ ∗

With my Carshalton flat costing me £120 per week in rent and my rarely staying there, I decided to let it go. I moved the last few pieces of my clothing to my mother's, which only left a fridge and the double bed Janice and I had brought from our North London flat. Rather than leave them for the landlord, I decided to give them away.

Tom's sister, Carrie, was in the process of moving to a new flat in Brixton and said she could do with them. I said that she could have them if she could arrange the transport.

Carrie was a couple of years younger than Tom and very different indeed. She was well aware of his many shortcomings, the lies, the deceit, the taking advantage of friends, but she invariably stood by him, while regularly taking him to task for his sins.

I got on well with her. She was honourable, straightforward and quite intelligent. The only trait she seemed to share with her brother was a propensity for promiscuous sex. She was very forward in a 'laddish' sense and had had affairs with many of Tom's friends and acquaintances over the years.

Although she had a lively personality, she wasn't particularly attractive. She was short and had a tendency to put weight on easily, which made her look dumpy. She tried to compensate for this by being outrageous.

It was quite clear that she looked up to me. I was far more sensible and honourable than most of her brother's friends. I got the feeling that she felt Tom was in good hands with me. Consequently, she was always perfectly proper around me.

Carrie arranged for a friend to hire a van. He met up with me, we collected the bed and fridge from Carshalton and delivered them to Brixton. After the friend left, I remained to talk to Carrie.

The conversation inevitably turned to the recent death of Janice and the various psychic incidents. Carrie confessed that she had had mildly psychic abilities since a child, but had deliberately ignored them for several years.

During a lull in the conversation, I noticed her looking at me pensively. As if suddenly coming to a decision, she spoke.

'Look, Norman, I like you and I don't want you to think I'm just saying this, but for the past ten minutes or so I've felt a spiritual presence. It's gone now, but I'm sure it was Janice.'

I stared at her closely, examining her expression to see if she was joking. But Carrie was eminently sensible and wouldn't have joked about something that I felt so deeply about.

'I feel a bit silly now, I don't want you to think I'm just trying to get your attention.' She looked down at the floor.

'Carrie,' I began, 'I know you wouldn't do that to me. Are you sure it was Janice?'

Carrie stated that she was sure, then went on to give instances where she had experienced psychic incidents in the past. I listened, enthralled. It seemed that psychic phenomena were far more common than it was generally believed. Suddenly, she stopped mid-sentence.

'Norman, Janice's spirit is back again,' she announced abruptly.

I stared at her and around her, but could see no change whatsoever, other than that she now looked decidedly uncomfortable, as if she were aware that something was hovering over her.

'What's it like, Carrie? Is it friendly? Does it mean any harm?' My questions were quick, breathless and almost whispered.

Carrie smiled and seemed to relax a bit. 'No, it's quite friendly,' she paused and was obviously thinking deeply. 'But other than that, I can't tell you anything,' she concluded. She began speaking again immediately. 'Oh, it's just gone.'

The incident brought us together, bridged any remaining gap between two strangers. I could tell she liked me and, in truth, I liked her. She was strong, intelligent and funny. Further, although she liked to go out at weekends and get off her face, for the rest of the time she had her life under control. Almost inevitably I asked her out.

I wasn't surprised when she accepted.

On Friday at 9.00pm I picked her up from her flat. I had been invited to a party at Camden. Liz, a lesbian girl I had met through Janice, was celebrating her birthday. Liz thought she was a man. She certainly dressed, acted and fought like one. But she was funny and had a wide circle of equally nutty friends. I knew it wouldn't be a dull evening.

Carrie and I arrived just after ten and the party had already begun. Liz welcomed us and we were introduced to as bizarre a group of partygoers as you would find this side of Bohemia. You could have spent the rest of the evening just trying to work out the sex of the various guests. The best part, as far as I was concerned, was that they wouldn't be at all judgemental. The fact that I was a 50-year-old guy with a 25-year-old girl went completely unremarked upon.

I had a couple of Es with me and Carrie and I took one each. I did recall something Tom had said about Carrie having a problem with Es in the past. I asked her about this, but she just threw her head back and laughed. Soon we were both out of it, bopping about to the music.

Like myself, Carrie liked to dance. In fact, she was a wicked dancer. She suggested we go on to a club. The Black Cap was close by. Twenty minutes later we were on the dance floor surrounded by the gays, the straights, the animal, vegetable and mineral that comprised the clientele.

We had a great time. We relaxed in each other's company and the E transported us into a happy, touchy, feely world of music-driven bliss. We staggered out of the club at just after 1.00am and returned to the party.

Liz's place was quiet, deserted and in darkness. As I rang her bell a neighbour popped her head out and said that there had been some trouble and the police had been called. We quickly got back in the car and I headed for Brixton and Carrie's flat.

The closer we got, the more I thought about what would come next. I guessed that Carrie would expect me to shag her. A number of things deterred me. Firstly, her brother was a friend of mine. Perhaps I was being old-fashioned, but I wondered how he would feel about it. Was it all too incestuous? In similar circumstances, would I feel betrayed if he shagged my sister?

Then there was the fact that Carrie was quite outrageous about her sexual liaisons. A couple of times I had heard her holding forth to a mixed group of friends about the minutiae of some steamy encounter.

The guy always ended up shocked, and the way Carrie told it, it invariably left the group shrieking with laughter. I didn't particularly want to become another funny story in Carrie's repertoire.

Lastly, I didn't really fancy her. Perhaps it was a combination of all the above, but it was also a physical thing. However, I was committed now. I would have to play it by ear. If we ended up in bed together, then I would do what duty demanded.

We climbed the stairs to her flat. As we entered, she turned and came easily into my arms. We kissed passionately and I felt myself respond. The problem for me was, I really liked this girl as a person. I could see sex getting in the way of our relationship.

She prised herself from me, explaining that there was something she had to do. She disappeared through a door to our right, which I knew to be the bedroom. I stood in the same spot, waiting.

In under a minute, she was back. As she came close I reached for her again, but she stopped short of me. I immediately noticed there had been a complete change in her attitude. Mediated through the effects of the E, I couldn't quite put my finger on what it was. However, she was distinctly colder and more distant.

As she spoke, there was an embarrassed look on her face.

'Norman, please don't be offended, but I really don't think that we should make love tonight.'

Now it was my turn to look embarrassed. I was nothing if not proud. There was no *quid pro quo* with me. If a woman didn't want to sleep with me, then I didn't want to sleep with her.

'Carrie,' I almost spluttered, 'that's OK. I've really had a great time. Perhaps we can do it again soon.'

Seeing I was about to leave, she stepped forward quickly and grabbed me by the arms.

'Oh, I don't want you to leave,' she said forcefully with just a hint of desperation in her tone. 'It's just that I don't feel that we should have sex.'

I knew something strange was going on, but the effect of the E was the complicating factor. It was difficult to establish what was actually real.

She led me into the bedroom and indicated that we would share the same bed. There was only one bed anyway, the one I had given her from my flat. I stripped down to my underpants and got in. In truth, I was quite tired now and was looking forward to sleep. Carrie put on a short nightie and climbed in next to me.

I reached out and put an arm around her shoulders. We lay cuddled together.

Suddenly, she sat bolt upright. 'I feel like doing something,' she announced energetically. 'Maybe we could go out and ...'

'Carrie,' I cut her off short. 'I'm absolutely fucked. I couldn't face getting in a car and driving anywhere.'

'OK, OK,' she replied, decidedly manic now. She jumped out of bed and disappeared from the room.

Two minutes later, she was back. There had been another change in her. She was altogether calmer now.

'Sorry about that,' she said softly. She climbed in next to me and cuddled close.

Hardly had we settled down again than she was up again.

'I must do something,' she announced manically. She jumped out of bed and stared around the room.

Even through the effects of the E, I was quite worried now. Perhaps she was having some sort of psychotic interlude brought on by the E. I tried to recall what Tom had said about her earlier problem. Maybe she was just freaked at the thought of spending the night with 'Norman the Murderer'. I quickly dismissed the latter as mere paranoia.

'You know, this is the one room in the flat that I didn't finish decorating,' she said conversationally, as if we were a couple discussing the décor. I noticed strips of wallpaper that had been partly peeled off.

Carrie came to a decision.

'I know, I'll finish stripping the wallpaper.' She began pulling at the hanging strips.

Now I really was worried. Stripping wallpaper at 2.00am was bizarre by any standards. I studied her carefully to try to determine if there was the possibility of her turning violent, because she was clearly disturbed. Just then, she rushed out of the room again.

When she returned, she had calmed down once more. She sat at a table across the room and began to read. It was all very confusing. However, confused, bemused, whatever, there was another feeling that was overwhelming me. I was absolutely dead tired. I just couldn't keep my eyes open. With a deep sigh, I turned on my side and fell instantly asleep.

When I awoke several hours later, Carrie was still bustling about the room. My head was clear now and perhaps so was hers. We seemed uncomfortable around each other, as if we had both been on a date that had turned sour. Neither of us would be at our ease until we parted.

I dressed, thanked her for a nice time and, quite formally, kissed her goodbye. As I walked from the flat, I examined the recent experience and tried to work out exactly what had happened. My life was full of bizarre sequences now, though. At the moment, the meaning was beyond me. I would have to file it away with all those other 'yet to be processed' memories. Once again, I yearned for Janice.

If anything, the earlier psychic incident with Jess had brought us closer. It had affected him deeply. He never mentioned Janice now and, if I told him of any psychic occurrence, he studiously avoided comment. He clearly regarded me as being much stronger in that department and possibly as someone who could protect him spiritually.

We still went out together. For a married man with two young children, he certainly had an active social life. On the Thursday following my Friday night out with Carrie, we went out in a foursome. With his wife away in the country somewhere, he had arranged a date with his babysitter and her mate.

Both were very young, barely in their twenties. While mine was pretty and plump, his was petitely dark and attractive. In the event, his was called away at the last minute. We went out in a threesome, with Jess playing 'gooseberry'.

It turned into a typically nutty, West End night out. We went from club to club, returning to Jess's place in the early hours of the morning.

My girl, Sally, was a sweet soul, if not a particularly bright one. Her head was full of all the silly things that obsess the minds of young girls in the teenage magazines. She was mightily impressed by the fact that I was a published author. It affected the way she was behaving. Clearly, she was playing a role.

We had danced in the clubs, she had drunk and we shared some Es that Jess had got. We were both turned on by each other. We rubbed together as we danced. In the darkened corner of one club, as we smooched sexily, she pulled out one breast for me to kiss. It was unspoken that we would sleep together later.

As we entered Jess's flat, he handed me the keys of another flat a couple of miles away. When I said that I didn't think I could find it in the state I was in, he suggested that we both sleep in a pull-out bed in his lounge.

We unfolded a divan settee and settled down. Jess wished us goodnight and climbed the short flight of stairs to his bedroom.

Sally was immediately embarrassed.

'I know Jess well. I come round here a lot,' she explained. 'I don't want to make love with him lying just up the stairs. I'm sure he will hear us.'

It was understandable.

'Don't worry about it,' I consoled. 'We'll be seeing each other again, won't we?'

Sally nodded her agreement.

'So there will be other times when we can make love,' I continued. She nodded again and snuggled close.

We lay in each other's arms, winding down from the helter-skelter passions of the evening. Suddenly, there was a sharp sound to the left side of the bed, on Sally's side. In the stillness, it stood out quite clearly. Not startlingly loud, but enough to grab the attention. I looked to try to determine its source.

A large, Welsh dresser stood to the left of the bed, its stained oak glinting dully in the half-light from a table lamp at the other side of the room. The sound seemed to have come from a point on its upper shelving, just above head height. It had been a sharp, wood on wood sound. As if someone had thrown a wooden child's brick against the oak of the dresser. But there was nothing to see now, if there ever had been. Already, I was beginning to feel uneasy. Things seemed to be starting again.

Sally hadn't noticed anything. Or rather, if she had, she hadn't reacted in any way. She still lay in my arms, completely relaxed, occasionally nuzzling her face against mine.

Crack, the sound came again, but louder and more intrusive. Sally jerked her head around to look for its source. I stared in the same direction, but there was nothing to be seen. Sally returned to gazing at the ceiling. Several minutes passed.

CRACK, it was a sound almost like a pistol shot, but with no resounding, concussive echo. I felt Sally jump beside me. Startled, she gaped at the dresser as if demanding an explanation of it.

'What was that?' she asked breathlessly, a catch of fear in her throat.

I had all too clear an idea of what it was. It was definitely something to do with Janice. But to explain, to go all through the entire, drawn-out story would take too long and be too tiresome. Instead I said, somewhat tongue-in-cheek, 'Perhaps it's a ghost.'

All at once, Jess was at the foot of the stairs, staring wide-eyed at us across the bed.

'Did you hear that bang up there, Jess?' I asked.

'Norman.' His tone was intense. 'I heard it from outside the house. The noise came from outside the house.' He sounded very scared.

Beside me, Sally was sitting bolt upright now. She looked backwards and forwards from the overwrought Jess to myself, searching for an explanation.

'Are you sure, Jess?' I asked.

'Norman,' he said with emphasis. 'For the last half-hour I've heard footsteps going up and down the gravel path in the back garden and each time I've looked out there was no one there.' His voice trailed off.

By now, Sally was frightened, too. When Jess went into the kitchen to make a cup of tea, she joined him. I was left to mull over what was happening by myself.

I wasn't the slightest bit scared. I knew it was Janice and that she meant me no harm. These incidents seemed to occur whenever I was in bed with a woman. In one way it was quite funny. Janice was policing me from beyond the grave, frightening my girlfriends and driving them away. My mind went back to the previous Friday with Carrie. I resolved to question her about it later.

For now, though, as far as romance was concerned, the evening was ruined. I could hear Sally and Jess muttering together quietly in the kitchen. No doubt he was telling her about previous incidents. I suppose I should have joined them and calmed their fears. All at once, though, I was terribly tired. I don't remember doing so, but I must have fallen asleep.

When I awoke in the morning, Sally had already left. With a mental shrug, I reasoned that it was never going to last anyway. In the cold light of day, though, the events of the previous evening seemed more serious. There could be little doubt about it, Janice was haunting me. That I didn't seem to mind was a tribute both to my continuing love for her and to my bizarre mystical outlook on life.

If things continued this way, I could see her isolating me from all my friends. And was it healthy for one of the living to be tied so closely to one of the dead? I felt that Janice's spirit meant me no harm, but some part of her had tried to do away with my mother. That in itself would have virtually finished me. If only I could determine which was Janice 1 and which was Janice 2. One solution, of course, would be to complete my mission quickly and destroy the latter.

As soon as I got home, I phoned Carrie at her flat. Quickly dispensing with pleasantries, I asked earnestly, 'Carrie, what exactly happened last Thursday?'

It was as if she had wanted to get it off her chest. It all poured out and I let her continue until she had finished. She told me of how everything was all right until she had gone into her bedroom. She was adamant that Janice's spirit was there. It was oppressive, emphasising that she mustn't have sex with me that night.

It had frightened her badly. She didn't want to tell me about it and she didn't want me to leave her alone in the flat. Perhaps she should have suggested that I sleep on the sofa in the other room, but maybe I would have refused and gone home.

The solution, of just lying next to me in what had once been my and Janice's bed, was no solution at all. As long as she was in the room with me, Janice's spirit would bear down on her oppressively and freak her out. The moment she left the room, the feeling would pass and she would be all right again.

It explained the transformations in her that I had witnesed. It was reassuring that I had found out what had happened, but, on the other hand, it was nothing to get complacent about.

I told Carrie about the events of the previous evening with Sally and Jess.

'Oh, Norman,' she said, 'what are you going to do?'

I confessed that I didn't know at the moment. Whatever it would be, I would have to do it on my own. I thanked her for her help and hung up.

* * *

For several days, my life returned to a semblance of normality. The next shock wasn't long in coming, though. My only consolation was that it was an entirely corporeal one.

It was the tone of the man's voice that put me off guard. I answered my phone and admitted that he was, in fact, speaking to Norman Parker.

'Oh, I'm Detective Sergeant Neil Thompson from King's Cross Police Station,' he said.

My heart did skip a beat, any active criminal's would. Only the truly blameless are completely unmoved when contacted by the police. I was immediately on my guard.

'I wonder if you would come down to King's Cross to see me,' continued DS Thompson seamlessly.

Now I was concerned. What could it be? Would I walk into the nick quite voluntarily and not walk out again? I searched my mind for anything that might have compromised me lately. There was nothing. The runs from Spain were still continuing uninterrupted.

I had hesitated noticeably. Sensing my reluctance, DS Thompson spoke again. 'I'll tell you what it's about, Mr Parker. It's about Janice.'

The last word was like a semantic bomb. It plunged into my consciousness and set every nerve ending jangling. I was as nervous with expectation as a child on his first day at school. 'What about Janice?' I heard myself croak.

'I'll be very frank, Mr Parker,' there was concern in the voice now, 'it's about Nigel Hampton. A woman called Louise McDonald has been arrested for hitting him over the head with a bottle. Nigel Hampton is friendly with her daughter, a seriously drug-addicted girl called Elsa. Elsa told her that Nigel Hampton had asked her to commit suicide with him by jumping in front of a train.'

I heard the words but the overall meaning refused to register. What did strike home though was the reference to suicide in front of a train.

'Can I come and see you right now?' I asked quickly.

He said that I could and gave me directions. Barely 20 minutes later I was parking my car at the back of King's Cross Police Station.

DS Neil Thompson was a well-built man in his early forties. His solid, angular, unsmiling face spoke of someone who had seen too much pain and misery. If I had to choose one word to describe him, it would have to be 'no-nonsense'. Everything about his manner said that he wouldn't pussy-foot about.

He met me at the front desk and quickly led me into a back office. When another officer made to follow, he shooed him away, closing the door with him still outside. He waved me to a chair and sat himself down. 'I'm Neil, call me Neil. Can I call you Norman?'

He stuck out his hand and I nodded agreement as I shook it.

He pointed to a tape machine that lay on a table next to us, the tape holder open and empty.

'You can see that there's no tape in that, Norman. You'll know I'm not secretly recording this when you hear some of the things I'm going to tell you. I could get in serious trouble.'

He waited for his words to sink in. I didn't intend to say much anyway. I had come to listen.

'We've been interested in Nigel Hampton for some time now. He's always hanging around the Cross and the vulnerable drug-addicted girls who go there. There have been a couple of incidents in which girls have died, ostensibly by suicide, where the last person seen with them was Nigel Hampton. We've never been able to prove anything, though.

'We knew that he had seen Janice occasionally. We know he was the last person to see her before she died under the train. What we're really concerned about now, though, is the girl he's with right now. She's a little blonde girl called Elsa, same age as Janice. In fact, Janice knew her. She's a hopeless heroin addict, injecting. She's also got a bad crack habit. We've warned her about Nigel Hampton. Her mother's warned her. But she won't stay away. He buys her the drugs she needs. Now she's told her mother that Hampton has asked her to commit suicide with him by jumping in front of a train. We're afraid that the same thing is going to happen to her as happened to Janice.'

My mind was racing to take it all in, analysing, synthesising, looking for underlying nuances of meaning. All the time, I was looking for any secret trap for me. Where did I fit in to all this? I was definitely 'Norman the Murderer' to the police. They almost certainly knew that I was active. Janice was dead, I could do nothing for her now. I would have to be careful that this wasn't some elaborate plot to bring me down.

'So what do you want me to do, Neil?' I asked evenly.

'To be honest, I don't really know.' He turned away and stared at the wall. He looked decidedly put out now, noticeably out of control. 'I'll admit that this case has got to me. No one has ever frightened me like Nigel Hampton frightens me. We think he's a serial killer. He talks vulnerable girls into suicide pacts, then encourages them to go through with it while he drops out at the last moment.'

It was heady stuff, but I wasn't really having any of it. From my point of view, there was one basic flaw. I had killed Janice. I finished with her and, feeling abandoned, she wrote suicide notes and jumped into the train. To believe anything else was to shirk my responsibility, to avoid the guilt that was my due. Perhaps Nigel Hampton had encouraged other girls to commit suicide, but Janice was my responsibility.

Suddenly, another thought dawned on me. The police knew of my violent background, that I had killed people in the past for minor things compared to this. Perhaps they were out to kill two birds with one stone here. No doubt Nigel Hampton was a thorn in their side. I was sure they had no great love for me. If they could convince me that Nigel Hampton had killed Janice, perhaps they thought that I would kill Nigel Hampton.

Lastly, there was the issue of being a 'grass'. To inform to the police was anathema to me. If I did think that someone had done me a wrong, I would deal with it in my own way. I certainly wouldn't involve the police.

Neil Thompson seemed disappointed by my silence.

'So what do you want me to do?' I repeated.

'Maybe if you saw Elsa,' he suggested. 'Told her about what happened to Janice. Can you help us at all with this Nigel Hampton?'

It was the constant repetition of his name that triggered the memory, one that I had entirely forgotten. Janice had told me that the night she had stayed with him, before flying on to meet me in Spain, the police had swooped on his house in Torrington. I mentioned it to Neil Thompson and he indicated that he already knew. That gave me another idea. Perhaps I could get to the bottom of the mystery of Janice's plane ticket, her showing up right where I was in Spain and the police coming on to my plane as I landed in England.

At first he ducked my question. Then, realising that if he didn't give me something, I wouldn't help him, he acquiesced. He admitted that it had all been part of an operation to catch me.

That they had been out to get me wasn't what concerned me. It was all part of the game if you were active. What did concern me though was that Janice had obviously been a part of it. Or rather, they had thought that she was.

It was all very confusing. I said I would go and find Elsa for him. I stood, shook his hand and did my best to suppress a shudder as I left.

Tracking down Elsa proved a lot more difficult than I had first thought. It was a safe bet that the girls round Ian's would know her. Sure enough, Emma was a personal friend of Elsa's sister and knew Louise, the mother. But Elsa was every bit the gypsy that Janice had been. All the girls claimed to know her, to have served time with her, even to have spotted her down the Cross recently, but none knew where she might be found right now.

In the end I settled for Emma, who took me to Elsa's sister. Anne was a pale, untidy-looking girl of about 25 who threw her hands up in despair when I asked her where I might find her sister. I told her about Janice's death and the danger I thought Elsa was in. She said that the best thing would be to talk to her mother.

Louise McDonald's reputation preceded her. According to Emma she was a minor legend in the locality. She had drunk and fought the length and breadth of the Caledonian Road for the past 30 years. And not just with her fists. Emma offered the opinion that Nigel Hampton was lucky that Louise had hit him with only a bottle.

It was with some trepidation that I was finally ushered into the presence of the great woman. After all the build-up, Louise was something of a disappointment. She was a small, wizened woman in her mid-fifties, who moved about with quick, rodent-like movements, as if permanently on her guard against some sneak attack.

Her eyes were hard and piercing. They burned not so much with fire, but with bitterness. Louise was not content with her place in the world, which was why she tried to blot it out with the drink. It was barely noon, yet it was clear she had already had a few.

Emma introduced me and Louise gave me a withering look.

'You've got something to tell me about my daughter?'

The accent was broad Scots, the tone threatening, as if I was poking my nose in where it wasn't wanted.

I explained about Janice's death and told her about what the police suspected of Nigel Hampton. The mention of the latter galvanised her from her previous indifferent state.

'Don't you worry about Nigel,' she cautioned darkly, as if I was some kind of supporter of his. 'I'll deal with him in my own way.'

That pronouncement virtually signalled the end of the conversation. It was clear to me that Louise didn't want my help and, in fact, almost resented my intrusion. As no one knew where Elsa was or could lead me to her, there was nothing more I could do. Consoling myself that I had done my best, I left with Emma.

* * *

With the inquest now imminent, all thoughts of Elsa and anyone else for that matter faded into obscurity. I knew it would be an ordeal for me, one that would solve nothing either. I knew all the facts that would be brought out. Sergeant Ford had kept me briefed about developments. And if I knew anything about courts, coroner's or otherwise, the verdict wouldn't reflect the evidence.

It was a bright spring day in the market town of Bishops Stortford. The Coroner's Court convened in an old Georgian building which also housed the Civic Offices. I arrived early and sat at the back of a long, narrow, pillared room. From here I could observe anyone who entered while, partially obscured by a pillar, remaining unobserved myself.

All the major players began to arrive. I reflected that it was very much like a play, each actor having his or her particular role. Mrs Harris arrived, all in black, accompanied by Luke. I stood and waved, but she ignored me. After they had sat down, Luke turned and waved surreptitiously.

Sergeant Ford, the two policemen who had come to my mother's flat and 'Sad Face' milled about in the margins between the seats. They all acknowledged me. From time to time they were joined by other men who looked quite awkward in their smart suits. I guessed these to be the train driver, the ticket office man and other railway personnel.

I was particularly looking out for Nigel Hampton. Although I had met him the time I drove Janice and pretended to be a minicab driver, I hadn't got a good look at him at all. Now I would try to weigh him up. Differing personae fought for supremacy — Nigel the multi-millionaire property dealer vied with Nigel the 'crack-head' serial killer, who competed against Nigel the rival for Janice's affections.

The proceedings started before he arrived and they now took all my attention. Witness followed witness, adding their particular piece of the puzzle. When Nigel Hampton was called, I fully expected him to be absent.

I was a good judge of men, having spent so many years living cheek by jowl with them in the prison situation. But from the back of the courtroom it was hard to characterise this Nigel Hampton.

The word 'nondescript' came to mind. Average build, in a stoop-shouldered, dissolute, crest-fallen sort of way. Thirtyish, pallid-faced, longish, sandy, thinning hair. Bemused-looking, weak-chinned, self-conscious, not at all a warrior who would challenge me for Janice's hand. And so I dismissed him as a rival and rested content in the knowledge that the third suicide note had been meant for me.

I still intended to have a word with him, though. Just to let him know that, if I thought for one second that he had harmed my Janice, I would visit a personal Armageddon on him. However, I was mindful of the fact that Janice had described him as a friend to her. I would be careful not to do anything that might distress her spirit. For if I was intent on the salvation of that spirit, I couldn't do anything to hurt it.

It came as no surprise to me when the Coroner ruled that it had been an accident. Mrs Harris had cut a sympathetic figure and it was clear that she rejected the suicide theory. In the grand scheme of things, it wasn't particularly important. My immediate concern was to confront Nigel Hampton.

As he slipped out of the courtroom, I was close behind him. Sergeant Ford shot me a worried look and made as if to intercept me, but I was too quick for him. However, I wasn't quick enough for Nigel Hampton. As I exited into the street, he was nowhere to be seen.

It temporarily confused me. I couldn't comprehend how he had disappeared so quickly. I walked the length of the block and rounded the corner. To my surprise, he was waiting for me.

Nostrils flaring, firmly in battle mode, I approached him quickly. He held out his hands as if to ward off any attack.

'Norman, I just want to talk to you,' he pleaded.

'That's good, 'cause I want to talk to you,' I rejoined deadpan.

'We can't talk here.' He looked furtively over each shoulder. 'Can you meet me at The White Horse in Torrington tomorrow?'

'What time?' I demanded.

'Will one o'clock do? There's only one White Horse, you'll find it easily enough.'

'See you at one tomorrow then,' I said menacingly. I watched as he turned and scurried away.

I was at Torrington early and spent half-an-hour just standing on the platform near the spot where Janice had died. I tried to picture some cosmic gateway, a point where Janice had made the transition from this dimension to the next, returning almost at will, albeit only in spirit form.

The bright morning sunlight highlighted a reality that was both solid and unyielding. Everything was bounded by harsh lines that clearly marked the parameters of their existence. Mysticism seemed as remote as the mountain passes of Hindustan.

After the brightness of the station, the saloon of The White Horse seemed as dingy as a cellar. I sat in a prominent place at the bar.

Precisely at 1.00pm, Nigel Hampton entered. He sidled up and sat on the bar-stool next to me. I dispensed with the handshake, ignoring his outstretched hand and asked him what he wanted to drink. As the barman went to fetch it, I turned and, with no preliminaries whatsoever, spoke.

'Nigel.' His eyes met and held mine as I said his name. 'Let me make something very clear to you.' My tone was calm, even, measured. 'If I thought for one minute that you had hurt my Janice ...'

'You'd kill me,' he interrupted, cutting me off mid-sentence. 'But I was a friend to Janice,' he added quickly. 'I would have never done anything to harm her.'

I looked long and deep into his eyes. They were clear and expressionless. I had known serial killers in prison and there was inevitably something steely about their gaze. As if they lived in a nightmare world, had witnessed terrible things, and their very vision was mediated through them.

'Janice told me about you, Norman,' he continued. 'She loved you. She would never sleep with me all the time she was with you.'

The last bit was added almost as an afterthought. It roused mixed feelings in me. Pleasure that Janice had been faithful to me, and pain that he had known her before. I felt grateful to this man, this friend of Janice and I owed it to him to be truthful.

'The police are bang after you, Nigel. They had me down the nick and told me about you.'

'Oh, what did they say?' he asked animatedly.

'They think you're a psycho,' I replied.

'Oh I am, I am,' he emphasised, laughing and sounding quite pleased with himself.

Mentally, I took a quick step backwards. This was a very bizarre reaction to what I had just told him. Perhaps I had misjudged him and should look at him anew. Instead of appraising him as a macho rival, maybe I should assess him in terms of the sicko 'nonce' cases of the jail-house.

'Aren't we all?' I answered quick as a flash to mask my change of attitude.

We made desultory conversation. Suddenly, I remembered Janice's plane ticket. Nigel said that it had all been very strange, as if the police wanted her to meet me in Spain at all costs. He said that she had had an open ticket that must have cost all of £300 and he hadn't paid for it.

It was all beginning to fall into place. They had been pressurising Janice to inform on me. That was why she had run away for three weeks just before Christmas. The poor soul was caught between loving me and wanting to be with me and being forced to betray me on pain of a long prison sentence if she didn't.

The shoplifting at Gatwick all made sense now. She was a good 'hoister', she would never have done that in a top-security place like an airport. No, she had deliberately got herself nicked so she wouldn't have to travel to Spain and compromise me.

If anyone had killed Janice, had driven her to her death, it was the police. Some bungling under-cover cop, in a misguided attempt to get me, had blackmailed her until she broke. I had always hated the police. I felt a new wave of rage against them wash over me.

There was nothing more to be said to Nigel now. Before I left I thanked him for being a friend to Janice. This time I did shake his hand.

* * *

With the inquest out of the way, we could now proceed with the funeral. Or rather, Mrs Harris could proceed with it, for she wasn't communicating with me at all now. I thought it ungenerous of her in view of the fact that she knew her daughter had loved me. But love was a far too uncontrolled an emotion for Mrs Harris to tolerate. A sense of order and the keeping up of appearances ranked far higher.

I welcomed the funeral and was mortified by it, both at the same time. Welcomed it in the sense that, at last, my Janice would be laid to rest and I would then have somewhere to go to feel close to her. Mortified in that it would be a very public occasion at which I was sure to break down and, further, it was her final, symbolic parting from the land of the living. At present, I was surviving one day at a time. After the funeral, what was there to look forward to?

From Luke I learned that Mrs Harris had invited mourners from her extended family and close circle of personal friends. The irony of this was that Janice had rarely if ever met her extended family and I was sure she had never even been allowed close to Mrs Harris's friends.

Whether I liked it or not, Janice's family and friends were drawn from among the 'street people' she associated with in North London. So, if the funeral was to be about Janice, then it was only right that they should be invited. I didn't go so far as to put posters up around King's Cross, but I did have cards printed asking anyone who wanted to attend the funeral to contact me.

By coincidence, Janice's body was lying in an undertaker's whose premises were at the end of the street where Emma lived. The start of the procession was timed for 10.00am, a bit early for the 'street people', but they knew that, if they didn't get there in time, there would be no lift to the cemetery.

Two distinct groups of mourners soon emerged on the broad pavement outside the undertaker's. Mrs Harris's crowd were smart and dignified and, save for their sombre dress, could have been bound for Royal Ascot. Apart from two exceptions, they were all black.

Ian and Charlie had clearly got straight out of bed to attend. Their clothes were creased and neither had shaved. Equally clearly, Judy and Emma were still hungover from whatever they had taken the night before, to steel themselves, no doubt, against the ordeal of the following day.

Jess had toned down his usual finery which he wore for Soho socialising, but he couldn't resist the bright-red waistcoat beneath the dark-blue jacket. Ivor and Bessie were propriety itself in their smart suits and highly polished shoes. They stood talking to Jess, halfway between the two main groups, as if not quite sure where they belonged.

Mrs Harris arrived on the stroke of 10.00am. Within seconds of her appearing, everyone made a move towards the waiting cars. Needless to say, no provision had been made in the official cars for anyone outside Mrs Harris's group. But I was ready for that. Ivor and Jess had both brought cars, as had I. We climbed in with room to spare, even including two scruffy girls who arrived at the last minute.

The chapel at St Marylebone Cemetery was small and quite beautiful. Its clean, Gothic lines were as counterpoint to the arboreal chaos of the surrounding trees. In the strong sunshine it gleamed like an exquisite jewel in a precious setting. God and man, in conjunction, had created something of great beauty.

Inside the chapel, though, only man held sway. Mrs Harris had arranged it so that her party sat down the left, close to the coffin, the chaplain and the organ. The rest of us were strung out across the pews to the right of the aisle.

I knew I would cry at some stage. In the event, even before the organ struck up, tears were streaming down my cheeks. The service passed in a blur. It was as if I had tunnel vision. I focused on the chaplain and never took my eyes off him until it was over. Awareness only returned as I stumbled outside into the daylight.

Then, as the cortége bearing the coffin moved off along an avenue towards Janice's final resting place, something very beautiful happened. Whether it was pre-planned or whether it was something that black people do at their funerals, I didn't know, but some mourners skipped along beside the hearse, singing.

All too soon, we were a crowd gathered around a hole in the ground, albeit a crowd in two parts. Mrs Harris's group gathered around the head of the grave where the chaplain was. The rest of us crowded together at the opposite end.

The chaplain led the prayers, the coffin was lowered into the ground and the grave-digger began frantically shovelling dirt into the hole. He must have over-exerted himself, for he was soon forced to rest. Quite incongruously, Charlie stepped forward and took the shovel from him. He began to scoop great shovelfuls of earth on to the coffin.

I hadn't been waiting for any particular time, but now seemed as good an opportunity as any for what I intended. Taking the gold engagement ring from my finger, I stepped forward and dropped it into the grave. From the moment of her twenty-fourth birthday it had been Janice's engagement ring. It was only fitting that she should have it now.

I had learned from Luke that Mrs Harris had organised a get-together for after the funeral. Once again, neither I nor any of Janice's street friends was invited. As if to protect me from this final snub, Jess and Ivor led me away. We set off with Bessie for our own private farewell drink to Janice.

In the aftermath of the funeral, I went through the events of the day over and over again. Mrs Harris had behaved very cruelly to me. Everyone who had known Janice said that I was the best thing that had ever happened to her. That I had treated her well and she had found more happiness with me than with anyone.

To be fair to her, Mrs Harris wouldn't have seen it that way. Perhaps she had grown used to Janice appearing, then disappearing into prison. At least when Janice was in prison, she knew where she was. And maybe she didn't mind the constant stream of low-life druggie boyfriends. They were never around long enough for her to have to deal with them.

But as soon as 'Norman the Murderer' had appeared, there was a great change in Janice. Admittedly, it was for the better. But then she had died. Perhaps it was only understandable that her mother should blame me. Anyway, grief did strange things to people. No doubt Mrs Harris was dealing with her grief as best she could and who was I to condemn her? For Janice's sake, if for no other reason, I would forgive her.

❋   ❋   ❋

As if I didn't have enough problems, the puff smuggling coup from Spain finally collapsed. Both greed and complacency had played a hand. The latest couriers had taken a Volvo estate car and packed it with almost 120 keys. They had even put nine-bars in the door panels so that the windows wouldn't wind down. Not surprisingly, they had been stopped at Customs and the cache had been found.

All I had really lost was my share and, of course, my sole means of earning a living at the moment. It was small comfort that Tom informed me that he was finally ready to do one of his techno-fraud money transfers with his special machine.

He had obtained details of an account with over £1m in it, as well as information of when the account holder would be going away on holiday. A hacker had to be paid, a signature forged and some new parts bought for the machine. It all cost money, my money. Almost before I knew it, I was in to the tune of £3,000.

In truth, I didn't particularly believe in the project. There had been several failures in the past. However, I was £90,000 strong at the moment and had given Tom my word that I would back him. As I handed over the money, I was sure I would never see it again.

In many ways, it was a last chance for Tom. The exotic Elaine had left him, love having proved no match for poverty. In her place was another extremely beautiful but badly damaged girl called Lucy. I really didn't know how he did it, because he was nothing to look at himself.

Lucy was tall, stunning and very sexy. She was phenomenally spirited which, compounded by a severe 'crack' problem, made her unstable and self-destructive. Like so many girls I was meeting, she had been sexually abused in her early teens. Now, ten years later, she was struggling to block the memory out.

If you studied her carefully, you could tell that the tough exterior was just a façade. However, it was a very effective one. In some ways, she was merely an appetite in motion. She appeared, took what she wanted, then moved on, often leaving chaos in her wake. Tom and his friends sometimes referred to her affectionately as 'Tank Girl' after the cartoon character. She was certainly violent and disruptive enough.

I didn't have a problem with her. I recognised her as another troubled spirit who had temporarily moved into my orbit. On the one occasion she had met Janice, she had got on well with her, which was no mean feat. At the moment, she was Tom's girlfriend and he said he needed her to do the signature. As far as I was concerned, it was his decision and I wouldn't interfere.

Tom and Lucy were kindred spirits as far as drugs were concerned. In fact, the basis of his appeal for her was probably the fact that he was forever off his face on a wide variety of illegal substances. The problem, as far as I was concerned, was that this made them very unreliable and difficult to deal with. And for something as sophisticated as a techno-fraud coup, precision was an absolute necessity.

To my surprise, and probably Tom's, too, the coup worked. Or to be precise, just over £1m had been sent electronically to an account in Spain. This was where I came in. I had found this Spanish account holder through friends of mine. Now, provided he could draw the money out, all I had to do was go to Spain to collect our share.

I was in Marbella the following day, staying at Ron's house. It was he who had introduced me to the account holder. Jacob was an ancient, retired Jewish banker who was deeply into the mysticism of the Kabbala. Knowing my interest in the subject, Ron had introduced us.

Our discussions were deep and far-ranging. Learning of my background in crime, Jacob had pronounced one day, 'Banking and crime are synonymous.' They were my sentiments entirely; that was why I lost little sleep over robbing banks. One thing led to another and Jacob mentioned his special bank account. The rest, as they say, is history.

Jacob lived in a large, old house in the hills above Marbella. Strangely for a Jew, both his middle-aged manservants were Arabs. A more sinister pair it would have been hard to find. I had been around sinister men all my life, but the two of them unnerved even me. It was a strange set-up entirely — Jacob, the old gloomy house and the two malignant Arabs.

On the way up to the house, I joked to Ron about being murdered for our shares. Ron laughed and dismissed it out of hand. I could tell he had never even considered the possibility. I wasn't quite so trusting. I had borrowed a small .32 calibre pistol. It nestled reassuringly at the base of my spine.

In the event, all that was needed to secure the money was a smile and a handshake. The smiles came from Ron and me. We were both of the firm opinion that Jacob could never have managed such a feat of facial dexterity, and the Arabs most certainly couldn't. They entered the room, solemn as pall-bearers, carrying a small, battered brown suitcase between them. Not that it was heavy. $750,000 in $100 bills doesn't weigh that much. Their role was as much ceremonial as anything.

I opened the case immediately. The crisp, new $100 bills in neat bundles looked quite out of place in the battered old suitcase. I wondered if there was something special about it, or whether Jacob was just too mean to buy a new one.

I accepted Jacob's assurance that all the money was there. I would count it as soon as we got back to Ron's place anyway. Still very much on my guard, I shook hands with Jacob and, keeping one eye on the two Arabs, made my way to the door.

We were on the path outside when Jacob called Ron back. There was a brief, whispered conversation, then he hurried to join me again.

'What was all that about?' I muttered out of the corner of my mouth.

'Tell you in the car,' replied Ron in similar vein.

We were at the bottom of the drive before I spoke again.

'Well, what did he say? That it's all counterfeit?'

Ron sat silent, as if weighing his words. Now I really was becoming suspicious.

'Well?' I repeated. 'What did he say?'

'It's nothing about the money,' intoned Ron darkly. 'I suppose you could say it's more to do with Janice.'

I sat bolt upright in my seat. If I had been driving I would have certainly lost control of the car. What could Jacob possibly know about Janice?

'Jacob said,' began Ron in a tone that clearly indicated that they were Jacob's words and not his, 'that there is something that is trying to take you over and you must fight it.'

He enunciated the words quite clearly so there would be no chance of a misunderstanding. The message was short and succinct. There could be no ambiguity. I didn't bother to ask him either to repeat or to explain. I sat there in silence.

Of late, I had become increasingly aware of a dark force within me, that beckoned me to my doom. It was something more than depression or my normal self-destructiveness. Undoubtedly, since Janice's death, the world had become an unrelievedly dark place for me. I found no pleasure in anything now. I felt even more isolated from the rest of humanity than at any time during my life sentence.

Life had become a curse rather than a blessing for me. I had tried to rejoin the human race. I had driven the evil from my heart and found God in my own peculiar way. Janice's love had warmed my icy spirit and I had found some peace. Peace from my rampaging, rumbustious, troubled spirit. Merciful peace.

Then, with Janice's death, it was all snatched away from me again. The loneliness and pain came rushing back, all the more poignant because I had found some respite. I had made a mess of this life and wouldn't be sorry when it was over. For the moment, I would blindly pursue my mission to destroy Janice 2. It would help to dissipate my rage and ward off feelings of impending self-destruction.

Ron left me to my thoughts. We didn't speak until we were back at his place. Subdued now, I counted the money. It was all there. Tom and I would get just over £160,000 each.

I immediately wired some money to Tom. The following day I collected him and Lucy from the airport. Tom was beside himself with joy, like a child who has pulled off a very clever trick. He was very naïve about crime. He treated it as if it were all some jolly game, only ever with rewards and never with sanctions. I hoped he would never have to learn the hard way. Tom wouldn't have lasted five minutes in Parkhurst.

There was no changing him, though. The irrepressible little boy would always out. I had playfully nicknamed him 'Boy Wonder'. He didn't like it at all, probably because it was too close to the mark, but even his sister said that it was rather apt. Funny nicknames apart, I would just have to do my best to contain him. My first task would be to prevent him from telling everyone what we had done.

He seemed almost surprised when I handed over his full share of £160,000. Always, in the past, his partners had robbed him of some portion of his share. He quickly paid me back the couple of grand he had borrowed from me over the recent months. The smile on his face said that he thought he had got off lightly.

We all had something to celebrate and Ron's house rang to the sound of loud music and laughter. Tom was in fine form. Already falling down drunk, he regaled Ron with details of his next proposed techno-fraud, one that would bring us even more money.

I joined in the celebrations with the others, but my heart wasn't in it. I now had in the region of £250,000 in cash. Not bad for someone so recently out of prison. But what did it mean? I was still desperately unhappy. I still missed Janice as much as I had the day she died. And I could see no end to it. I couldn't begin to contemplate the thought of someone eventually taking her place.

The saying 'money isn't everything' ran through my head like a constant refrain. In my case, that had certainly proved to be correct. What was I to do now? I had achieved wealth and, by contemporary standards, success. Yet still I felt unfulfilled and restless. What would be my next goal? I had only the mission to destroy Janice 2 to concentrate on. In my heart of hearts, I feared it would destroy me, too.

Tom suddenly tired of just sitting about drinking. He wanted to go out. He wanted to spend some money. After months of living from hand to mouth, he wanted to enjoy the pleasure of his new-found wealth.

'What's the use of having money if you can't spend it?' he shouted.

The immediate problem was that it was now after one in the morning. Unlike England though, people would still be out and about. Ron suggested that we go to Puerto Banus. He excused himself and stumbled off to bed.

On a weekday, even Banus was largely deserted. We had a drink in a couple of bars where the barmen outnumbered the customers. It was a beautiful night, still warm from the heat of the day, but with a slight, cool breeze that came off the sea. We decided to stroll through the streets of Banus.

Suddenly, we came to a designer sports shop that was still open. Its windows were full of expensive jet skis, wet-suits, tennis rackets and equipment for every conceivable sport. With a small shriek of delight, Tom rushed inside with Lucy following close behind.

I had never known him to express any interest in sport. He had rarely been straight long enough to be able to participate. And Lucy most definitely wasn't 'sporty'. Yet soon they were excitedly rummaging though racks and racks of brightly coloured sports gear.

'Aaah ...'

It was both an exclamation and a sigh of pleasure. Tom held aloft a brightly painted skate-board. He discussed its merits animatedly with Lucy, then bought it. He hurried outside to try it.

So, at 2.00am, having recently stolen over £1m quite bloodlessly, I strolled through the streets of Puerto Banus in slow pursuit of the rest of my 'gang'. Boy Wonder was in front, negotiating the pavement obstacles on his new skate-board, occasionally letting out a 'whoop' when he did some particularly clever trick. Tank Girl tottered along behind, an erotic fantasy in her high heels and skimpy blue dress. I brought up the rear, looking through the eyes of a writer at this life of mine that so regularly insisted on imitating art. I could only wonder what would come next.

LIFE
AFTER LIFE

In pursuit of a lifestyle more in keeping with his new-found wealth, Tom decided that we should rent a nice apartment. Ron's house had always been perfectly adequate for me, but it wasn't something I was going to argue over. I didn't intend to throw my money away, but perhaps I could indulge myself a bit more now.

Tom suggested that I leave the choice of apartment to him. I had already promised Ron I would accompany him to buy a new car, so I went off with him, while Tom and Lucy went apartment hunting.

I had no intention of buying a car myself. I was only in Spain one week out of four and hire cars always sufficed. However, as Ron perused the stock of a Marbella car showroom, I suddenly found myself looking at a gunmetal-blue Mustang.

'Why don't you buy it?' said Ron from behind me.

To be honest, the thought hadn't even crossed my mind.

'You'll get that for about £6,000 English money,' cajoled Ron.

It certainly made me think. Compared with what I had, £6,000 was small change. And whereas I would have never bought such an attention-grabbing car in England, in the anonymity of Spain I could get away with it.

In the event, Ron couldn't see anything he liked. I drove away in a shiny, gunmetal-blue Mustang with a white, convertible soft top. Even the extrovert Tom was overawed.

'Great choice, Norm,' he conceded, 'it will go with the apartment.'

I suppose that should have warned me. I was suspicious when he said that it should have cost £1,200 per week, but he got it for the bargain price of £800. You could get a luxury villa for less than a third of that.

The apartment was in an exclusive block that lay between Marbella's high street and the sea. An alarm bell rang when Ron informed me that a well-known local dignitary had an apartment there, as did a couple of Colombian drug dealers. He said that to buy one would cost about £500,000.

The block stood in its own grounds and was surrounded by a high wall topped by a steel fence. Entry was by way of an electronic gate that was operated by an armed guard from inside a bullet-proof, glass vestibule.

The hallways and staircases were vast expanses of white marble. Whole walls were of glass, revealing the manicured gardens and Olympic-size pool. To describe our flat as a three-bedroom apartment did no justice at all to its scale. Each bedroom was easily three times the size of an English counterpart. You could have got four full-size snooker tables in the lounge alone. The kitchen wouldn't have looked out of place in a small hotel and the marble-floored balcony was so long that Boy Wonder skate-boarded it.

I suppose I should have been annoyed. If the police did look at us, we could never explain how we could afford to live there. However, in the desperate frame of mind I was in at the time, it gave me a much-needed lift. I was going back to England in ten days. I told Tom that, after I left, he should look for a reasonably priced villa.

Living cheek by jowl with Tom and Lucy, it soon became apparent that they weren't ideally suited. When they were both off their faces they could tolerate each other, but when they were down the sparks would fly. Tom was arrogant, Lucy massively independent, both were quite selfish. I suppose it was only a matter of time.

* * *

I woke suddenly, realising that something had disturbed me, but not knowing what. Most sound didn't penetrate the marble-clad walls of my mausoleum-like bedroom. From the darkness outside the window I could tell it was still early.

BANG, BANG, BANG. Three sounds like pistol shots shattered the early morning stillness. With several hundred thousand dollars still in the flat, my first concern was that it was a police raid. I jumped out of bed.

BANG, BANG, BANG. Three more concussions came from the direction of the lounge. I ran along the hallway, feet sliding on the polished marble, and skidded into the lounge. Tom had Lucy by the hair; she had her hands around his throat. They wrestled across the room and fell full-length on the sofa, screaming at the tops of their voices.

As they rose, still wrestling, I was on them. I tore them apart and threw Tom bodily across the sofa. Grabbing Lucy by the throat, I ran her into the main bedroom and threw her across the bed. I quickly shut the door behind me.

'What the fuck's going on?' I roared at her.

She jumped to her feet and faced me angrily.

'How would you like to keep waking up and find him lying next to you wanking?' she shouted back.

There really was no answer to such a question. In fact, it was so bizarre that it temporarily confused me. I stood there with my mouth open, blinking.

'That cunt's a fucking pervert!' continued Lucy, *fortissimo*.

It shocked me out of my inaction.

'Lucy, for fuck's sake, keep it down,' I pleaded. 'We've still got all the money in the flat.'

That seemed to calm her somewhat, but she still stood there fuming, fists clenched in anger.

'Lucy, I don't want to get involved in your and Tom's sex life,' I began.

'Oh, that's it,' she interrupted. 'I suppose I'm just supposed to lie there and put up with it. Just like you fellas to stick together.'

'Lucy, I'm not taking sides.'

'Well, it fucking sounds like it to me,' she shouted. 'You tell him that if he ever touches me again, I'll fucking kill him!'

That gave me the excuse to go and talk to Tom. He was pacing the lounge, muttering to himself. I had never seen him so angry.

'That fucking, crack-head cunt,' he began as I entered the room.

'Tom, keep it down,' I cautioned. He lowered his voice.

'Well, she's a fucking lunatic. That's her with me. I want her out of the flat.'

It seemed that the rift was irreconcilable. As much as I didn't want Lucy to go off on her own, to keep them together might lead to a serious incident. The last thing we wanted right now was to attract attention to ourselves. Perhaps it was best that they parted.

Lucy already had a sizeable sum of money. She had been to Marbella several times before and had friends there. I helped her pack and took her to a hotel. She had forced me to choose.

Tom and I weren't out of the woods yet. The police could come after us at any moment. In the circumstances, I would have to stick by my mate and crime partner. In the final analysis, Lucy was only his bird.

The incident only highlighted for us the dangers of still having all the money around us. We would have to find somewhere to hide it, but where? To rent a safety deposit box might attract attention. Many of the drug dealers buried large sums in the grounds of their villas, but we didn't have this option. However, it did give me an idea.

JD had once warned me that many of the Spanish along the coast were well aware that resident drug dealers often were forced to bury large sums of cash. It was something of a local hobby to look out for suspicious gardening work at unusual hours. There were apocryphal tales of stashes that had been discovered and stolen.

The answer was to bury the stash away from prying eyes, in a spot where it wouldn't be accidentally stumbled upon.

'Where would we find such a place around here?' queried Tom.

'We won't find one around here,' I answered.

It was a 90-minute drive to Janice's place in the mountains, by the bridge over the gorge. On the road that led to Coripe, we didn't so much as see another car. We parked and Tom went one way and I another. I walked along a dirt track, then climbed halfway up a hillside. I buried my money in two plastic boxes, beneath a large rock.

If I had been seen, it was only by the local wildlife. It was a long way to come when I wanted more money, but it was perfectly safe. It was also quite fitting that I should have buried it at Janice's place. I was sure that she would watch over it for me.

* * *

Although Tom and Lucy had said goodbye to England semi-permanently, I had several reasons to go back. Apart from promoting my writing career and a couple of deals I was involved in, my mother still lived there.

I decided to return through Holland. English airports were always high-profile places, so I would fly to Amsterdam and take the ferry. I was in no hurry and cost wasn't a factor, so I stayed overnight and toured the city the following day.

Somehow, I found myself in a large bookshop. It had an extensive section on magic. As I perused one book, I came upon a chapter on exorcism — suddenly I was engrossed.

'The Devil hates nothing so much as a good Gospel,' read one part of the text. The reference was to the first 13 verses of the Gospel of St John. It was called *Il Principio* and had been used since medieval times as a potent charm to drive out evil spirits. An idea began to form. I had a strong feeling that I was meant to find this book. I bought it.

The ferry crossing was smooth. Amidst the vastness of the sea one could only conclude that each individual was completely insignificant in the grand scheme of things. I passed through Customs with only a cursory check and was soon on a train to London.

I had left my mobile with my mother, as it didn't receive in Spain. As soon as I walked through the door, she showed me a record of calls she had taken and said that Emma had called several times and wanted to speak to me urgently. She wasn't on the phone herself, though, so I would have to wait until she called again.

I looked down the list of callers and saw that Neil Thompson's name was amongst them. I wondered what he wanted from me. I wouldn't rush to call him. If he didn't call again, he wouldn't hear from me.

Emma wasn't long in calling. Her voice sounded strained, panicky.

'Norman, Elsa's dead. She was found dead in the streets near King's Cross early Sunday morning. That Nigel Hampton was with her the night before.'

There were too many strange things going on in my life to say I was stunned, but it did make me think. I wondered if there was anything I could have done to save her.

'What did she die of?' I asked.

'They don't know yet, they're still doing tests,' replied Emma.

'How's Louise taking it?'

It was a superfluous question really. I didn't particularly care about her feelings, but I expected there would be repercussions. I wasn't to be disappointed.

Emma lowered her voice as if that would prevent anyone who was listening from hearing.

'Don't say I said so, but there's a load of her relatives down from Scotland. They've been scouring the Cross for days, looking for Nigel

Hampton.'

This was worrying news for me. If anything happened to Nigel Hampton, I would be among the prime suspects. And with a bunch of nutty Jocks about to fall on him at any time, I would have to be with people who would support me if I wanted an alibi. The first thing, though, was to phone Neil Thompson. I could guess what he wanted to talk to me about now.

Within the hour, I was facing him across the interview room table at King's Cross. Neil looked suitably grim. It wasn't an 'I told you so' look but, clearly, he was searching his conscience to see if there was anything more he could have done.

I couldn't believe that Nigel Hampton could be so brazen as to do in another girl in circumstances which he knew would make him the prime suspect. Neil wasn't so sure.

'If he talks some girl into deliberately taking an overdose with no witnesses around, how can we prove it?' he argued.

He told me that he knew about Louise's relations who were looking for Nigel Hampton. At that point, I felt that I should make my own position perfectly clear.

'Let me emphasise this, Neil,' I said with passion, 'I don't give a fuck about Nigel Hampton. For a start, I don't believe he pushed Janice into the train. And even if he did, what could I do about it? I'd be one of the first people you'd come to if anything happened to him. No, Neil, the way I look at it is that if I was going to wish anything for him, I'd wish exactly what he's already got — a £600-a-day crack habit. It's killing him slowly and painfully. Why should I put him out of his misery?'

Neil looked thoughtful. I guessed he was weighing up whether I meant what I had said. The irony for me was that I had changed so much, I couldn't have done away with Nigel Hampton, whatever he had done. A couple of times, Boy-Boy had offered to have him 'ironed out'. The euphemism didn't detract from the enormity of the act. I had already irrevocably compromisd my immortal soul by my earlier crimes. It had taken me so long to claw my way back to a comparative state of grace. To be party to another supremely evil act would undo all that I had achieved.

How would I explain that to Neil, though? Would he have understood it? Then, would he have believed me? Other than if something happened to Nigel Hampton, I didn't really care what he believed. As I said my goodbye there was the strong implication that I wouldn't be seeing him again.

* * *

By now, I had thoroughly read the book on magic that I had bought in Holland. I had gone through the chapter on exorcism so many times that I virtually knew it by heart. It seemed quite straightforward. If one read *Il Principio* at the spot where the evil spirit was supposed to be, it would be driven out.

'Right, you fucker,' I muttered under my breath to that disembodied entity that was Janice 2. I had my plan, all I had to decide on was the time and the place.

It was rapidly approaching the summer solstice, a time when all the forces of nature would be at their most powerful. I reasoned that this could only give the exorcism greater impetus. I further reasoned that, in order to add to its power, it should be done by three of us, a trinity.

Ian readily agreed. In truth, it was little more than a day out to him, an escape from the dreary world of his basement flat, coupled with the possibility of a drink, too.

Judy was more thoughtful when I asked her. Although her faith had lapsed many years previously, she had been brought up a Catholic. There was still the innate fear of evil spirits that came from her Afro-Caribbean background but, even though we weren't still going out together, she would have done anything for me. And for Janice, too, for that matter.

Along with myself, we had our trinity. However, Judy was so unpredictable, even she never knew where she would be from one day to the next. She could go missing for days, lying somewhere completely out of it. Then there was the everpresent possibility of her being nicked shoplifting. I would need a more reliable stand-in.

Jess looked distinctly dubious when I first asked. He still hadn't completely returned to his normal, abrasive, knock-about 'Jock mode'. As if he was now aware that there was a force in the world that could negate even his effervescent spirit. Only someone who knew him well would notice it, but the experience with Janice 2 had definitely diminished him.

But he was a good friend to me and my appeal to him was from the heart. Further, although he wasn't so bold as to admit it openly, secretly I felt he welcomed the opportunity to hit back at Janice 2.

I was up at the crack of dawn on the morning of the solstice and ran on the common. Perhaps it was only my imagination, but the very air seemed to be alive with a zest and vitality that bespoke a positive affirmation of all that was good and wholesome.

I picked Jess up at about 10.00am. His mood was sombre but determined. As we set off together, sitting silently next to each other in the car, it triggered off an earlier memory. I was a young man again, setting off with a partner-in-crime to go on a 'bit of work'. The guns were in the boot, the intended target a bank or security van. The tart taste of early morning nervousness was fresh in our mouths.

There were definite parallels with the present situation. This too was a 'bit of work'. However, our only weapon was the prayer book we carried and our only reward would be salvation.

As usual, Ian's place was in darkness when we arrived. The interchangeable residents didn't operate by the same clock as the rest of the world. Bedtime was usually that moment when they passed out from whatever they had imbibed earlier.

I had reminded Ian and Judy the previous evening about our mission on the morrow. Even so, I was agreeably surprised to find them both in the flat. I woke them and, within 20 minutes, they were ready to leave. As the four of us set off for St Marylebone Cemetery I mused that, by any standards, corporeal or spiritual, we were certainly a motley crew.

I had timed the ceremony, for that was how I had referred to it, to take place precisely at noon. I reasoned that that was when the solstice powers would be at their height. I would take the leading role, reading the prayers. The others would join in, reading *Il Principio* from the sheets I had prepared for them.

I stood at the foot of Janice's grave, Jess, Ian and Judy gathered in a rough semi-circle at its head. I must have cut an incongruous figure with my kappel on my head and my prayer shawl about my neck, but appearances didn't figure in my list of priorities on this particular day.

I read the two prayers from my Talmud that I read every morning of my life. I fired up my spirit by thinking of all the years I had prayed in my cell to sustain me through my life sentence. I visualised the times Janice and I had prayed together, reading these very prayers. Then we were ready. I looked up.

Judy was standing, fists clenched, eyes tightly shut. Ian stared into the middle-distance, his fragmented mind transported to some mystical land where Janice could still be found. A tear had formed in the corner of one eye and had run down his cheek, leaving a glistening track in its wake. Jess shifted uneasily from foot to foot, sheer nervousness preventing him from standing still.

'Ready?' I intoned.

The question sounded like a challenge. All three looked at me and nodded. We began to read *Il Principio*.

There was no thunder and lightning, nor the faintest trace of fire and brimstone. I hadn't expected there would be. In the event, it was a thoroughly understated, rather ragged performance. Jess spoke out clearly with me, while Ian and Judy mispronounced words and hurried to keep up. It didn't matter at all. It was the intention that counted.

Soon it was over. The three of them looked at me sheepishly as if to say, 'Is that all there is to it?' There was a definite air of anti-climax as we walked back to the car.

Jess had other commitments and Judy had to go in search of her first pipe of the day, but the presence of Ian would suffice for the next leg of the mission. I thanked them and dropped them both off. We headed for Wandlebury.

It was the motion, the journeying, that reasserted the sense of mission. By ourselves now, Ian suddenly became more animated. He made a rather raddled Sancho Panza to my driven Don Quixote, but the presence of my old prison pal was decidedly comforting for me. I realised that there were some things from my prison life that I missed, not least the solidarity, the loyalty, and the way friends sacrificed themselves for each other. Qualities that seemed sadly missing from this contemporary, free world that I had found.

We made for an odd couple, standing on the side of Wandlebury hill, my prayer shawl blowing in the wind as we recited *Il Principio* again. I imagined worshippers gathered there on this day in ancient times, times when the worlds of spirits and men were more closely intertwined. I mused that the pagan deities of Gog and Magog might welcome our words, but I took grim satisfaction from the bolt of sheer torment I was firing into the third, demonic deity. 'Hold that, you fucker,' I said wordlessly.

That only left Torrington. I wanted to be there at 5.10pm when the Bishops Stortford train went through. The timing was symbolic, but symbolism would be important on this day.

It was the first time Ian had been to the station. He nodded knowingly as I pointed out the relevant spots in Janice's demise. We had arrived early and another through train hurtled past as we waited. Ian cowered back. 'God,' he exclaimed, 'I didn't realise that was what hit Janice.'

It set the mood. This was by far the most public spot where we would perform the exorcism today. I wasn't aware of any British Rail regulations covering prayer meetings on stations, but I felt there must be some. It was with grim determination that I donned my kappel and prayer shawl for this final recitation.

For once, British Rail was running on time. I read my morning prayers then, precisely as we began the first verse of *Il Principio*, the 5.10 to Bishops Stortford barrelled through the station.

I was deep in thought as we drove back to London. With nothing tangible to show, I wondered what I had achieved by my actions. Ian was eager for the drink I had promised him and whittered animatedly in the seat beside me. I was in no hurry to get back. I drove at about 60mph in the middle lane of the M1.

Apart from the arthritis, I had never been ill in my life. Blackouts, fainting fits, whatever, were completely alien to me. My conscious state had always been sharp and firmly focused.

Suddenly, a long, dark tunnel opened up right in front of my eyes. It disappeared downwards, wormhole-like, its sides marked with raised corrugations. Inexorably, I felt my consciousness being pulled into it. All the while, I was still aware of Ian chattering next to me, the sound of the car and the view through the windscreen.

Mentally, I struggled with whatever it was that sought to pull me in. Rationality dictated that my full attention should be focused on driving the car. A sense of panic surged in me as I realised that it was irresistible. With a psychic scream, I tumbled into its depths.

Before I knew it, I was back again. The reality that rushed through the windscreen showed that I must have swerved into the inside lane. I heard Ian next to me saying urgently, 'Norm, are you all right? Norm?'

I quickly looked in the car mirrors to check that I hadn't swerved into the path of anything. Fortuitously, there was little traffic southbound on this stretch of motorway. I mused that it was lucky it had happened when and where it did.

I assured Ian I was OK, saying that I was tired and must have dozed off. I ignored his further enquiries. In truth, I didn't know what had happened and wanted some time to examine the experience for myself.

It most definitely wasn't a blackout. My remaining senses had been too alive for that. Also, I was clearly conscious of some entity wrestling with me to pull me into the hole. Its intent was definitely malignant. My recent obscene curse at Wandlebury came back to me. 'And you fucking hold that,' rejoined the echo. Chastened, I acknowledged my combatant. The realisation dawned that this would be a fight to the death.

* * *

I sat for a while with Ian when we got back from Torrington. Judy, Charlie, Georgie, Charlotte and even Juby dropped in during the evening. Ian had spoken of our proposed solstice ceremony and word had got round. They were all fascinated by the idea and wanted to know what had happened.

In truth, there wasn't much to tell. I described the ceremony at the three different places. For the first time, I described the experience on the motorway. Blackouts and fainting fits were commonplace for all of them, but the way I related the details must have been sufficiently different to move them. All sat there grim-faced.

'Oh, just like *The Twilight Zone*,' said Charlotte suppressing a shiver.

It was late when I got home. There was a note pinned to the front door which read, 'Norman, see Mary, flat 42, urgently.'

Mum's flat was in darkness when I entered. There was nothing unusual in that, she was often in bed by this time. I looked into her room. The bed was empty, the room deserted. This was very unusual. Where would she be at 10.30 at night?

I ran up the two flights of stairs to Mary's flat. She was an elderly lady who often sat with my mum and ran errands for her. Mary had clearly gone to bed. When she finally came to the door, she was bleary-eyed and in her nightdress. She waved me inside, but I declined.

'Mary. What's happened to my mum?' I demanded.

'I would have phoned you but I didn't have your mobile number.' Mary looked harassed and worried both at the same time. 'She's had a fall. She's in Roehampton Hospital ...'

I was already on my way. Cutting Mary off mid-sentence, I turned and ran back down the stairs. Soon I was in my car, racing towards

Roehampton Hospital.

The night nurse was helpful, but firm. She wouldn't disturb the ward by letting me in to see my mother. She reassured me that, although she had broken her hip in the fall, she was perfectly all right. She had been sedated and was sleeping peacefully. I could see her the following day.

Later, as I lay in bed and went over the events of the day, I was sure that my mum's fall was somehow related to what I had done. Wordlessly, I cursed myself for my arrogance in thinking I could take on a mystical, vengeful crusade, without there being some price to pay.

My mother seemed very small and frail as she lay in her bed in the geriatric ward of Roehampton Hospital. She had always carried her age well, but now she looked every day of her 84 years. Her mind was still quite clear, though. Despite being obviously in pain, she told me what had happened the previous day.

It was just after noon. She remembered the time, because the *12 O'Clock News* had just started. As she went to sit down to watch it, she had noticed a bird out on the balcony. There was a netting screen to keep the pigeons out, but this one bird, a large black bird, was trying to get under the netting.

She had gone out on to the balcony to shoo it away. Once it was beyond the netting it would have been trapped. As she opened the balcony door and stepped over the threshold, she had missed her footing. She had fallen heavily, hitting her head and knocking herself out. When she awoke, she was lying on the floor of the balcony, in excruciating pain from a hip injury. She was unable to move.

She had lain there for several hours, alternately drifting in and out of consciousness. At times, when she had been able, she had called for help, but no one had heard her. All the while, the large black bird had sat on the edge of the balcony, looking down at her.

Eventually, she had been found by Mary. They had rushed her to hospital and operated. Her hip would be permanently damaged. There would be a long period of convalescence in a private nursing home close to where we lived. It would all be paid for by her insurance. It had been suggested to her that it might be best if she stayed there permanently, where there would be professional staff to care for her 24 hours a day.

We discussed it at length. She argued that she didn't want to leave me alone in the flat. I told her of my new life in Spain. She said that each time I returned I could visit her in the nursing home.

It was a life-changing event for me. Even though I had been away in prison for 24 years, there had always been a strong bond between my mother and me. She had always been there for me. Now, in some ways, this accident had set me free.

It was all clearly linked to the ceremony at Janice's grave. My mother had fallen at precisely the time when I had been reading the prayers. It was too much of a coincidence.

And the bird, the large black bird. Birds were always portentous in mysticism and usually of ill omen. This one had lured my mother to her fall. I could see the hand of Janice 2 behind it. It filled me with a terrible resolve. Suddenly, I had no fear. I saw quite clearly what I must do.

✳ ✳ ✳

The street alongside King's Cross station was silent and deserted now, the heat and crowds of the day but a distant memory. A cool wind blew its length, lightly disturbing the detritus strewn across its pavements. The local church clock struck, its solitary chime echoing eerily along the thoroughfare. It was the time of night when all decent people were home in bed.

Rudy Waters lounged in the doorway of the derelict shop. This was his time. When light ruled, during the day, this was the domain of the shoppers, the travellers and the passers-by. Now, in the hours of darkness, he held sway.

He looked further down the street to where two girls loitered close to another shop doorway. Skimpily clad, they shivered in the cool night breeze, occasionally shaking their shoulders and rubbing themselves with their hands in a vain attempt to warm themselves.

Rudy smiled a humourless smile. They would be warm soon enough, he mused. Some late-night punter would come by to sample what they were offering. That would put more money in his pocket, for these were his girls. Not that they were related to him, or were even friends. They were his by conquest. He had just appeared, like he had done so many times before, and told them that now they worked for him.

Mostly, they were girls on their own. Even if they did have boyfriends, Rudy was big enough and vicious enough to frighten them away. The girls had no choice but to work. Invariably, they had a drug habit that had to be fed.

Suddenly, he shouted down the street. The girls had stepped into the doorway, temporarily to warm themselves out of the wind. As they reappeared, he shook his fist at them. The punters wouldn't see them in the doorway.

The blonde girl, the smaller of the two, shot him a weak smile. His facial expression changed not one bit. He would take her again tonight, just as he had two nights previously. She had briefly struggled, then cried. She said that she had thought he was her friend. That did bring a smile to his face. He had no need of friends. When you were strong, you could just take what you wanted.

He had noticed the black motorbike and its two riders earlier, when it had cruised slowly up the street. He had paid it little heed, thinking they were probably two shy punters looking over the local talent. Now, as it cruised to a halt just opposite his doorway, he scrutinised them more closely.

There was little to see really. Both riders were dressed from head to toe in black leathers, their faces obscured by the smoked glass of their helmets. As Rudy watched, the pillion rider climbed off the bike and walked purposefully towards him.

Even now, he felt no sense of alarm. This was his patch, no one had ever dared challenge him in all the months he had been coming here. Coolly, he looked the approaching biker up and down. Only at the last moment did he see the black object gleaming dully in his hand.

Rudy spun from the doorway and made as if to run. He became aware of two things simultaneously. There was a loud explosion and an excruciating, searing pain in his right thigh. He screamed and felt himself falling. There were more explosions and it seemed as if his left leg was on fire. Then another explosion, and he felt a duller pain in his right leg again.

Instinctively, he turned as he lay on the pavement. This way, at least he would have the opportunity of pleading for his life with his nemesis. He extended his arms towards the black-clad figure in supplication.

The figure raised the black gun and pointed it directly at Rudy's head. He cowered away, screwing up his face in the process. 'No,' he moaned. Insanely, an image ran through his mind. It was the scene from *True Romance* where Clarence was about to shoot the Gary Oldman character in the face. Rudy recalled what came next. 'No,' he moaned more forcefully.

The figure bent over him. He heard the voice from behind the visor.

'You won't be raping any more helpless birds, you dirty cunt,' it growled. He watched, horrified, as the gun traversed down his body and out of sight.

When it came, the sound and the pain were one. As the searing, white light detonated into his consciousness, he was aware of only one thing before he passed out. It had originated in his groin.

LIFE AFTER LIFE

As I travelled about making the final preparations for my return trip to Spain, I had the uncanny feeling that I was experiencing certain commonplace things for the last time. So I examined them more carefully, fondly, savouring the memory of times past.

There was now another stop on my daily rounds of ricocheting from friend to friend to acquaintance. Besides my regular visits to Susan's grave, I would often sit by Janice's for hours, sometimes going straight from one to the other. I mused that I'd been spending a lot of my time with the dead of late.

I had already packed, but my flight wasn't until much later in the day. I would set out on a round of last goodbyes, taking in the graves of both Susan and Janice.

As I neared Mortlake Cemetery, I recalled the time I had brought Janice there. Now she and Susan were united in death. I wondered if their spirits had met, if they had discussed me, if they were looking over me right now. Alive to the world of the spirits now, I was sure they were.

I always had the same feeling of expectation as I approached Susan's grave. It was a nervousness in the pit of my stomach, as if I were about to stand before some awful power to be judged. On this day, I felt it more acutely than ever.

I parked by the field of graves, then walked along a gravel path counting the rows. It was an unnecessary ritual. I could have found my way to her grave blindfolded now. I turned into the row and

349

stopped abruptly.

Although the day was bright and warm, a cold chill ran right through my body. I hardly needed any further proof that the realm of the spirits could rudely intrude into this corporeal world. However, unless I denied the evidence of my senses, what lay before me was incontrovertible.

The familiar headstone stood as it always had, the beatific angel smiling sadly from its alcove. But the grave beneath!

It was as if it had been blasted with a bolt from above. An entire section at the head of the grave had caved in to the depth of over a foot. A smaller, deeper hole winked darkly at me as my gaze plumbed its depths.

It was summer. It hadn't been particularly dry and there had been no torrential rain. The obvious solution of a subsidence wasn't obvious at all in the circumstances. I walked the rows of surrounding graves and they were all intact. If Susan's grave had in fact subsided, then it was the only one. Further, subsidence was for recent graves. Susan's was 33 years old.

Strangely, I wasn't at all surprised. I considered it to be another round in my timeless battle with Janice 2. I smiled grimly at the thought that she had sent me a sign. I would be sending her one all too soon now.

*   *   *

Tom collected me from Malaga airport in a taxi. Only I was allowed to drive the Mustang. As we headed towards Marbella, he regaled me excitedly with details of the villa he had rented for us.

If I had thought that he had sated his desire for profligacy by the renting of the apartment, I was to be disappointed. The villa that perched atop a hill overlooking Marbella was a vision in extravagance. It had been built by Arabs at a cost of over $2m. While it was aesthetically breathtaking, functionally it left a lot to be desired. The views however, as Tom hastened to reassure me, were stunning.

The Mustang, gleaming from a fresh cleaning, nestled snugly in the carport. I had left it parked outside Ron's house. I avoided asking who had driven it there lest it seemed I was being ungrateful.

The welcoming party was waiting by the pool. The fact that it was all stage-managed by Tom seemed irrelevant in the circumstances.

Elaine rushed to greet me, closely followed by Nicky, a young, mixed-race musician whom I remembered from Tom's circle in London, and Aisha and Dolly, two of Tom's former girlfriends.

As they helped me carry my luggage inside, I shot an arch look at Tom and glanced from him to Elaine.

'Oh I meant to tell you, Norm. I phoned Elaine and asked her to fly over and join me,' he began bravely, only lapsing into sheepishness at the very end.

I shrugged, as if to say it was entirely his decision. He would have to live with her. However, I couldn't help but reflect on a love that had been smothered by poverty but could now only be resurrected by wealth. It was surely a sign of the times.

'One thing, Tom,' I muttered *sotto voce* as I pulled him aside. 'I'm not mean by any stretch of the imagination. But I'm fucked if I'm paying the bills for all your mates.'

'No, no, Norm,' he reassured. 'You're only half in on the rent.'

'And what's that set me back?' I enquired.

'The villa costs £400 a week,' he replied, a guilty flicker in his eye.

As I nodded my approval, I saw relief flare in his eyes. I reflected that, after the extravagance of the apartment, I had got off quite lightly.

I found it very difficult to settle into my new lifestyle. On the face of it, it should have been simplicity itself. It certainly was the stuff of most men's dreams.

I went shopping with Tom in Marbella and soon had a wardrobe full of designer label clothes. With my shiny Mustang parked outside my $2m villa, I suppose I more than qualified as the archetypal, eligible bachelor.

Night after night I dressed up and went out to all the best clubs along the coast with Tom, Nicky and the girls. Everywhere we went, we were fêted. Our crowd was inevitably the centre of attention, if not when first we arrived, then certainly by the time we left. Tom and Nicky were past masters at manipulating the social scene. Nicky was an accomplished musician. He would take over a piano, playing and singing while the girls danced sexily around him, occasionally pausing to kiss each other full on the lips. It scandalised the more reserved Spanish girls and titillated their men. We were invited to every party.

But it was all so shallow and mercenary. Each interaction became a transaction as hard-faced women assessed their proposed partner for the evening. I hadn't taken a vow of celibacy, but I found one virtually forced on me. If you had to buy or barter for it, then it wasn't love. And love was all that would heal me at the moment.

Soon, it became very boring. I found myself asking why I should go through the motions of going out, just to stand in some noisy bar where I could hardly hear myself think, talking to some anonymous stranger with whom I had little in common. I came to realise why most of them took coke and drank heavily.

I regularly began to stay in during the evenings. With Tom and the others out clubbing until the early hours, I had the villa to myself. I would sit by the pool with the sound system gently playing, looking out over the rolling hills of the Spanish coast as the light slowly failed.

Sometimes, if I closed my eyes tightly and focused intently, I could visualise Janice sitting opposite me in one of the poolside chairs. Then, if I opened my eyes quickly, her image would briefly hover, before dissipating into nothingness.

'Oh, "Little Girl", if only you had waited to share this with me.'

If Tom noticed my behaviour or perceived my state of mind, he never remarked on it. However, he was permanently lost to his world of coke and booze now. He drifted, almost like some disembodied spirit, from one sensation to the next. I knew he wouldn't miss me when I left. Perhaps he wouldn't even notice.

Strangely enough, it was Elaine who brought something quite significant to my attention. She had been reading *Parkhurst Tales* and asked who had chosen the cover. The image was the one of the tattooed arm of a convict handcuffed to the uniformed arm of a warder — simplistic but effective. I had been given a choice of only six photos to choose from and this had seemed the most relevant.

I explained this to Elaine and enquired why she had asked.

'It's the tattoo on the convict's arm,' she replied, 'I thought you had the photo done specially.'

I asked her to indicate what she was referring to. She pointed to the heavily tattooed arm.

'There,' she said, 'just above the wrist, the tattoo of "Janice".'

I had looked at the photo 1,000 times, but had never closely examined it. Now I peered intently at its detail. Sure enough, there among the scribble of other tattoos was the name 'Janice'.

How strange. It stood out quite clearly, but I had never noticed it before. 'Janice' wasn't that common a name either and I hadn't even met her when I had chosen the photo. Somehow, it was all quite fitting.

As the day of my departure approached, I cleared my mind and purified my body. I prayed every morning without fail and never took the talisman or Janice's ring from around my neck, except to shower. I ate only rice, fish and fruit and drank only bottled water. I ran every morning and spent an hour every evening stretching and meditating. I went to bed early and slept long, dreamless sleeps.

On the evening before my departure, I secretly packed the few things I would need and left early the next morning. Tom and the others had been in bed for only a few hours. They were sleeping soundly. I didn't wake them. There was nothing to say that they would have understood.

The drive up into the mountains calmed my spirit as it always did. I arrived at Janice's place just as the sun was beginning to warm the hills. I drove off the road, up a dusty track and parked behind one of the derelict houses. The Mustang was invisible from the road, no one would find it there.

I went to where I had buried my money and put the talisman inside. Jess would find it when he followed the instructions I had left. He would distribute some of the money as directed, but the talisman he would have to deal with by himself. I reflected on how right Israel Regardie had been when he had said that all magic for powers was evil. The talisman belonged with Mammon, so it was fitting that it lay with the money I had strived so hard to obtain.

I climbed a rocky hillside to a little plateau that nestled in the lee of a large rock. It was cool here in the shade. The view over the surrounding countryside was panoramic. From here I could see, but not be seen.

I spread out around me the few things I would need. I squatted cross-legged, with my Talmud, a copy of *Il Principio* and a bottle of water within easy reach. Wearing my kappel and prayer shawl, I fasted as I read from the Talmud and recited *Il Principio* over and over again.

I watched the sun set and the moon rise. In the chill of the night, I took the blanket from beneath me and draped it about my shoulders. In the darkness, I reached inside myself and found that little place where I used to go when in solitary confinement.

My spirit, fired in the furnace of solitude, was an awesome and wondrous thing to behold. I examined 'the Beast' and bent it to my will. I would need its strength in the ordeal that was to come. I talked with God about death and argued with the Devil about the meaning of life. As dawn broke and the sun rose again, I stood and felt the power course through my body. I was ready.

The Mustang was where I had left it. I drove to a petrol station and put it through the car wash. It emerged, sleek and glistening.

I went into the washroom, where I washed, shaved and put on fresh clothes. Then I was on the road again.

To the east of Marbella, there is a part of the motorway that runs closely parallel to the sea. With the azure blue waters of the Mediterranean on one side and the massy, rugged cliffs on the other, the *autovia* sweeps majestically through El Faro. At one point, rounding a bend, there is a stretch of road that runs straight as an arrow to the foot of a massive white rock-face before cutting sharply around it to continue on towards Marbella.

Sometimes, when the sun is at the right angle and there is no cloud, a trick of light occurs. The sunlight, reflecting off the sea, lights up the straight stretch of road and the white rock-face at its end, creating a continuous, brightly shining 'avenue of light', that seemingly stretches to infinity. If ever there were to be a cosmic gateway in this earthly dimension, I felt that this was where it would be.

I had timed this run regularly. As I rounded the bend into the straight stretch of road, I had reached the thirteenth and final verse of *Il Principio*.

The shining, gunmetal-blue bullet that was the Mustang hurtled along the 'avenue of light' towards the cosmic gateway. As it met and became one with the transluscent rock-face, I felt a surge of pure energy. It was a consummation devoutly to be wished, blissful union with Janice.